Macroeconomic Policy

Macroeconomic Policy

Robert J. Barro

Harvard University Press
Cambridge, Massachusetts
London, England
1990

Library of Congress Cataloging in Publication Data

Barro, Robert J.
  Macroeconomic policy/Robert J. Barro.
    p. cm.
  Includes bibliographical references.
  ISBN 0-674-54080-8 (alk. paper)
  1. Monetary policy. 2. Fiscal policy. 3. Economic policy.
  4. Finance, Public. 5. Economic development. 6. Macroeconomics.
  I. Title.
  HG230.3.B37 1990   89-71679
  339.5—dc20   CIP

Contents

Macroeconomic Policy

Introduction

The new classical macroeconomics analyzes macro phenomena under the twin disciplines of rational behavior and cleared markets. The use of rational expectations has often been stressed, but this feature is just one way in which the approach relies on microeconomic foundations. More generally, models in the new classical tradition allow for optimization subject to budget constraints by various economic agents. The models generate predictions and policy evaluations (along the lines suggested by Robert Lucas 1976) by taking account of the reactions implied by individuals' conditions of optimization.

Many analyses assume that private agents are rational but treat the government's behavior as mechanical. More recently, macroeconomists have incorporated some concept of optimization subject to budget constraints in the modeling of the government's behavior. These approaches allow for positive analyses of the government; in particular, the theories can be tested by comparing the hypothesized behavior of policy variables, such as the money supply and budget deficits, with the behavior that shows up in data.

One area where the new classical macroeconomics has made major contributions, and where the positive approach to governmental action has been crucial, concerns the distinction between rules and discretion. An older literature, represented by Simons (1936) and Friedman (1960), argued that rules would be preferable to discretion. The main reasons were the incomplete knowledge and inappropriate objectives of policymakers. A weakness of this approach is that a "benevolent" policymaker who took account of imperfect information seemed to have no incentive to use a rule to bind himself or herself in advance to a particular course of actions. Therefore, in the framework used by Simons and Friedman, discretion would be superior to rules in many circumstances.

1

Kydland and Prescott (1977) refocused the topic by viewing a rule as a mechanism enabling policymakers to make commitments that people could rely on. Even when policymakers are well intentioned and competent, such commitments typically improve outcomes by generating more efficient choices of investment, production, and so on. In the absence of adequate enforcement mechanisms, however, policymakers are often motivated to depart, ex post, from the path dictated by their "commitments." Because people anticipate these breakdowns, expectations do not accord with the initially announced policy. Consequently, people alter their levels of investment, production, and so on, and the outcomes are typically less desirable than those that would have resulted had commitments been feasible.

Many macroeconomists accepted Kydland and Prescott's analysis as a telling critique of standard policy analysis. But it was less clear how to build on their arguments to form a more satisfactory understanding of government policy. In reaction, David Gordon and I thought of the strategic interactions between the government and the private sector as a basis for a positive theory of monetary and other policies (in "A Positive Theory of Monetary Policy in a Natural-Rate Model"). We showed that the approach had empirical implications for the behavior of money and other policy variables. Subsequently, we linked the analysis to developments in applied game theory, and we included the policymaker's reputation as an influence on policy choice (in "Rules, Discretion, and Reputation in a Model of Monetary Policy"). In circumstances where the interaction between the policymaker and the private sector was ongoing (a "repeated game"), the value of reputation can sometimes substitute effectively for formal rules or commitments. In some cases, however, the reputational equilibria break down; and in other cases there are multiple equilibria. Although research in this area is very active, the understanding of how society coordinates on a particular reputational equilibrium is still primitive.

Aside from my two articles with David Gordon (Chapters 2 and 3), Part I of this book includes three other chapters in the area of rules versus discretion. The first (Chapter 1) is a survey of the field. (For additional discussion of this area, see Rogoff 1989.) Chapter 4 applies the framework to the inflation tax. The final chapter in this section (5) uses the Kreps and Wilson (1982) sequential-equilibrium approach to study monetary policy when people are uncertain about some characteristics of the policymaker.

The new classical approach began in the early 1970s with research that stressed the real effects of monetary disturbances. (For a survey, see Barro 1981.) Initially, the major challenge seemed to be to reconcile equilibrium models, which tend to generate close approximations to monetary neutrality, with a strong role for monetary disturbances in business cycles. The work in this area, which featured major contributions by Robert Lucas and by Thomas Sargent and Neil Wallace, had a major impact on the way most macroeconomists now carry out their research. But I believe that the particular program of research ultimately failed to explain why nominal disturbances would be of major significance for real variables.

More recently, some macroeconomists reconsidered the empirical evidence and concluded that the role of money in business fluctuations had been overstated. That is, this role is neither as large nor as pervasive as many economists had believed. Chapter 6 supports this conclusion by finding little effect of monetary shocks on real rates of return. Chapter 7, coauthored with Robert King, raises a number of theoretical problems in models where monetary disturbances are central sources of business cycles.

The final chapter in Part II (Chapter 8) is perhaps the natural conclusion of my transition to models where the real effects of money are deemphasized. In this model monetary policy has no effect on real variables but does determine the price level and nominal interest rate. I use the idea that the central bank targets nominal interest rates to generate a positive theory of the money supply, the price level, and the nominal interest rate. Then I use data on policy variables to test this theory.

Because empirical and theoretical findings suggested a deemphasis of monetary disturbances, I found it reasonable to focus more of my research on fiscal policy. Theoretical arguments in this area have centered on analyses (pro and con) of the Ricardian theory of budget deficits. I view this theory, which says that taxes and budget deficits are basically equivalent, as a logical application of the new classical macroeconomics to the fiscal area.

The Ricardian analysis starts with the government's budget constraint and notes that government expenditures have to be paid by taxes now or by taxes later, but not by taxes never. This no-free-lunch view implies that, as long as the present value of government purchases does not change (and default on government bonds is ruled out), public debt and budget deficits cannot alter the present value of taxes. Then, if households care about the total present value of taxes, the Ricardian equivalence result holds. That is, shifts in budget deficits, with an unchanged behavior of government purchases, have no impact on consumption, investment, interest rates, and so on.

Chapter 9 in Part III summarizes various aspects of the debate on the Ricardian theory of budget deficits. Many reasons for departures from strict Ricardian equivalence can be advanced, and I discuss reasons such as finite lifetimes, imperfect credit markets, uncertainty, and non–lump-sum taxes. But my main conclusion is that—as in the case of the Modigliani–Miller theorem in corporate finance—the Ricardian theorem is the right starting point for analyses of intertemporal government finance.

Chapter 10 uses one reason for departure from strict Ricardian equivalence—effects from the timing of income taxes—to generate a positive theory of budget deficits. Basically, the government adjusts its deficit or surplus to smooth out the pattern of tax collections over time. This tax-smoothing model fits the U.S. experience on public debt reasonably well from World War I until 1983. (Budget deficits since 1984 are significantly above the values that the historical relation would predict.) Again, this approach uses data on a policy variable to test a model where the government acts in a sensible manner. Chapter 11 uses the same approach for a direct analysis of tax rates.

Macroeconomists have probably spent too much time thinking about budget deficits—which relate to how government spending is financed—and not enough about the macroeconomic effects of government expenditures and the public services related to these expenditures. Chapter 12 considers some macroeconomic effects of U.S. government purchases, with stress on the distinctions between temporary and permanent spending and between defense and nondefense purchases. Chapter 13 analyzes the macroeconomic consequences of military spending over the long-term British history. This research also considers the interplay between spending and budget deficits, effectively applying the analysis in my previous research (especially Chapter 10) to the experience of the United Kingdom.

Looking ahead, I believe that game-theoretic approaches to government policy will continue to be an important area of research in macroeconomics. I anticipate that investigators, instead of focusing on monetary models, increasingly will apply this analysis to topics such as fiscal policy, international debt, and government regulation. Two other areas of recent macroeconomic research are theories of endogenous economic growth and real models of business fluctuations (real business-cycle theory). Each of these areas stresses real disturbances; but the former focuses on long-term economic development, whereas the latter deals with short-term business fluctuations. Many economists (including myself) are working in these fields, and the results are promising. One area of particular interest is the interaction of real models of growth and fluctuations with the analyses of government policy that are discussed in this book.

References

Barro, R. J. 1981. *Money, Expectations, and Business Cycles.* New York: Academic Press.

Friedman, M. 1960. *A Program for Monetary Stability.* New York: Fordham University Press.

Kreps, D. M., and R. Wilson. 1982. "Reputation and Imperfect Information." *Journal of Economic Theory* 27(2):253–279.

Kydland, F. E., and E. C. Prescott. 1977. "Rules rather than Discretion: The Inconsistency of Optimal Plans." *Journal of Political Economy* 85(3):473–491.

Lucas, R. E. 1976. "Econometric Policy Evaluation: A Critique." *Carnegie-Rochester Conference Series on Public Policy* 1:19–46.

Rogoff, K. 1989. "Reputation, Coordination, and Monetary Policy." In *Modern Business Cycle Theory,* ed. R. J. Barro. Cambridge, Mass.: Harvard University Press, pp. 236–264.

Simons, H. C. 1936. "Rules versus Authorities in Monetary Policy." *Journal of Political Economy* 44(1):1–30.

Rules versus Discretion

Rules versus Discretion

1 Developments in the Theory of Rules versus Discretion

The older literature on rules versus discretion focused on the intentions and capability of the policymaker. Arguments for rules were based on imperfect knowledge about the economy and on policymakers' tendencies to further inappropriate ends, possibly motivated by interest groups.[1] But an intelligent policymaker could take account of incomplete information about the economy when deciding on the optimal discretionary policy. Then if the policymaker was also well meaning, there was no obvious defense for using a rule to bind his hands in advance. Discretion seemed to be synonymous with flexibility, which one had no reason to deny to a smart, benevolent policymaker.

This perspective on rules versus discretion was changed by Kydland and Prescott (1977), who looked at rules as a form of commitment. A commitment amounts to a binding contract, which specifies in advance the actions that someone will take, possibly contingent on some exogenous variables that everyone can observe. In contrast, under discretion a person promises only to take those future actions that will best further his objectives later on. (Such promises are easy to keep!) Thus discretion is the special case of a rule or contract in which none of today's provisions restrict a person's future actions. In the area of private business dealings, it is natural to think about optimal forms of contracts, which would not usually be pure discretion. Similarly, for public policy, the perspective becomes the optimal form of rules or prior restrictions— even the smart, benevolent policymaker is likely to desire and use an ability to make binding promises.

From *Economic Journal* (1986) supplement. The present chapter is an extension of results contained in a previous paper (Barro 1984). I have benefited from research support from the National Science Foundation.

1. See, for example, Friedman (1960, chap. 4).

Kydland and Prescott discuss various areas of public policy in which commitments are important. One example is patents, which encourage inventions but also restrict the supply of goods ex post. Under discretion a policymaker who cares about "social welfare" would invalidate old patents ("once and for all") but continue to issue new ones. However, the perception of this policy by potential inventors has adverse effects on new inventions, which soon become old inventions. Hence the optimal policy contains a mechanism to preclude or at least inhibit the abolition of old patents. Then the details of this policy involve the standard trade-off between the incentive to invent and the ex post restriction of supply.

The manner of committing future actions varies with the area of public policy. In some cases, such as the duration and scope of patents, the rules are set out in formal law. Then the costs of changing laws (possibly coming under constitutional restrictions against ex post facto laws) enforces the government's commitments. In the case of the Gold Standard Act in the United States, however, the existence of a law proved in 1933 to be inadequate protection for those who held gold or made contracts denominated in gold.[2]

More often a government's commitments rely on the force of reputation, whereby people's expectations of future policy are tied in some fashion to past behavior. For instance, if a government defaults on its debts, then potential bondholders are deterred by the perception that future defaults are more likely. If a municipality sharply raises property taxes, and thereby reduces property values, then potential residents are deterred from moving in. But, as a general matter, the linkages between past actions and expectations of future behavior are difficult to formalize in a model.

Monetary Policy under Discretion

A major contribution of Kydland and Prescott was the recognition that monetary policy involves the same issues about commitments that are involved in areas such as patents, default on government debt, and imposition of levies on previously accumulated capital (via changes in property taxes or in other taxes that fall on capital). In the case of

2. For a discussion of the abrogation of gold clauses in public and private contracts, see Yeager (1966, p. 305). Additional discussions are in Nussbaum (1950, pp. 283–291) and McCulloch (1980).

patents it is obvious that a policymaker must worry about the link between current actions—such as eliminating past patents or changing the form of patent law—and people's perceptions about the value of presently issued patents. Similarly, the monetary authority must consider the interplay between today's choices—whether to engineer a monetary expansion or to change the "law" governing monetary policy—and people's beliefs about future money and prices.

Consider the example about the Phillips curve, as discussed in Kydland and Prescott (1977) and in Barro and Gordon (1983a,b). These models involve the following main ingredients. First, monetary policy works by affecting the general price level. In the simplest setting the monetary authority can use its instruments to achieve perfect control over the price level in each period. Second, unexpected increases in the price level (but not expected changes in prices) expand real economic activity. In other words, there is an expectational Phillips Curve. Third, the representative person and, hence, the benevolent policymaker value these expansions of activity at least over some range (which means that existing distortions make the "natural" level of output too small). In order to focus on the distinction between rules and discretion, the models assume unanimity about the public's desires and a willingness of the policymaker to go along with this objective. This is, there are no principal-agent problems. Finally, inflation is itself undesirable—people value it only as a device to create unexpected inflation and thereby higher levels of economic activity.[3]

This setup for inflation is structurally similar to the patent example. At any point in time the policymaker is motivated to generate unexpected inflation in order to stimulate the economy. (The analogue is the expansion of supply by means of an abolition of past patents.) But people understand these incentives in advance and therefore form high expectations of inflation. Accordingly, the policymaker must choose a high rate of inflation just to stay even—that is, in order for unexpected inflation to be zero. Finally, this high inflation imposes costs on the economy. (The parallel is the decrease in inventions because of the expectation that current patents will not be honored later.)

Barro and Gordon (1983a,b) analyze the equilibria for monetary policy and inflation for the Phillips-curve model. In the case of pure discre-

---

3. The analysis can be extended to incorporate the standard inflation tax or other real effects from anticipated inflation. Then the best rate of inflation need not be zero.

tion, the policymaker has no mechanisms for committing the future behavior of money and prices. Rather, he has a free hand to maximize social welfare at each point in time, while treating past events as givens. In this situation there is an incentive at each point in time to create surprise inflation in order to generate an economic boom. But individuals understand this motivation and formulate their expectations accordingly. Thus, actual inflation cannot end up being systematically higher or lower than expected inflation.

Overall, two conditions must be satisfied in equilibrium. First, people's expectations of inflation are correct on average, which is a rational-expectations condition. Second, although the policymaker retains the power in each period to fool people via inflation surprises, he is not motivated to exercise this power. For this second condition to hold, the policymaker's drive to create unexpected inflation must be balanced by the marginal cost of inflation itself. In other words, inflation must be high enough so that the marginal cost of inflation equals the marginal benefit from inflation surprises. Only then will the chosen rate of inflation—which ends up equal on average to the rate that people expect—be incentive compatible in the sense of according with the policymaker's desire to maximize social welfare at each point in time. The important point is that this equilibrium involves inflation that is high, but not surprisingly high. Therefore, the economy bears the costs of high inflation but does not receive the rewards that would arise from unexpected inflation.

The solution just described rests on the presence of benefits from surprise inflation, but it does not depend on the existence of the expectational Phillips curve. An alternative model recognizes that surprise inflation amounts to a capital levy on assets, such as money and government bonds, that are denominated in nominal terms. At a point in time, unexpected inflation works like a lump-sum tax as a device for generating government revenue. Given that other taxes are distorting, the policymaker (and the representative person in the economy) would value the use of this lump-sum tax. Therefore, this model parallels the previous one with the Phillips curve, even though the source of benefit from unexpected inflation is different. There is an analogous discretionary equilibrium with high inflation, but with no tendency for unexpected inflation to be positive or negative.[4]

4. See Barro (1983) for an elaboration of this model.

In the example of the Phillips curve, the incentive to create surprise inflation hinges on the desire to expand economic activity. But this incentive depends in turn on some distortions that make the natural rate of output too low. The disincentive effects from income taxes and transfer programs are possible sources of these distortions.[5] Similarly, in the example where the government values surprise inflation as a lump-sum tax, there must be an underlying environment in which alternative taxes are distorting. In both cases the existence of initial distortions underlies the prediction of high inflation. Calvo (1978) discusses the general role of existing distortions in these types of models. The main point is that the bad outcomes under discretion depend on the presence of these distortions.

Barro and Gordon (1983b) view the discretionary equilibrium as a positive theory of monetary policy and inflation under present-day monetary arrangements. Aside from predicting high average inflation and monetary growth, the model indicates the reactions to changes in the benefits from unexpected inflation or in the costs of actual inflation. For example, a rise in the natural rate of unemployment can raise the benefits from lowering unemployment through surprise inflation. It follows that a secular rise in the natural unemployment rate will lead to a secular rise in the mean rates of monetary growth and inflation. Similarly, the policymaker would particularly value reductions of unemployment during recessions. The implication is that monetary growth will be countercyclical, although such a policy can end up with no effect on the amplitude of business cycles.

A higher stock of nominally denominated public debt raises the benefits from capital levies via surprise inflation. The model then implies that more public debt will lead to higher values of monetary growth, inflation, and nominal interest rates (although not to higher unexpected inflation). In other words, the prediction is that deficits will be partly monetized. A similar analysis suggests that indexation of the public debt for inflation—which removes some of the benefits from surprise inflation—will tend to lower inflation and monetary growth. This prediction comes from the positive theory of the money-supply process rather than from direct effects of indexation on the economy. Finally, a higher level of government spending tends to raise the benefits from lump-sum taxa-

5. These taxes and transfers may themselves be warranted as necessary counterparts of (valuable) government expenditures. Hence there is no implication that the government is failing to optimize on the fiscal side.

tion, because the deadweight losses from other taxes would be higher. This change leads again to higher rates of inflation and monetary growth. The endogenous response of monetary growth implies that government expenditures are inflationary.

The model assumes that actual inflation is costly, but it does not explain the source of these costs. Two frequently mentioned possibilities are the administrative expenses for changing prices and the transaction costs associated with economizing on cash holdings. The positive analysis of monetary policy implies that a downward shift in the costs of inflation will lead to more inflation. If people think that inflation is not a serious problem, the economy will end up with a lot of inflation!

The analysis implies also that each flicker in the benefits from inflation surprises or in the costs of inflation will be reflected in variations in inflation. In contrast to an environment in which the government stabilizes prices, there will be substantial random fluctuations of inflation and monetary growth. Further, the variances of prices and money will be larger the greater the random fluctuations in the variables that influence the benefits from inflation shocks. For example, if there are frequent supply shocks (which alter the natural rate of output), then inflation and monetary growth will be volatile.

Monetary Rules

The results under discretion contrast with those under rules, which are regimes where the policymaker can and does make commitments about future monetary growth and inflation. Under discretion, the equilibrium involved high inflation but no tendency toward surprisingly high inflation. Hence, the economy suffered the costs from high inflation but secured none of the benefits from inflation surprises. The policymaker can improve on this outcome if he can commit himself ex ante to low inflation. If this commitment is credible—which means that some mechanism prevents violations ex post—then people also anticipate low inflation. Therefore, the equilibrium would exhibit low and stable inflation,[6] with the same average amount of surprise inflation (zero) as before.

---

6. More generally, one can choose the average inflation rate that is optimal from the standpoint of the usual inflation tax.

These results support a form of constant-growth-rate rule—although applied to prices rather than to the quantity of money per se.

There is a tension in this type of rules equilibrium because the policy-maker may retain the capacity to produce large social gains at any point in time by "cheating"—that is, by generating surprisingly high inflation. Then there may be a temporary economic boom or at least a substantial amount of government revenue obtained via a distortion-free tax. But, if such cheating were feasible and desirable, then people would understand the situation beforehand. In this case the low-inflation equilibrium would be untenable. (Sometimes people say that this equilibrium is time inconsistent, although it is actually not an equilibrium at all.) Rather, there would be a high-inflation, discretionary equilibrium, as described earlier. Hence the enforcement power behind the low-inflation rule is crucial. There must be a mechanism for binding the policymaker's hands in advance, so that (surprisingly) high inflation cannot be generated later, even if such a choice looks good to everyone ex post. Note that the rationale for this binding of hands applies even though (or actually especially if) the policymaker is well meaning. This type of commitment is necessary in order for low inflation to be incentive compatible and hence credible.

Although the low-inflation, rules equilibrium is superior to the high-inflation, discretionary equilibrium, the rules equilibrium is still not first best. The benefits from inflation surprises—for example, from lower unemployment or from the generation of distortion-free government revenue—reflect some external effects that have not been eliminated. It is the desire to approach the first-best solution via inflation surprises that threatens the viability of the low-inflation equilibrium. The pursuit of the first best tends to push the economy away from the second best of a rule with low inflation and toward the third best of discretionary policy with high inflation. Again, this perspective highlights the importance of the enforcement power that makes a rule sustainable.

Contingent Rules

More generally, the optimal rule may set money or prices contingent on exogenous events, rather than being noncontingent. In some models, such as those where the monetary authority has superior information about the economy, a contingent reaction to business-cycle variables may help to smooth out business fluctuations. However, the direct communication of the government's information may be a substitute for the feedback response of money.

Another example of contingent response is the association of wars with high growth rates of money and prices. High wartime inflation constitutes surprisingly high inflation from the standpoint of an earlier time at which a war was not anticipated. In an equilibrium the counterpart must be surprisingly low inflation during peacetime. This type of contingent rule may be desirable because it generates lots of easy revenue via the capital levy from unexpected inflation during emergencies. In particular, it is possible to hold down distortions from the income tax at the most important times, such as during wars.[7] Although the necessary accompaniment is a loss of revenue during the nonemergencies, the net effect of this contingent policy is likely to be beneficial.[8]

Under the gold standard, governments did in fact tend to go off gold during wartime, as Britain did during the Napoleonic period and around World War I and as the United States did during the Civil War. This procedure enables a government to pursue the type of contingent policy for inflation that I sketched above. In this sense a movement off gold in wartime is not necessarily a violation of the rules. However, the subsequent return to gold at the previous parity—as occurred in Britain in the 1820s and 1920s and in the United States in the 1870s—was probably an important part of the enforcement process.

One difficulty with contingent rules is that they may be difficult to verify. It is easy to confuse contingencies with the type of cheating that I described earlier. Further, the policymaker would be inclined to explain away high inflation as the consequence of some emergency rather than as a failure to conform with the rules. Canzoneri (1984) points out that this situation involves asymmetric information whereby the public can-

7. The government's ability to run deficits lessens this incentive but does not eliminate it. Contingent on a bad draw, such as war, it tends to be desirable to trigger the distortion-free capital levy.

8. Such an outcome obtains in the model of Lucas and Stokey (1983), which is exposited by Persson and Svensson (1984). These models feature public debt with a contingent real payoff, which turns out to be high during peacetime and low in wartime. If government bonds are nominally denominated and noncontingent (for reasons that escape me), the contingent behavior of inflation achieves the same end.

not verify the nature of the policymaker's actions even after the fact. These considerations favor a rule that is relatively simple, such as a constant-growth-rate rule for prices or money. In any case the contingencies should be limited to well-defined events, such as major wars. Although this limitation may miss some gains from contingent action, the greater ease of enforcement makes it less likely that the situation will degenerate into a high-inflation, discretionary equilibrium.

The Policymaker's Reputation

Barro and Gordon (1983a) examine some possibilities for substituting the policymaker's reputation for formal rules. In this setting people's expectations of future inflation depend in some way on past performance. Unlike the case of pure discretion, the policymaker's choice of today's inflation rate assigns some weight to the effect on future inflationary expectations. Such considerations motivate the policymaker to hold down the rates of inflation and monetary growth.

The example considered in Barro and Gordon (1983a) is an application of repeated games as developed by Friedman (1971). Reputational equilibria emerge in which the rates of inflation are weighted averages of that under discretion and that under a constant-growth-rate rule. The higher the policymaker's discount rate, the greater the weight attached to the discretionary result. From a positive standpoint, the findings are qualitatively in line with those under discretion. The main difference is that the reactions of inflation to various shocks—such as shifts in the natural rate of unemployment or in the size of government—are now smaller in magnitude. Hence the variances (as well as the means) of inflation and monetary growth are smaller than they are under discretion.

One difficulty with these types of reputational equilibria is that they depend on an infinite horizon for the game between the policymaker and the public. If there is a known, finite end point for the game, reputational considerations have no weight in the final period. Because this outcome is anticipated, the force of reputation is also nil in the next to last period, and so on, working backward up to the current period. In other words, a finite horizon causes the reputational equilibria to unravel.[9] However, if the game terminates in any period with a probability less than one—but there is no known finite horizon—the repeated-games approach goes through. In this case the probability of termination effectively adds to the policymaker's discount rate in the solution.

In some contexts, such as those where a term of office with fixed length is important, the finiteness of the horizon eliminates the type of reputational equilibria considered in Barro and Gordon (1983a). Even when an infinite horizon is tenable, there are difficulties with multiple equilibria. This multiplicity of solutions reflects the bootstrap character of the reputational equilibria. Namely, if people base future beliefs on the policymaker's actions in some arbitrary fashion, then the policymaker is motivated in a range of cases to validate these beliefs. Hence various equilibria conform with rational expectations as well as with period-by-period optimization by the policymaker.

In Barro and Gordon (1983a) the equilibria can be indexed by the length of the period over which people expect high future inflation when they observe high current inflation. In Friedman (1971) the analogous "punishment interval" is infinite, whereas in the basic model of Barro and Gordon (1983a) it is one period. Because the punishment does not arise in equilibrium in these models, the only effect of a longer interval is more deterrence against choosing high inflation. Therefore a longer interval is at least as good as a shorter one.

Canzoneri (1984) uses the approach of Green and Porter (1984), who treat the length of the punishment interval as a parameter. In Canzoneri's model the policymaker has private information about the economy, which the private agents can never observe directly. This information sometimes gives the policymaker good reason to inflate on a contingent basis. But people cannot tell whether he is instead acting in a discretionary manner to exploit low inflationary expectations. It therefore turns out that the punishments, which take the form of high expected inflation, occur from time to time as part of the equilibrium. Because these punishments are undesirable per se, a longer punishment interval imposes costs, which trade off against a greater deterrent value. Therefore the optimal punishment interval tends to be finite. Nevertheless, it is unclear what process would cause the interval to take on either this optimal value or some other value. Hence the problem of multiple equilibria remains. The solutions also still unravel if the horizon is finite.

9. This result, as applied to the "prisoner's dilemma" problem, appears in Selten (1978).

Reputation in Models with Different Types of Policymakers

The basic difficulty in the preceding treatment of reputation is that there is nothing to learn about in the models. The policymaker gains more or less reputation for high or low inflation; yet people know everything about the policymaker's objectives and abilities from the outset. Therefore the link between performance and beliefs has the bootstrap character mentioned before, rather than building directly on the revelation of information.

A basis for learning arises if potential policymakers differ in ways that are not immediately observable. These differences could involve preferences for inflation versus unemployment, capacities for making commitments about future monetary growth and inflation, lengths of horizons, and so on. Observed choices for inflation or monetary growth may alter the probabilities that people rationally attach to the policymaker's being of one type or another. Then this process would determine the connection between performance and expectations of future inflation or other variables. The policymaker, who knows his own type, takes this learning and expectational process into account when deciding how to act. In particular, the policymaker may wish to influence people's beliefs in one way or another. A full analysis of reputation considers these incentives, as well as the rationality of the public's expectations. Aside from giving content to notions of reputation and learning, this approach turns out to have two other advantages. First, the results no longer depend on an infinite horizon; and second, the equilibrium is often unique.

Models of this type have been applied to problems in the area of industrial organization by Kreps and Wilson (1982) and by Milgrom and Roberts (1982). Applications of their method to monetary policy include those by Backus and Driffill (1985), by Tabellini (1983), and by Barro (1986). In the following, I sketch an example of this application.

Suppose that there are two types of policymakers. Type I makes a serious commitment to low inflation. Type II is incapable of commitments but acts in the usual discretionary manner to trade off the costs of inflation against the benefits of inflation surprises. (Results are similar if the type I people worry more than the type II about inflation.) People cannot tell directly which policymaker is in office but must make inferences from the observed choices for monetary growth and inflation. Specifically, there is some prior probability that the policymaker is of type I. Then, as long as good performance (low inflation) is observed, people upgrade this possibility via Bayes' law. In other words, an additional period of low inflation makes people more confident that the policymaker is committed to low inflation. The type II policymaker takes account of this inference process when deciding how to behave. Notably he may be motivated to choose low inflation for a while in order to acquire some (false) reputation for being type I. Thereby, the type II person can hold down inflationary expectations, which helps to lower the overall costs to the economy. In particular, a low value of expected inflation creates an opportunity for large gains through inflation surprises once the type II policymaker decides to reveal his true nature.

For typical parameter values, the equilibrium involves an interval over which expected inflation is a weighted average of the low committed value and the higher value associated with discretion. The type I policymaker faithfully generates low inflation in each period. But, because people fear that he may be type II, this low inflation rate is below the expected rate. The implied string of negative inflation surprises imposes costs, which may take the form of a recession. In an environment where the policymaker's type is uncertain, these costs are necessary in order to fulfill the type I person's commitment to low inflation.

If the policymaker turns out to be type II, then he mimics the low inflation of the type I person for some interval. But the probability rises over time that the type II person will opt for high inflation. In particular, as he approaches the end of his term in office (finite horizon), this probability approaches one. Thus, there is eventually a surge in inflation, which is mostly unanticipated. The inflation is surprising partly because the policymaker might have been type I and partly because the timing of the type II person's surge is uncertain. In any event the surprise inflation generates benefits, perhaps in the form of a temporary economic boom. Having opted for high inflation, the type II policymaker reveals his incapacity for commitments. Therefore the equilibrium in later periods involves high (and expectedly high) inflation, as in the usual model of discretionary behavior.

Because of the benefit for the inflation shock it turns out that the overall results are actually better ex post if the policymaker happens to be a "bad guy" (type II) rather than a "good guy" (type I). On the other hand, outcomes also improve if policymakers are more likely ex ante to be type I. Basically, a higher prior probability of being type I reduces inflationary expectations, an outcome that is desirable regardless of the policymaker's type. From a normative standpoint, these findings do not favor the systematic choice of type II people to run the government. After all, one cannot simultaneously raise the prior probability of the policymaker's being committed to low inflation (type I) and also pick uncommitted people (type II) more often ex post.

The results just described have the virtue of stemming from a unique equilibrium and of applying even when the horizon is finite. The model also determines a process of learning about the policymaker's type in a context of incomplete information. It provides a meaningful concept of reputation, which is the probability that people rationally attach at each point in time to the policymaker's being of one type or another.

On the other hand, the analysis may be too sensitive to the traits of individual policymakers. In this model the behavior of inflation depends on the realization of the policymaker's type with respect to the capacity for commitments, tastes for inflation versus unemployment, and so on. It may be preferable to have a theory that predicts inflation without assigning a major role to the individual characteristics of the persons who happen to be in office. But if there are no differences in potential policymakers, then there seems to be nothing to learn from performance. In that case we are back to the previous difficulties in modeling the policymaker's reputation.

Types of Monetary Rules

In this section I assume that the choice is among types of monetary rules rather than between regimes with rules or no rules (that is, rules versus discretion). The choices are often divided between quantity rules and price rules. In the former category the policymaker aims for a target path of a monetary aggregate, such as the monetary base, or $M1$, or a still broader concept of money. Friedman's (1960, chap. 4) proposal for a constant-growth-rate rule for $M2$ falls into this class. From October 1979 until late 1982, the Federal Reserve claimed to be following a policy of this general type, which was framed in terms of monetary targets. But it is hard to see from the data that the growth of monetary aggregates became notably more stable—say, from quarter to quarter. On the other hand, interest rates did show unprecedented volatility, a result that many people think related to the Fed's new policy.

Under a price rule the monetary authority uses its direct instruments—which might be open-market operations, the discount rate, a pegged exchange rate, or a set price of gold—to achieve a desired path for some target price. The target might be a general index of prices, the prices of specified commodities, an interest rate, or the exchange rate itself. Examples of price rules are the gold standard, other commodity standards, a regime with a fixed exchange rate, and Irving Fisher's (1920) stable-money proposal for varying the price of gold in order to stabilize the overall cost of living. A policy of pegging a nominal interest rate is also a price rule, but an incomplete one. This type of rule requires some additional specifications in order to pin down the levels of prices and other nominal variables (see, for example, Sargent and Wallace 1975 and McCallum 1984). Therefore an interest-rate rule is not a substitute for a rule that specifies the quantity of some monetary aggregate or the level of some price.

Generally, people care about a variety of current and future prices rather than about the quantities of monetary aggregates per se. Therefore, the case for a quantity rule must rely on ease of implementation and verification.[10] Even this argument is compromised by the monetary authority's tendency to shift from one target aggregate to another whenever it finds it convenient to do so on other grounds (see Hetzel 1984). Such a regime involves feedback from unspecified ultimate targets to money, rather than actually being a quantity rule.

In discussing Friedman's monetary rule, Tobin (1965, p. 472) notes the difficulty in providing an unambiguous definition of money. Then he criticizes "Friedman and his followers" because they seem to be saying that "we don't know what money is, but whatever it is, its stock should

10. I do not mean to argue that a constant-growth-rate rule for money, if implemented in the United States, say, 30 years ago, would have been inferior to actual monetary policy. A quantity rule is likely to be better than discretion. Also, the difference between a quantity rule, say, for M1, and a rule for stabilizing the general level of prices derives from movements in the real demand for M1. But shifts in this demand—especially the changes in velocity that are induced by shifting nominal interest rates—would probably have been mild if the monetary authority had adhered for a long time to a constant-growth-rate rule. However, when starting from a state of high and volatile nominal interest rates, there are serious problems in the implementation of a quantity rule. One problem is the possibility of severe deflation during the transition to lower inflation, because real cash balances must rise dramatically. The advantage of a price rule is that it allows for large infusions of nominal money during the transition. Further, because this monetary expansion arises only in response to the actual behavior of prices, there is no threat to the credibility of the system.

grow steadily at 3 to 4 per cent per year." In fact, a workable monetary rule would seem to entail settling on some definition of money and then dictating the behavior of this concept. Ex ante the precise definition of money may matter little. Yet it is important to stick with the chosen definition in order to avoid discretionary behavior. Otherwise the monetary authority could always find a revised definition that delivers the desired behavior ex post.

As in the case of quantity rules, the argument for focusing on a narrow band of prices, such as gold or an exchange rate, is that such regimes are relatively easy to operate and monitor. Otherwise, it would be preferable to stabilize a broad index of prices, possibly using the price of gold, as in Fisher's proposal, or some other price instrument to attain the desired behavior of prices in general.

At the risk of engaging in normative economics (see below), I would advocate a modified Fisherian regime in which open-market operations, rather than the price of gold, were used to achieve a target path of a general price index, such as the deflator for the gross national product (GNP).[11] This type of regime involves a form of feedback, whereby a price level above target for a specified length of time triggers lower growth of the monetary base, and vice versa for a price level below target. The objective might involve a moving path of prices, which allows for nonzero inflation. However, the ease of monitoring the system, as well as prevention of "once-and-for-all" discretionary adjustments to the level of prices, argues for specifying the target as a constant price level. This setup would also produce a convenient monetary unit, which is one that maintains a nearly constant purchasing power.[12] One possible drawback of this scheme is that it severely limits the government's revenue from printing money. However, it would be possible to permit deviations from the target price level—and thereby permit more revenue from money creation—during major wars. This kind of provision parallels the tendency under previous monetary regimes for governments to depart from gold in wartime.

A credible rule of this type works to stabilize prices even if there are lags in observations of price indexes, or in the feedback reaction of money to past prices, or in the effects of (exogenous changes in) money

---

11. Simons (1936), who was concerned mostly with the superiority of rules over authorities, also favored a price rule over a quantity rule.

12. See Hall (1982) for a related discussion.

on the price level. In particular, if prices rise above target, then people know that future monetary actions will eventually bring prices back down to target. The exact timing of the monetary reaction is not crucial. In any event the expectation of future deflation raises the current real demand for money, a result that lowers today's price level. Hence there is a form of stabilizing speculation that improves the functioning of the system.

Overall, the proposed rule would generate a near-zero mean inflation rate and a small forecast variance of future price levels. In such a regime the prices of individual commodities would be accurate guides for the allocation of resources. As in Hayek (1945), monetary policy would provide for a stable economic background that enhances the flow of information and thereby promotes efficiency.

Recently some people have suggested that monetary policy should aim at stabilizing nominal GNP rather than the general price level (see, for example, Hall 1980 and Taylor 1984). Because nominal GNP is the product of real GNP and the GNP deflator, this rule prescribes inverse feedback of money to two things: first, excesses of real GNP above target and, second, excesses of the deflator over target. By contrast, the price-stabilization rule dictates feedback only to the second item; given the price level, fluctuations in real GNP do not induce any reactions of monetary instruments.

To evaluate proposals for stabilizing nominal GNP, one has to ask why feedback from real GNP to money is desirable. This reaction must mean that the monetary authority does a poorer job of stabilizing the overall price level. That is, there are occasions when the policymaker accepts greater departures of the price level from target in order to effect the desired response of money to fluctuations in output. But then there must be some gain from these monetary reactions to output that justifies the accompanying increase in fluctuations of the general price level.

In many theories associated with the new classical macroeconomics, such as those of Sargent and Wallace (1975), the regular reaction of money to real activity does not smooth out the business cycle.[13] Because people know that recessions inspire monetary accelerations, there are no

---

13. This conclusion also obtains in purely real theories of business cycles. In other models monetary activism can affect the character of the business cycle, but not in a desirable manner. In these cases it follows immediately that feedback from output to money should be avoided.

systematic surprises. Then, if only the surprise movements in money matter for real variables, there would be no implications for the business cycle. It follows that it would be preferable to limit monetary policy to the objective of stabilizing the general price level. Any broadening of this objective threatens people's accurate perceptions of prices (an outcome that has adverse real effects) but provides no offsetting benefits.

On the other hand, Keynesian theories with sticky prices suggest that regular feedback from output to money can (usefully) smooth out fluctuations in real economic activity. Hence, although it means an increase in the volatility of prices, it is nevertheless worthwhile for money to react systematically to variations in real GNP.

In effect, the proposal to stabilize nominal GNP is an attempt to unite the principal warring factions of macroeconomists. The new classicists are supposed to be happy because monetary policy is governed by a rule, and that rule does entail stabilization of some nominal magnitude. Then the feedback response of money to real GNP is to be regarded as a minor nuisance, most of which the private sector can hopefully filter out.

Keynesians are supposed to be happy with the scheme because it allows for an active response of money to recessions and booms. Presumably, most Keynesians would also accept the feedback from prices to money, although they may not opt for the equal weighting attached to fluctuations in real GNP versus fluctuations in the general price level. Apparently, the main thing that Keynesians have to give up is their commitment to discretionary monetary policy, which seems little to ask.

The choice between the two objectives—stabilizing the general price level versus stabilizing nominal GNP—corresponds to the weights one attaches to the validity of the two competing viewpoints about macroeconomics. (Surely one of these views must be correct!) If one attaches little weight to Keynesian theories with sticky prices, then the policymaker's preferred objective would be stabilization of the general price level.

Positive versus Normative Theories of Government Policy

I have been vague in this chapter about whether I am engaging in positive or normative economics. In Barro and Gordon (1983a) we intended to carry out a positive analysis of monetary policy, given that the existing institutions dictated an environment of discretion. In this setting the policymaker could not opt for a rule, under which there would be meaningful commitments about future money and prices. Given these institutional constraints, we analyzed the day-to-day operating characteristics of the monetary authority. We also observed that the advice of economists would not be especially relevant at this level.

Gordon and I contrasted the results under discretion with those under a rule, which was an alternative institution where the policymaker could and did make some commitments about future money and prices. For this comparison between discretion and rules to be interesting, it must be that both setups are feasible under some circumstances. That is, at some level there must be a choice of whether to create an institutional arrangement that does or does not permit commitments about future money and prices. Because the process of creating institutions involves substantial lumpy costs, changes would occur infrequently. But the choices should be as much subject to positive analysis as are those about day-to-day operations under a given institutional mode. Further, if an economist labels the actual institutional selection as inferior to the nonchosen option, then what does that labeling mean? Possibly the economist has unearthed new knowledge, but other possibilities are more likely. Although Buchanan and Tullock (1962) and Buchanan (1962) argue the opposite, it is unclear why the advice of economists is more pertinent at the level of institutional choice than it is at the level of day-to-day operations.

I suppose the answer is that economists' advice has some role as part of the economy's overall production process. Then the value of this advice is measured in the same way as that of other factors of production. Namely, economists' market wages—rather than claims of saving the economy vast sums through policy advice—tell us something about the group's productivity. Although the wages of economists are fairly high (in the United States), they still represent a negligible proportion of the GNP.

References

Backus, D., and J. Driffill. 1985. "Inflation and Reputation." *American Economic Review* 75(3):530–538.

Barro, R. J. 1983. "Inflationary Finance under Discretion and Rules." *Canadian Journal of Economics* 16(1):1–16.

———— 1984. "Rules versus Discretion." Presented at the Conference on Alternative Monetary Regimes, Dartmouth College, Hanover, New Hampshire.

———— 1986. "Reputation in a Model of Monetary Policy with Incomplete Information." *Journal of Monetary Economics* 17:3–20.

Barro, R. J., and D. Gordon. 1983a. "Rules, Discretion and Reputation in a Model of Monetary Policy." *Journal of Monetary Economics* 12(1):101–121.

———— 1983b. "A Positive Theory of Monetary Policy in a Natural Rate Model." *Journal of Political Economy* 91(4):589–610.

Buchanan, J. M. 1962. "Predictability: The Criterion of Monetary Constitutions." In *In Search of a Monetary Constitution*, ed. L. B. Yeager. Cambridge, Mass.: Harvard University Press, pp. 155–183.

Buchanan, J. M., and G. Tullock. 1962. *The Calculus of Consent*. Ann Arbor: University of Michigan Press.

Calvo, G. 1978. "On the Time Consistency of Optimal Policy in a Monetary Economy." *Econometrica* 46(6):1411–28.

Canzoneri, M. B. 1984. "Monetary Policy Games and the Role of Private Information." Unpublished manuscript. Federal Reserve Board.

Fisher, I. 1920. *Stabilizing the Dollar*. New York: Macmillan.

Friedman, J. W. 1971. "A Noncooperative Equilibrium for Supergames." *Review of Economic Studies* 38(113):1–12.

Friedman, M. 1960. *A Program for Monetary Stability*. New York: Fordham University Press.

Green, E., and R. Porter. 1984. "Noncooperative Collusion under Imperfect Price Information." *Econometrica* 52(1):87–100.

Hall, R. E. 1980. "Monetary Policy for Disinflation." Remarks prepared for the Federal Reserve Board, October.

———— 1982. "Explorations in the Gold Standard and Related Policies for Stabilizing the Dollar." In *Inflation: Causes and Effects*, ed. R. Hall. Chicago: University of Chicago Press, for the National Bureau of Economic Research, pp. 111–122.

Hayek, F. A. 1945. "The Use of Knowledge in Society." *American Economic Review* 35(4):519–530.

Hetzel, R. 1984. "The Formulation of Monetary Policy." Unpublished manuscript. Federal Reserve Bank of Richmond.

Kreps, D., and R. Wilson. 1982. "Reputation and Imperfect Information." *Journal of Economic Theory* 27(2):253–279.

Kydland, F. W., and E. C. Prescott. 1977. "Rules rather than Discretion: The Inconsistency of Optimal Plans." *Journal of Political Economy* 85(3):473–491.

Lucas, R. E., and N. Stokey. 1983. "Optimal Fiscal and Monetary Policy in an Economy without Capital." *Journal of Monetary Economics* 12(1):55–93.

McCallum, B. T. 1984. "Some Issues Concerning Interest Rate Pegging, Price Level Determinacy and Real Bills Doctrine." National Bureau of Economic Research Working Paper No. 1294.

McCulloch, J. H. 1980. "The Ban on Indexed Bonds." *American Economic Review* 70(5):1018–21.

Milgrom, P., and J. Roberts. 1982. "Predation, Reputation, and Entry Deterrence." *Journal of Economic Theory* 27(2):280–312.

Nussbaum, A. 1950. *Money in the Law, National and International.* Brooklyn, N.Y.: Foundation Press.

Persson, T., and L. Svensson. 1984. "Time-Consistent Fiscal Policy and Government Cash-Flow." *Journal of Monetary Economics* 14(3):365–374.

Sargent, T. J., and N. Wallace. 1975. "Rational Expectations, the Optimal Monetary Instrument, and the Optimal Money Supply Rule." *Journal of Political Economy* 83(2):241–254.

Selten, R. 1978. "The Chain-Store Paradox." *Theory and Decision* 9(2):127–159.

Simons, H. 1936. "Rules versus Authorities in Monetary Policy." *Journal of Political Economy* 44(1):1–30.

Tabellini, G. 1983. "Accommodative Monetary Policy and Central Bank Reputation." Unpublished manuscript. Los Angeles: University of California.

Taylor, J. 1984. "What Would Nominal GNP Targeting Do to the Business Cycle?" Presented at the Carnegie-Rochester Conference, Rochester, New York, April.

Tobin, J. 1965. "The Monetary Interpretation of History." (Review article) *American Economic Review* 55(3):464–485.

Yeager, L. B. 1966. *International Monetary Relations.* New York: Harper and Row.

2 A Positive Theory of Monetary Policy in a Natural Rate Model

With David B. Gordon
Board of Governors of the Federal Reserve System
Washington, D.C.

The primary purpose of this chapter is to develop a positive theory of monetary policy and inflation. On the one hand, the theory turns out to accord with two perceptions about the world in recent years:

1. Average rates of inflation and monetary growth are excessive relative to an efficiency criterion.
2. There is a tendency to pursue activist, countercyclical monetary policies.

Yet the model exhibits three other properties:

3. The unemployment rate—our proxy for real economic activity—is invariant with monetary policy (neglecting the familiar deadweight-loss aspect of inflation).
4. The policymaker and the public all act rationally, subject to their environments.
5. The policymaker's objectives reflect the public's preferences.[1]

From *Journal of Political Economy* (1983) 91(4):589–610; © 1983 by The University of Chicago. Useful suggestions were provided on earlier drafts by Ken Arrow, Gary Becker, Bob Brito, Ben Eden, Donald Gordon, Herschel Grossman, Bob Hall, Bob Lucas, Bill Oakland, Alan Stockman, and Larry Weiss. This research was supported in part by the National Science Foundation.

1. The model that we consider is sufficiently simple to allow for unanimity about desirable governmental actions.

Natural rate models with rational expectations—such as that developed by Sargent and Wallace (1975)—suggest that the systematic parts of monetary policy are irrelevant for real economic activity. Some empirical evidence on the real effects of monetary disturbances in the post–World War II United States (for example, Barro 1977, 1981) is consistent with this result—in particular, there is some support for the proposition that anticipated monetary changes are neutral with respect to output, unemployment, and so on. On the other hand, these empirical studies and others indicated the presence of countercyclical monetary policy at least for the post–World War II United States—rises in the unemployment rate appear to generate subsequent expansions in monetary growth. Within the natural rate framework, it is difficult to reconcile this countercyclical monetary behavior with rationality of the policymaker.[2] A principal object of our analysis is to achieve this reconciliation.

The natural rate models that have appeared in the macroeconomics literature of the last decade share the characteristic that policy choice is over a class of prespecified monetary rules. With the policy rule predetermined, there is no scope for ongoing policymaking; discretionary policy choice is excluded a priori. If private agents can deduce the characteristics of the monetary process once it is implemented, it defines their expectations. Thus the policy decision is made subject to the constraint that agents' expectations of future monetary policy will equal the realization. This framework allows the analysis to be reduced to a pair of single-agent decision problems, which can be considered independently. But this approach cannot deal with the game-theoretic situation that arises when policy decisions are made on an ongoing basis.

In our framework an equilibrium will include the following features:

(a) a decision rule for private agents, which determines their
    actions as a function of their current information;

2. Many people respond with a willingness to view public policy as irrational. Despite the obvious attractions of this viewpoint, it does leave us without a theory of systematic governmental behavior. An earlier attempted reconciliation with rationality (Barro 1977, p. 104) relied on public finance considerations associated with cyclical changes in the revenue obtained from printing money. This avenue appears to be quantitatively insufficient to explain the facts about countercyclical monetary response. However, the revenue motive for money creation is important in some extreme cases. See, for example, Hercowitz (1981) for an analysis of monetary behavior and government spending during the German hyperinflation.

(b) an expectations function, which determines the expectations of private agents as a function of their current information; and

(c) a policy rule, which specifies the behavior of policy instruments as a function of the policymaker's current information set.

The outcome is said to be a rational-expectations equilibrium if, first, the decision rule specified in (a) is optimal for agents given their expectations as calculated under (b); and, second, it is optimal for the policy-maker, whose actions are described by (c), to perform in accordance with agents' expectations (b), given that the policymaker recognizes the form of the private decision rules under (a). Faced by a maximizing policy-maker, it would be unreasonable for agents to maintain expectations from which they know it will be in the policymaker's interest to deviate.

If policy is precommitted, the only reasonable expectations that agents can hold are those defined by the rule. But, if policy is sequentially chosen, the equality of policy expectations and realizations is a character-istic of equilibrium—not a prior constraint. We have to determine which expectations agents can reasonably expect to be realized.

We view the policymaker as attempting to maximize an objective that reflects "society's" preferences on inflation and unemployment. (Addi-tional arguments for the preference function are mentioned later.) Al-though the equilibrium involves a path of unemployment that is invari-ant with policy, the rational policymaker adopts an activist rule. The extent of countercyclical response depends on, among other things, soci-ety's relative dislikes for inflation and unemployment. This result ap-pears paradoxical, because the policymaker pursues an activist policy that ends up having no desirable effects—in fact, unemployment is unal-tered but inflation ends up being excessive. This outcome reflects the assumed inability of the policymaker—that is, of the institutional appa-ratus that is set up to manage monetary affairs—to commit its course of future actions. This feature has been stressed in an important paper by Kydland and Prescott (1977). If commitment were feasible through legal arrangements or other procedures, the countercyclical aspect of mone-tary policy would disappear (and, abstracting from costs of erecting and maintaining institutions, everyone would be better off). When this type of advance restriction is precluded, so that the policymaker sets instru-ments at each date subject only to the initial conditions prevailing for that date (which do not include restraints on policy choices), the equilib-rium may involve an activist form of policy. This solution conforms to optimal behavior of private agents subject to a rationally anticipated policy rule. It corresponds also to optimality for the policymaker each period, subject to agents' decision rules. Although an equilibrium obtains, the results are suboptimal, relative to outcomes where commitment is permitted. Given an environment where this type of policy commitment is absent—such as that for the United States and other countries in recent years—the results constitute a positive theory of monetary growth and inflation.

We illustrate the results with a simple model, which comes from an example in Kydland and Prescott (1977, pp. 477–480). We augment their example along the lines detailed in Gordon (1980) to include a theory of expectations formation. People form their expectations by effectively solving the problem that the optimizing policymaker will face. The policymaker's problem is then conditioned on the expectations function of private agents. Ultimately, there are no systematic differences between expected and realized inflation. But this property emerges as part of the equilibrium rather than as a constraint on the policy problem.

The Model of Unemployment and Inflation

The unemployment rate U_t, which is a convenient proxy for the overall state of real activity, equals a "natural rate," U_t^n, plus a term that depends negatively on contemporaneous unexpected inflation, $\pi_t - \pi_t^e$,

$$U_t = U_t^n - \alpha(\pi_t - \pi_t^e), \quad \alpha > 0. \tag{2.1}$$

For convenience, we treat the "Phillips curve slope" parameter, α, as a constant.[3] Given the relevant inflationary expectations, π_t^e, Eq. (2.1) is assumed to reflect the maximizing behavior of private agents on decentralized markets. The formulation of π_t^e is detailed below. Equation (2.1) could be reformulated without changing the main conclusions by expressing U_t as a reduced-form function of monetary shocks.

---

3. The prior expectation of inflation for period t could be distinguished from the expectation that is conditioned on partial information about current prices. This distinction arises in models (for example, Lucas 1972, 1973; Barro 1976) in which people operate in localized markets with incomplete information about contemporaneous nominal aggregates. In this setting the Phillips curve slope coefficient, α, turns out to depend on the relative variances for general and market-specific shocks.

The natural unemployment rate can shift over time due to autonomous real shocks, ε_t. A single real disturbance is allowed to have a persisting influence on unemployment, output, and so on. This behavior is modeled as

$$U_t^n = \lambda U_{t-1}^n + (1 - \lambda)\overline{U}^n + \varepsilon_t, \quad 0 \le \lambda \le 1, \tag{2.2}$$

where ε_t is independently, identically distributed with zero mean. If $0 < \lambda < 1$ applies, then the realization for the shock ε_t affects future natural unemployment rates in the same direction. However, the effect dissipates gradually over time—Eq. (2.2) implies that the long-run mean of the natural unemployment rate is $\overline{U}^n$, a constant. For convenience, we assume that U_t in Eq. (2.1) depends only on contemporaneous unexpected inflation, $\pi_t - \pi_t^e$, and not on lagged values. These additional terms could be introduced without changing the main results (see below). Thus the main thrust of our analysis is compatible with either monetary or real theories of business cycles.

The policymaker's (and society's) objective for each period is summarized by a cost, Z_t, which depends on that period's values for the unemployment rate and inflation. We assume a simple quadratic form,

$$Z_t = a(U_t - kU_t^n)^2 + b(\pi_t)^2; \quad a, b > 0, 0 \le k \le 1. \tag{2.3}$$

We do not consider any divergence across individuals in their assessments of relative costs for unemployment and inflation.

The first term in Eq. (2.3) indicates that costs rise with the departure of the unemployment rate from a target value, kU_t^n, which depends positively on the contemporaneous natural rate. In the absence of external effects, $k = 1$ would correspond to an efficiency criterion—that is, departures of U_t from U_t^n in either direction would be penalized. In the presence of unemployment compensation, income taxation, and the like, the natural unemployment rate will tend to exceed the efficient level—that is, privately chosen quantities of marketable output and employment will tend to be too low. The inequality $k < 1$ captures this possibility.[4] Not surprisingly, we shall need some existing distortion in the economy—that is, $k < 1$—in order to generate activist policy in our model. This result conforms with those stressed by Calvo (1978a).

4. The target unemployment rate is $U_t^* = kU_t^n < U_t^n$. The formulation implies also that $\partial U_t^* / \partial U_t^n < 1$. The last condition, which we use for some conclusions, is more difficult to justify.

Governmental decisions on taxes and transfers will generally influence the value of k. However, given that some government expenditures are to be carried out, it will generally be infeasible to select a fiscal policy that avoids all distortions and yields $k = 1$. We assume that the government's optimization on the fiscal side—which we do not analyze explicitly—results in a value of k that satisfies $0 < k < 1$. The choice of monetary policy is then carried out conditional on this value of k.

Equation (2.3) regards departures of π_t from zero as generating costs. Economists have not come up with convincing arguments to explain why inflation is very costly. However, direct costs of changing prices would fit most easily into our model. More generally, the form of the cost function could be changed to include a term in $(\pi_t - \bar{\pi}_t)^2$, where $\bar{\pi}_t$ might involve the optimal rate of taxation on cash balances. A later section expands the analysis to consider the revenue from money creation.

We assume that the policymaker controls an instrument—say, monetary growth, μ_t—which has a direct connection to inflation, π_t, in each period. This specification neglects any dynamic relation between inflation and monetary growth or a correlation between $(\pi_t - \mu_t)$ and the real disturbances, ε_t, ε_{t-1}, ... In effect, we pretend that the policymaker chooses π_t directly in each period. We discuss later what happens when we allow a separation between inflation and monetary growth.

The choice of π_t at each date is designed to minimize the expected present value of costs, as calculated at some starting date zero. That is, the objective is to minimize

$$E \left[\sum_{t=1}^{\infty} \frac{Z_t}{(1 + r)^t} \right] \Bigg| I_0, \tag{2.4}$$

where I_0 represents the initial state of information and r is a constant, exogenous real discount rate. It should be stressed that the policymaker's objective conforms with society's preferences.

The determination of inflation and unemployment can be characterized as a game between the policymaker and a large number of private-sector agents. The structure of this game is as follows. The policymaker enters period t with the information set, I_{t-1}. The inflation rate, π_t, is set based on I_{t-1} in order to be consistent with the cost-minimization objective that we set out in expression (2.4). Simultaneously, each individual formulates expectations, π_t^e, for the policymaker's choice of inflation for period t. These expectations are based on the same information set, I_{t-1}, as that available to the policymaker. Most important, in forming inflationary expectations, people incorporate the knowledge that π_t will emerge from the policymaker's cost-minimization problem that we specified in Eq. (2.4). Finally, the choices for π_t and π_t^e, together with the random disturbance, ε_t, determine U_t and the cost, Z_t, in accordance with Eqs. (2.1)–(2.3).

The Expectations Mechanism

To determine π_t^e, agents must consider the policymaker's optimization problem, which determines the choice of π_t. Suppose for the moment that the policymaker, when selecting π_t, treats π_t^e and all future values of inflationary expectations, π_{t+i}^e, as given. Variations in π_t affect unemployment through the usual Phillips curve mechanism in Eq. (2.1). As the model is set out, this effect would not carry forward to direct effects on future unemployment rates, although this channel of persistence could be incorporated. We assume that the current choice of inflation, π_t, also implies no direct constraints on future choices, π_{t+i}. Therefore, with current and future inflationary expectations held fixed, the determination of π_t involves only a one-period trade-off between higher inflation and lower unemployment in accordance with the cost function of Eq. (2.3).

In the present framework the determination of π_t^e is divorced from the particular realization of π_t. At the start of period t, agents form π_t^e by forecasting the policymaker's "best" action, contingent on the information set, I_{t-1}. The expectation, π_t^e, is not conditioned on π_t itself. Therefore the policymaker faces a choice problem in which π_t^e is fixed while π_t is selected. Further, in formulating π_t^e, the private agents understand that the policymaker is in this position.

The connection between π_t and future inflationary expectations, π_{t+i}^e, is less clear. As noted before, the present model allows for no direct connection between π_t (even with π_t^e held fixed) and future "objective" characteristics of the economy. There is also no scope for learning over time about the economy's structure; in particular, π_t supplies no additional information about the objective or technology of the policymaker. Accordingly, we are inclined to search for an equilibrium in which π_{t+i}^e does not depend on "extraneous" past variables, such as π_t. However, the severing of a link between π_t and π_{t+i}^e eliminates some possibly interesting equilibria in which the government can invest in its reputation—

that is, in "credibility." The nature of these solutions is discussed later. For present purposes we examine situations in which future expectations, π^e_{t+i}, are invariant with π_t.

Given that future values of U and π^e are independent of π_t, there is no channel for π_t to affect future costs, Z_{t+i}. Therefore the objective posed in expression (2.4) reduces to the one-period problem of selecting π_t in order to minimize $E_{t-1}Z_t$.

In a solution to the model, the public will view the policymaker as setting π_t in accordance with the information set, I_{t-1}, which is available at the start of period t. Suppose that people perceive this process as described by the reaction function, $h^e(I_{t-1})$.[5] Therefore inflationary expectations—formed on the basis of I_{t-1}—are given by[6]

$$\pi^e_t = h^e(I_{t-1}). \tag{2.5}$$

A solution to the model involves finding a function $h^e(\cdot)$, such that setting $\pi_t = h^e(I_{t-1})$ is a solution to the policymaker's cost-minimization problem, given that $\pi^e_t = h^e(I_{t-1})$. Expecting inflation as specified by $h^e(\cdot)$ must not contradict the policymaker's minimization of expected costs, as set out in Eq. (2.3). The previous discussion suggests that lagged values of inflation will not appear as parts of the solution, $h^e(\cdot)$. That is, we are looking for an equilibrium where $\partial \pi^e_t / \partial \pi_{t-i} = \partial h^e / \partial \pi_{t-i} = 0$ applies for all $i > 0$. We also look for a solution where the policymaker understands that π^e_t is generated from Eq. (2.5).

The unemployment rate is determined from Eq. (2.1) after substituting for U^n_t from Eq. (2.2) and for π^e_t from Eq. (2.5) as

$$U_t = \lambda U^n_{t-1} + (1 - \lambda)\bar{U}^n + \varepsilon_t - \alpha[\pi_t - h^e(I_{t-1})]. \tag{2.6}$$

Costs for period t follow by substituting for U_t and π^e_t in Eq. (2.3) as

$$Z_t = a\{(1 - k)[\lambda U^n_{t-1} + (1 - \lambda)\bar{U}^n + \varepsilon_t]$$
$$- \alpha[\pi_t - h^e(I_{t-1})]\}^2 + b(\pi_t)^2. \tag{2.7}$$

5. In the present setting the policymaker has no incentive to randomize policy choices—therefore, the reaction function ends up being purely deterministic.
6. Because there are many private agents, they neglect any effect of their methods for formulating π^e_t on the policymaker's choice of π_t.

Given that inflationary expectations for period t are $\pi_t^e = h^e(I_{t-1})$, the policymaker selects π_t to minimize $E_{t-1}Z_t$. The first-order condition, $(\partial/\partial\pi_t)(E_{t-1}Z_t) = 0$, implies that the chosen inflation rate, denoted by $\hat{\pi}_t$, satisfies the condition

$$\hat{\pi}_t = \frac{a\alpha}{b}\{-\alpha[\hat{\pi}_t - h^e(I_{t-1})] + (1 - k)[\lambda U_{t-1}^n + (1 - \lambda)\bar{U}^n]\}. \quad (2.8)$$

The property, $E(\varepsilon_t | I_{t-1}) = 0$, has been used here. The second-order condition for a minimum is satisfied.

Although the policymaker is not constrained to follow the anticipated rule, $h^e(I_{t-1})$, the public understands the nature of the policymaker's optimization problem in each period. In particular, people understand that the actual choice, $\hat{\pi}_t$, satisfies Eq. (2.8). Therefore rationality entails using Eq. (2.8) to calculate $h^e(I_{t-1})$ in Eq. (2.5). Consistency requires that $h^e(I_{t-1}) = \hat{\pi}_t$. The unexpected inflation term, $\hat{\pi}_t - h^e(I_{t-1})$, then cancels out in Eq. (2.8), and the formula for the expectations function becomes

$$\pi_t^e = h^e(I_{t-1}) = \frac{a\alpha}{b}(1 - k)[\lambda U_{t-1}^n + (1 - \lambda)\bar{U}^n] \quad (2.9)$$

$$= \frac{a\alpha}{b}(1 - k)E_{t-1}U_t^n.$$

Equilibrium Policy

By the construction of the problem, a policymaker who faces the expectations given in Eq. (2.9) will be motivated from the first-order condition of Eq. (2.8) to choose an inflation rate, $\hat{\pi}_t$, that coincides with π_t^e. That is, the equilibrium involves

$$\hat{\pi}_t = \frac{a\alpha}{b}(1 - k)E_{t-1}U_t^n = \pi_t^e. \quad (2.10)$$

Since $\hat{\pi}_t = \pi_t^e$, $U_t = U_t^n$ applies also as part of the equilibrium.

Equation (2.10) provides an equilibrium (Nash equilibrium) in the following sense. Given the public's equilibrium perceptions, $\pi_t^e = h^e(\cdot)$, minimization of $E_{t-1}Z_t$ (for a given value of π_t^e) induces the policymaker to choose $\hat{\pi}_t = h^e(\cdot)$ in each period.[7] Expectations are rational and individuals optimize subject to these expectations—as summarized in Eqs. (2.1) and (2.2).

To provide perspective on the present framework, consider an alternative manner in which the policymaker's choice problem could have been formulated. Policy could have been viewed as the once-and-for-all choice of reaction function, $h(\cdot)$, so that $\pi_t^e = h^e(\cdot) = h(\cdot)$ holds automatically in every period for all choices of $h(\cdot)$. This perspective applies, for example, to the analysis of macro policy in Sargent and Wallace (1975). In their setting the choice of the function $h(\cdot)$ affects not only π_t but also π_t^e in each period. The independence of π_t^e from π_t is broken in the context of a once-and-for-all selection of policy functions. The condition $\pi_t - \pi_t^e = \pi_t - h^e(I_{t-1}) = 0$ is then a constraint on the policy problem and can be substituted into Eq. (2.7). In particular, with π_t^e guaranteed to move one-to-one with changes in π_t, the policymaker must regard unemployment, $U_t = U_t^n$, as invariant with $h(\cdot)$. Given the simple objective from Eq. (2.3), which penalizes departures of π_t from zero, the choice of $h(\cdot)$ that minimizes EZ_t for all periods is a variant of the constant-growth-rate rule,[8]

$$\pi_t^* = h(I_{t-1}) = 0. \tag{2.11}$$

Note that $U_t = U_t^n$ obtains again as part of this solution.

Given the public's perceptions, $\pi_t^e = h^e(I_{t-1})$, U_t depends on the term, $\pi_t - \pi_t^e = \pi_t - h^e(I_{t-1})$. People have observed (Taylor 1975; Friedman 1979) that the policymaker can fool the public and reduce unemployment ("temporarily") by setting $\pi_t > \pi_t^e = h^e(I_{t-1})$ in period t. This possibility is ruled out in the case where policy amounts to a once-and-for-all binding choice of $h(\cdot)$. However, there may be no mechanism in place to constrain the policymaker to stick to the rule, $h(I_{t-1})$, as time evolves. This consideration leads to the setup for policy choice that we assumed before—namely, for given initial conditions in each period, including the expectations mechanism, $\pi_t^e = h^e(I_{t-1})$, set π_t in order to minimize $E_{t-1}Z_t$. The policymaker is not required to select an inflation rate that equals the given expected inflation rate. However, people also realize

---

7. Note that no equilibrium exists if the policymaker gives no direct weight to inflation—that is, if $b = 0$. More generally, we require that the marginal cost of inflation, π_t, be positive at a point where $\pi_t = \pi_t^e$.

8. If Z_t in Eq. (2.3) depended on $(\pi_t - \bar{\pi}_t)^2$, $\pi_t^* = \bar{\pi}_t$ would emerge.

that the policymaker has the power to fool them at each date. Since the formation of expectations takes this potential for deception into account, a full equilibrium will ultimately involve $\pi_t = \pi_t^e$. The crucial point is that—unlike the case of a once-and-for-all choice of policy rules, the policymaker does not regard $\pi_t = \pi_t^e$ as occurring automatically for all possible choices of π_t. For this reason the (noncooperative) equilibrium does not correspond to Eq. (2.11).

Compare the equilibrium solution, $\hat{\pi}_t$ from Eq. (2.10), with the choice, $\pi_t^* = 0$, which arises from a once-and-for-all selection of policy rules. The equilibrium solution delivers the same unemployment rate and a higher rate of inflation at each date. Therefore, the equilibrium cost, $\hat{Z}_t$, exceeds that, Z_t^*, which would arise under the rule. (Note that, with U_t the same in both cases, costs end up depending only on the path of the inflation rate.) Of course, this conclusion neglects any costs of setting up or operating the different institutional environments. Notably, the costs of enforcing commitments are excluded. With this cost neglected, the present type of result provides a normative argument (and positive theory?) for policy rules—that is, for commitment on future choices of π_t. We highlight these aspects of our results in a later section.

It may be useful to demonstrate directly that $\pi_t = 0$ is not an equilibrium for the case where the policymaker optimizes subject to given expectations in each period. Conjecture that $\pi_t^e = h^e(I_{t-1}) = 0$ holds. In this case the choice of $\pi_t > 0$ would reduce unemployment for period t. A trade-off arises between reduced costs of unemployment and increased costs from inflation. The balancing of these costs determines the chosen inflation rate, as shown in Eq. (2.8). Under the assumed conditions (marginal cost of inflation is zero at $\pi_t = 0$ and marginal benefit from reduced unemployment is positive when $U_t = U_t^n$), the selected inflation rate will be positive. However, since people understand this policy choice, the result $\pi_t > 0$ is inconsistent with the conjecture that $\pi_t^e = 0$. Zero inflation is not a reasonable expectation for individuals to hold.

An analogous argument can be used to find the positive rate of inflation that does provide an equilibrium. If a small positive value for π_t^e had been conjectured, the policymaker would still have been motivated to select $\pi_t > \pi_t^e$, which would be inconsistent with equilibrium. The equilibrium obtains when π_t^e is sufficiently high, so that $\pi_t = \pi_t^e$ is the policymaker's best choice, given this value of π_t^e. At this point the policymaker retains the option of choosing $\pi_t > \pi_t^e$ (or $\pi_t < \pi_t^e$) to accomplish a trade-off between lower unemployment and higher inflation (or vice versa).

However, the level of π_t^e is sufficiently high that the marginal cost of inflation just balances the marginal gain from reducing unemployment.[9] The inflation rate that corresponds to this equilibrium condition is given in Eq. (2.10).

The rules-type equilibrium, given in Eq. (2.11), is often referred to as the optimal, but time-inconsistent, solution (see, for example, Kydland and Prescott 1977, p. 480). The term *time inconsistent* refers to the policymaker's incentives to deviate from the rule when private agents expect it to be followed. On the other hand, the discretionary equilibrium, given in Eq. (2.10), is often called the suboptimal, but time-consistent, solution. This terminology is deceptive in that it suggests that these decision rules represent alternative solutions to the same problem. Although the objective function and decision rules of private agents are identical, the problems differ in the opportunity sets of the policymaker.

In one case, constraints on future policy actions are infeasible, by assumption. In the other case, rules are enforceable, so that the policymaker can commit the course of future policy (and thus of expectations). In the former case, the time-inconsistent solution is not an equilibrium, given the problem faced by the policymaker. In the latter case, the incentives to deviate from the rule are irrelevant, since commitments are assumed to be binding. Thus the time-inconsistency of the optimal solution is either irrelevant—when commitments are feasible—or else this solution does not solve the problem actually faced by the policymaker.

Properties of the Discretionary Equilibrium

Assume now that the policymaker cannot make binding commitments, so that optimization occurs period by period, as we have been assuming for most of our analysis. Under this discretionary regime, the solution for $\hat{\pi}_t$ in Eq. (2.10) constitutes a positive theory of inflation and monetary growth. The major implications are

1. The average inflation rate exceeds the value (zero in this model) that would be optimal if policy rules were feasible. Therefore an exogenous shift from a regime that involved some commitment on nominal

---

9. Consider the more general case where $Z_t = Z(U_t - kU_t^n, \pi_t)$ and $U_t = U_t^n - f(\pi_t - \pi_t^e)$. The first-order condition entails $f' = (\partial Z/\partial \pi_t)/[\partial Z/\partial (U_t - kU_t^n)]$. This expression is evaluated in equilibrium at $\pi_t = \pi_t^e$ and $U_t = U_t^n$. An equilibrium will be found if $\partial Z/\partial \pi_t$ rises sufficiently with π_t (as it does in the quadratic case considered in the text) or if f' declines sufficiently with π_t. Given the last condition, it is no longer essential that inflation involve increasing marginal costs—$\partial^2 Z/\partial \pi_t^2 > 0$.

values—such as a gold standard or possibly a system with fixed exchange rates—to one without such restraints would produce a rise in the average rates of inflation and monetary growth.

2. Within a discretionary regime, the rate of inflation rises if the policymaker attaches greater benefits to unexpected inflation. One change that generates this outcome is an increase in the long-run average of the natural unemployment rate, $\bar{U}^n$. In fact, the natural unemployment rate rose significantly in the United States over the last 10–15 years.

3. The benefits from surprise inflation depend on the gap between the natural unemployment rate and the target rate. In the model this gap reflects distortions, such as income taxation, which deter work effort and production. An increase in these distortions shows up as a decrease in the parameter k, which leads to a higher rate of inflation. One source of this change is the growth of government. Thus more government is inflationary in the model.

4. An adverse shock to the unemployment rate (that is, $\varepsilon_t > 0$) tends to persist over time. Then, as in the case of an increase in U^n, the benefits from inflation shocks increase. Thus the rational policymaker behaves countercyclically, in the sense that inflation and monetary growth react positively to increases in unemployment. In a larger model it would be possible to distinguish the countercyclical response of monetary growth from that of inflation. However, these two variables are directly linked in the present model. See the discussion below.

5. The mean rate of inflation and the extent of countercyclical response rise with α—the Phillips curve slope parameter in Eq. (2.1)—and the relative value of the cost coefficients, a/b, attached to unemployment versus inflation. In particular, if inflation is not very costly—as many economists have argued—then the parameter b is small and we wind up having a lot of inflation.

Some of the results listed above are the sorts of normative implications for aggregate demand policy that are delivered by Keynesian models in which policymakers can exploit a systematic (possibly dynamic) trade-off between inflation and unemployment. However, in the present model,

6. Unemployment, $U_t = U_t^n$, is invariant with the systematic parts of inflation and monetary growth.[10] In this sense policy ends up with no effect on real economic activity.

Some people have argued that policymakers do not face a "cruel

---

10. Formally, changes in the parameters a, b, α, or k—which alter $E_{t-1}\hat{\pi}_t$ for all dates t in Eq. (2.10)—have no significance for the time path of unemployment.

choice" between inflation and unemployment in a natural rate environment. This argument is misleading in a context where monetary institutions do not allow for policy choice to be committed. Although $U_t = U_t^n$ emerges in equilibrium—that is, unemployment is invariant with policy in this sense—policymakers do optimize in each period subject to the appropriate givens, which include the formation of expectations. Given these expectations, the choice of π_t does influence the unemployment rate "right now"—that is, for date t. The social trade-off between unemployment and inflation, as expressed by the preference ratio, a/b, is central to the policymaker's decision.[11] No cruel choice arises, and $\pi_t = 0$ follows only if the policymaker can commit future actions. Within the present model, this outcome is infeasible. Counseling stable prices (or constant and small rates of monetary growth) in this environment is analogous to advising firms to produce more output with given inputs. Policymakers in a discretionary regime really are finding the optimal policy, subject to the applicable constraints, when they determine a countercyclical monetary reaction with positive average rates of inflation.

Extensions to the Model

Monetary Growth as the Policy Instrument

In Barro and Gordon (1981) we developed a simple model to treat monetary growth, rather than inflation, as the instrument of policy. We allowed for control errors in the supply of money, as well as stochastic shifts to velocity.

In equilibrium we found that the discretionary policymaker would set the monetary instrument in order to equate the mean of the inflation rate to the value determined in Eq. (2.10). The actual inflation rate, however, differs from its mean because of shocks to money supply and velocity. Therefore surprises in money or in velocity lead to unexpected inflation, $\pi_t - \pi_t^e$, which affects unemployment through the mechanism of the Phillips curve in Eq. (2.1). So the unemployment rate does not

---

11. We are tempted to say that setting $\pi_t < \hat{\pi}_t$ in Eq. (2.10) would deliver $U_t > U_t^n$. (As an analogue, a firm that ends up in equilibrium with an ordinary rate of return would end up with below-normal rates of return if it did not strive to maximize profits at all times.) However, the choice of $\pi_t < \hat{\pi}_t$ is inconsistent with the prescribed form of the policymaker's objective.

always equal the natural rate in this model. In particular, positive shocks to money or velocity reduce the unemployment rate.

We found also that some disturbances would generate divergent reactions of monetary growth and inflation. The differences involve the behavior of real money demanded, which responds to changes in output (that is, in the unemployment rate) and to shifts in the expected rate of inflation.

Persisting Effects of Nominal Shocks

We can modify the model to allow the effects of inflation shocks to persist over time—that is, we can change Eq. (2.1) to allow U_t to depend on current and lagged values of $(\pi - \pi^e)$. This extension complicates the policymaker's first-order condition in Eq. (2.8) to include effects from a distributed lead of prospective values of unemployment and inflation. Ultimately, the equilibrium is altered in that expected future values of U and π appear as influences on $\hat{\pi}_t$ in Eq. (2.10).

Our basic analysis is compatible with either monetary or real disturbances as the impulses underlying the business cycle. Both of the shocks mentioned in the previous section (monetary control errors and velocity shocks) are potential nominal sources of such disturbances, but systematic monetary policy is not. Without some informational asymmetry, the policymaker is, in equilibrium, incapable of counteracting the real effects of exogenous disturbances, whatever their source.

Revenue from Money Creation and Depreciation of Public Debt

An important element in our model is the negative effect of unexpected inflation on the unemployment rate. Because the policymaker likes a lower unemployment rate, he attaches a benefit to positive inflation surprises. In finding the discretionary equilibrium, the crucial item is this benefit from unexpected inflation—the underlying Phillips curve does not matter per se. In fact, there are other reasons for the policymaker to value unexpected inflation. These include the revenue from money creation and the inverse effect of inflation on the real value of public debt.

Surprise inflation constitutes an unanticipated capital levy on holdings of the government's nominal liabilities. As with other capital levies, this form of tax—when not foreseen—can raise revenue at little deadweight loss. Therefore, from the standpoint of public finance, the policymaker would attach some benefits to surprise inflation. Further, we can identify some variables that influence the extent of these benefits. These include (1) the deadweight losses associated with other methods of taxation; (2) the volume of government expenditure, because a greater share of output absorbed by the government is likely to raise the marginal deadweight loss from conventional taxes; (3) the extent of temporary government spending, as in wartime, which may have an especially strong effect on the marginal cost of alternative taxes; (4) the position of the money-demand function (a higher level makes surprise inflation more rewarding); and (5) the outstanding real quantity of nominally denominated public debt.

Because people understand the attractions of ex post capital levies, they will attempt to forecast the policymaker's incentives to exploit such situations. Therefore, as we saw in our earlier example about the Phillips curve, systematic surprises to inflation cannot arise in equilibrium. In an equilibrium the inflation rate is high enough so that the marginal cost of inflation to balance the marginal benefit from a hypothetical unit of surprise inflation.[12] Whereas, before, the benefit involved reductions in unemployment, now the benefit concerns increased governmental revenues. Therefore, any items that people know about in advance and that shift around the benefits from those revenues will end up raising the equilibrium rate of inflation. So, from our earlier examples, we find that the inflation rate rises with an increase in government spending, especially during wartime. A higher outstanding quantity of real public debt also raises the equilibrium inflation rate.

In contrast with the simple model of the Phillips curve, realizations of unexpected inflation occur when there are unanticipated changes in the benefits from governmental revenues.[13] For example, when an unpredicted war starts, the policymaker will exercise some of his power to depreciate the real value of money and bonds. From an ex ante standpoint, this possibility is balanced by the more favorable returns on

---

12. In Calvo's (1978b) model of inflationary finance, the policymaker attaches no cost to inflation. Therefore there is no discretionary equilibrium with a finite inflation rate under rational expectations. The details of the case where inflation is viewed as costly are worked out in Barro (1983).

13. We would get this type of result in our earlier model if the unemployment rate depended on unanticipated inflation, $\pi_t - E_{t-1}\pi_t$, where the forecast, $E_{t-1}\pi_t$, is formed before all data from period $t - 1$ are available.

money and bonds during peacetime. In particular, the nominal interest rate paid on government bonds provides a satisfactory distribution of real returns, given the dependence of these returns on conditions of war or peace, and so forth.

The significance of rules is similar to that in our previous model. For the case of public debt, the indexation of returns for inflation is a simple form of rule. Indexation eliminates the government's power, ex post, to use inflation to depreciate the real value of its debts. From our perspective, we predict that the implementation of an indexing rule lowers the equilibrium growth rates of prices and money. However, this conclusion holds unambiguously only if the costs from inflation do not change. If the existence of the government's indexed bonds reduces the costs attached to inflation—that is, the b-coefficient in the cost function from Eq. (2.3)—then an opposing force emerges.

Reputational Equilibria

A different form of equilibrium may emerge in which the policymaker forgoes short-term gains for the sake of maintaining a long-term "reputation." Consider again the initial setting where costs depend on unemployment and inflation, as they do in Eq. (2.3). The "rules equilibrium" generates $U_t = U_t^n$ and $\pi_t = 0$, while the noncooperative, period-by-period solution yields the inferior outcome, $U_t = U_t^n$ and $\pi_t = \hat{\pi}_t > 0$.

Another possible form of solution, which has been discussed in the related game theory literature (for example, in Friedman 1971), takes the following form. Private agents anticipate the cooperative result,[14] $\pi_t = 0$, unless they have seen something else. Once observing a different value for inflation, agents henceforth expect the noncooperative policy, $\pi_t = \hat{\pi}_t$.[15] Confronted by this behavior, the policymaker has two options: first, $\pi_1 = \hat{\pi}_1$ can be chosen in period one. In conjunction with the initial expectation, $\pi_1^e = 0$, the choice of $\pi_1 = \hat{\pi}_1$ generates a favorable first-period trade-off between low unemployment, $U_1 < U_1^n$, and high inflation. For the first period the policymaker prefers this outcome to the

14. The result is not fully cooperative because of the underlying externality, which makes the natural unemployment rate "too high."

15. The reaction can be modified so that $\pi_t^e = \hat{\pi}_t$ applies only for a finite time period. However, a shorter "punishment interval" makes it more difficult to induce the policymaker to opt for the cooperative result.

rules solution, where $U_1 = U_1^n$ and $\pi_1 = 0$. In subsequent periods individuals would set $\pi_t^e = \hat{\pi}_t$. Therefore, the policymaker selects $\pi_t = \hat{\pi}_t$ as the best possible response, given expectations. In other words the noncooperative equilibrium, $U_t = U_t^n$ and $\pi_t = \hat{\pi}_t$, arises from period 2 on.

The policymaker's second option is to set $\pi_t = 0$ in each period. Since $\pi_t^e = 0$ is sustained under this policy, the cooperative solution, $U_t = U_t^n$ and $\pi_t = 0$, obtains in all periods. Under this option the policymaker forgoes the hypothetical short-run gain in order to sustain credibility and thereby enjoy the benefits of future cooperative outcomes.

From the policymaker's viewpoint, the central new feature is the linkage between current policy choices and subsequent inflationary expectations. In particular, the policymaker knows that $\pi_t^e = 0$ will apply only if $\pi_{t-i} = 0$ has been set at all previous dates. Whether the reputational equilibrium will arise depends on the policymaker's weighing of the benefits from the two possible modes of behavior. In particular, it will not arise if the hypothetical one-period benefit from low unemployment outweighs the present value of the losses from higher inflation in future periods. A high discount rate makes this outcome more likely.[16]

There are many features that can cause the reputational equilibrium to break down. First, any known finite horizon for the game rules out these types of equilibria. The cooperative solution is clearly nonsustainable in the final period—working backward, period by period, this breakdown can be shown to be transmitted to all earlier periods.[17] However, if the game ends only probabilistically, the reputational equilibrium might be sustainable. A higher probability of termination effectively raises the discount rate that applies to outcomes in future periods. This higher discount rate lowers the benefits from long-term reputation (low inflation) relative to those from short-run gains (low unemployment). Accordingly, although a finite expected horizon for the game does not make the reputational equilibrium impossible, it does make it more difficult to maintain.

16. The form of behavior described under the first option cannot arise in equilibrium in the present model. If this option were attractive for the policymaker, private agents would anticipate this outcome. In that case $\pi_t^e = 0$ would not be maintained. The noncooperative solution, $U_t = U_t^n$ and $\pi_t = \hat{\pi}_t$, would then arise for all periods, including the first. However, there will always exist some intermediate values of π_t, where $0 \leq \pi_t < \hat{\pi}_t$, such that a cooperative solution based on π_t would be sustainable. Assuming an infinite horizon for the problem (see below), a sufficiently high value of π_t within this interval must make option 2 preferable to option 1. However, the admissible range for π_t would depend on the realizations for U_t^n and other variables.

17. Some attempts to avoid this conclusion in analogous contexts have been explored in, for example, Radner (1979) and Kreps and Wilson (1980).

Second, at least the simple form of cooperation is lost if option 1 becomes preferable to option 2 during any period. In the present example, a run-up in the natural unemployment rate might make the hypothetical short-run benefit from reduced unemployment exceed the present value of losses from higher future inflation.

Third, in a context of partial information, agents may have difficulty verifying the underlying monetary policy. Some form of stochastic decision rule would have to be implemented. Policymakers would have a corresponding incentive to cheat: such situations would be characterized by claims that inflation or monetary growth was not caused by past governmental actions. Similarly, policymakers would desire to proclaim the end of a previous regime that involved excessive inflation in order to restore matters to the "first period" in which $\pi_1^e = 0$ was based on trust rather than on performance.

The essential problem is the lack of an objective link between current actions, π_t, and future expectations, π_{t+i}^e. An enforced rule ties actual and anticipated values together. In this sense the reputational equilibrium amounts to a fragile approximation to the rules equilibrium. Despite the apparent difficulties with sustaining reputational equilibria, casual observation suggests that reputational forces, unreinforced by formal rules, can generate satisfactory outcomes in some areas. Further investigation seems warranted into the factors that allow reputational equilibria to be sustained.[18]

Rules versus Discretion Once Again

The presence or absence of precommitment is the most important distinction between rules and discretion. However, it is useful to consider two other points that have arisen in the previous literature.

1. Policy is described by a once-and-for-all choice of reaction function, $h(I_{t-1})$, but discretion allows I_{t-1} to encompass a larger set of arguments than does a rule. This viewpoint makes rules look like pointless constraints on the options of the policymaker. From this perspective, rules are defensible only if the policymaker is incompetent or nontrustworthy, in the sense of using an inappropriate objective. However, it may be true that complicated rules cannot be adequately monitored and enforced.

18. See Barro and Gordon (1983) for our further work in this area.

Then, we may need to consider the operating characteristics of simple rules, which allow only for limited contingencies.

2. Ignorance about the workings of the economy favors a simple rule for policy. Although this outcome is possible, the conclusion is not general. It is readily imaginable that uncertainty about variables or about model structure would magnify the number of factors to which feedback was justified.

The important dimension of a rule is its capacity to restrict the manner in which future policy choices will be made. In many private arrangements, as with governmental policies, efficiency requires the potential for advance commitments—that is, for contractual obligations. Kydland and Prescott (1977) describe numerous areas of public policy in which formal or implicit prior restraints on future actions are important, including patents, floodplain projects, and energy investments. Other areas include repudiation of national debt and taxation of capital income generally. Actual methods for framing governmental policies seem to be successful to different degrees in each case.

In the unemployment–inflation example, the outcome is suboptimal relative to that generated by a policy rule, if we disregard the costs of erecting and enforcing the rules. The "optimal" solution, $\pi_t = 0$ and $U_t = U_t^n$, is then attainable through a (costlessly operating) mechanism that restricts future governmental actions on inflation. Under a discretionary regime, the policymaker faces an unemployment–inflation trade-off at each date and performs accordingly. The policymaker does as well for the public as possible within an environment where commitments—that is, long-term contracts with the public—are precluded. Rather than rules being less flexible than discretion, the situation is reversed. Discretion amounts to disallowing a set of long-term arrangements between the policymaker and the public. Purely discretionary policies are the subset of rules that involve no guarantees about the government's future behavior.[19]

19. If the desirability of commitments on monetary growth and inflation is accepted, there are numerous procedures within the present model that can generate outcomes that are equivalent to those produced by a once-and-for-all choice of rules. Discretion, for example, could be maintained, but the parameters of the policymaker's preferences could be artificially manipulated to generate a noncooperative solution where $\hat{\pi}_t = 0$. This result follows if the policymaker gives infinite weight to inflation ($b = \infty$), gives zero weight to unemployment ($a = 0$), or regards the natural unemployment rate as optimal ($k = 1$). In the context of discretionary policy, outcomes may improve if there is a divergence in preferences between the principal (society) and its agent (the policymaker).

Monetary Institutions and Policy Choice

The spirit of this chapter is to characterize monetary growth and inflation as reflections of optimal public policy within a given institutional setup. Under a discretionary regime, the policymaker performs optimally subject to an assumed inability to commit future actions. The framework assumes rationality in terms of the day-to-day actions that are carried out repeatedly within the given institutional mode. The intention here is to model the regular behavior of a monetary authority, such as the Federal Reserve. Excessive inflation, apparently unrewarding countercyclical policy response, and reactions of monetary growth and inflation to other exogenous influences can be viewed as products of rational calculation under a regime where long-term commitments are precluded.

The model stresses the importance of monetary institutions, which determine the underlying rules of the game. A purely discretionary environment contrasts with regimes, such as a gold standard or a paper-money constitution, in which monetary growth and inflation are determined via choices among alternative rules. The rule of law or equivalent commitments about future governmental behavior are important for inflation, just as they are for other areas that are influenced by possibly shifting public policies.

We are less comfortable about specifying fruitful approaches to framing positive theories of monetary institutions.[20] If we had retained the optimality criterion that we utilized for analyzing day-to-day monetary actions, and if we had assumed that the costs of implementing and enforcing monetary rules were small, then discretionary monetary policy would not be observed. Within the natural rate setting of our model, a positive theory would predict the selection of a rule (or its equivalent)—and the establishment of an accompanying enforcement apparatus—that would guarantee low and relatively stable rates of inflation.

Presumably, the substantial setup costs that are associated with erecting monetary or other institutions mean that changes in regime will be observed only infrequently. The relatively small experience with alterna-

20. The distinction between choices of institutions and selections of policies within a given regime parallels Buchanan and Tullock's (1962) dichotomy between decisions at the constitutional and operating levels of government. Buchanan (1962) stressed the importance of the constitutional perspective in designing a satisfactory monetary policy.

tives suggests the potential for substantial, persisting errors. Although we would be uncomfortable attempting to forecast a systematic direction of error in future institutional choices, we might be willing to label a particular past choice—such as the movement away from the remnants of the gold standard and fixed exchange rates—as a mistake.

The distinction between institutional choice and operating decisions within a given regime relates also to the economist's role as a policy adviser. In our model the economist has no useful day-to-day advice to offer to the monetary authority.[21] If monetary institutions were set optimally, then the economist's counsel would also not enter at this level. The most likely general role for policy advice consists of identifying and designing improvements in present policy institutions. In the monetary area the major issue concerns arrangements that are preferable replacements for the present discretionary setup. We would like to know which mechanisms—such as commodity standards and legal restrictions on the behavior of paper money—would effectively (and cheaply) restrict the course of future money and prices.

References

Barro, R. J. 1976. "Rational Expectations and the Role of Monetary Policy." *Journal of Monetary Economics* 2:1–32.

—— 1977. "Unanticipated Money Growth and Unemployment in the United States." *American Economic Review* 67:101–115.

—— 1981. "Unanticipated Money Growth and Economic Activity in the United States." In *Money, Expectations, and Business Cycles: Essays in Macroeconomics,* ed. R. J. Barro. New York: Academic Press, pp. 137–172.

—— 1983. "Inflationary Finance under Discretion and Rules." *Canadian Journal of Economics* 16:1–16.

21. Perhaps this observation accounts for the Federal Reserve's attitude toward the unsolicited advice economists provide to it. The Federal Reserve appears interested mostly in "efficient" operation within a given policy regime—specifically, on what to do right now. Although many economists offer advice of this sort, there is little reason to believe that these suggestions would improve on the Fed's period-by-period optimization. More recently, much of economists' advice to the Fed has amounted to proposals for altering the underlying rules of the game. It is likely that the Federal Reserve is powerless to utilize these types of constitutional suggestions.

Barro, R. J., and D. B. Gordon. 1981. "A Positive Theory of Monetary Policy in a Natural-Rate Model." Working Paper No. 807. Cambridge, Mass.: National Bureau of Economic Research.

——— 1983. "Rules, Discretion and Reputation in a Model of Monetary Policy." *Journal of Monetary Economics* 12:101–121.

Buchanan, J. M. 1962. "Predictability: The Criterion of Monetary Constitutions." In *In Search of a Monetary Constitution,* ed. L. B. Yeager, Cambridge, Mass.: Harvard University Press, pp. 155–183.

Buchanan, J. M., and G. Tullock. 1962. *The Calculus of Consent.* Ann Arbor: University of Michigan Press.

Calvo, A. 1978a. "On the Time Consistency of Optimal Policy in a Monetary Economy." *Econometrica* 46(a):1411–28.

——— 1978b. "Optimal Seigniorage from Money Creation: An Analysis in Terms of the Optimum Balance of Payments Deficit Problem." *Journal of Monetary Economics* 4(b):503–517.

Friedman, B. M. 1979. "Optimal Expectation and the Extreme Information Assumptions of 'Rational Expectations' Macromodels." *Journal of Monetary Economics* 5:23–41.

Friedman, J. W. 1971. "A Non-Cooperative Equilibrium for Supergames." *Review of Economic Studies* 38:1–12.

Gordon, D. B. 1980. "Dynamic Equilibria with Purposive Policymaking." Unpublished manuscript. Chicago: University of Chicago.

Hercowitz, Z. 1981. "Money and the Dispersion of Relative Prices." *Journal of Political Economy* 89:328–356.

Kreps, D. M., and R. B. Wilson. 1980. "On the Chain-Store Paradox and Predation: Reputation for Toughness." Unpublished manuscript. Stanford: Stanford University.

Kydland, F. E., and E. C. Prescott. 1977. "Rules rather than Discretion: The Inconsistency of Optimal Plans." *Journal of Political Economy* 85:473–491.

Lucas, R. E., Jr. 1972. "Expectations and the Neutrality of Money." *Journal of Economic Theory* 4:103–124.

——— 1973. "Some International Evidence on Output-Inflation Tradeoffs." *American Economic Review* 63:326–334.

Radner, R. 1979. "Collusive Behavior in Noncooperative Epsilon-Equilibria of Oligopolies with Long but Finite Lives." Unpublished manuscript. Murray Hill, N.J.: Bell Telephone Laboratories.

Sargent, T. J., and N. Wallace. 1975. "Rational Expectations, the Optimal Monetary Instrument, and the Optimal Money Supply Rule." *Journal of Political Economy* 83:241–254.

Taylor, J. B. 1975. "Monetary Policy during a Transition to Rational Expectations." *Journal of Political Economy* 83:1009–22.

3 Rules, Discretion, and Reputation in a Model of Monetary Policy

With David B. Gordon
Board of Governors of the Federal Reserve System
Washington, D.C.

In a discretionary regime the monetary authority can print more money and create more inflation than people expect. The benefits from this surprise inflation may include expansions of economic activity and reductions in the real value of the government's nominal liabilities. Because people understand the policymaker's incentives, however, these types of surprises—and their resulting benefits—cannot arise systematically in equilibrium. People adjust their inflationary expectations to eliminate a consistent pattern of surprises. In this case the potential for creating inflation shocks, ex post, means that in equilibrium the average rates of inflation and monetary growth—and the corresponding costs of inflation—will be higher than otherwise. Enforced commitments on monetary behavior, as embodied in monetary or price rules, eliminate the potential for ex post surprises. Therefore the equilibrium rates of inflation and monetary growth can be lowered by shifts from monetary institutions that allow discretion to ones that enforce rules.

When monetary rules are in place, the policymaker has the temptation each period to "cheat" in order to secure the benefits from inflation shocks. (Because of existing distortions in the economy, these benefits can accrue generally to private agents rather than merely to the policy-

From *Journal of Monetary Economics* (1983) 12:101–121. We have benefited from discussion at the Conference on Alternative Monetary Standards, and from seminars at Chicago, Northwestern, and Iowa. We are particularly grateful for comments from Gary Fethke, Roger Myerson, José Scheinkman, and John Taylor. Part of this research was supported by the National Science Foundation.

maker.) However, this tendency to cheat threatens the viability of the rules equilibrium and tends to move the economy toward the inferior equilibrium under discretion. Because of the repeated interactions between the policymaker and the private agents, it is possible that reputational forces can support the rule. That is, the potential loss of reputation—or credibility—motivates the policymaker to abide by the rule. Then the policymaker forgoes the short-term benefits from inflation shocks in order to secure the gain from low average inflation over the long term.

We extend the positive theory of monetary policy from the preceding chapter (Chapter 2) to allow for reputational forces. Some monetary rules, but generally not the ideal one, can be enforced by the policymaker's potential loss of reputation. We find that the resulting equilibrium looks like a weighted average of that under discretion and that under the ideal rule. Specifically, the outcomes are superior to those under discretion—where no commitments are pertinent—but inferior to those under the ideal rule (which cannot be enforced in our model by the potential loss of reputation). The results look more like discretion when the policymaker's discount rate is high, but more like the ideal rule when the discount rate is low. Otherwise, we generate predictions about the behavior of monetary growth and inflation that resemble those from our previous analysis of discretionary policy. Namely, any change that raises the benefits of inflation shocks—such as a supply shock or a war—leads to a higher growth rate of money and prices.

The Policymaker's Objective

As in our earlier analysis, we think of the monetary authority's objective as reflecting the preferences of the representative private agent. Ultimately, we express this objective as a function of actual and expected rates of inflation. Specifically, benefits derive from positive inflation shocks (at least over some range), but costs attach to higher rates of inflation.

The Benefits from Surprise Inflation

We assume that some benefits arise when the inflation rate for period t, π_t, exceeds the anticipated amount, π_t^e. One source of benefits—discussed in Barro and Gordon (1983) and in an example from Kydland and Prescott (1977, p. 477)—derives from the expectational Phillips curve. Here, unanticipated monetary expansions, reflected in positive values for $\pi_t - \pi_t^e$, lead to increases in real economic activity. Equivalently, these nominal shocks lower the unemployment rate below the natural rate. By the natural rate, we mean here the value that would be ground out by the private sector in the absence of monetary disturbances. This natural rate can shift over time because of supply shocks, demographic changes, shifts in governmental tax and transfer programs, and so on. The natural rate also need not be optimal; in fact, the benefits from surprise inflation arise when the policymaker views the natural rate as excessive. For example, unemployment tends to be too high on average if the distortions from income taxation, unemployment compensation, and the like make the average level of privately chosen work and production too low. Because of the externalities from these distortions, the government (and the private agents) would value stimulative policy actions that lower the unemployment rate below its natural value.

Other sources of benefits from surprise inflation involve governmental revenues. Barro (1983) focuses on the proceeds from inflationary finance. The expectation of inflation (formed the previous period), π_t^e, determines people's holdings of real cash, M_{t-1}/P_{t-1}. Surprise inflation, $\pi_t - \pi_t^e$, depreciates the real value of these holdings, and thereby allows the government to issue more new money in real terms, $(M_t - M_{t-1})/P_t$, as a replacement. The policymaker values this inflationary finance if alternative methods of raising revenue—such as an income tax—entail distortions. Hence the benefit from surprise inflation depends again on some existing externality. Calvo (1978) discusses the necessity of existing distortions in this type of model.

The revenue incentive for surprise inflation relates to governmental liabilities that are fixed in nominal terms, rather than to money, per se. Thus the same argument applies to nominally denominated, interest-bearing public debt. Suppose that people held last period the real amount of government bonds, B_{t-1}/P_{t-1}. These bonds carry the nominal yield, R_{t-1}, which is satisfactory given people's inflationary expectations over the pertinent horizon, π_t^e. Surprise inflation, $\pi_t - \pi_t^e$, depreciates part of the real value of these bonds and therefore lowers the government's future real expenditures for interest and repayment of principal. In effect, surprise inflation is again a source of revenue to the government. Quantitatively, this channel from public debt is likely to be more significant than the usually discussed mechanism, which involves revenue from printing high-powered money. For example, the outstanding public debt for the United States in 1981 is around $1 trillion,[1] and a surprise inflation of 1% would lower the real value of this debt by about $10 billion. Hence this channel produces an effective lump amount of revenue of about $10 billion for each extra 1% of surprise inflation. By contrast, the entire annual flow of revenue through the Federal Reserve from the creation of high-powered money is about the same magnitude ($8 billion in 1981, $13 billion in 1980).

The attractions of generating revenue from surprise inflation are clear if we view the depreciation of real cash or real bonds as an unexpected capital levy. As with a tax on existing capital, surprise inflation provides for a method of raising funds that is essentially nondistorting, ex post. Once people have built up the capital or held the real cash or real bonds, the government can extract revenue without disincentive effects. Of course, the distortions arise—for capital, money, or bonds—when people anticipate, ex ante, the possibility of these capital levies ex post. Therefore these forms of raising revenue will not end up being so desirable in a full equilibrium where people form expectations rationally. But, for the moment, we are just listing the benefits that attach, ex post, to surprise inflation.

The Costs of Inflation

The second major element in our model is the cost of inflation. Costs are assumed to rise, and at an increasing rate, with the realized inflation rate, π_t. Although people generally regard inflation as very costly, economists have not presented very convincing arguments to explain these costs. Further, the present type of cost refers to the actual amount of inflation for the period rather than to the variance of inflation, which could more easily be seen as costly. Direct costs of changing prices fit reasonably well into the model, although the quantitative role of these costs is doubtful. In any event the analysis has some interesting conclusions for the case where the actual amount of inflation for each period is not perceived as costly. Then the model predicts a lot of inflation!

1. For this purpose we should actually look at the privately held component of the funded national debt, which was about $700 billion in 1981.

The Setup of Our Example

We focus our discussion on the simplest possible example, which illustrates the main points about discretion, rules, and reputation. Along the way, we indicate how the results generalize beyond this example.

The policymaker's objective involves a cost for each period, z_t, which is given by

$$z_t = (a/2)(\pi_t)^2 - b_t(\pi_t - \pi_t^e) \quad \text{where} \quad a, b_t > 0. \tag{3.1}$$

The first term, $(a/2)(\pi_t)^2$, is the cost of inflation. Notice that our use of a quadratic form means that these costs rise at an increasing rate with the rate of inflation, π_t. The second term, $b_t(\pi_t - \pi_t^e)$, is the benefit from inflation shocks. Here we use a linear form for convenience.[2] Given that the benefit parameter, b_t, is positive, an increase in unexpected inflation, $\pi_t - \pi_t^e$, reduces costs. We can think of these benefits as reflecting reductions in unemployment or increases in governmental revenue.

We allow the benefit parameter, b_t, to move around over time. For example, a supply shock—which raises the natural rate of unemployment—may increase the value of reducing unemployment through aggressive monetary policy. Alternatively, a sharp rise in government spending increases the incentives to raise revenue via inflationary finance. In our example, b_t is distributed randomly with a fixed mean, $\bar{b}$, and variance, σ_b^2.[3] (Hence we neglect serial correlation in the natural unemployment rate, government expenditures, and so on.)

The policymaker's objective at date t entails minimization of the expected present value of costs,

$$Z_t = E\left[z_t + \frac{1}{1 + r_t} z_{t+1} + \frac{1}{(1 + r_t)(1 + r_{t+1})} z_{t+2} + \cdots\right], \tag{3.2}$$

2. Chapter 2 uses a term of the form $[\phi_t - \lambda(\pi_t - \pi_t^e)]^2$, where $\phi_t > 0$ depends on the natural unemployment rate for the period. Then the policymaker values inflation shocks—that is, $\pi_t > \pi_t^e$—only over some range. But, the general nature of the results does not change if we substitute this more complicated form. Also, we could modify the cost of inflation to depend on $(\pi_t - \bar{\pi}_t)^2$, where $\bar{\pi}_t$ is the optimal inflation tax on cash balances.

3. In some models, such as Lucas (1973) and Barro (1976), the coefficient b_t depends on the forecast variance of inflation. Most of our results would not be affected if we allowed for this type of dependence. However, this element matters when we compare across regimes that have different forecast variances for inflation.

where r_t is the discount rate that applies between periods t and $t + 1$. We assume that r_t is generated from a stationary probability distribution. (Therefore we again neglect any serial dependence.) Also, the discount rate is generated independently of the benefit parameter, b_t. For the first period ahead, the distribution of r_t implies a distribution for the discount factor, $q_t = 1/(1 + r_t)$. We denote the mean and variance for q_t by $\bar{q}$ and σ_q^2, respectively.

The policymaker's monetary instrument enables him to select the rate of inflation, π_t, in each period. The main points of our analysis do not change materially if we introduce random discrepancies between inflation and changes in the monetary instrument. For example, we could have shifts in velocity or control errors for the money supply. Also, the policymaker has no incentive to randomize choices of inflation in the model.

We begin with a symmetric case where no one knows the benefit parameter, b_t, or the discount factor for the next period, q_t, when they act for period t. Hence the policymaker chooses the inflation rate, π_t, without observing either b_t or q_t. Similarly, people form their expectations, π_t^e, of the policymaker's choice without knowing these parameters. Later on we modify this informational structure.

Discretionary Policy

Chapter 2 discusses discretionary policy in the present context as a non-cooperative game between the policymaker and the private agents. In particular, the policymaker treats the current inflationary expectation, π_t^e, and all future expectations, π_{t+i}^e for $i > 0$, as given when choosing the current inflation rate, π_t. Therefore π_t is chosen to minimize the expected cost for the current period, Ez_t, while treating π_t^e and all future costs as fixed. Because future costs and expectations are independent of the policymaker's current actions, the discount factor does not enter into the results. The solution from minimizing Ez_t, where z_t is given in Eq. (3.1), is

$$\hat{\pi}_t = \frac{\bar{b}}{a} \quad \text{(discretion)}. \tag{3.3}$$

We use carets to denote the solution under discretion. (With other cost functions, π_t would depend also on π_t^e.)

Given rational expectations, people predict inflation by solving out the policymaker's optimization problem and forecasting the solution for $\hat{\pi}_t$ as well as possible. In the present case they can calculate exactly the choice of inflation from Eq. (3.3)—hence the expectations are

$$\pi_t^e = \hat{\pi}_t = \frac{\bar{b}}{a}. \qquad (3.4)$$

Since inflation shocks are zero in equilibrium—that is, $\hat{\pi}_t - \pi_t^e = 0$—the cost from Eq. (3.1) ends up depending only on $\hat{\pi}_t$. In particular, the cost is

$$\hat{z}_t = \left(\frac{1}{2}\right) \frac{(\bar{b})^2}{a} \quad \text{(discretion)}. \qquad (3.5)$$

Policy under a Rule

Suppose now that the policymaker can commit himself in advance to a rule for determining inflation. This rule can relate π_t to variables that the policymaker knows at date t. In the present case no one knows the parameters b_t and q_t at date t. But everyone knows all previous values of these parameters. Therefore the policymaker can condition the inflation rate, π_t, only on variables that are known also to the private agents. (The policymaker could randomize his choices, but he turns out not to have this incentive.) Therefore the policymaker effectively chooses π_t and π_t^e together, subject to the condition that $\pi_t^e = \pi_t$. Then the term that involves the inflation shock, $\pi_t - \pi_t^e$, drops out of the cost function in Eq. (3.1). Given the way that we modeled the costs of inflation—namely, as $(a/2)\pi_t^2$—it follows immediately that the best rule prescribes zero inflation at all dates.

$$\pi_t^* = 0 \quad \text{(rule)}. \qquad (3.6)$$

We use an asterisk to denote the results from a rule. Equation (3.6) amounts to a constant-growth-rate rule, where the rate of growth happens to be zero.

Finally, we can calculate the costs under a rule from Eq. (3.1) as

$$z_t^* = 0 \quad \text{(rule)}. \qquad (3.7)$$

The general point is that the costs under the rule, z_t^*, are lower than those under discretion, $\hat{z}_t$ from Eq. (3.5). The lower cost reflects the value of being able to make commitments—that is, contractual agreements between the policymaker and the private agents. Without these commitments, inflation ends up being excessive—specifically, $\hat{\pi}_t > 0$—but no benefits from higher inflation result.

Cheating and Temptation

As noted by others (for example, Taylor 1975; B. Friedman 1979), the policymaker is tempted to renege on commitments. In particular, if people expect zero inflation—as occurs under the rule—then the policymaker would like to implement a positive inflation rate to secure some benefits from an inflation shock. Further, this desire does not stem from a peculiarity in the policymaker's tastes. Rather, it reflects the distortions that make inflation shocks desirable in the first place.

How much can the policymaker gain in period t by cheating? Assume that people have the inflationary expectation, $\pi_0^e = 0$, which they formed at the start of period t. If the policymaker treats this expectation as a given, the choice of π_t that minimizes z_t is the one that we found before under discretion[4]—namely,

$$\tilde{\pi}_t = \frac{\bar{b}}{a} \quad \text{(cheating)}. \tag{3.8}$$

We use tildes to denote values associated with cheating. The expected cost follows from Eq. (3.1) as

$$E\tilde{z}_t = -\frac{(\bar{b})^2}{2a} \quad \text{(cheating)}. \tag{3.9}$$

The general point is that this expected cost is lower than that, $z_t^* = 0$, from following the rule. We refer to the difference between these expected costs as the temptation to renege on the rule—or simply as the

---

4. With a different cost function, the result for $\tilde{\pi}_t$ generally differs from that under discretion, $\hat{\pi}_t$.

temptation. In the present case we have

$$\text{temptation} = E(z_t^* - \tilde{z}_t) = \frac{(\bar{b})^2}{2a} > 0. \tag{3.10}$$

At the present stage we have three types of outcomes. Ranging from low costs to high, these are

1. cheating (with people expecting the rule), $E\tilde{z}_t = -(\bar{b})^2/2a$,
2. rule, $z_t^* = 0$,
3. discretion, $\hat{z}_t = (\bar{b})^2/2a$.

Discretion is worse than the rule because first, no inflation shocks arise in either case, but second, the commitment under the rule avoids excessive inflation. However, the rule is only a second-best solution. Cheating—*when people anticipate the rule*—delivers better results, because the inflation shock eliminates part of the existing distortion in the economy (which is worth the extra inflation). But the cheating outcome is feasible only when people can be systematically deceived into maintaining low inflationary expectations. In our subsequent analysis this cannot happen in equilibrium. However, the incentive to cheat determines which rules are sustainable without legal or institutional mechanisms to enforce them. There is a tendency for the pursuit of the first best—that is, the cheating outcome—to generate results that are poorer than the second best (rules) and closer to the third best (discretion).

Enforcement of Rules

Generally, a credible rule comes with some enforcement power that at least balances the temptation to cheat. We consider here only the enforcement that arises from the potential loss of reputation or credibility. This mechanism can apply here because of the repeated interaction between the policymaker and the private agents.[5] Specifically, if the policymaker engineers today a higher rate of inflation than people expect, then everyone raises their expectations of future inflation in some

---

5. This type of repeated game is discussed in Friedman (1971).

manner. Hence, in a general way, the cost of cheating today involves the increase in inflationary expectations for the future.

Consider a rule that specifies the inflation rate, π_t^*, for period t. The rule might prescribe $\pi_t^* = 0$, as before, or it might dictate some nonzero rate of inflation. Generally, the rule can specify some dependence of π_t^* on the realizations of all variables through date $t - 1$—that is, the values for date t are still not observed when π_t^* is set.

We postulate the following form of expectations mechanism, which we eventually show to be rational:

$$\pi_t^e = \pi_t^* \quad \text{if} \quad \pi_{t-1} = \pi_{t-1}^e, \quad \text{and} \tag{3.11a}$$

$$\pi_t^e = \hat{\pi}_t \quad \text{if} \quad \pi_{t-1} \neq \pi_{t-1}^e. \tag{3.11b}$$

In other words if the previous inflation rate, π_{t-1}, accords with expectations, π_{t-1}^e, then people trust the government to perform in line with its announced rule for period t—that is, $\pi_t^e = \pi_t^*$. But, if the actual value departs from expectations last period, $\pi_{t-1} \neq \pi_{t-1}^e$, then people do not expect the government to follow its rule this period—hence $\pi_t^e \neq \pi_t^*$. Rather, private agents anticipate that the policymaker will optimize subject to given expectations, which defines a discretionary situation. Hence expectations are $\pi_t^e = \hat{\pi}_t$, where $\hat{\pi}_t$ is again the discretionary outcome.

If the government follows its rule in every period, then it also validates expectations each period. The first part of Eq. (3.11) then says that the government maintains its reputation (or credibility) in each period. On the other hand, if the government cheats during period t, then the second part of Eq. (3.11) says that the next period's expectations are the ones associated with discretion, $\hat{\pi}_{t+1}$. Then, if in period $t + 1$ the government chooses the discretionary inflation rate, $\hat{\pi}_{t+1}$ (which is optimal given that expectations are $\hat{\pi}_{t+1}$), the actual and expected inflation rates coincide, although at the discretionary levels. Accordingly, Eq. (3.11a) says that people anticipate the rules outcome, π_{t+2}^*, for the following period. In other words the "punishment" from violating the rule during period t is that the discretionary (noncooperative) solution obtains during period $t + 1$. But credibility is restored as of period $t + 2$—that is, things carry on as of date $t + 2$ as though no previous violation had occurred. Therefore the mechanism in Eq. (3.11) specifies only one period's worth of punishment for each "crime."[6] Other equilibria exist that have punishment intervals of different length, as we discuss later on.

Consider our previous rule where $\pi_t^* = 0$. Suppose that the policymaker has credibility in period t; so $\pi_t^e = 0$. If the policymaker cheats during period t, then his best choice of inflation is $\tilde{\pi}_t = \bar{b}/a$ from Eq. (3.8). (Note that Eq. 3.11 says that the size and length of the punishment do not depend on the size of the crime.) Then the policymaker gains the temptation, $E(z_t^* - \tilde{z}_t) = (\bar{b})^2/2a$, from Eq. (3.10).

The cost of this violation is that discretion, rather than the rule, applies for period $t + 1$. Hence the policymaker realizes next period the cost, $\hat{z}_{t+1} = (\bar{b})^2/2a$, from Eq. (3.5), rather than that, $z_{t+1}^* = 0$, from Eq. (3.7). Since costs for period $t + 1$ are discounted by the factor $q_t = 1(1 + r_t)$ in Eq. (3.2), the expected present value of the loss is

$$\text{enforcement} = E[q_t(\hat{z}_{t+1} - z_{t+1}^*)] = \bar{q}(\bar{b})^2/2a. \tag{3.12}$$

We use the term *enforcement* to refer to the expected present value of the loss from transgressions.

The policymaker abides by the rule during period t—that is, sets $\pi_t = \pi_t^*$—if the enforcement is at least as great as the temptation. Otherwise, he opts for the cheating solution, $\pi_t = \tilde{\pi}_t$ (and suffers the consequences next period). But, when forming expectations for period t, π_t^e, people know whether the policymaker will find it worthwhile to cheat. Hence, if the cheating solution is preferable to the rule, then the expectation, $\pi_t^e = \pi_t^* = 0$, is irrational. Therefore people would not stick with the expectation mechanism from Eq. (3.11). The rules that can apply in equilibrium are those that have enough enforcement to motivate the policymaker to abide by them, given the expectations mechanism in Eq. (3.11). Then the equilibrium satisfies two properties. First, the expectations are rational. In particular, each individual's projection, π_t^e, is the best possible forecast of the policymaker's actual choice, π_t, given the way the policymaker behaves and given the way others form their expec-

---

6. Green and Porter (1981) used an analogous model for oligopoly pricing. There, the observation of a low price triggers $(T - 1)$ periods of punishment, during which firms behave in a Cournot manner.

tations. Second, the policymaker's choice, π_t, maximizes his objective, given the way people form their expectations.[7]

In equilibrium, rules satisfy the enforceability restriction,

$$\text{temptation} = E(z_t^* - \tilde{z}_t) \leq \text{enforcement} \qquad (3.13)$$

$$= E[q_t(\hat{z}_{t+1} - z_{t+1}^*)].$$

This condition says that the costs incurred today by following the rule, rather than cheating, are not greater than the expected value of having the cooperative (rules) outcome next period, rather than the discretionary outcome. Consider now whether the proposed rule, $\pi_t^* = 0$, satisfies the enforceability restriction. From Eq. (3.10), the temptation is $(\bar{b})^2/2a$, whereas from Eq. (3.12), the enforcement is $\bar{q}(\bar{b})^2/2a$.[8] Since $\bar{q} < 1$, the temptation is strictly greater than the enforcement. Hence the ideal rule, $\pi_t^* = 0$, is not enforceable, at least given the expectations mechanism from Eq. (3.11). Therefore zero inflation is not an equilibrium in our model. (With a different form of cost function, rather than Eq. 3.1, the ideal rule may or may not be enforceable.)

The Best Enforceable Rule

We look here for the best enforceable rule—that is, the one that minimizes expected costs, subject to the constraint that the enforcement be at least as great as the temptation. In the present setting, where the parameters b_t and q_t are unobservable at date t, the best rule has the simple form

$$\pi_t^* = \pi. \qquad (3.14)$$

7. The expectations mechanism from Eq. (3.11) cannot be rational if the game has a known, finite end point. Then, no punishment arises for crimes in the last period. If we work backward, the solution unravels period by period. Our framework assumes no known termination date for the game, although the game may end probabilistically. Then a higher probability of termination shows up as a higher discount rate—that is, as a lower mean discount factor, $\bar{q}$. For some related game-theory literature, see Selten (1978), Kreps and Wilson (1980), and Milgrom and Roberts (1982).

8. The two terms are equal when $\bar{q} = 1$ only because of the specific cost function from Eq. (3.1). Generally, equality would arise for a value of $\bar{q}$ that is either above or below one.

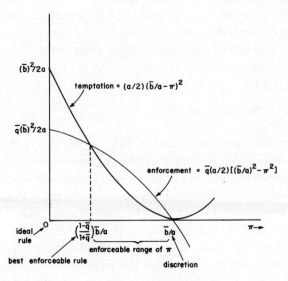

Figure 3.1. Temptation and enforcement

That is, the rule specifies constant inflation (a constant-growth-rate rule). But we already know that the ideal rule, $\pi = 0$, is not enforceable. Given this, the enforceability restriction turns out to hold with equality for the best enforceable rule.

Using the procedures described before, we can calculate the temptation and enforcement associated with the rule, $\pi_t^* = \pi$. (Note that $\pi_t^e = \pi$ also applies here.) The results are

$$\text{temptation} = E(z_t^* - \tilde{z}_t) = \left(\frac{a}{2}\right)\left(\frac{\bar{b}}{a} - \pi\right)^2, \quad \text{and} \tag{3.15}$$

$$\text{enforcement} = \bar{q} \cdot E(\hat{z}_{t+1} - z_{t+1}^*) = \bar{q}\left(\frac{a}{2}\right)\left[\left(\frac{\bar{b}}{a}\right)^2 - \pi^2\right]. \tag{3.16}$$

We graph the temptation and enforcement versus the inflation rate, π, in Fig. 3.1. (This figure was suggested to us by John Taylor.) At $\pi = 0$, the temptation follows from Eq. (3.10) as $(\bar{b})^2/2a$. Then, as π rises, the gain from cheating diminishes—hence the temptation falls. Finally, when π equals the discretionary value, $\bar{b}/a$, the temptation equals zero, because the cheating solution and the rule prescribe the same inflation rate, $\bar{b}/a$, at this point. (As π increases further, the temptation increases, because—for given expectations—the policymaker prefers the discretionary inflation rate, $\bar{b}/a$, to higher rates of inflation.)

The enforcement equals $\bar{q}(\bar{b})^2/2a$ when $\pi = 0$, from Eq. (3.12). Then, as π rises, the enforcement declines, because the cost from losing reputation becomes smaller when the rule prescribes a higher rate of inflation. As with the temptation, the enforcement equals zero when π equals the discretionary value, $\bar{b}/a$. Here, when the policymaker cheats, people expect the same rate of inflation—namely, the discretionary amount $\bar{b}/a$—as when the policymaker abides by the rule. Consequently, there is no enforcement. (When π increases further, the enforcement becomes negative—that is, the policymaker prefers the punishment, where people anticipate the inflation rate $\bar{b}/a$, to the maintenance of the rule, where people expect an inflation rate that exceeds $\bar{b}/a$.)

Notice that Fig. 3.1 determines a range of announced inflation rates that can be equilibria. Specifically, the enforcement is at least as large as the temptation for values of π in the interval, $(\bar{b}/a)(1 - \bar{q})/(1 + \bar{q}) \le \pi \le \bar{b}/a$. Among these, we focus on the value of π that delivers the best results in the sense of minimizing the expected costs from Eq. (3.2). We can rationalize this focus on one of the possible equilibria by allowing the policymaker to choose which value of π to announce in some initial period. Then, as long as this value is in the enforceable range, we assume that the private agents follow along. That is, they all use the announced value of π as the basis for assessing the policymaker's performance (in accordance with Equation 3.11).[9] Within this setup, the policymaker will, in fact, announce the value of π that leads to a minimum of expected costs.

The best of the enforceable rules occurs where the curves for temptation and enforcement intersect in the interior of Fig. 3.1. (The curves also intersect at the discretionary value, $\pi = \bar{b}/a$, but expected costs are higher at this point.) Hence the announced inflation rate is

$$\pi^* = \left(\frac{\bar{b}}{a}\right)\left(\frac{1 - \bar{q}}{1 + \bar{q}}\right) \qquad \text{(best enforceable rule)}, \qquad (3.17)$$

9. But recall that the equilibrium is itself noncooperative. In particular, each agent calculates the best forecast, π_t^e, of the policymaker's actions, while taking as given the way the policymaker behaves and the way other agents form their expectations.

for which the expected cost in each period is

$$Ez_t^* = \left[\frac{(\bar{b})^2}{2a} \right] \left[\frac{1 - \bar{q}}{1 + \bar{q}} \right]^2 \tag{3.18}$$

Notice that, with $0 < \bar{q} < 1$, the inflation rate, π^*, is intermediate between the ideal rule, 0, and discretion, $\bar{b}/a$. In fact, the best enforceable rule is a weighted average of the ideal rule and discretion, with the weights depending on the mean discount factor, $\bar{q}$. A relatively small value of $\bar{q}$, which means a high rate of discount on future costs, implies a relatively high weight on discretion—that is, a high value of π^*. This result applies because a decrease in $\bar{q}$ weakens the enforcement (Eq. 3.16), and thereby requires π^* to increase to maintain the equality between the enforcement and the temptation.

Generally, an increase in the mean discount factor, $\bar{q}$, reduces π^*, with π^* tending toward zero (the ideal rule) as $\bar{q}$ tends to one.[10] On the other hand, π^* tends to $\bar{b}/a$—the discretionary result—as $\bar{q}$ tends to zero. (A zero discount factor means zero enforcement, so only discretion is credible.) Notice that any force that influences the mean discount factor, $\bar{q}$, has a corresponding effect on inflation. For example, during a war a low value of $\bar{q}$ leads to high inflation (via high monetary growth).

The expected cost from Eq. (3.18) is also intermediate between that from the ideal rule, which is zero, and that for discretion, which is $(\bar{b})^2/2a$. Remember that the ideal rule is itself a second-best solution, which is inferior to cheating when people anticipate the ideal rule. But cheating cannot occur systematically when people understand the policymaker's incentives and form their expectations accordingly. Rather, the lure of the better outcome from cheating creates the temptation, which makes the ideal rule nonenforceable. Hence the attraction of the first best makes the second best unattainable. We end up with a cost that exceeds the second best (the ideal rule) but is still lower than the third best (discretion).

The other feature of our results is the dependence of the inflation rate, π^*, on the ratio of cost parameters, $\bar{b}/a$. This ratio pertains to the benefit from inflation shocks, which depends on $\bar{b}$, relative to the costs of inflation, which depends on the parameter a. An increase in the ratio,

---

10. This last condition depends on the specifics of our example. However, the direction of effect for $\bar{q}$ on π^* applies generally.

$\bar{b}/a$, raises the temptation, relative to the enforcement, and thereby raises π^*. In particular, if inflation is not very costly, so that the parameter a is small, then we end up with a lot of inflation. Also, anything that raises the mean benefit attached to an inflation shock, $\bar{b}$, leads to higher inflation (but not to more benefits from inflation shocks). In Chapter 2, which focused on the results under discretion, we discussed some changes in the economy that can affect the benefits from inflation shocks. For example, the parameter $\bar{b}$ tends to be high in the following cases:

- when the natural unemployment rate is high;
- during a recession;
- during a war or other period where government expenditures rise sharply;
- when the deadweight losses from conventional taxes are high; and
- when the outstanding real stock of nominally denominated public debt is large.

In each case we predict that the high value of $\bar{b}$ triggers a high value of π^*—that is, a high rate of monetary expansion by the policymaker. This view accounts for[11]

- a rise in the mean inflation rate along with a rise in the natural unemployment rate (as seen in the United States over the last 10–15 years);
- countercyclical response of monetary policy;
- high rates of monetary expansion during wartime;
- high rates of monetary growth in some less-developed countries; and
- an inflationary effect from the outstanding real stock of public debt.

Contingent Rules

We get some new results when we modify the informational structure in ways that motivate the policymaker to employ a contingent rule. Then

11. Some of these results can also be explained by changes in the optimal tax rate on cash balances, which applies to the systematic part of inflation. For example, this effect is probably important for monetary growth during wartime and in less-developed countries.

the inflation rate varies each period in accordance with the state of the economy.

Suppose that the policymaker knows the values of the benefit parameter, b_t, and the discount factor, q_t, when choosing the inflation rate, π_t. If people also condition their expectations, π_t^e, on b_t and q_t, then the results change little from those already presented. So we focus on the case where π_t^e is still generated without knowledge of the contemporaneous variables b_t and q_t.

One possibility is that the policymaker receives information more quickly than private agents. However, our setup does not require this informational asymmetry. For example, when setting demands for real money balances or holdings of real government bonds, people have to forecast rates of inflation. Once people hold the government's nominal liabilities, their real wealth changes when subsequent inflation shocks occur. Therefore, although the government and private agents may have the same information at any point in time, the agents' decisions (on how much real money and bonds to hold) depend on expectations of inflation that were formed earlier. Therefore we can think of π_t^e as not being conditioned on the realizations b_t and q_t. However, these realizations can influence the actual inflation rate, π_t.

The situation is less clear for the example of the Phillips curve. In models where only unperceived nominal disturbances matter for real variables—as in Lucas (1972, 1973) and Barro (1976)—the pertinent value for π_t^e is the one based on contemporaneously available information. However, some models with long-term nominal contracting (Gray 1976; Fischer 1977; Taylor 1980) suggest that inflationary expectations formed at earlier dates will matter for today's choices of employment, production, and so forth. Then the situation resembles that from above where people choose their holdings of money and bonds based on forecasts of inflation. However, the rationality of the Gray–Fischer–Taylor contracts has been questioned (Barro 1977).

Discretion

We find the results under discretion in the same way as before. Specifically, we get

$$\hat{\pi}_t = \frac{b_t}{a}. \tag{3.19}$$

Now the policymaker reacts to the actual value of the benefit parameter, b_t, rather than to its mean, $\bar{b}$. However, people's expectations—not conditioned on b_t—are $\pi_t^e = \bar{b}/a$. Although $\pi_t^e = E\hat{\pi}_t$, the realizations for b_t now generate departures of inflation from its expectation; the inflation shocks—and the corresponding benefits from them—are sometimes positive and sometimes negative.

The costs under discretion are now

$$\hat{z}_t = \frac{(b_t)^2}{2a} - \left(\frac{b_t}{a}\right)(b_t - \bar{b}). \tag{3.20}$$

The results correspond to those from before [Eq. (3.5)] if $b_t = \bar{b}$. Looking one period ahead, we can calculate

$$E\hat{z}_{t+1} = \left(\frac{1}{2a}\right)[(\bar{b})^2 - \sigma_b^2]. \tag{3.21}$$

The new term is the variance of the benefit parameter, σ_b^2.

The Ideal Contingent Rule

When b_t is observed, the ideal rule no longer prescribes zero (or constant) inflation at all times. Rather, the policymaker conditions the inflation rate on the realizations of the benefit parameter. The present example is simple enough to write out the ideal contingent rule in closed form. Specifically—abstracting from enforcement problems—the best rule turns out (after a large amount of algebra) to be

$$\pi_t^* = \left(\frac{1}{a}\right)(b_t - \bar{b}). \tag{3.22}$$

As before, the prior mean of inflation, $\pi_t^e = E\pi_t^*$, is zero. But, realized inflation exceeds its expectation—and benefit from inflation shocks arise—when b_t exceeds its mean, $\bar{b}$. Conversely, inflation is below its expectation—so costs from unexpectedly low inflation occur—when b_t is below its mean.

Note that inflationary expectations are always zero, but the policy-maker creates surprisingly low inflation (that is, deflation) when the benefit parameter takes on relatively low values. These realizations may show up as a recession or as other costs from a negative inflation shock. Yet, ex post, it would clearly be preferable to have zero, rather than negative, inflation. Then we would avoid the negative inflation shock and also have smaller costs due to inflation [which are $(a/2)(\pi_t)^2$]. So the negative inflation shocks may appear pointless. Yet the ideal rule says that the policymaker should "bite the bullet"—that is, cause a recession through contractionary monetary policy—under some circumstances. The reason is that the surprisingly low rule of inflation when the benefit parameter, b_t, is low is the counterpart of the surprisingly high rate of inflation when the benefit parameter is high. Choosing zero rather than negative inflation for the low states means that the prior expectation of inflation is higher than otherwise. Then the policymaker achieves lower benefits in the states where b_t is relatively high. In fact, it is worthwhile to incur some costs in the low states—namely, bite the bullet through unex-pectedly low inflation—in order to "buy" the unexpectedly high infla-tion and the corresponding benefits in the high states. In effect the policymaker invests in credibility when it is relatively cheap to do so—namely, when b_t is low—in order to cash in on this investment when it is most important—that is, when b_t is high.

The costs associated with the ideal rule turn out to be

$$z_t^* = -\left(\frac{1}{2a}\right)[(b_t)^2 - (\bar{b})^2].\tag{3.23}$$

Again, we obtain our previous results (Eq. 3.7) if $b_t = \bar{b}$. Looking ahead one period, the expectation of these costs is

$$Ez_{t+1}^* = -\left(\frac{1}{2a}\right)\sigma_b^2.\tag{3.24}$$

Because the policymaker can match the variations in b_t with appropriate responses in π_t, the expected costs fall with an increase in the variance of the benefit parameter, σ_b^2.[12]

---

12. However, we did not enter the variance of inflation directly into the cost function of Eq. (3.1). If we had done so, this result could change.

As before, we can show that the ideal rule is not enforceable in our model.[13] Therefore we go on now to examine the best enforceable, contingent rule.

Enforceable Contingent Rules

We look at rules that express the inflation rate, π_t^*, as a stationary function of the state, which specifies the values of the two variables b_t and q_t. Given that the ideal rule is unattainable, the best enforceable rule in our model turns out to equate the temptation to the enforcement *for all realizations of b_t and q_t*.[14] The temptation cannot exceed the enforcement for any of these realizations if the rule is to be credible. Further, if the enforcement exceeds the temptation in some state, then we can do better by changing the inflation rate for that state. That is, we bear more costs than necessary by having excessive enforcement.

The present example is sufficiently simple to work out the results in closed form. The solution for inflation turns out to be a linear function of b_t and of $\sqrt{q_t}$—that is,[15]

$$\pi_t^* = c_1 + c_2 b_t + c_3 \sqrt{q_t}, \tag{3.25}$$

where the c's are constants, which have to be determined. If we conjecture that the rule for inflation takes the form of Eq. (3.25), then we can work out the temptation and enforcement as functions of the parameters, c_1, c_2, c_3, and the realizations for b_t and q. We then determine the value of the c coefficients to equate the temptation to the enforcment for all values of (b_t, q_t). Since Eq. (3.25) has the correct form, this operation turns out to be feasible. The results are

$$c_1 = 0, \quad c_2 = \frac{1}{a}, \quad c_3 = -2 \left(\frac{\bar{b}}{a}\right) \frac{\sqrt{\bar{q}}}{1 + \bar{q}}, \tag{3.26}$$

13. When considering the ideal rule, the temptation and enforcement turn out to be independent of the realization for b_t. Further, the temptation exceeds the enforcement for all discount factors, q_t, that are less than one.

14. With other cost functions, the enforcement may exceed the temptation for some realizations. In particular, we then find that the inflation rate does not react to variations in q_t in some regions.

15. The enforcement is linear in q_t. But, the temptation involves the square of the inflation rate. Therefore, if π_t is linear in $\sqrt{q_t}$, then the temptation also involves terms that are linear in q_t.

where $\sqrt{\bar{q}}$ is the mean of $\sqrt{q_t}$. Hence the best enforceable contingent rule for inflation is[16]

$$\pi_t^* = \left(\frac{b_t}{a}\right) - 2\left(\frac{\bar{b}}{a}\right)\left(\frac{\sqrt{\bar{q}} \cdot \sqrt{q_t}}{1 + \bar{q}}\right). \tag{3.27}$$

The enforceable rule can again be viewed as a weighted average of the ideal rule—Eq. (3.22)—and discretion—Eq. (3.19). In particular, the mean rate of inflation is positive but lower than that associated with discretion, which is $\bar{b}/a$. The relative weights depend on the discount factor—both on the parameters of the probability distribution for q_t and on the realized value. Given the parameters of the distribution, a higher realization for q_t means a lower inflation rate, π_t^*.[17]

Note that the realization of the discount factor does not affect current benefits and costs from inflation but does influence the amount of enforcement. Thus the ideal rule does not depend on q_t in Eq. (3.22). But, for low realizations of q_t, low inflation rates are not credible, because the temptation would exceed the enforcement. Therefore the best enforceable rule does depend on q_t in Eq. (3.27).

The inflation rate now moves around with fluctuations in the benefit parameter, b_t, or in the discount factor, q_t. In particular, relatively high realizations for b_t and relatively low ones for q_t lead to unexpectedly high inflation. Conversely, the policymaker "bites the bullet"—that is, creates negative inflation shocks—when the benefit parameter is lower than normal or the discount factor is higher than normal. The reasoning here is similar to that from before. It is worthwhile to suffer negative inflation shocks in some cases—that is, for low values of b_t or high values of q_t—to sustain low prior expectations of inflation. Then large gains are attained in the cases where the benefit parameter, b_t, is high or the discount factor, q_t, is low. These last cases are likely to be emergencies—such as wars or other times where economic activity or government revenues are valued especially highly. In effect, the policymaker bites the bullet during the nonemergencies to invest in credibility—an investment that yields returns during the emergencies.

---

16. The solution reduces to the previous one in Eq. (3.17) if there is no random variation in b_t and q_t. Then, $b_t = \bar{b}$, $q_t = \bar{q}$, and $\sqrt{\bar{q}} = \sqrt{\bar{q}}$.

17. Given the variance for $\sqrt{q_t}$ and the realized value of $\sqrt{q_t}$, a higher value of $\sqrt{\bar{q}}$ also lowers π_t^*. This follows by using the formula $\bar{q} = \text{var}(\sqrt{q_t}) + (\sqrt{\bar{q}})^2$.

The Length of the Punishment Interval

So far our results apply when the length of the punishment interval is fixed at one period. That is, the length of time for which the discretionary outcome obtains, conditional on cheating, equals the length of time over which the policymaker can enjoy the results of his cheating. (The last interval essentially defines the length of the period.) Given the length of the punishment interval, we obtained a unique reputational equilibrium by allowing the policymaker to announce the best one. But if we look at different punishment intervals (which can be either greater or smaller than one period), then we find an array of reputational equilibria. At this point, we have no satisfactory way to resolve this problem of multiple equilibria. However, we have some observations.

First, we know that the length of the punishment interval cannot be zero. That is, the policymaker cannot instantly restore a lost reputation. If he could, there would be no enforcement, and the only equilibrium would be the discretionary one.

We can calculate the effect of longer punishment intervals on expected costs. In the present model the punishments—that is, discretionary outcomes—never occur as part of a reputational equilibrium. Hence we always do at least as well if we increase enforcement, which corresponds here to raising the length of the punishment interval. In particular, it always looks desirable in this model to have an infinite interval, which amounts to a form of "capital punishment."

We can modify the model so that punishments take place occasionally.[18] For example, suppose that inflation depends partly on the policymaker's actions and partly on uncontrollable events. Further, assume that people cannot fully sort out these two influences on inflation, even ex post. Then people adopt a form of control rule where the policymaker loses reputation if the observed inflation rate exceeds some critical value. But, because of the uncontrollable element, this loss of reputation—and hence, the punishment—actually occur from time to time. Then, in contemplating a more severe form of punishment, we have to weigh the losses when punishments occur against the benefits from greater enforcement. Thus it is likely that the optimal punishment interval would be finite. (From a positive standpoint, however, it does not

18. Green and Porter (1981) have this feature in their model of oligopoly pricing.

necessarily follow that the equilibrium with this punishment interval will be selected.)

Finally, another possibility is to introduce uncertainty about the policymaker's preferences. Then people try to learn about these preferences by observing behavior. Further, the policymaker knows that people learn from his actions, and acts accordingly. Kreps and Wilson (1980) and Milgrom and Roberts (1982), who use this general type of model, show that unique equilibria sometimes obtain.[19] But we have not yet pursued this route in our context, because it relies on differences in tastes among potential policymakers. Unfortunately, we have nothing interesting to say about the sources of these differences. But possibly this idea would become meaningful if we identified policymakers with shifting interest groups, each of which were affected differently by variations in inflation.

Observations

Our analysis provides an example of a reputational equilibrium for monetary policy. The results amount to a combination of the outcomes from discretion with those from the ideal rule. Previously, we analyzed discretion and rules as distinct possible equilibria. Now, the relative weights attached to the discretionary and rules solutions depend on the policymaker's discount rate and some other factors. From a predictive standpoint for monetary growth and inflation, the results modify and extend those that we discussed previously.

In some environments the rules take a contingent form, where inflation depends on the realization of the benefit parameter or the discount factor. Here the policymaker sometimes engineers surprisingly low inflation, which is costly at a point in time. Thus the monetary authority "bites the bullet" and pursues a contractionary policy, given some states of the world. By acting this way, the policymaker sustains a reputation that permits surprisingly high inflation in other states of the world.

We have difficulties with multiplicity of equilibria, which show up also in the related game-theory literature. Here the problem arises in determining how long a loss of reputation persists. In an extended version of

---

19. Also, the solution does not necessarily degenerate to the discretionary equilibrium when the game has a known, finite end point. See note 7.

the model, we can figure out the optimal length for this interval of punishment. But from a positive standpoint, it is unclear which equilibrium will prevail.

References

Barro, R. J. 1976. "Rational Expectations and the Role of Monetary Policy." *Journal of Monetary Economics* 2:1–32.

——— 1977. "Long-Term Contracts, Sticky Prices, and Monetary Policy." *Journal of Monetary Economics* 3:305–316.

——— 1983. "Inflationary Finance under Discretion and Rules." *Canadian Journal of Economics* 16:1–16.

Barro, R. J., and D. B. Gordon. 1983. "A Positive Theory of Monetary Policy in a Natural-Rate Model." *Journal of Political Economy* 91:589–610.

Calvo, G. 1978. "On the Time Consistency of Optimal Policy in a Monetary Economy." *Econometrica* 46:1411–28.

Fischer, S. 1977. "Long-Term Contracts, Rational Expectations and the Optimal Money Supply Rule." *Journal of Political Economy* 85:191–205.

Friedman, B. 1979. "Optimal Expectations and the Extreme Information Assumption of 'Rational Expectations' Macromodels." *Journal of Monetary Economics* 5:23–42.

Friedman, J. W. 1971. "A Non-Cooperative Equilibrium for Supergames." *Review of Economic Studies* 38:861–874.

Gray, J. A. 1976. "Wage Indexation: A Macroeconomic Approach." *Journal of Monetary Economics* 2:221–236.

Green, E. J., and R. H. Porter. 1981. "Noncooperative Collusion under Imperfect Price Information." Unpublished manuscript. Pasadena: California Institute of Technology.

Kreps, D. M., and R. Wilson. 1980. "On the Chain-Store Paradox and Predation: Reputation for Toughness." Unpublished manuscript. Stanford: Stanford University.

Kydland, F. E., and E. C. Prescott. 1977. "Rules rather than Discretion: The Inconsistency of Optimal Plans." *Journal of Political Economy* 85:473–491.

Lucas, R. E. 1972. "Expectations and the Neutrality of Money." *Journal of Economic Theory* 4:103–124.

——— 1973. "Some International Evidence on Output-Inflation Tradeoffs." *American Economic Review* 63:326–334.

Milgrom, P., and J. Roberts. 1982. "Predation, Reputation and Entry Deterrence." *Journal of Economic Theory* 27(2):280–312.

Selten, R. 1978. "The Chain-Store Paradox." *Theory and Decisions* 9:127–159.

Taylor, J. 1975. "Monetary Policy during a Transition to Rational Expectations." *Journal of Political Economy* 83:1009–22.

——— 1980. "Aggregate Dynamics and Staggered Contracts." *Journal of Political Economy* 88:1–23.

4   Inflationary Finance under Discretion and Rules

Inflationary finance has often been studied in the context of a once-and-for-all choice of the monetary growth rate. See, for example, Bailey (1956) and Phelps (1973). The nominal interest rate is the tax rate levied on real cash balances. The effects of this tax on governmental revenues and excess burden can be analyzed in a manner similar to that for taxes on labor income, produced commodities, and so forth. The special characteristics of money concern the tendency for monopoly on the supply side and the possibility that the marginal cost of production (for real balances) is near zero.

Cagan (1956, 77ff.) observed that surprise inflation is also a source of government revenue. The discussions in Auernheimer (1974) and Sjaastad (1976) link surprise inflation to unanticipated capital losses on real cash (or, more generally, on any governmental obligations whose payment streams are fixed in nominal terms). The revenue obtained through surprise inflation amounts to an ex post capital levy. As with other capital levies, this form of tax—when not foreseen—can raise revenue at little deadweight loss.

Since people understand the attractions of ex post capital levies, they will attempt to forecast, ex ante, the government's tendency to exploit such situations. So, in deciding to hold money or other nominal liabilities of the government, people will take into account the government's power to engineer ex post "surprises," which depreciate the real value of these claims. (Default on public debts and high rates of taxation on "old"

From *Canadian Journal of Economics* (1983) 16(1):1–16. An earlier version of this chapter was presented at the Peterkin Symposium on Foundations of Monetary Policy and Government Finance, Rice University, April 1982. I have benefited from research support by the National Science Foundation.

capital are similar phenomena.) The expected cost of holding money takes into consideration the likelihood of these subsequent capital losses. Further, in making optimal forecasts of these losses, people essentially have to model the monetary authority's behavior. Specifically, people would project the reaction of monetary growth to a set of state variables, which include the position of the money-demand function. In a full rational expectations equilibrium, no systematic inflation surprises can occur. Prices may be higher or lower than predicted because of the realizations of some random events, but the government cannot be systematically generating proceeds from surprise inflation.

Although a regular pattern of inflation surprises cannot arise in equilibrium, the government's capacity to create these shocks, ex post, influences the position of the equilibrium for the growth rates of money and prices. If the policymaker could commit himself in advance to resist the ex post benefits from surprise inflation, then the equilibrium rates of monetary growth and inflation are likely to be lower. Monetary and price rules provide such commitments to varying degrees. In contrast, a purely discretionary regime has no scope for these types of restrictions on subsequent monetary behavior. This type of distinction between rules and discretion has been stressed by Kydland and Prescott (1977).

Calvo (1978) studied a model in which the government was interested only in maximizing its revenue from inflationary finance. In a purely discretionary setup, where people have rational expectations, there is no finite equilibrium solution for monetary growth and inflation. In the model in this chapter, the government's objective is modified to trade off costs of inflation against the benefits from revenues. A finite equilibrium is then determined under purely discretionary monetary policy. The implied growth rates of money and prices depend on some stochastic state variables, which include the government's valuation of revenues (which may vary with the overall level of government spending or with aggregate business conditions), and the position of the money-demand function.

The results under discretion are contrasted with those obtainable from monetary rules. I consider rules that allow for a full set of state-contingent responses, as well as those of simple form that do not allow for full contingencies. The constant-growth-rate rule is of the latter type. Although state-contingent rules can unambiguously outperform discretion (abstracting from costs of enforcing the rules), the ranking of discretion and simple rules is uncertain. The rules have the benefit of internalizing all linkages between monetary behavior and inflationary expectations. However, discretion (and fully contingent rules) allow for a flexible response to changes in circumstances, which has some value in the model under study.

Setup of the Model

It is convenient to develop the model in a framework of discrete time. The length of the period is denoted by τ, which has units of time, say, of years. Since the length of the period plays no economic role in the present model, I ultimately focus on the results when τ is allowed to approach zero.

The government determines the nominal money stock at the start of period t to be the amount M_t. No private issues of money are considered. The growth rate of money from period $t - 1$ to t is $\mu_t \equiv (1/\tau) \cdot \log(M_t/M_{t-1})$, which has units of per year. The general price level for period t is P_t; so real balances are M_t/P_t. I focus here on holdings of money, although the approach can be applied also to government bonds that have prescribed nominal pay-outs. The inflation rate from period $t - 1$ to t is $\pi_t \equiv (1/\tau) \log(P_t/P_{t-1})$, which is measured per year.

Let I_t denote the information set that each person has during period t. (The government will have equivalent information when setting the money stock, M_t.) This information set includes knowledge of P_t and M_t. Based on this information, everyone calculates the expected rate of inflation from period t to $t + 1$,

$$\pi_{t+1}^e \equiv E(\pi_{t+1}|I_t) = 1/\tau \ [E(\log P_{t+1}|I_t) - \log P_t]. \tag{4.1}$$

Demand for real balances during period t depends inversely on π_{t+1}^e, and positively on a stochastic scale variable, A_t. I use the semilogarithmic form, as in Cagan (1956),

$$M_t/P_t = A_t \cdot \exp(-\alpha\pi_{t+1}^e). \tag{4.2}$$

The logarithm of the scale variable, A_t, is generated from a random-walk process,

$$\log A_t = \log A_{t-1} + a_t, \tag{4.3}$$

where a_t is white noise. The variance of a_t, σ_a^2, is proportional to the period length, τ. People know the value of A_t at the start of period t—that is, A_t and a_t are contained in the information set, I_t.

Taking logarithmic first differences of Eq. (4.2) and using Eq. (4.3) and the definitions of μ_t and π_t leads to the condition,

$$\pi_t \tau = \mu_t \tau + \alpha(\pi_{t+1}^e - \pi_t^e) - a_t. \tag{4.4}$$

Note that $\pi_t^e = (1/\tau)\,[E(\log P_t|I_{t-1}) - \log P_{t-1}]$. Equation (4.4) indicates that the inflation rate, π_t, is above (below) the monetary growth rate, μ_t, to the extent of the proportionate fall (rise) in real money demanded from period $t - 1$ to t. The change in real money demanded reflects either a change in expected inflation, $\pi_{t+1}^e - \pi_t^e$ (multiplied by the proportionate sensitivity of money demand, α), or a proportionate change in the scale variable, $a_t = \log(A_t/A_{t-1})$.

The government's real revenue from money creation for period t is

$$R_t = (M_t - M_{t-1})/P_t = (M_t/P_t) - (M_{t-1}/P_{t-1})(P_{t-1}/P_t). \tag{4.5}$$

Substituting for the real-balance terms from Eq. (4.2), and using the condition $P_{t-1}/P_t = \exp(-\pi_t \tau)$, leads to the expression,

$$R_t = A_t \exp(-\alpha\pi_{t+1}^e) - A_{t-1}\exp(-\alpha\pi_t^e - \pi_t \tau). \tag{4.6}$$

For given inflationary expectations between periods t and $t + 1$, π_{t+1}^e, there is a given amount of real cash that people will hold during period t, $(M_t/P_t) = A_t \exp(-\alpha\pi_{t+1}^e)$. Given this term, governmental revenue will be higher if the real value of money carried over from the previous period, $M_{t-1}/P_t = A_{t-1}\exp(-\alpha\pi_t^e - \pi_t \tau)$, can be reduced. Therefore, if π_{t+1}^e could be held fixed (and for a given value of the prior expectation, π_t^e), revenue would be enhanced by choosing monetary growth, μ_t, in order to engineer a higher value of π_t. Higher inflation depreciates more real cash and thereby allows the policymaker to provide more new real cash as a replacement. Of course, this procedure works best when π_{t+1}^e is insulated from the determination of μ_t and π_t—that is, when people do not anticipate a repetition of the high rate of depreciation in the real value of their money. The model has to clarify the interconnections among anticipated inflation rates, π_{t+1}^e and π_t^e, monetary growth, μ_t, and inflation, π_t. This analysis requires a theory of expectations, as well as a model of the policymaker's incentives to choose different rates of monetary expansion. The discussion deals first with the objectives of the policymaker. The solution to this problem—which private agents are assumed to understand—ultimately provides the basis for the theory of expectations.

The Policymaker's Objective

The government likes more revenues from money creation—perhaps because the alternatives are either extra revenue obtained from distorting taxation or less (valuable) public expenditure. For any period the policymaker values each unit of real revenue from money issue by the positive amount, θ_t. This valuation would be higher in times when alternative revenue sources require greater welfare losses at the margin. Possibly, θ_t would be especially high in wartime, in other periods where government expenditures have risen sharply from previous levels, or in recessions. In this model changes in the logarithm of the θ_t parameter are regarded as unpredictable—that is, I use the random-walk specification,

$$\log \theta_t = \log \theta_{t-1} + \varepsilon_t, \tag{4.7}$$

where ε_t is white noise and independent of a_t in Eq. (4.3). The variance of ε_t, σ_ε^2, is proportional to the period length, τ. People know the value of θ_t at the start of period t—that is, θ_t and ε_t are included in the information set, I_t.

The policymaker is also concerned with costs from inflation. The usual liquidity costs, which are associated with the quantity of real money demanded during period t, involve the expected inflation rate between periods t and $t + 1$, π_{t+1}^e. The actual inflation rate between periods $t - 1$ and t, π_t, is assumed to entail separate costs from the standpoint of the policymaker. There might be costs of changing prices, per se, as well as losses from unexpected inflation. The costs of inflation, as perceived by the policymaker, are written as the function $\phi(\pi_t, \pi_{t+1}^e)$. These costs have units of commodities per year. The total costs incurred over period t, which has length τ, are equal to $\tau\phi(\pi_t, \pi_{t+1}^e)$.

Overall, the government's objective concerns the net costs of inflation for each period, Z_t, as calculated from

$$Z_t = \tau\phi(\pi_t, \pi^e_{t+1}) - \theta_t R_t \qquad (4.8)$$

$$= \tau\phi(\pi_t, \pi^e_{t+1}) - \theta_t[A_t\exp(-\alpha\pi^e_{t+1}) - A_{t-1}\exp(-\alpha\pi^e_t - \pi_t\tau)],$$

where the formula for R_t has been substituted from Eq. (4.6). The cost function satisfies the properties, $\partial\phi/\partial\pi_t > 0$ and $\partial\phi/\partial\pi^e_{t+1} > 0$. The valuation placed on revenue, $\theta_t R_t$, is subtracted from the costs ascribed to actual and expected inflation. In general the policymaker would seek to minimize the expected sum of net costs—that is, of the various Z_t— where each period's cost is expressed in present-value terms. The expectations of each Z_t would be evaluated as of some appropriate starting date.

The Choice of Monetary Growth under Discretion

The analysis of discretionary policy follows the general line of argument presented in Barro and Gordon (1983a). The policymaker selects the monetary growth rate, μ_t, for each period. Under discretion, there are—by definition—no possibilities for prior constraints or commitments that would restrict the subsequent choices of monetary growth rates.

At date t the expectation of inflation that was formed last period, π^e_t, cannot be altered. Suppose for the moment that current and future inflationary expectations, $\pi^e_{t+1}, \pi^e_{t+2}, \ldots$, are also treated as givens by the policymaker during period t. The choice of μ_t then determines π_t from Eq. (4.4), given the exogenous disturbance, a_t. The value for μ_t also determines the real revenue for period t, R_t, from Eq. (4.6) (given the values of A_t and A_{t-1}). Therefore, we can compute the full effect of μ_t on the contemporaneous net cost, Z_t, in Eq. (4.8). With the various π^e_{t+i}'s held fixed (and future μ_{t+i}'s unrestricted by current actions), there are no effects in this model of the choice of μ_t on future Z_{t+i}'s. Therefore, the optimizing policymaker would choose μ_t in order to minimize the contemporaneous net cost, Z_t. Note that the neglect of future costs does not derive from myopia of the policymaker. Rather, with given expectations, the policymaker has no way at date t to influence these future costs.

More generally, the π_{t+i}^e's will be related to expectations of future μ_{t+i}'s. Hence, the π_{t+i}^e's can be held fixed above only if the choice of μ_t has no implications for expectations of the μ_{t+i}'s. In the present context each μ_{t+i} will emerge from a minimization problem that starts from date $t + i$. The choice of μ_t and the resulting value for π_t do nothing to alter the objective characteristics of this problem for any future period. Therefore it is reasonable to look for an equilibrium solution to the model where the μ_{t+i}'s are invariant with the selection of μ_t. (Note that there is nothing to learn about in this model; in particular, people already know the government's objective and "technology.") With the μ_{t+i}'s held fixed, it is reasonable also to hold fixed the π_{t+i}^e's when μ_t varies. In other words there will be a sensible equilibrium that satisfies this condition.[1]

A discretionary policymaker treats inflationary expectations as givens when choosing the monetary growth rate, μ_t. Therefore, as shown before, the choice of μ_t affects only the contemporaneous cost, Z_t. Hence the choice of μ_t follows from the first-order condition, $(\partial Z_t / \partial \mu_t)|\pi_t^e$, $\pi_{t+1}^e, \ldots = 0$, as

$$\partial \phi / \partial \pi_t - \theta_t A_{t-1} \exp(-\alpha \pi_t^e - \pi_t \tau) = 0. \tag{4.9}$$

This calculation uses the conditions, $(\partial \pi_t / \partial \mu_t)|\pi_t^e, \pi_{t+1}^e = 1$ (from Eq. (4.4)), and $(\partial \pi_{t+1}^e / \partial \mu_t)|\pi_{t+1}^e = 0$. (The period length, τ, appears multiplicatively in both terms in Eq. (4.9) and has been canceled out.) Rewriting Eq. (4.9) yields the condition,

$$\partial \phi / \partial \pi_t = \theta_t A_{t-1} \exp(-\alpha \pi_t^e - \pi_t \tau) \tag{4.10}$$

$$= \theta_t (M_{t-1} / P_{t-1}) \exp(-\pi_t \tau).$$

The monetary growth rate, μ_t, is chosen so that the marginal cost of (actual) inflation equals the marginal benefit from additional revenue. The latter quantity equals the valuation per unit of revenue, θ_t, times the marginal effect of μ_t on revenue, R_t. With π_{t+1}^e and π_t^e held fixed, it follows from Eqs. (4.5) and (4.6) that $\partial R_t / \partial \mu_t = \tau (M_{t-1} / P_{t-1}) \exp(-\pi_t \tau)$. Notice that, because π_{t+1}^e is held fixed when μ_t changes, the marginal

1. This analysis neglects the possibility that the policymaker can build up a reputation for low inflation. Such reputational equilibria may or may not exist in the present type of model. For a discussion of the possibilities, see Barro and Gordon (1983b).

cost of expected inflation does not enter into the first-order condition. Similarly, with inflationary expectations taken as given, there are no effects of current monetary growth on the real money demanded for periods $t - 1$ and t.

To obtain closed-form results, I specialize the cost function to the convenient form,

$$\phi(\pi_t, \pi_{t+1}^e) = (k_1/b)\exp(b\pi_t) \tag{4.11}$$
$$+ (k_2/b)\exp(b\pi_{t+1}^e); \quad k_1, k_2, b > 0.$$

The exponents, b, could differ in the two cost terms without affecting most of the results. Equation (4.11) implies positive and increasing marginal costs for actual and expected inflation. (π_t and π_{t+1}^e are also entered in separable form in this example.) With this specification of costs, Eq. (4.10) implies

$$k_1\exp(b\pi_t) = \theta_t A_{t-1}\exp(-\alpha\pi_t^e - \pi_t\tau). \tag{4.12}$$

Rearranging terms and taking logarithms of both sides yields

$$(b + \tau)\pi_t + \alpha\pi_t^e = \log(\theta_{t-1}A_{t-1}/k_1) + \varepsilon_t, \tag{4.13}$$

where [from Eq. (4.7)] $\varepsilon_t = \log(\theta_t/\theta_{t-1})$. Given the formula for π_t in Eq. (4.13), the implied choice for μ_t (given π_{t+1}^e, π_t^e, and a_t) can be determined from Eq. (4.4).

Rational Expectations

Equations (4.4) and (4.13) determine actual rates of inflation and monetary growth, π_t and μ_t, as functions of exogenous variables and the expected inflation rates, π_t^e and π_{t+1}^e. In order to close the model these expectations must be determined. I use a rational expectations condition, $\pi_{t+1}^e = E(\pi_{t+1}|I_t)$ and $\pi_t^e = E(\pi_t|I_{t-1})$. The information set, I_t, includes observations of all variables for date t, including M_t, P_t, θ_t, and A_t. People also use knowledge of the model's structure to calculate these expectations. Most important, everyone understands that the policy-maker chooses μ_t in each period to minimize costs, Z_t from Eq. (4.8), while treating π_t^e and π_{t+1}^e as givens. Hence they know that Eq. (4.13) holds. In a full equilibrium, people's inflationary expectations, π^e_{t+1} and π^e_t, will be consistent with well-informed projections of the policymaker's future choices of monetary growth. Although the policymaker is not restricted to validating these expectations (which will appear to him as givens in each period), the first-order condition in Eq. (4.10) will lead to a free choice to do so in equilibrium. That is, in equilibrium the policymaker will not be motivated to deviate systematically from people's prior expectations.

People form the expectation, π^e_t, based on the information available in period $t - 1$. The variables, θ_{t-1} and A_{t-1}, are known at this date. Therefore, taking expectations of Eq. (4.13), conditional on the information set I_{t-1}, the expected inflation rate must satisfy

$$\pi^e_t = \left(\frac{1}{b} + \alpha + \tau\right)\log\left(\frac{\theta_{t-1}A_{t-1}}{k_1}\right), \tag{4.14}$$

where I have used the condition, $E(\varepsilon_t|I_{t-1}) = 0$. The formula for π^e_t can be substituted back into Eq. (4.13) to calculate the actual inflation rate, π_t. The form of Eq. (4.14) can be updated by one period to determine π^e_{t+1}, the anticipated rate of inflation between periods t and $t + 1$. Then the results for π^e_t, π^e_{t+1}, and π_t can be substituted into Eq. (4.4) to determine the monetary growth rate, μ_t.

The period length, τ, is now assumed to be negligible relative to the parameters, b and α. As $\tau \to 0$, the full solution to the model is

$$\pi_t = (1/b + \alpha)\log(\theta_{t-1}A_{t-1}/k_1) + (1/b)\varepsilon_t, \tag{4.15}$$

$$\pi^e_t = (1/b + \alpha)\log(\theta_{t-1}A_{t-1}/k_1), \tag{4.16}$$

$$\pi^e_{t+1} = (1/b + \alpha)\log(\theta_t A_t/k_1), \tag{4.17}$$

$$\mu_t = (1/b + \alpha)[\log(\theta_{t-1}A_{t-1}/k_1) - \alpha\varepsilon_t/\tau + ba_t/\tau],^2 \tag{4.18}$$

where $\varepsilon_t = \log(\theta_t/\theta_{t-1})$ and $a_t = \log(A_t/A_{t-1})$.

The solution for monetary growth and inflation is an equilibrium in the following sense. First, at a point in time, the policymaker treats π^e_t as given and regards π^e_{t+1} as generated from the expectations mechanism in Eq. (4.17)—in particular, π^e_{t+1} is invariant with the choice of μ_t. Given

---

2. As $\tau \to 0$, the resulting revenue per unit of time, R_t/τ, can be written as $(R_t/\tau) = [A_{t-1}/(b + \alpha)](\theta_{t-1}A_{t-1}/k_1)^{-\alpha/(b+\alpha)}[\log(\theta_{t-1}A_{t-1}/k_1) + b(a_t/\tau) - \alpha(\varepsilon_t/\tau)] = \mu_t(M_t/P_t)$.

π_t^e and π_{t+1}^e, and the relation of π_t to μ_t from Eq. (4.4), the setting for μ_t in Eq. (4.18) satisfies the policymaker's first-order condition for minimizing Z_t, as specified in Eq. (4.13). Second, the expectations mechanisms in Eqs. (4.16) and (4.17) are rational—that is, $\pi_t^e = E(\pi_t|I_{t-1})$ and $\pi_{t+1}^e = E(\pi_{t+1}|I_t)$, given that monetary growth for each period follows the form of Eq. (4.18).

Notice from Eq. (4.10) that the marginal cost of inflation, $\partial\phi/\partial\pi_t$, must be positive in equilibrium. Therefore, if $k_1 = 0$, then the policymaker attaches no cost to actual inflation, π_t, and no finite equilibrium values for π_t and μ_t are determined in Eqs. (4.15) and (4.18). This case corresponds to the one explored by Calvo (1978), where the discretionary policymaker considers only the maximization of revenue, R_t.

Economists often have trouble explaining why inflation is costly. If these costs are small, the parameter k_1 will be small. Remember that this coefficient refers to the cost of the actual inflation rate, π_t. The smaller the parameter k_1, the greater will be the growth rates of prices and money in Eqs. (4.15) and (4.18). In other words, if inflation is not very costly, the model predicts that we will have a lot of inflation! Recall that the costs of expected inflation, π_{t+1}^e, involve the parameter k_2. This coefficient has no effect on the discretionary choices of inflation and monetary growth in Eqs. (4.15) and (4.18).

Within a discretionary setup, where the policymaker can make no commitments about future policy choices, the results provide a positive theory of monetary growth and inflation. As long as $k_1 > 0$, inflation and monetary growth depend on the two variables that move around in the model: θ and A. A higher level for θ_{t-1} (given the value of $\varepsilon_t = \log(\theta_t/\theta_{t-1})$) means a greater value placed on revenues. Hence, in an equilibrium where the first-order condition from Eq. (4.13) is satisfied, the values of π_t and μ_t are higher.[3] Similarly, a higher level for real money demand A_{t-1} [given $a_t = \log(A_t/A_{t-1})$] encourages the revenue objective relative to the cost of inflation.[4] Therefore, π_t and μ_t rise with A_{t-1}.

---

3. If $a_t = \varepsilon_t = 0$, then the equilibrium amount of revenue per unit of time (note 2) rises with θ_{t-1} if and only if $\mu_t < 1/\alpha$; that is, if and only if the monetary growth rate is below the revenue-maximizing value for the context of a once-and-for-all choice of μ.

4. Secular growth, which leads to a steady increase in real money demand, would tend to be accompanied by a parallel rise in the cost parameter, k_1. These changes leave π_t and μ_t unaltered over time.

Although expectations are rational, surprises do occur because of the stochastic terms in the model. The amount of unexpected inflation follows from Eqs. (4.15) and (4.16) as

$$\pi_t - \pi_t^e = (1/b)\varepsilon_t. \tag{4.19}$$

When the valuation of revenue rises unexpectedly—that is, when $\varepsilon_t = \log(\theta_t/\theta_{t-1}) > 0$—inflation is unexpectedly high. This result obtains because the policymaker is motivated by the rise in θ to incur a higher marginal cost of inflation. The positive value for ε_t means also a rise in the expected inflation rate—that is, $\pi_{t+1}^e - \pi_t^e > 0$ from Eqs. (4.16) and (4.17). Because of the reduction in real money demanded, we need a downward shift in μ_t to satisfy Eq. (4.4) (hence the term $-\alpha\varepsilon_t/\tau$ in the expression for μ_t in Eq. (4.18).[5] Expected future rates of monetary expansion rise with ε_t.

A surprise shift in the level of real money demanded, $a_t = \log(A_t/A_{t-1})$, does not generate unexpected inflation (although it does produce unanticipated monetary growth). Given A_{t-1}, a higher value for a_t means a higher level of A_t. Revenue rises from Eq. (4.6) in accordance with the term $(M_t/P_t) = A_t\exp(-\alpha\pi_{t+1}^e)$. However, with π_{t-1}^e treated as invariant with the choice of μ_t, a shift in this term leaves unaltered the value of π_t that satisfies the policymaker's first-order condition. The term a_t does influence the relation between monetary growth and inflation in Eq. (4.4). This element raises μ_t for a given value of π_t. A positive value for a_t also raises anticipated future rates of monetary growth, which means an increase in π_{t+1}^e. This element lowers μ_t for a given value of π_t in Eq. (4.4). On net, a_t leads to an (unexpected) expansion of μ_t.[6]

The model determines the variance of the inflation rate over various horizons. If we use Eq. (4.15) and the random-walk specifications for $\log(\theta_t)$ and $\log(A_t)$ (from Eqs. 4.3 and 4.7), then the variance of the inflation rate is

$$\text{var}(\pi_t|I_0) = (1/b + \alpha)^2(t - 1)(\sigma_\varepsilon^2 + \sigma_a^2) + (1/b)^2\sigma_\varepsilon^2, \tag{4.20}$$

---

5. As $\tau \to 0$, the variance of ε_t/τ approaches infinity. In other words, jumps in the money stock are required to maintain equality between money supply and demand at all points in time. However, the policymaker acts in this model to avoid jumps in the price level (see Eq. 4.15).

6. The term, a_t/τ, appears in Eq. (4.18). The variance of this term approaches infinity as $\tau \to 0$. Hence, jumps in the money stock can occur, as discussed in note 5.

where I_0 is the information available in period zero. The variance of the inflation rate depends on the variances of the two innovation terms, σ_ε^2 and σ_a^2. The forecast variance for π_t increases linearly with the distance in time, t. The variance for the log of any future price level, $\log(P_t)$, can also be determined as a function of σ_ε^2, σ_a^2, and t.[7]

Discretion versus Rules

Constant State Variables

In the discretionary regime the policymaker holds fixed current and future inflationary expectations when deciding on period t's rate of monetary growth. The policymaker does this because he cannot make any commitments about future policy choices. But since inflation is related to monetary behavior, this result means that the discretionary policymaker is unable to internalize some effects of his actions. Recall the form of the objective function from Eq. (4.8),

$$Z_t = \tau\phi(\pi_t, \pi_{t+1}^e) - \theta_t[A_t\exp(-\alpha\pi_{t+1}^e) - A_{t-1}\exp(-\alpha\pi_t^e - \pi_t\tau)].$$

The discretionary policymaker has no way to consider the effects of monetary behavior on inflationary expectations, which influence costs, $\phi(\pi_t, \pi_{t+1}^e)$, and revenues, through the terms $\exp(-\alpha\pi_{t+1}^e)$ and $\exp(-\alpha\pi_t^e)$.

The difference between discretion and policy rules—or commitments—can best be clarified by initially suppressing the variations over time in the state variables, θ_t and A_t. Assume now that $\theta_t = \theta$, and $A_t = A$; thus $\varepsilon_t = a_t = 0$ holds for all t. The discretionary solutions now dictate constant rates of monetary growth and inflation. The results follow from Eqs. (4.15)–(4.18) as

$$\pi = \pi^e = \mu = (1/b + \alpha)\log(\theta A/k_1). \tag{4.21}$$

Suppose that the policymaker could restrict himself in advance to a particular value for future monetary growth. That is, the policymaker rules out the possibility of altering his subsequent behavior, even if such

---

7. The variance of the monetary growth rate, μ_t, is infinite. However, the variance of the log of the future money stock, $\log(M_t)$, is finite.

alterations would appear advantageous ex post. In this case there would be a linkage between the policymaker's choice of (constant) monetary growth, μ, and the values of inflationary expectations. Namely, $\pi_t^e = \mu$ would hold for all periods t. Rather than treating expectations as givens at any point in time, the policymaker would now choose monetary growth subject to the condition that $\pi_t^e = \mu$ holds for all t.[8] Because the state variables are constant, it also follows here (from Eq. (4.4) that $\pi = \mu$, and (from Eq. 4.6) that $R/\tau = \mu(M/P)$.

The policymaker's objective still entails minimization of net costs, which are now the same for all periods (see, however, note 8):

$$Z = \tau\phi(\pi, \pi^e) - \theta R \tag{4.22}$$

$$= \tau(k_1/b)\exp(b\pi) + \tau(k_2/b)\exp(b\pi^e) - \tau\theta\mu A\exp(-\alpha\pi^e).$$

Given that $\pi^e = \pi = \mu$ holds, the optimizing value for the monetary growth rate, denoted by μ^*, satisfies the first-order condition,

$$(k_1 + k_2)\exp(b\mu^*) = \theta A(1 - \alpha\mu^*)\exp(-\alpha\mu^*).$$

This condition can be rewritten as

$$(b + \alpha)\mu^* = \log\left(\frac{\theta A}{k_1 + k_2}\right) + \log(1 - \alpha\mu^*).$$

If $\alpha\mu^*$ is much less than one (which means that μ^* is well below the purely revenue-maximizing rate), then $\log(1 - \alpha\mu^*) \approx -\alpha\mu^*$. The approximate solution for μ^* can then be written as

$$\mu^* \approx \left(\frac{1}{b + 2\alpha}\right)\log\left(\frac{\theta A}{k_1 + k_2}\right), \tag{4.23}$$

if $\alpha\pi^*$ is much less than one. Because people anticipate this monetary behavior under a rule, their expectations, $(\pi^e)^*$, accord with μ^* and with the actual inflation rate—that is, $\pi^* = (\pi^e)^* = \mu^*$.

---

8. In some initial period where the rule is implemented, say date 0, expectations need not be realized. That is, $\pi_0^e \neq \mu$ may apply. Under reasonable assumptions, this element has a negligible impact on the policymaker's once-and-for-all choice of the monetary growth rate.

Compare the choice of monetary growth under a rule, μ^*, with the value of μ from Eq. (4.21), which arises under discretion. The growth rates of money and prices tend to be higher under discretion for two reasons.[9] First, the discretionary policymaker cannot influence inflationary expectations, his choices do not depend on the costs of expected inflation. Therefore the cost parameter k_2 is absent from Eq. (4.21) but is present in Eq. (4.23). Similarly, the discretionary policymaker cannot make commitments that take account of the negative effect of higher anticipated inflation on real money demanded. This factor enters into the rules solution of Eq. (4.23) through the parameter, 2α. For the discretionary solution in Eq. (4.21), α appears instead of 2α.

Alternatively, suppose that μ^* were conjectured to be the equilibrium rate of monetary growth under discretion. This rate of monetary expansion minimizes net costs in Eq. (4.22), given that π^e and π move one-to-one with μ. But, if π^e (at all dates) were set by the formula in Eq. (4.23), the discretionary policymaker—who is not bound to set $\mu = \mu^*$—would not find this rate of monetary growth to be advantageous. Rather, a (surprisingly) higher value for monetary growth, which depreciates more of the initial real balances, would be preferred.[10] The increase in costs due to added inflation would be more than outweighed by the gains from additional revenue. Of course, agents would not then maintain their inflationary expectations at the value indicated in Eq. (4.23). The full equilibrium under the assumption of an unrestricted policymaker is the discretionary outcome that is specified in Eq. (4.21).

Net costs, Z, are lower under the monetary rule (μ^* in Eq. 4.23) than under discretion (μ in Eq. 4.21). It is unclear whether revenues are higher under rules or discretion. Since monetary growth is higher under discretion (note 9), revenues will also surely be higher under discretion if the rate μ from Eq. (4.21) is below the purely revenue-maximizing rate, which is $1/\alpha$ in this model. Using Eq. (4.21), we find that this condition holds if $(\theta A/k_1) < \exp[(b + \alpha)/\alpha]$. (Because the discretionary policymaker cannot internalize the full consequences of his monetary behavior, it is

9. Equations (4.21) and (4.23) imply that $\mu - \mu^* = [1/(b + \alpha)] \log[(k_1 + k_2)/k_1] + [\alpha/(b + \alpha)(b + 2\alpha)] \log[\theta A/(k_1 + k_2)]$. $\mu > \mu^*$ follows unambiguously if $\log(\theta A/k_1 + k_2) > 0$, that is, if $\mu^* > 0$ in Eq. (5.23).

10. This preference does not require any difference of opinion between the policymaker and the typical member of the private sector. The valuation of revenues, θ_t, reflects some externality (for example, from distorting taxation). The inflation surprise lowers the welfare loss from this existing distortion.

conceivable that he would choose a monetary growth rate that exceeds the revenue-maximizing rate.)

Changes in the State Variables

Given constant state variables, θ and A, discretion and rules generate constant values for monetary growth, which are μ and μ^* respectively. When θ and A move randomly over time, the discretionary choice of monetary growth also moves randomly, as shown in Eq. (4.18). What does a monetary rule dictate when the state variables change? Suppose that we interpret a rule as a commitment to a prescribed functional relation between μ_t and the pertinent state variables, θ_t, A_t, ε_t, a_t, and so on. Then we could solve for the rule that minimizes the expected sum of net costs—that is, the Z_t's—in present-value terms. The expectations would be evaluated as of some starting date (see below). Although the best contingent rule cannot be written out in closed form, it is clear that such a rule would outperform discretion.[11] Basically, the contingent rule differs from discretion only because it allows the policymaker to internalize the relation between monetary behavior and inflationary expectations. The consideration of this linkage can only deliver better outcomes, regardless of whether θ and A are constants or variables. (Note also that discretion is one form of "rule" that is admissable to a policymaker who can choose among all possible contingent forms of action.)

Some properties of the optimal, fully contingent rule are clear at this stage. First, neither the growth rate of prices nor that of money would generally be constant. Typically, it will be better to allow inflation and monetary growth to react to changes in the state variables, θ_t and A_t. That is, inflation is one form of tax. Generally, the optimal rate of this tax will vary with the valuation of revenues, θ_t, and with the base of the stuff being taxed, A_t. Recall that the variable θ_t could change with a shift in government expenditures or with changes in the excess burdens associated with alternative methods of taxation.

---

11. Rules would also deliver a variance for the inflation rate that differs from the one generated under discretion in Eq. (5.20). In a larger model the forecast variance for the price level might enter into the cost function, Z in Eq. (5.8), or in the money-demand function.

Second, since the movements in θ_t and A_t are unpredictable, we shall also have unanticipated changes in the growth rates of money and prices. Sometimes people will experience surprise capital losses on their cash, and sometimes they will get surprise gains. For example, holders of money may do badly in wartime but do well in peacetime. But, the ex ante return on money is satisfactory for the holders of money. The realized return depends on exogenous events such as war or peace and on the contractual relation between the returns (that is, the rate of inflation) and these events. As long as people can verify that the policymaker is sticking to the rules, they cannot complain about the government's behavior in specific cases. Further, unanticipated inflation, when it occurs in accordance with the rules, would not produce changes in the forms of money-demand functions.

A fully contingent rule can work only if people can verify that the policymaker's commitments are being honored in each state of nature that has occurred—and would be honored in each hypothetical state. It can plausibly be argued that only simple commitments can be adequately monitored and enforced. (The fact that the optimal contingency rule cannot be written out in closed form in the present model may or may not be evidence in this context.) Rules with a full set of contingencies may be infeasible. Then the operational choice would be between discretion and simple rules. Discretion has the advantage of responding flexibly to movements in the state variables. (This flexibility is valuable in a model, such as the present one, where it is desirable to alter monetary behavior in response to changes in the state variables.) The nature of the response and the choice of average monetary growth under discretion are "wrong," however, because they fail to internalize the connection between monetary behavior and inflationary expectations. That is, the discretionary policymaker lacks the valuable option of making binding promises (long-term contracts with the public) about his future actions. A simple rule exercises this option but misses the flexibility of response to changes in the state variables.

To illustrate, suppose that $\log \theta_t$ again moves as the random walk,

$$\log \theta_t = \log \theta_{t-1} + \varepsilon_t. \tag{4.24}$$

For simplicity, continue to assume that $A_t = A$ applies for all t. Suppose that the only admissible form of rule is a constant-growth-rate rule. At some starting date, 0, the policymaker makes a once-and-for-all, binding selection of the monetary growth rate, $\hat{\mu}$. Since A_t is constant, we also have, for all periods after period 0, $\hat{\pi} = \hat{\pi}^e = \hat{\mu}$. Further, revenue per unit of time is constant in all periods after period 0 at the amount, $\widehat{R/\tau} = \hat{\mu}(\widehat{M/P}) = \hat{\mu}A\exp(-\alpha\hat{\mu})$. Net costs for any period $t \geq 1$ are therefore given by

$$Z_t = [\tau(k_1 + k_2)/b]\exp(b\hat{\mu}) - \tau\theta_t\hat{\mu}A\exp(-\alpha\hat{\mu}). \tag{4.25}$$

The expected net costs for any period $t \geq 1$, as calculated at date 0, are

$$E(Z_t|I_0) = [\tau(k_1 + k_2)/b]\exp(b\hat{\mu}) - \tau\hat{\mu}A\exp(-\alpha\hat{\mu})E(\theta_t|I_0), \tag{4.26}$$

where I_0 is the information available at date zero.

Suppose that ε_t in Eq. (4.24) is normally distributed with zero mean and variance, $\sigma_\varepsilon^2 = \sigma_\tau^2$. The parameter σ^2 represents the variance over a period of unit length. Then, conditioned on I_0, $\log(\theta_t)$ is normally distributed with mean $\log(\theta_0)$ and variance $\sigma^2\tau t$. (Note that t is measured in periods and τ in years per period, so τt is measured in years.) The expectation of θ_t is then

$$E(\theta_t|I_0) = \theta_0\exp[(\sigma^2/2)\tau t], \tag{4.27}$$

where I have used the standard formula for the mean of a log-normal variate (Aitchison and Brown, 1957, chap. 2). Note that a random walk for $\log(\theta_t)$ means a drift in θ_t at rate $\sigma^2/2$ per year.

Suppose that we neglect matters for period 0 (as we did in note 8), which would otherwise bring in the initial state of inflationary expectations, π_0^e.[12] (The policymaker may be able to "cheat once" by picking $\hat{\mu} \neq \pi_0^e$.) Assume that the policymaker cares about the sum of expected present values of net costs from period 1 onward. That is, $\hat{\mu}$ is chosen to

12. Under reasonable assumptions, this element would not have a significant impact on the policymaker's once-and-for-all choice of monetary growth rate. We would also have to consider whether the implementation of the monetary rule were anticipated at earlier dates—that is, it may be inappropriate to treat π_0^e as an arbitrary parameter.

minimize the quantity

$$V \equiv \sum_{t=1}^{\infty} E(Z_t|I_0)\exp(-r\tau t) \tag{4.28}$$

$$= \sum_{t=1}^{\infty} \{[\tau(k_1 + k_2)/b]\exp(b\hat{\mu} - r\tau t)$$

$$- \tau\hat{\mu}A\theta_0\exp[-\alpha\hat{\mu} - (r - \sigma^2/2)\tau t]\},$$

where r is an exogenous, constant real discount rate, expressed per unit of time. I assume that $r > \sigma^2/2$, which generates a finite sum on the right side of Eq. (4.28). (That is, the discounting outweighs the drift in θ_t.) As $\tau \to 0$, the sum can be evaluated as

$$V = \left(\frac{k_1 + k_2}{rb}\right)\exp(b\hat{\mu}) - \frac{\hat{\mu}A\theta_0\exp(-\alpha\hat{\mu})}{(r - \sigma^2/2)}. \tag{4.29}$$

Assuming that $\alpha\hat{\mu}$ is much less than one—that is, that $\hat{\mu}$ is well below the purely revenue-maximizing rate—the value of $\hat{\mu}$ that minimizes V is given by

$$\hat{\mu} \approx \left(\frac{1}{b + 2\alpha}\right)\log\left[\left(\frac{\theta_0 A}{k_1 + k_2}\right)\left(\frac{r}{r - \sigma^2/2}\right)\right]. \tag{4.30}$$

A comparison of Eq. (4.30) with Eq. (4.23) indicates that the new feature is the variance term, σ^2. If σ^2 is higher, relative to r, the value of the monetary growth rate, $\hat{\mu}$, is increased. Essentially, the policymaker recognizes that the mean of θ_t advances over time in accordance with the value of σ^2. Given the assumed inability to match μ_t to θ_t at each date, the policymaker compensates partially by picking a higher value for $\hat{\mu}$ at the start. Of course, as time passes, the rate $\hat{\mu}$ is likely to depart further and further from the rate that would have been chosen on a fully contingent basis. There might eventually be sufficient pressure to generate a breakdown in the constant-growth-rate rule. But to analyze this situation, we would have to specify precisely the conditions that motivate a departure of monetary growth from the value $\hat{\mu}$. We would then have a rule that allows for limited contingencies, although not for a full set of these contingencies.

It is possible to compare the outcomes from a constant-growth-rate rule, as specified in Eq. (4.30), with those generated under discretion, as shown in Eq. (4.21). It is now uncertain which method of operation delivers the lower sum of expected present values of net costs (say, from period 1 onward). The expected costs can be calculated explicitly for the two cases, although the results are hard to interpret. Generally, the relative sizes of the two expected costs depend on the parameter values, α, b, A, k_1, k_2, σ^2, and r. For example, a high value for k_2 tends to favor the simple rule, because discretion does not internalize the responses associated with this parameter. However, a higher value for σ^2 favors discretion, because the flexibility of adjustment becomes more significant as σ^2 rises.

Observations

The interaction between monetary behavior and inflationary expectations determines the time path of inflation. To understand this interaction and the mechanisms by which expectations are generated, we have to model the money-supply process. In the present analysis monetary behavior reflects the government's desire for inflationary finance, subject to some concern about the costs of inflation. The outcomes depend heavily on the characteristics of monetary institutions. Specifically, there are important distinctions between discretion and rules. In a purely discretionary regime the monetary authority can make no meaningful commitments about the future behavior of money and prices. Under an enforced rule—such as a serious gold standard or statutes that restrain monetary growth—it becomes possible to make these commitments, which amount to long-term contracts with holders of the government's liabilities. Thereby the policymaker can internalize some linkages between monetary actions and inflationary expectations. Some of these connections are missing under discretion.

The analysis distinguishes fully contingent rules from commitments of a simple form, such as a constant-growth-rate rule for the money supply. Abstracting from costs of erecting and enforcing the rules, discretionary monetary policy is always inferior to a fully contingent rule. The comparison with limited rules is ambiguous. The rules allow the internalization of some links between policy actions and inflationary expectations, but discretion permits some desirable "flexibility" of monetary growth.

Generally, monetary institutions are important in two respects. First, the characteristics of these institutions, such as discretion versus rules, matter for predicting the actual course of monetary growth and inflation. That is, institutional features matter at the level of positive analysis. Second, it may be that economists' normative analysis of governmental policy is usefully directed toward changes in institutions rather than to day-to-day operating procedures within a given regime. Whether this is so depends on a positive theory of institutional choice, which is not well developed.

References

Aitchison, J., and J. A. C. Brown. 1957. *The Lognormal Distribution*. Cambridge: Cambridge University Press.

Auernheimer, L. 1974. "The Honest Government's Guide to the Revenue from the Creation of Money." *Journal of Political Economy* 82:598–606.

Bailey, M. J. 1956. "The Welfare Cost of Inflationary Finance." *Journal of Political Economy* 64:93–110.

Barro, R. J., and D. B. Gordon. 1983b. "A Positive Theory of Monetary Policy in a Natural-Rate Model." *Journal of Political Economy* 91:589–610.

—— 1983a. "Rules, Discretion and Reputation in a Model of Monetary Policy." *Journal of Monetary Economics* 12:101–121.

Cagan, P. 1956. "The Monetary Dynamics of Hyperinflation." In *Studies in the Quantity Theory of Money*, ed. M. Friedman. Chicago: University of Chicago Press, pp. 25–117.

Calvo, G. 1978. "Optimal Seigniorage from Money Creation." *Journal of Monetary Economics* 4:503–517.

Kydland, F. E., and E. C. Prescott. 1977. "Rules rather than Discretion: The Inconsistency of Optimal Plans." *Journal of Political Economy* 85:473–491.

Phelps, E. S. 1973. "Inflation in the Theory of Public Finance." *Swedish Journal of Economics* 75:67–82.

Sjaastad, L. 1976. "Why Stable Inflations Fail." In *Inflation in the World Economy*, ed. M. Parkin and G. Zis. Manchester: Manchester University Press, pp. 73–86.

5 Reputation in a Model of Monetary Policy with Incomplete Information

In Chapter 3 David Gordon and I (1983b) built on the work of Kydland and Prescott (1977) and others to distinguish rules versus discretion in monetary policy. When the policymaker could make binding commitments (rules), it was feasible to achieve low average inflation. This result was superior to that attainable with no commitments (discretion), where inflation tended to be high, but not surprisingly high. Because of the incentive to create inflation surprises ex post (stemming from a desire to relieve some existing distortions in the economy), only high inflation turned out to be incentive-compatible for the policymaker who was not bound by a rule.

In Chapter 4 we considered reputational forces that might substitute for formal rules (Barro and Gordon 1983a). When future inflationary expectations were tied to current actions, the discretionary policymaker was motivated to keep inflation down. Thereby we found that an equilibrium entailed lower inflation, which corresponded to a weighted average of the outcome under a rule and that under discretion. However, there were two shortcomings of this approach. First, the reputational possibility hinged on an infinite horizon (otherwise the guaranteed cheating in the last period leads to an unraveling of the solution). Second, the equilibrium was not unique.[1] From the positive standpoint of using the model to predict the policymaker's behavior—and thereby to predict monetary growth and inflation—this last feature is at least unfortunate.

From *Journal of Monetary Economics* (1986) 17:3–20. I am grateful for comments from David Backus, David Gordon, Vittorio Grilli, and Michael Jones. This research was supported by the National Science Foundation.

1. This problem appears also in the related literature from game theory—see Friedman (1971) and Green and Porter (1984).

Kreps and Wilson (1982) and Milgrom and Roberts (1982) have dealt with analogous problems in the area of industrial organization by introducing uncertainty about one of the player's objectives. In the present context there could be uncertainty either about the policymaker's preferences or about his technology for making commitments. Then the extent of reputation or credibility would correspond to an outside observer's subjective probability that the policymaker is of one type or another. In general, current policy actions influence this probability and thereby affect the way that people learn about the policymaker's true type. In addition, the policymaker takes this learning process into account when deciding how to perform. Aside from giving content to notions of reputation and learning, this approach has the advantage of not depending on an infinite horizon and of sometimes delivering a unique perfect equilibrium. In the following sections I apply this analysis to the setting of monetary policy.[2]

Setup of the Model

As in previous models (Chapters 3 and 4), costs for period t depend on actual and unexpected inflation,

$$z_t = z(\pi_t, \pi_t - \pi_t^e), \tag{5.1}$$

where π_t is actual inflation for period t and π_t^e is the representative person's forecast of π_t made at the beginning of period t. I assume $\partial z/\partial|\pi_t| > 0$ and $\partial z/\partial(\pi_t - \pi_t^e) < 0$ in the relevant range. Thus costs rise with the magnitude of inflation, $|\pi_t|$, but fall with surprise inflation, $\pi_t - \pi_t^e$. The benefit from surprise inflation can reflect some existing distortions, such as taxation of market income or unemployment insurance, that lead to inefficiently low levels of employment and output. Through the standard mechanism of the expectational Phillips curve, surprise inflation (reflecting surprise monetary expansion) raises output and is thereby beneficial. Alternatively, the use of surprise inflation as a capital levy on nominally denominated government obligations is desir-

2. Previous discussions of this approach in the context of monetary policy include Barro and Gordon (1983a, p. 119), Backus and Driffill (1984, 1985), Tabellini (1983), and Horn and Persson (1985, sec. 6).

able because it lessens the need for distorting income taxes or other types of non–lump-sum taxes (see Barro 1983). For a given value of surprise inflation, $\pi_t - \pi_t^e$, the minimum of costs in Eq. (5.1) occurs at $\pi_t = 0$. (The model can readily be modified so that the minimum obtains at an arbitrary value $\bar{\pi}$.)

The policymaker strives to minimize the expected present value of costs,

$$\mathrm{E}\left[z_t + \frac{z_{t+1}}{(1 + r)} + \cdots + \frac{z_T}{(1 + r)^{T-t}}\right],$$

where $r > 0$ is the exogenous and constant real discount rate and T is the terminal period, which is discussed below. Because everybody agrees on the merits of this objective, there is no principal-agent problem in the model.

In the case where the policymaker makes a serious advance commitment to inflation—so that $\pi_t^e = \pi_t$ follows at once from general knowledge of this commitment—the cost-minimizing value of the inflation rate is $\pi_t = 0$ for all periods. The corresponding cost for each period is normalized to zero—that is, $z(0, 0) = 0$.

In a discretionary situation—where commitments are precluded—the policymaker takes current and future inflationary expectations as given. Then the cost-minimizing inflation rate for period t is some value $\hat{\pi}_t$, which generally depends on π_t^e—that is,

$$\hat{\pi}_t = \phi(\pi_t^e). \tag{5.2}$$

Since people understand the policymaker's behavior, it also follows here that $\pi_t^e = \hat{\pi}_t = \phi(\pi_t^e)$; so surprise inflation, $\hat{\pi}_t - \pi_t^e$, is zero. For a given form of the cost function in Eq. (5.1) (with appropriate curvature properties), the equilibrium determines some number $\hat{\pi}$, which is such that $\hat{\pi} = \phi(\hat{\pi})$. This result is the discretionary equilibrium discussed in previous research. The cost for each period in this equilibrium is

$$z_t = \hat{z} = z(\hat{\pi}, 0) > 0. \tag{5.3}$$

Hence the outcome is higher costs than under the zero-inflation rule. This result follows because the absence of commitments leads to inflation that is high but not surprisingly high.

Suppose now that there are two types of policymakers. Type 1 is capable of commitments and binds himself to the outcome $\pi_t = 0$ for each period. Type 2 has no capacity to make commitments and simply strives at each date t to minimize the expected present value of costs, $E[z_t + z_{t+1}/(1 + r) + \cdots + z_T/(1 + r)^{T-t}]$, where costs for each period satisfy Eq. (5.1).[3] Although the policymaker knows his own type, the private agents cannot discern this type directly. Instead they attempt to infer the true type from observed performance, which means that they learn from experience. The policymaker of type 2, who is not bound by commitments, understands this learning process and may be motivated to exploit it when making choices of inflation rates. Throughout I assume that the parameters of the cost function in Eq. (5.1), as well as the real interest rate r, are time invariant and common knowledge.

The policymaker is installed at the beginning of period 0 and remains in power through period T. Thus, the game between the policymaker and the private agents has a known, finite horizon.[4] (The value of T is common knowledge.) In some circumstances the horizon can be identified with the term of office. However, that perspective may be too narrow, since various mechanisms can motivate lame-duck officeholders to behave. The horizon can also be interpreted in terms of the persistence of differences across policymakers with respect to capacity for commitments (or preferences about inflation). In other words, the distinction between type 1 and type 2 may not be permanent. Then a large value of T signifies that this designation by type holds up for a long time. The form of the subsequent results continues to apply when the horizon becomes arbitrarily long.

If people knew that the policymaker was of type 2, then the (perfect, Nash) equilibrium would be the discretionary one, $\pi_t = \hat{\pi}$, as described before.[5] Further, since the type 1 person always picks $\pi_t = 0$, the policymaker of type 2 can conceal his identity only by choosing zero inflation.

3. It is basically equivalent if the policymakers differ by their relative weights for the costs and benefits of inflation. But in the present formulation each policymaker has the same tastes, which just reflect the preferences of the "representative person." The suggestion of uncertainty about whether one player has or has not made a commitment appears in Milgrom and Roberts (1982, p. 303) and has also been used by Tabellini (1983).

4. The game may also end probabilistically in each period. This possibility, discussed in Barro and Gordon (1983a, p. 110), effectively adds to the discount rate, r, in the objective function.

5. This result holds with a known, finite horizon. With an infinite horizon, there are other "reputational" equilibria, as considered in Barro and Gordon (1983a).

The motivation for doing this is to hold down subsequent inflationary expectations, which helps to keep down future costs. However, since the game ends in period T, there is no gain from masquerading as a type 1 person after this period. Therefore, the policymaker of type 2 definitely picks $\pi_t = \hat{\pi}$ in period T.

Suppose that there is an interval $(\tau, T - 1)$ for some $\tau \geq 0$, during which the policymaker of type 2 randomizes the choice of inflation between 0 and $\hat{\pi}_t = \phi(\pi_t^e)$. (Recall that the value $\hat{\pi}_t$ minimizes costs for period t when expectations are given.) The motivation for randomizing can arise only if the true type has not yet been revealed—specifically, if $\pi_t = 0$ applied in each prior period. Accordingly, let p_t be the probability that a type 2 policymaker sets $\pi_t = 0$, conditional on having chosen zero inflation in all previous periods. Then the conditional probability of picking $\pi_t = \hat{\pi}_t$ is $1 - p_t$. The period $(\tau, T - 1)$ is the one where $0 < p_t < 1$ is supposed to apply. In this interval the probability of selecting $\pi_t = 0$ is neither zero nor one, but it is in the interior of this range.

Let α_t be the representative person's subjective probability made at the start of period t that the policymaker is of type 1. The probability for period 0, α_0, is a given value and is common knowledge. In the absence of other information, α_0 would be the fraction of the population of potential policymakers who are capable of commitments (and are therefore of type 1).

The two possible outcomes for inflation at date t are $\pi_t = 0$ or $\pi_t = \hat{\pi}_t = \phi(\pi_t^e)$. The former occurs if the policymaker is of type 1 (probability α_t) or if the policymaker is of type 2 (probability $1 - \alpha_t$) but masquerades as a type 1 person (conditional probability p_t). Hence the value $\hat{\pi}_t$ emerges only if the policymaker is of type 2 (probability $1 - \alpha_t$) and does not masquerade (conditional probability $1 - p_t$). For later use, let $\tilde{p}_t$ be the representative person's perception of p_t. Then expected inflation for period t is

$$\pi_t^e = \hat{\pi}_t(1 - \alpha_t)(1 - \tilde{p}_t). \tag{5.4}$$

Equation (5.4) indicates the best forecast of period t's inflation rate, π_t, given α_t and $\tilde{p}_t$. Note that, since there are many private agents, no individual has the incentive to pretend that his expectations are different from this value of π_t^e. In particular, each person takes as given the policymaker's behavior and everyone else's method for formulating expectations. It follows that there is no reason for atomistic agents to behave strategically—each one just aims for the best forecast of inflation, given how everyone else is acting.[6] (Presumably, accurate forecasts of inflation aid in other individual decisions, which are unnecessary to detail for present purposes.)

As people observe "good behavior" from the policymaker—that is, $\pi_t = 0$—they revise upward the probability that the policymaker is of type 1. The adaptation formula follows from Bayes' law as

$$\alpha_{t+1} \equiv \text{Prob(type } 1|\pi_t, \pi_{t-1}, \ldots = 0) \qquad (5.5)$$

$$= \frac{\text{Prob(type } 1|\pi_{t-1}, \ldots = 0) \cdot \text{Prob}(\pi_t = 0|\text{type } 1)}{\text{Prob}(\pi_t = 0|\pi_{t-1}, \ldots = 0)}$$

$$= \frac{\alpha_t \cdot 1}{\alpha_t + (1 - \alpha_t)\bar{p}_t}.$$

Note that if $0 < \alpha_t < 1$ and $0 \le \bar{p}_t < 1$, then $\alpha_{t+1} > \alpha_t$. In other words, the observation of $\pi_t = 0$ raises the probability that the policymaker is of type 1. From the standpoint of a type 2 policymaker, this learning process means that masquerading as a type 1 person builds up one's image as someone who is committed to low inflation.

The Incentives of Policymakers

Consider now the incentives of a policymaker of type 2. Let $V_t(\alpha_t)$ be the minimized expected present value of costs from date t onward, $E[z_t + z_{t+1}/(1 + r) + \cdots + z_T/(1 + r)^{T-t}]$, conditional on having chosen zero inflation in all previous periods. In this case the policymaker has a certain amount of current reputation, as summarized by the value of α_t. The overall cost, $V_t(\alpha_t)$, equals the expected cost for period t, $E(z_t)$, plus

6. Backus and Driffill (1985) treat π_t^e as a dichotomous variable, which in the present context would take on only the values 0 or $\hat{\pi}_t$. In this case π_t^e cannot be interpreted as expected inflation. In another paper, Backus and Driffill (1984) consider a two-sided game in which the private sector and the policymaker each behave strategically. This setting is inappropriate if the private sector consists of a large number of independent agents, as I assume in the present paper. The assumption of a monolithic private sector might be applicable to a monopoly trade union that bargains for an economy-wide wage rate— which is the setting imagined by Horn and Persson (1985, sec. 6). However, if the private sector acts collectively, then it is unclear why there is an existing distortion (externality) that underlies the benefit from unexpected inflation in Eq. (5.1).

the expected present value of costs from date $t + 1$ onward. With probability p_t the policymaker sets $\pi_t = 0$, which generates the amount of reputation α_{t+1} shown in (5.5). In this case the minimized expected present value of costs beginning at date $t + 1$ is $V_{t+1}(\alpha_{t+1})$. With probability $1 - p_t$ the policymaker sets $\pi_t = \hat{\pi}_t$. Then the reputation is lost ($\alpha_{t+1} = \alpha_{t+2} = \cdots = 0$) and the costs each period are the discretionary ones $\hat{z}$ from Eq. (5.3). The present value (expressed in terms of period t units) of this flow from date $t + 1$ through date T is $(\hat{z}/r) \cdot [1 - 1/(1 + r)^{T-t}]$. Putting these results together implies

$$V_t(\alpha_t) = E(z_t) + \frac{1}{1 + r} \cdot p_t V_{t+1}(\alpha_{t+1}) \tag{5.6}$$

$$+ (1 - p_t) \left(\frac{\hat{z}}{r}\right) \left[1 - \frac{1}{(1 + r)^{T-t}}\right],$$

for $\tau \le t \le T - 1$ and where α_{t+1} satisfies Eq. (5.5). The value for $E(z_t)$ is given by

$$E(z_t) = p_t \cdot z(0, -\pi_t^e) + (1 - p_t) \cdot z(\hat{\pi}_t, \hat{\pi}_t - \pi_t^e), \tag{5.7}$$

where $\pi_t^e = \hat{\pi}_t(1 - \alpha_t)(1 - p_t)$ from Eq. (5.4). Note that $z(\hat{\pi}_t, \hat{\pi}_t - \pi_t^e) < z(0, -\pi_t^e)$, since $\hat{\pi}_t$ minimizes period t's costs for given inflationary expectations.

The policymaker of type 2 selects p_t at the start of period t to minimize the expected present value of costs. At the same time—that is, without seeing the value for p_t or the realization of π_t—the representative person perceives that the probability of a type 2 policymaker choosing zero inflation is $\hat{p}_t$. However, there is nothing to constrain the policymaker at a point in time to set $p_t = \hat{p}_t$. The policymaker does not commit himself in advance to pick zero inflation with some designated probability—in fact, there is no commitment even to pursuing a mixed strategy. Further, the private agents cannot verify ex post what probability the policymaker used. If people could observe this probability (and hence verify it), then they would know that the policymaker was of type 2. (The type 1 person does not pursue a mixed strategy.)[7] Therefore the analysis will go through only if the probability, p_t, is unobservable to the public, even ex post. The only thing that people observe—at the start of the next

7. I am grateful to Michael Jones for this point.

period—is the value of π_t from the previous period. At a point in time the uncommitted policymaker can choose any value of p_t that he wishes, which includes the pure strategies of picking $\pi_t = 0$ or $\pi_t = \hat{\pi}_t$ with probability 1. Thus the outcome $p_t = \hat{p}_t$ can emerge only if this choice for p_t is at least as good for the policymaker as any other value of p_t, *given people's perceptions* $\hat{p}_t$, the value of α_t, and the structure of the optimization problem as laid out in Eqs. (5.6) and (5.7).

Note that, for given $\hat{p}_t$, $V_t(\alpha_t)$ is a linear function of p_t in Eq. (5.6).[8] Thus, if $V_t(\alpha_t)$ were increasing in p_t, then the policymaker would set $p_t = 0$ ($\pi_t = \hat{\pi}_t$), whereas if $V_t(\alpha_t)$ were decreasing in p_t, then he would set $p_t = 1$ ($\pi_t = 0$). For the policymaker to be willing to randomize—that is, to set p_t in the interior where $0 < p_t < 1$—it must be that $V_t(\alpha_t)$ is independent of p_t. This independence holds for a linear function if and only if

$$0 = \partial V_t(\alpha_t)/\partial p_t|_{\hat{p}_t, \alpha_t} \tag{5.8}$$

$$= z(0, -\pi_t^e) - z(\hat{\pi}_t, \hat{\pi}_t - \pi_t^e) + \frac{V_{t+1}(\alpha_{t+1})}{1 + r} - \frac{\hat{z}}{r}\left[1 - \frac{1}{(1+r)^{T-t}}\right].$$

Eq. (5.8) applies in the interval, $(\tau, T - 1)$, where randomization occurs $(0 < p_t < 1)$.

The result in Eq. (5.8) implies that the minimized expected present value of costs, V, must satisfy the condition

$$\frac{V_{t+1}(\alpha_{t+1})}{1 + r} = -z(0, -\pi_t^e) + z(\hat{\pi}_t, \hat{\pi}_t - \pi_t^e) \tag{5.9}$$

$$+ \left(\frac{\hat{z}}{r}\right)\left[1 - \frac{1}{(1+r)^{T-t}}\right],$$

for $\tau \leq t \leq T - 1$. Using this result to substitute out for V_t and V_{t+1} in Eq. (5.6) leads to the basic condition that supports randomization of policy,[9]

$$z(\hat{\pi}_t, \hat{\pi}_t - \pi_t^e) + \frac{1}{1 + r}\hat{z} \tag{5.10}$$

$$= z(0, -\pi_t^e) + \frac{1}{1 + r}z(\hat{\pi}_{t+1}, \hat{\pi}_{t+1} - \pi_{t+1}^e),$$

8. Given $\hat{p}_t$, the term $V_{t+1}(\alpha_{t+1})$ is independent of p_t. Note that α_{t+1} in Eq. (5.5) depends on $\hat{p}_t$, rather than p_t, because p_t is unobservable even at the start of period $t + 1$.
9. The result for period $T - 1$ uses the condition $p_T = 0$, which implies $V_T(\alpha_T) = E(z_T) = z(\hat{\pi}_T, \hat{\pi}_T - \pi_T^e)$.

for $\tau \leq t \leq T - 1$. The left side of Eq. (5.10) is the present value of costs over period t and $t + 1$ if the policymaker reveals himself today by setting $\pi_t = \hat{\pi}_t = \phi(\pi_t^e)$. Then the cost next period is the discretionary one $\hat{z}$. The right side of Eq. (5.10) is the present value of costs for the two periods if the policymaker masquerades today ($\pi_t = 0$) but reveals himself tomorrow [$\pi_{t+1} = \hat{\pi}_{t+1} = \phi(\pi_{t+1}^e)$]. (In either case the costs are $\hat{z}$ from date $t + 2$ onward, so these terms do not appear in Eq. 5.10.) To be willing to randomize over π_t—without having made a commitment to do so—the policymaker must be indifferent between cheating today or cheating tomorrow—hence the equality of costs in Eq. (5.10).

Rearranging terms in Eq. (5.10) yields

$$z(0, -\pi_t^e) - z(\hat{\pi}_t, \hat{\pi}_t - \pi_t^e) \tag{5.11}$$

$$= \frac{1}{1 + r} [\hat{z} - z(\hat{\pi}_{t+1}, \hat{\pi}_{t+1} - \pi_{t+1}^e)],$$

for $\tau \leq t \leq T - 1$. The left side of Eq. (5.11) is the "temptation to cheat" today (refer to Barro and Gordon 1983a, p. 107) by setting $\pi_t = \hat{\pi}_t$ rather than $\pi_t = 0$. (The difference in costs is positive since the value $\hat{\pi}_t$ minimizes today's cost.) The right side is the "enforcement power," which motivates the policymaker to maintain a low-inflation reputation today by choosing $\pi_t = 0$. The gain from deferring high inflation is the difference between the discretionary cost $\hat{z}$ (which arises in period $t + 1$ if $\pi_t = \hat{\pi}_t$) and the lower cost from setting $\pi_{t+1} = \hat{\pi}_{t+1} = \phi(\pi_{t+1}^e)$ (which can arise only if $\pi_t = 0$).

Properties of the Equilibrium

Equation (5.11) prescribes a time path for expected inflation that must hold in order for the policymaker of type 2 to be willing to randomize at each date t. Thus far I have explored in detail the implications of this condition only for the case of the simple cost function that I used previously (Barro and Gordon 1983a). Namely, the cost function from Eq. (5.1) is now specialized to

$$z_t = z(\pi_t, \pi_t - \pi_t^e) = \frac{a}{2}(\pi_t)^2 - b(\pi_t - \pi_t^e), \tag{5.12}$$

where $a, b > 0$ and common knowledge. As I discuss later, it appears that the main results are not very sensitive to modifications of this cost function.

The specification of costs from Eq. (5.12) yields the inflation rate that minimizes costs for given expectations:

$$\hat{\pi}_t = \hat{\pi} = b/a, \tag{5.13}$$

which is independent of π_t^e. (This result follows because z_t in Eq. 5.12 is linear in π_t^e.) The terms that appear in Eq. (5.11) are given by

$$z(0, -\pi_t^e) - z(\hat{\pi}_t, \hat{\pi}_t - \pi_t^e) = b^2/2a,$$

$$\hat{z} = b^2/2a,$$

$$z(\hat{\pi}_{t+1}, \hat{\pi}_{t+1} - \pi_{t+1}^e) = -b^2/2a + b\pi_{t+1}^e.$$

Then the condition for the path of expected inflation in Eq. (5.11) becomes

$$\pi_t^e = \left(\frac{1-r}{2}\right)\left(\frac{b}{a}\right), \tag{5.14}$$

for $\tau + 1 \leq t \leq T$, where $b/a = \hat{\pi}$ in this model. For the cost function given in Eq. (5.12), randomization requires that expected inflation be constant.

Equation (5.4) implies that expected inflation must also satisfy

$$\pi_t^e = (b/z)(1 - \alpha_t)(1 - p_t). \tag{5.15}$$

Here I have substituted the actual probability p_t for the perceived probability $\hat{p}_t$. That is, since the policymaker of type 2 is guaranteed to be indifferent over the choice of probabilities, I look at the behavior that is consistent with people's perceptions. The question of why an agent would be motivated to pursue just the right mixed strategy seems to arise whenever behavior is not committed and the equilibrium entails randomization. However, the resulting equilibrium will satisfy the condition that the policymaker not prefer any other course of action.

Equations (5.14) and (5.15) dictate a relationship over time between the probability α_t that the policymaker is of type 1 and the probability p_t that the type 2 person masquerades as a type 1, namely,

$$(1 - \alpha_t)(1 - p_t) = \frac{(1 - r)}{2}, \tag{5.16}$$

for $\tau + 1 \leq t \leq T$. It is apparent from Eq. (5.16) that a rising path of reputation α_t (from the updating formula in Eq. (5.5)) must be accompanied by a declining path of p_t. As the type 2 person builds reputation via good past performance (α_t rises as long as zero inflation is observed), it must be that the probability of continued good performance by a type 2 person, p_t, diminishes. Note also that the left side of Eq. (5.16) is positive, which requires $r < 1$ on the right side. If $r \geq 1$, the discount rate is so high that the threat of lost reputation is insufficient ever to motivate the type 2 person to select zero inflation. Hence, $\pi_t = \hat{\pi} = b/a$ ($p_t = 0$) emerges from the start if $r \geq 1$. Some further discussion of this result appears below.

The determination of the equilibrium path of α_t and p_t follows by combining Eq. (5.16) with Bayes' rule for updating α_t. The latter condition, stated in Eq. (5.5), is

$$\alpha_{t+1} = \frac{\alpha_t}{\alpha_t + (1 - \alpha_t)p_t}, \tag{5.17}$$

for $\tau \leq t \leq T - 1$. With the addition of the boundary condition, $p_T = 0$, Eqs. (5.16) and (5.17) determine the path of α_t and p_t for $t = \tau + 1, \ldots, T,$[10] up to the determination of the starting date for randomization τ.

The computations involve a first-order linear difference equation in α_t, which has the solution

$$\alpha_t = \left(\frac{1 + r}{2}\right)^{T+1-t}, \tag{5.18}$$

$$p_t = \left[\left(\frac{1 + r}{2}\right) - \left(\frac{1 + r}{2}\right)^{T+1-t}\right] \Big/ \left[1 - \left(\frac{1 + r}{2}\right)^{T+1-t}\right], \tag{5.19}$$

10. This calculation does not yet use Eq. (5.17) at $t = \tau$.

for $\tau + 1 \leq t \leq T$. Note that α_t rises over time [since $(1 + r)/2 < 1$], while p_t falls. As $t \to T$, p_t approaches 0, while α_t tends toward the value $(1 + r)/2$.

The starting date for randomization, τ, depends mainly on the length of the horizon, T, and the initial probability α_0 of being type 1. Consider the value of t—not necessarily an integer—that would equate the result for α_t in Eq. (5.18) to α_0. The result, denoted by t^*, is

$$t^* = T + 1 - \log(\alpha_0) \Big/ \log\Big(\frac{1 + r}{2}\Big). \tag{5.20}$$

The solution for τ is the largest integer contained in t^*—denoted $\text{int}(t^*)$—subject to the condition that $0 \leq \text{int}(t^*) < T$, which corresponds to

$$\Big(\frac{1 + r}{2}\Big)^T \leq \alpha_0 < \Big(\frac{1 + r}{2}\Big). \tag{5.21}$$

Hence,

$$\tau = \text{int}\Big[T + 1 - \log(\alpha_0) \Big/ \log\Big(\frac{1 + r}{2}\Big)\Big], \tag{5.22}$$

subject to the inequalities in (5.21).[11]

Finally, the probability p_τ of masquerading in period τ is determined so that the updating formula in Eq. (5.17) holds at date $t = \tau$, given that $\alpha_{\tau+1}$ satisfies Eq. (5.18) and $\alpha_\tau = \alpha_0$. The resulting probability p_τ is somewhat above that indicated in Eq. (5.19) (plugging in $t = \tau$), unless the value t^* in Eq. (5.20) happens to be exactly an integer.

Assuming that $\tau > 0$, the policymaker of type 2 sets $\pi_t = 0$ with probability 1 at dates prior to τ (beginning with the starting date 0). In this situation the horizon is long enough so that the policymaker prefers $p_t = 1$ to randomization. Since $p_t = 1$ during this interval, expected inflation π_t^e is zero. Therefore the costs are those associated with a full commitment to zero inflation, namely, $z(0, 0) = 0$. Since $p_t = 1$, it also

---

11. This result corresponds to that in Backus and Driffill (1985, p. 536). Their other findings differ somewhat from mine because they view the private sector as randomizing its choice of expected inflation (see note 6).

follows (from Eq. 5.17) that there is no updating of beliefs about the policymaker during this period. That is, $\alpha_t = \alpha_0$ for $0 \le t \le \tau$.

If the prior probability α_0 is very low, or the horizon T is relatively short, $\alpha_0 < [(1 + r)/2]^T$ would hold. In this case there is no interval during which $p_t = 1$ obtains. The starting point for randomization is then $\tau = 0$, but the formulas for α_t and p_t in Eqs. (5.18) and (5.19) continue to apply for $0 < t \le T$.

In this situation the initial probability of masquerading p_0 must be such as to build up the right amount of reputation for period 1— namely, $\alpha_1 = [(1 + r)/2]^T$ from Eq. (5.18)—contingent on $\pi_0 = 0$ being realized. The smaller the value of α_0, the lower p_0 must be in order for the correct value of α_1 to be generated from the updating formula in Eq. (5.17). The solution for this initial probability is

$$p_0 = \left(\frac{\alpha_0}{1 - \alpha_0}\right)\left[1 - \left(\frac{1 + r}{2}\right)^T\right] \Big/ \left(\frac{1 + r}{2}\right)^T. \tag{5.23}$$

In one sense the solutions for (α_t, p_t) in Eqs. (5.18) and (5.19) apply no matter how small the initial probability α_0 that the policymaker is of type 1. However, as $\alpha_0 \to 0$, $p_0 \to 0$ in Eq. (5.23). Therefore it becomes increasingly likely that $\pi_0 = \hat{\pi} = b/a$, which means that the discretionary outcome would obtain in all succeeding periods. Further, as $\alpha_0 \to 0$ and $p_0 \to 0$, it also follows that $\pi_0^e = \hat{\pi}(1 - \alpha_0)(1 - p_0)$ tends to $\hat{\pi} = b/a$. Accordingly, for very small values of α_0, it becomes likely that a close approximation to the discretionary result will emerge from the outset.

A small value of α_0 does have to be weighed against the length of the horizon T, since the relevant condition is $\alpha_0 < [(1 + r)/2]^T$. For any finite α_0, an infinite horizon T rules out this inequality. Therefore, with an infinite horizon, the condition $\alpha_0 > 0$ implies that there will be a starting interval (of infinite length) during which $p_t = 1$ applies.

As the horizon T approaches infinity, the situation approaches that of a fully committed rule where $\pi_t = \pi_t^e = 0$ obtains for all t. In this case the present value of costs approaches zero. The policymaker of type 2 retains the option of cheating today (or in any period) by setting $\pi_t = \hat{\pi}$, thereby attaining the lower one-period cost, $z(\hat{\pi}, \hat{\pi}) = -b^2/2a$. But the revelation of his identity implies that the subsequent outcomes are the discretionary ones, $\pi_t = \pi_t^e = \hat{\pi}$, with $z_t = \hat{z} = b^2/2a$. With an infinite horizon, the net effect of cheating in the current period on the present value of costs is therefore

$$-\frac{b^2}{2a} + \left(\frac{b^2}{2a}\right)\left[\frac{1}{1+r} + \frac{1}{(1+r)^2} + \cdots\right] = \left(\frac{b^2}{2a}\right)\left(\frac{1-r}{r}\right).$$

The previously mentioned condition $r < 1$ ensures that cheating delivers a higher present value of costs than that from setting $\pi_t = 0$ for all finite t. In other words, if $T \to \infty$ and $r < 1$, the potential loss of reputation is sufficient to enforce the low-inflation outcome for a type 2 policy-maker.[12]

The final possibility is a very high starting probability of being type 1—specifically, $\alpha_0 > (1 + r)/2$ in expression (5.21). In this case (if $r < 1$), the policymaker sets $p_t = 1$ for the entire interval, $0 \le t \le T - 1$, before switching to $p_T = 0$ in the last period. Thus there is no period of random-ization—or of accumulation of reputation in the sense of a rising value of α_t—when the policymaker starts with a level of reputation α_0 that exceeds the critical level, $(1 + r)/2$.

Figure 5.1 shows the equilibrium path for the probabilities α_t and p_t. These values apply for a policymaker of type 2, assuming that $[(1 + r)/2]^T < \alpha_0 < (1 + r)/2$. Prior to date τ, the figure shows $p_t = 1$ and $\alpha_t = \alpha_0$. During this period $\pi_t^e = \pi_t = 0$. Then at date τ there is a discrete decline in p_t, but α_t has not yet changed. From date $\tau + 1$ onward, the probability p_t of masquerading as a type 1 person follows the declining path shown in Eq. (5.19), while the probability α_t of being type 1 follows the rising path given by Eq. (5.18). Along this path, expected inflation, π_t^e, is the constant $(1 - r)b/2a$. Finally, at date T, the value of p_T is zero, while α_t equals $(1 + r)/2$. [Note that $\pi_T^e = (1 - \alpha_T)b/a = (1 - r)b/2a$, which is the same value as in the interval between $\tau + 1$ and $T - 1$.][13]

---

12. This result did not obtain in Barro and Gordon (1983a) because the loss of reputa-tion lasted for only one period in that model. Since cheating reveals one's identity in the present case, the punishment interval is effectively infinite when the horizon is infinite.

13. It is possible to rule out other equilibria in this model by showing that they are inconsistent with rational expectations, given the incentives of a type 2 policymaker. For example, if $\alpha_t > 0$ and $r < 1$, then $p_t > 0$ must hold for all $t < T$. Hence there is no interval—analogous to that before date τ—where the high-inflation outcome $\hat{\pi}$ occurs deterministically. If $\hat{p}_t = 0$ were conjectured, then the choice $\pi_t = 0$ implies $\alpha_{t+1} = 1$ and $\pi_{t+1}^e = 0$. Then the choice $\pi_{t+1} = \hat{\pi}$ delivers a low cost for period $t + 1$ (with the discretion-ary outcomes arising thereafter). This behavior turns out to generate a lower present value of costs (if $r < 1$) than those from setting $\pi_t = \hat{\pi}$, which means going along at date t with the perception $\hat{p}_t = 0$. The result demonstrates that $\hat{p}_t = 0$ leads to $p_t = 1$. It follows that $\hat{p}_t$ is irrational for all $t < T$ if $\alpha_t > 0$ and $r < 1$. Similarly, it is possible to rule out $\hat{p}_t < 1$ for $t < \tau$ or $\hat{p}_t = 1$ for $t \ge \tau$.

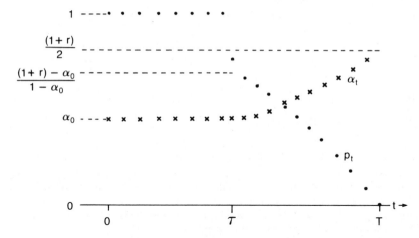

Figure 5.1. Behavior of probabilities α_t and p_t—before date τ, $p_t = 1$ and $\alpha_t = \alpha_0$; from date $\tau + 1$ until date T, α_t and p_t satisfy Eqs. (5.18) and (5.19), respectively; for date τ, $\alpha_\tau = \alpha_0$ while p_t is somewhat above the value implied by Eq. (5.19)

The length of the interval, $T - \tau$, where randomization occurs follows from Eq. (5.22) as

$$T - \tau = \mathrm{int}\left[\log(\alpha_0)/\log\left(\frac{1+r}{2}\right)\right] - 1. \tag{5.24}$$

Since $0 < \alpha_0 < 1$ and $0 < r < 1$, this interval falls (or does not change) with a higher prior probability α_0 of being type 1. Accordingly, a higher value of α_0 implies a longer interval, $(0, \tau - 1)$, during which the zero-inflation outcome occurs with probability 1. It also follows from Eq. (5.24) that a higher value of the discount rate r raises (or leaves unchanged) the randomization interval, $T - \tau$. In effect, a higher value of r lessens the value of reputation and thereby decreases the length of the period, $(0, \tau - 1)$, during which low inflation arises for sure. Table 5.1 shows the length of the interval, $T - \tau$ (in numbers of "periods"), from Eq. (5.24) for various values of the parameters α_0 and r. (The numbers apply subject to the condition that each be less than or equal to the value $T - 1$.)

Note that a change in α_0 alters the length of the randomization interval, $T - \tau$, but does not change the path of (α_t, p_t) during this interval. The main consequence of a higher value of α_0 is the increase in the

Table 5.1. Length of interval for randomization[a]

r	α_0				
	0.05	0.10	0.25	0.50	0.75
0	3	2	1	0	0
0.05	3	2	1	0	0
0.10	4	2	1	0	0
0.25	5	3	1	0	0
0.50	9	7	3	1	0
0.75	21	16	9	4	1

a. The table shows the value $T - \tau = \text{int}[\log(\alpha_0)/\log((1 + r)/2)] - 1$, where "int" indicates the largest integer contained in the bracketed term. The numbers apply subject to the condition $\alpha_0 > [(1 + r)/2]^T$ from expression (5.21), which requires that each number in the table be less than or equal to $T - 1$.

length of the period, $(0, \tau - 1)$, during which actual and expected inflation equal zero.[14] Correspondingly, there is a decrease in the length of the period, $(\tau + 1, T)$, for which expected inflation is the higher amount $\pi^e = (1 - r)b/2a$. These effects mean that the cost realized by either a type 1 or type 2 policymaker are lower the higher the value of α_0. Therefore the greater the fraction of committed persons in the population of potential policymakers, the better the outcomes for either type of policymaker.

This finding does not mean that the results improve if the policymaker turns out, ex post, to be of type 1. Before date τ the outcomes are identical (at $\pi_t = \pi_t^e = 0$) for either type. For date τ onward, the results continue to be the same for each as long as the policymaker of type 2 masquerades by choosing zero inflation. But at some point the type 2 person "cheats" by setting $\pi_t = \hat{\pi} = b/a$, which exceeds the expectation $\pi_t^e = (1 - r)b/2a$. Thereafter the outcomes for this policymaker are the discretionary ones, where $\pi_t = \pi_t^e = \hat{\pi}$. To see the implications for overall costs, recall that a policymaker of type 2 employs a mixed strategy only because the present value of costs is invariant to the time of cheating, except that cheating surely occurs by date T. Therefore pretend that cheating ($\pi_t = \hat{\pi}$ for the first time) occurs exactly at date T. In this case the outcomes for type 1 and type 2 coincide through date $T - 1$.

14. For a given τ, an increase in α_0 also raises the value of p_τ for the initial period of randomization. Hence π_t^e declines when α_0 rises.

Then at date T, where inflationary expectations are $\pi^e_T = (1 - r)b/2a$, the type 1 person sets $\pi_T = 0$, while type 2 sets $\pi_T = \hat{\pi} = b/a$. Thereby the type 2 person secures lower costs at date T. (The value $\hat{\pi}$ minimizes costs for given expectations, which is the case here.) It follows that the overall present value of costs is lower if the policymaker turns out to be of type 2. Because of the benefit from the one period of surprisingly high inflation, the outcomes are better if the randomly selected policymaker happens to be the kind that is incapable of commitments.

Ex ante, the expected costs weigh the type 1 realization by the probability α_0 and the type 2 by $1 - \alpha_0$. It turns out that these expected costs are lower the higher the value of α_0.[15] Outcomes tend to be better if the policymakers come from a pool that contains a higher fraction of those who are capable of commitments. This result is consistent with the previous conclusion that costs are smaller if the realization for the choice of policymaker is type 2.

I have assumed that the policymaker of type 1 always sets inflation at the committed value 0. Zero inflation is optimal with the assumed cost function if commitments are not only made but are also fully believed. In the present context credibility is tempered by the possibility that the policymaker is type 2. In this case the best value to commit to need no longer be zero inflation. It would be possible to determine the sequence of committed values, $\pi_t = \pi^*_t$, which minimizes the overall expected present value of costs (weighing type 1 outcomes by α_0 and type 2 by $1 - \alpha_0$). Conceivably these values would then be the ones announced each period by both types of policymakers, where type 1 makes a serious commitment and type 2 only masquerades with some probability. However, I have not yet made much progress in figuring out the properties of the resulting path of π^*_t.

Alternative Cost Functions

A surprising aspect of the result is that expected inflation remains constant during the period after date τ. That is, $\pi^e_t = \pi^e = [(1 - r)/2](b/a)$ as long as people observe zero inflation. The choice of zero inflation does enhance credibility in the sense that the probability α_t of being type 1

15. This can be shown by direct calculation of the present value of costs for the two types, pretending now that the type 2 person cheats in period τ—that is, sets $\pi_\tau = \hat{\pi}$.

rises over time. But the falling probability p_t of good behavior by a type 2 policymaker offsets this effect and keeps expected inflation constant. Thus the results are discouraging from the perspective of relying on reputation to lower inflationary expectations.

To see whether these results depend on the simplified cost function in Eq. (5.12), I modified the function to include a quadratic term in unexpected inflation. The new specification is

$$z_t = \frac{a}{2} (\pi_t)^2 - b(\pi_t - \pi_t^e) + \frac{c}{2} (\pi_t - \pi_t^e)^2. \tag{5.25}$$

The last term, with $c > 0$, could represent the distortion from incorrect information about the general price level. Now unexpected inflation conveys benefits on net (by relieving other distortions) only if the surprise is not too large—specifically, if $\pi_t - \pi_t^e < 2b/c$.

The new cost function in Eq. (5.25) does imply that the discretionary inflation rate, $\hat{\pi}_t$, rises with expected inflation—specifically,

$$\hat{\pi}_t = (b + c\pi_t^e)/(a + c). \tag{5.26}$$

The condition for randomization of policy in Eq. (5.11) becomes a first-order difference equation in expected inflation. The equation is quadratic in π_{t+1}^e and π_t^e. There is one value for expected inflation, call it π^e, such that expected inflation would be constant over time.[16] That is, $\pi_t^e = \pi^e$ implies $\pi_{t+1}^e = \pi_t^e = \pi^e$. By taking a linear expansion of the quadratic terms around the stationary value π^e, one can solve the difference equation explicitly. The result is that π_t^e follows damped oscillations around the rest point π^e.[17] Further, the departure of inflationary expectations from π^e for the initial period of randomization τ—and hence for all subsequent dates t—derives from the discrete length of periods and

---

16. The second root of the quadratic equation turns out to be inadmissible because it is inconsistent with $\alpha_t \geq 0$ and $p_t \geq 0$. The admissible root is

$$\pi^e = \frac{b}{c} \left\{ 1 + \frac{c}{a} [a(1 - r) + c]/[a + c(1 + r)] \right\}^{1/2} - \frac{b}{c}.$$

17. The solution is $\pi_t^e - \pi^e = (\pi_\tau^e - \pi^e)(-\gamma)^{t-\tau}$, where $\gamma = (c/a)(1 + r)$ and τ is the first period for randomization. The oscillations of π_t^e around π^e are damped as long as $(c/a)(1 + r) < 1$.

the associated integer restriction on τ. Otherwise, $\pi_t^e = \pi^e$ would apply at each date.

The main conclusion is that the modification of the cost function produces no tendency for π_t^e to fall during the period of randomization. The condition that π_t^e is constant no longer holds precisely but is a reasonable approximation to the solution. My conjecture is that this result would hold even with more complicated specifications of costs. It seems that expected inflation would approximate the (single?) value that corresponds to the rest point, $\pi_{t+1}^e = \pi_t^e$, in Eq. (5.11).

Predictions for Inflation and Other Variables

Consider again the simplified model where costs are given by Eq. (5.12). When viewed as a positive theory, the model has predictions for the behavior of inflation (and underlying monetary growth), which depend on whether the policymaker turns out to be of type 1 or type 2. With probability α_0 the policymaker is of type 1 and thereby makes a serious commitment to zero (or more generally low) inflation. There may be an interval of length τ over which expected inflation is also zero. [This applies if $r < 1$ and $\alpha_0 > [(1 + r)/2]^T$.] But [if $r < 1$ and $\alpha_0 < (1 + r)/2$] there is a subsequent interval of length $T - \tau$ where expectations are higher—namely, $\pi^e = (1 - r)b/2a$—but the policymaker continues to choose zero inflation. Correspondingly, the economy suffers from a string of surprisingly low inflation, which might show up as a recession or as an increase in distorting taxes. Thus the committed policymaker continually "bites the bullet" in the sense of tolerating the losses from surprisingly low inflation in order to maintain the low-inflation reputation. Nevertheless, this process does not succeed in reducing inflationary expectations. Credibility does rise over time in the form of a growing belief α_t that the policymaker is of type 1. But the offsetting reduction over time in the probability p_t that a type 2 person would select low inflation keeps expected inflation constant.

If the policymaker turns out to be of type 2 (which occurs with probability $1 - \alpha_0$), then [if $r < 1$ and $\alpha_0 > [(1 + r)/2]^T$], there is again a period of length τ where $\pi_t = \pi_t^e = 0$ obtains. Subsequently, as long as $\pi_t = 0$ is chosen, the path mimics that of the type 1 person. But, with the rising probability $1 - p_t$, the policymaker opts for high inflation, $\hat{\pi}$, which generates some short-run benefits from a positive inflation shock (which reflects an underlying shock to money). From then on, the outcomes are the discretionary ones where actual and expected inflation are both high $(\pi_t = \pi_t^e = \hat{\pi})$.

One characteristic of the equilibrium is a string of inflation rates that are below expectations. In the period after date τ, where expectations are $\pi^e = (1 - r)b/2a$, the type 1 person surely picks $\pi_t = 0 < \pi^e$, while the type 2 person has this realization with conditional probability p_t. The observation of a sequence of forecast errors of one sign may make it appear that expectations are irrational. In fact, these outcomes must be weighed against the probability—$(1 - \alpha_t)(1 - p_t)$—that the policymaker is of type 2 and will engineer a large positive surprise for inflation. Taking this element into account, the expectations are rational in the equilibrium solution.

According to the model, a long history of data—with occasional changes in the identity of the policymaker (or of the policy "regime")— would display a large number of relatively small negative inflation shocks that are offset by a small number of large positive surprises. The average value for unexpected inflation is zero, but there are substantial runs of negative realizations. The result resembles the "peso problem" for a "fixed" exchange rate. In these cases the occasional discrete devaluations of a currency offset the strings of errors when the expected devaluation exceeds the realized devaluation of zero (which applies when the exchange rate remains fixed).[18] For a discussion of the devaluation model under rational expectations, see Blanco and Garber (1985).

Observations

The introduction of uncertainty about the policymaker's type allows for meaningful notions of reputation and learning. Thereby the approach avoids some difficulties with multiple equilibria. Also, policymakers are no longer required to plan over an infinite horizon.

The results are interesting because they show how surprisingly low or high inflation can emerge as part of the equilibrium. The extended interval where inflation is below expectations seems to correspond to notions of the policymaker's "biting the bullet." That is, the costs from

18. This case applies when the exchange rate either remains fixed or is devalued by a discrete amount. Appreciations of the currency are not considered in this model.

surprisingly low inflation are accepted in order to enhance one's reputation for low inflation. (But the failure of expected inflation to fall here is a puzzling finding.) The uncommitted policymaker manages to create surprisingly high inflation for a period. This result corresponds to the idea that a surge in inflation can provide benefits in the "short run." But, as is also usually supposed, the long-term cost is that people raise their expectations of inflation. Thus—like the discretionary policymaker in previous models—the uncommitted policymaker ends up with an interval where inflation is high, but not surprisingly high.

One shortcoming of the approach is that it relies on differences in types of policymakers. In the present context these differences relate to capacities for making commitments. But divergences in preferences for "inflation versus unemployment" would generate similar results. It would seem preferable to generate predictions for inflation that depended less on individual traits of policymakers and more on basic institutional features. But if all potential policymakers were the same, there would be nothing to learn from seeing their actions. Then the model reduces to ones studied previously, which had the shortcomings mentioned before.

References

Backus, D., and J. Driffill. 1984. "Rational Expectations and Policy Credibility Following a Change in Regime." Unpublished manuscript. Kingston, Ontario: Queens University.

——— 1985. "Inflation and Reputation." *American Economic Review* 75(3):530–538.

Barro, R. J. 1983. "Inflationary Finance under Discretion and Rules." *Canadian Journal of Economics* 16(1):1–16.

Barro, R. J., and D. B. Gordon. 1983a. "Rules, Discretion and Reputation in a Model of Monetary Policy." *Journal of Monetary Economics* 12:101–121.

——— 1983b. "A Positive Theory of Monetary Policy in a Natural-Rate Model." *Journal of Political Economy* 91:589–610.

Blanco, H., and P. M. Garber. 1985. "Recurrent Devaluation and Speculative Attacks on the Mexican Peso." Unpublished manuscript. Rochester, N.Y.: University of Rochester.

Friedman, J. W. 1971. "A Non-Cooperative Equilibrium for Supergames." *Review of Economic Studies* 38(113):1–12.

Green, E., and R. Porter. 1984. "Noncooperative Collusion under Imperfect Price Information." *Econometrica* 52(1):87–100.

Horn, H., and T. Persson. 1985. "Exchange Rate Policy, Wage Formation, and Credibility." Unpublished manuscript. Stockholm: Institute for International Economic Studies.

Kreps, D. M., and R. Wilson. 1982. "Reputation and Imperfect Information." *Journal of Economic Theory* 27(2):253–279.

Kydland, F. E., and E. C. Prescott. 1977. "Rules rather than Discretion: The Inconsistency of Optimal Plans." *Journal of Political Economy* 85:473–491.

Milgrom, P., and J. Roberts. 1982. "Predation, Reputation, and Entry Deterrence." *Journal of Economic Theory* 27(2):280–312.

Tabellini, G. 1983. "Accommodative Monetary Policy and Central Bank Reputation." Unpublished manuscript. Los Angeles: University of California.

PART II

Money and Business Fluctuations

6 Intertemporal Substitution and the Business Cycle

Intertemporal-substitution variables play a major role in the new "equilibrium" models of the business cycle. A central feature of these models is the response of supply to perceived temporary opportunities for unusual rewards to working or producing—that is, to relatively high anticipated real rates of return. In some cases, as in explanations for the nonneutrality of money, the intertemporal-substitution mechanism is combined with confusions between general inflation and shifts in relative prices. In these circumstances the expectations of high returns are not borne out by the behavior of subsequently realized returns. In other settings, such as temporary increases of government purchases in wartime, economic expansion is stimulated by accurately perceived rises in real rates of return.

The first part of this chapter summarizes the theoretical role of intertemporal-substitution variables in the new classical macroeconomics. Some of this discussion draws on material from my survey paper (Barro 1981b). The later parts of this section stress empirical hypotheses concerning the contemporaneous and lagged effects of monetary and government-purchases variables on realized real rates of return.

The next section describes briefly some previous empirical findings that relate to the business-cycle role of intertemporal-substitution variables. This discussion is followed by some new empirical evidence on realized real rates of return. The analysis deals with returns on New York Stock Exchange (NYSE) stocks and on Treasury Bills. The princi-

From *Carnegie-Rochester Conference Series on Public Policy* (1981) 14:237–268. Prepared for presentation at the Carnegie-Rochester Conference, Rochester, April 1980. I have benefited from suggestions by Bob King, Ben McCallum, Charles Plosser, and Bill Schwert. The research underlying this chapter was supported by the National Science Foundation.

pal results concern reduced form effects of monetary and government-purchases variables on these realized returns.

Setup of the Model

Consider the type of model where goods and services are traded in a large number of localized markets or "islands," indexed by a parameter z. A simple version of the imperfect-information–intertemporal-substitution story, due to Phelps (1970) and Lucas and Rapping (1969) and related to ideas advanced by M. Friedman (1968), allows individuals to receive current information on local prices $P_t(z)$ but lagged information about the economy-wide average price level P or other nominal aggregates like the money stock. The underlying idea is that local prices reflect a mixture of the unperceived nominal aggregates and a variety of local factors that are specific to markets, individuals, occupations, and so on. Fluctuations in these local elements, which involve changes in the composition of technology and tastes, reevaluation of individual talents or opportunities, and the like, are viewed as having far more significance than general business conditions for individual fortunes (Lucas 1977, pp. 19–20). In particular, the exploitation of these local opportunities may require rapid and large responses by individuals, whether in terms of accepting or offering a job, making a sale, undertaking an investment project, and so on. With imperfect information, individuals attempt to purge the general price component from their observed price signals to make the appropriate allocative decisions.

Specifically, suppliers in a local market compare their observed current price or wage opportunities with expectations of prices or wages at alternative times and places. In a simplified setting where individuals visit only one market each period and where intermarket mobility over time is sufficient to make all markets look equally attractive one period ahead, the margin of substitution will involve a comparison of $P_t(z)$ with $E_z P_{t+1}$, which is the expectation formed today in market z of next period's general price level. In this setting the expected price for "next period" represents the perceived long-run average reward for the pertinent type of labor service or other good. Changes in current actual prices (wages) relative to anticipated future prices (wages) are viewed as inducing substantial intertemporal substitution on the supply side. In particular, the temporary nature of the perceived wage or price offer implies a substitution toward current activities and away from planned effort at an array of future dates. Similar intertemporal substitution would not arise in the case of a perceived permanent change in a relative price variable, such as the current real wage rate.

The relation of observed to anticipated prices appears as the central relative price variable in the models of Lucas (1972, 1973), Sargent (1973), Sargent and Wallace (1975), Barro (1976), and others. The precise form of the relative price variable differed across models. For example, Lucas (1973, p. 327) wrote his supply variable in logarithmic terms as $P_t(z) - E_z P_t$—that is, $E_z P_t$ appears without explanation instead of $E_z P_{t+1}$. However, most of his results would be unaffected by this difference in form.

Sargent (1973, p. 434) and Sargent and Wallace (1975, p. 242) used the variable $P_t - E_{t-1} P_t$, where $E_{t-1} P_t$ is the average expectation formed last period of this period's price level. A direct comparison of P_t with $E_{t-1} P_t$ is difficult to reconcile with the intertemporal-substitution or search stories of labor supply. Notably, in contrast to the intertemporal-substitution model, the Sargent–Wallace setup seems to predict a supply response to a contemporaneously understood monetary change that was not predicted at date $t - 1$. However, in many cases the contemporaneous expectations, $E_z P_t$ or $E_z P_{t+1}$, would be formed by updating the prior value, $E_{t-1} P_t$, for the information contained in current data. If current information is limited to that contained in a local price observation, $P_t(z)$, then a formulation based on a variable like $P_t(z) - E_{t-1} P_t$ may be indistinguishable from one involving $P_t(z) - E_z P_t$. For example, if the Bayesian updating rule appears in linear form as $E_z P_t = \theta P_t(z) + (1 - \theta) E_{t-1} P_t$, where the θ coefficient would depend on the relative values of price variances across markets and over time (see Lucas 1973, p. 328, and Barro 1976, p. 9), then $P_t(z) - E_z P_t = (1 - \theta)[P_t(z) - E_{t-1} P_t]$—that is, the two forms of relative price variables would be linearly related. The two specifications would be distinguished only by structural breaks that shifted the value of the θ parameter or by the existence of additional variables, such as war conditions or foreign shocks, that provided extra contemporaneous information about the general price level.

The impact of a variable like $P_t - E_{t-1} P_t$ has been rationalized along long-term nominal contracting grounds by Gray (1976) and Fischer

(1977). The argument is that previous expectations of current prices determine some portion of current contractual nominal wages, which would then be compared with current prices to determine the supply of commodities by firms. This interpretation was disputed in Barro (1977) on the grounds that efficient contracts would not permit variables like employment to be influenced by perceived, purely nominal disturbances.

A direct comparison of next period's expected nominal price with currently observed prices is appropriate only if stores of value earn a zero nominal rate of return—that is, if fiat money is the only available asset. More generally, as noted in Lucas and Rapping (1969), McCallum (1978), Barro (1980), and King (1978), the anticipated future prices would effectively be discounted by the available nominal interest rate over the applicable horizon. Instead of specifying a supply response to $P_t(z)$ relative to $E_z P_{t+1}$, which is a measure of the anticipated one-period real rate of return on money from the perspective of market z, the pertinent variable would be the expected real rate of return based on the holding of assets that earn a nominal interest rate R_t.

Equilibrium business cycle models typically incorporate a positive speculative response of supply to perceived excesses of observed prices over anticipated (future) normal values—that is, to unusual real rate of return opportunities. An analogous type of speculation implies a negative effect of the same type of relative price variable on the demand side (Barro 1976, p. 5; B. Friedman 1978, p. 76). In a specification that employs an anticipated real rate of return measure as the relative price variable, the aggregate demand equation when considered as an average over the markets would exhibit the conventional negative substitution effect of expected real interest rates on consumption and investment.

Suppose that aggregate supply and demand are influenced by the same relative price variable—for example, by an anticipated real rate of return with comparable information on prices, and so forth on both sides of each local market. If the other right-hand-side variables for supply and demand are exogenous real variables, then an equilibrium solution would involve a dichotomy between monetary variables and the real sector. The equation of supply to demand would determine output and the anticipated real rate of return in each local market as functions of the exogenous real variables. Therefore, in this type of model, it is essential for obtaining a link between nominal disturbances and real variables that the monetary shocks impact directly on excess commodity demand.[1] One possibility would be a real balance-type effect on commodity demand or supply. In Lucas's (1972, p. 106) overlapping-generations model in which money is the only store of value, a positive real balance effect on aggregate demand corresponds to the older generation's incentive to spend all of its savings from the previous period.[2] For the context of households that have access to interest-bearing assets and that effectively plan over an infinite horizon (perhaps because they have an operative bequest motive), it was argued in Barro (1980, sec. 1) that the principal direct monetary effect on excess commodity demand would involve the discrepancy between the money stock and its contemporaneously perceived value. Essentially, this setup ignores the wealth effect corresponding to changes in the excess burden due to anticipated inflation. The formulation implies, in particular, that equal increases in total money and in the desired money stock have no direct effect on excess commodity demand. The distinction between this type of specification of the monetary wealth effect and the real balance-type specification arises primarily in analyses of anticipated inflation, which involve changes in real balances but no changes in money relative to perceived money. If last period's money stock is viewed as observable, the latter variable becomes the unperceived part of current money growth, denoted by $m_t - E_z m_t$.

A simple log-linear model of local commodity markets that reflects the above discussion is (Barro 1980, sec. 1).

$$y_t^s(z) = a_s r_t(z) - \beta_s(m_t - E_z m_t) + \varepsilon_t^s(z), \tag{6.1}$$

$$y_t^d(z) = -a_d r_t(z) + \beta_d(m_t - E_z m_t) + \varepsilon_t^d(z), \tag{6.2}$$

1. In Sargent (1973, p. 434) and Sargent and Wallace (1975, p. 242), supply depends on $P_t - E_{t-1}P_t$, whereas demand depends on an expected real interest rate. Therefore a direct monetary effect on excess commodity demand is unnecessary. Similarly, in Lucas (1973, pp. 327–328), nominal income is exogenous and supply depends on $P_t(z) - E_z P_t$. Models where a separate form of relative price variable influences investment demand, as in Lucas (1975, p. 1124), do not require a direct real balance-type effect on aggregate demand. Although I regard this general route as promising, a fully satisfactory setup with different forms of relative price variables has not yet been constructed.

2. This model assumes also (p. 105) that new money enters as governmental transfers that are proportional to individual money holdings. The implicit interest rate on holding money in this circumstance leads to neutral effects of changes in the anticipated monetary growth rate.

where $y_t(z)$ is the log of local output, $r_t(z) \equiv P_t(z) - E_z P_{t+1} + R_t$ is the anticipated one-period[3] real rate of return from the perspective of market z (neglecting effects associated with the variance of future prices), $P_t(z)$ is the log of the local price, P_t is the average of the logarithms of prices across markets, R_t is a one-period nominal interest rate on an asset that is assumed to be traded economy-wide, $(a_s, a_d) > 0$ are relative price elasticities, $(\beta_s, \beta_d) > 0$ are "wealth" elasticities, and the $\varepsilon_t(z)$'s are local disturbance terms that add to zero in summations across the markets. In the present setup there is only one form of interest-bearing asset—notably, the model does not encompass imperfect substitutability between bonds and equity claims. Further, some of the results depend on a setup that allows individuals to observe an economy-wide nominal interest rate rather than a preset global real rate of return. Constants, economy-wide real shocks, or systematic effects on natural outputs could readily be added to Eqs. (6.1) and (6.2).

The assumptions that goods do not travel across markets during a period and that local prices are completely flexible generate the equilibrium condition for each commodity market, $y_t^s(z) = y_t^d(z)$. Equations (6.1) and (6.2) then imply conditions for local output and expected real rate of return, which can be written as

$$y_t(z) = (1/a)(a_s\beta_d - a_d\beta_s)(m_t - E_z m_t) \tag{6.3}$$
$$+ (a_s/a)\varepsilon_t^d(z) + (a_d/a)\varepsilon_t^s(z),$$

$$r_t(z) = (1/a)[\beta(m_t - E_z m_t) + \varepsilon_t(z)], \tag{6.4}$$

where $a \equiv a_s + a_d$, $\beta \equiv \beta_s + \beta_d$, $\varepsilon_t(z) \equiv \varepsilon_t^d(z) - \varepsilon_t^s(z)$.

Properties of the Model

Equations (6.3) and (6.4) are not final solutions for $y_t(z)$ and $r_t(z)$ because they contain the endogenous expectation $E_z m_t$. Further, the model would have to be closed to determine R_t and the array of $P_t(z)$'s by

3. The neglect of future anticipated real rates of return is satisfactory because these values are constant in the present setup. This type of model stresses departures of currently perceived returns from normal values rather than changes in the normal rate of return.

specifying some sort of portfolio-balance condition. However, for present purposes, the main results can be obtained by studying the intermediate Eqs. (6.3) and (6.4).[4]

Association between Money Shocks and Output

The direction of association of output with money shocks in Eq. (6.3) depends on the relative magnitudes of some elasticities. The speculative supply coefficient a_s, which is stressed in these types of models, entails a positive relation, but the demand coefficient a_d has an opposite implication. A sufficient condition for obtaining the "normal" net positive relation is that money shocks impact directly mostly on the demand side; that is, $\beta_d \gg \beta_s$. The direct monetary effect on supply—which can be viewed as reflecting a wealth effect on demand for leisure—is, in fact, typically assumed to be negligible in macroanalysis.

Behavior of Rates of Return

As stressed by Sargent (1973, pp. 442–444), there is a direct tie between departures of output from its natural value (which is itself treated as constant on average across markets in the present setting) and departures of the anticipated real rate of return from the natural rate. Because money shocks impact positively on excess commodity demand, the relative price variable $r_t(z)$ moves positively with $m_t - E_z m_t$ in Eq. (6.4) to maintain clearing of the local commodity market.

It should be stressed that the pertinent variable above is the anticipated real rate of return rather than the realized value. In models with an economy-wide nominal interest rate where monetary aggregates are not observed contemporaneously, the realized and anticipated returns tend to move in opposite directions in response to a money shock. For

4. The absence of actual or expected price levels from the right side of Eqs. (6.3) and (6.4) depends on some features of the specification in Eqs. (6.1) and (6.2). For example, this absence would not obtain if commodity supply and demand depended on the level of real cash balances, with either the actual or expected price level used as a deflator for nominal money. These changes would require an analysis of expectational equilibrium and portfolio balance before discussing any solution properties. Ultimately, the substantive differences would involve the real effects of anticipated inflation, as indicated in the text.

example, consider a setting where nominal aggregates are observed with a one-period lag, where money growth rates are serially uncorrelated, and where no elements of persistence in output are introduced (see below). Under these conditions, a change in this period's money stock would be reflected one-to-one in next period's price level. Because of incomplete current information about nominal aggregates,[5] equilibrium-expected future prices end up rising by less than the actual (full current information) mean value of future prices—that is, by less than one-to-one with the current money stock. Portfolio balance typically requires the implied increase in current real money balances to be accompanied by a decrease in the current economy-wide nominal interest rate.[6] The rise in the anticipated real rate of return is consistent with these results because the decline in the nominal interest rate is smaller in magnitude than the rise in current prices relative to expected future prices (that is, than the magnitude of decline in locally expected inflation rates). Note, however, that the mean (full current information) realized real rate of return must have fallen, because nominal interest rates have declined and the rise in the mean of actual future prices is greater than that of current prices.

The inverse effect of money shocks on current nominal interest rates is not a central element in the above story. Positive serial correlation in the money-growth process can reverse this effect, essentially by introducing the feature that the perceived parts of current money shocks signal future money creation and general inflation, which lead to increases in the current economy-wide nominal interest rate. This change leaves unaltered the conclusions regarding anticipated real rates of return. Unperceived monetary injections continue to raise anticipated real rates of return as indicated in Eq. (6.4). (The rise in the nominal interest rate cancels the effects of anticipated general inflation in the formula for expected real rates of return.)

The effects on realized real rates of return in models with an economy-wide market that sets a nominal interest rate are generally dependent on the nature of the serial dependence in the money-growth process. Positive serial correlation—which characterizes the post–World War II U.S. experience—implies that a current money shock has an

5. Models where the current information set includes observations on a local commodity price and a global nominal interest rate were considered in Barro (1980) and King (1978).

6. This decrease may not occur if the induced rise in current output has a strong effect on current real money demand.

even larger effect on the actual (full current information) mean value of future prices relative to the effect on currently anticipated (partial current information) future prices. The mechanism involves the inverse effect on next period's money demand of the inflationary expectations that arise after the current money shock has been fully perceived. Because of this effect, the presence of positive serial correlation in the money-growth process reinforces the inverse effect of money shocks on realized real rates of return.

The preceding story applies to the effects of unperceived monetary movements on contemporaneously expected real rates of return and on subsequently realized returns. If nominal aggregates are observed with a one-period lag, the present type of model would not account for effects of money shocks on output or expected real returns that last beyond the initial "period." Persisting effects of monetary and other disturbances have been explained in a number of models, such as those of Lucas (1975) and Sargent (1979, chap. 26), from consideration of stock-adjustment effects. A key element in these models is the existence of "excess capacity" in periods following the positive shock to aggregate demand. For example, the initial monetary-induced response of investment, production, and employment is reflected later in increased stocks of capital, inventories, employees, and so on. Because of stock-adjustment costs in a generalized sense, these high levels of stocks boost commodity supply[7] beyond the time at which nominal disturbances are fully understood. However, the spur to aggregate demand—which was provided initially by the direct impact of the nominal shock—must now be generated by a reduction in expected real rates of return—that is, by a decline in prices relative to expected discounted future prices.[8] Because incomplete in-

---

7. Elements of adjustment costs on the demand side—for example, the planning costs for investment that were stressed by Kydland and Prescott (1980, pp. 176ff.)—would imply maintenance of high levels of aggregate demand in periods subsequent to a shock (which would be followed by later periods of increased capacity). These effects reinforce the persistence of high output but offset the inverse effect on real rates of return in some future periods. Similarly, an inverse effect of monetary shocks on producers' finished-goods inventories (as opposed to inventories of goods-in-process and materials), which were stressed by Blinder and Fischer (1978), would tend to sustain high levels of demand. Overall, the excess capacity effect would be dominant in future periods if the principal initial effect of monetary disturbances is on work and production rather than on consumption. In this circumstance the aggregate of future stocks—whether held by businesses or by consumers—will end up higher than they otherwise would be.

8. As above, changing expectations of future money growth and associated general inflation would not alter the conclusions about expected real rates of return.

formation is not a part of this excess-capacity effect, the reduction in expected real returns would now coincide with a decline in the (full current information) mean value of subsequently realized returns.

To summarize, unperceived monetary disturbances would induce a contemporaneous increase in expected real returns, to be followed (when information on nominal aggregates becomes available and when the excess capacity effect becomes important) by a drop in expected returns. Realized real rates of return would be reduced throughout the period subsequent to a monetary shock.

Effects of Government Purchases

Intertemporal-substitution effects associated with movements in government purchases have been stressed in papers by Hall (1979) and Barro (1981a). These effects arise in the context of temporary purchases, such as wartime expenditures, which have a strongly positive impact on aggregate demand.[9] Long-run changes in the share of gross national product absorbed by government purchases have a corresponding inverse effect on households' permanent disposable income, which tends to eliminate the net impact of these purchases on aggregate demand.[10]

The positive effect of temporary government purchases on aggregate demand induces a rise in current commodity prices relative to expected, discounted future prices—that is, an increase in expected real rates of return. This price movement restores commodity-market clearing through a combination of reduced private demand and increased aggregate supply. The positive supply response reflects the intertemporal substitution of factor services and final products toward periods with relatively high (discounted) values of wages and prices, which signal unusual rewards for intensive work effort and production. This behavior implies that periods with high levels of government purchases relative to "normal," such as wartime, will also be periods with relatively high

9. Direct substitution in utility or production functions of government purchases for private consumption or investment expenditures, as stressed by Bailey (1971, pp. 152–155), offsets the positive aggregate demand effect of temporary government purchases.

10. This argument is independent of the method of public finance if households view deficits as equivalent to current taxation. The full direct offset of private for public demands arises when privately desired capital stocks are invariant with the level of government purchases.

levels of output. The substitution effects set off by temporary government purchases have been stressed by Hall (1979, sec. 2), who pointed out also that this mechanism differs in some important respects from the response of supply to monetary misperceptions that occurs in some business-cycle theories that stress intertemporal-substitution effects, as discussed above. The effect of temporary government purchases on the time arrangement of work and production does not rely on elements of misperception with respect to the general price level or other variables. In particular, the hypothesized positive effect of temporary government purchases on anticipated real rates of return carries over in this case to a positive effect on the (full current information) mean of subsequently realized returns.

Lagged effects of temporary government purchases on output and real rates of return are ambiguous. If the private plant and personnel that produce to government order were entirely nonspecific for this purpose, the persistence effects of shifts in government purchases would parallel those of monetary shocks. In particular, the excess capacity prevailing in future periods would tend to maintain high levels of output. Future real rates of return would be depressed in this case. However, the opposite conclusions emerge when factors are specific to government-ordered work. Therefore, the primary theoretical hypothesis is for a positive effect on real rates of return (and output) of the contemporaneous value of temporary government purchases.

For empirical purposes I utilize a series for the "normal" ratio of government purchases to GNP that was constructed in Barro (1981a, pt. 2). A time-series analysis of total government purchases was used to relate the expected value of future purchases to currently observed variables. Shifts in the ratio of federal plus state and local nondefense purchases to GNP appear to be permanent, in the sense that the most recent observation of this variable provides the best prediction for future values.[11] Similar behavior characterizes movements in the defense-purchases ratio when these changes do not accompany wars. The only temporary movements that were isolated were the shifts in defense purchases that were associated with wars. This behavior is exhibited for the period since 1941 by the series labeled $(g^w - g^{\bar{w}})$ in Table 6.1, where g^w is the ratio of real defense purchases to real GNP, and $g^{\bar{w}}$ is the

---

11. Neither this ratio nor the defense-purchases ratio exhibited significant drift. A drift does appear since 1929 in the ratio of transfers to GNP.

Table 6.1. Values of variables

Date	DM^a	DMR^b	$(g^w - g^{\bar{w}})^c$	RMV^d	RT^e	$D(WPI)^f$	$D(PGNP)^g$	τ^h
1941	0.160	−0.017	0.054	−0.095	0.001	0.171	—	0.24
1942	0.179	−0.030	0.214	0.163	0.003	0.059	—	0.17
1943	0.265	0.062	0.349	0.261	0.004	0.015	—	0.25
1944	0.162	−0.050	0.392	0.198	0.004	0.015	—	0.32
1945	0.150	0.010	0.341	0.337	0.004	0.020	—	0.36
1946	0.068	0.003	0.041	−0.049	0.004	0.282	—	0.35
1947	0.034	0.001	−0.011	0.037	0.006	0.124	0.075	0.23
1948	0.004	−0.005	−0.009	0.038	0.010	−0.016	0.013	0.15
1949	−0.010	−0.012	−0.021	0.190	0.011	−0.050	−0.013	0.17
1950	0.026	0.022	−0.002	0.275	0.012	0.161	0.084	0.24
1951	0.044	0.013	0.026	0.200	0.016	−0.017	0.014	0.30
1952	0.049	0.011	0.026	0.132	0.018	−0.028	0.017	0.26
1953	0.024	−0.016	0.013	0.007	0.019	0.009	0.014	0.15
1954	0.015	−0.002	−0.001	0.427	0.010	−0.007	0.015	0.18
1955	0.031	0.006	−0.017	0.235	0.018	0.016	0.026	0.17
1956	0.012	−0.012	−0.017	0.092	0.027	0.043	0.040	0.13
1957	0.005	−0.013	−0.017	−0.106	0.033	0.017	0.018	0.07
1958	0.012	−0.004	−0.018	0.374	0.018	0.005	0.020	0.06
1959	0.037	0.006	−0.020	0.128	0.034	−0.001	0.021	0.10
1960	−0.001	−0.036	−0.021	0.015	0.029	0.005	0.006	0.15
1961	0.021	−0.004	−0.019	0.246	0.024	−0.002	0.020	0.20
1962	0.022	−0.015	−0.020	−0.078	0.028	−0.003	0.016	0.27
1963	0.029	−0.003	−0.019	0.199	0.032	0.005	0.014	0.24
1964	0.039	0.003	−0.018	0.154	0.036	0.000	0.019	0.27

1965	0.042	0.003	-0.013	0.134	0.040	0.035	0.027	0.27
1966	0.044	0.002	0.000	-0.089	0.049	0.015	0.032	0.26
1967	0.039	-0.002	0.013	0.248	0.043	0.010	0.038	0.28
1968	0.068	0.029	0.016	0.129	0.053	0.031	0.046	0.27
1969	0.061	0.015	0.009	-0.093	0.067	0.047	0.055	0.17
1970	0.038	-0.008	-0.003	0.035	0.065	0.023	0.050	0.19
1971	0.065	0.021	-0.011	0.157	0.044	0.039	0.046	0.23
1972	0.068	0.009	-0.013	0.168	0.041	0.068	0.041	0.27
1973	0.072	0.009	-0.017	-0.173	0.070	0.163	0.078	0.30
1974	0.053	-0.007	-0.016	-0.284	0.079	0.159	0.110	0.29
1975	0.042	-0.017	-0.015	0.340	0.058	0.043	0.056	0.22
1976	0.050	-0.013	-0.017	0.245	0.050	0.047	0.052	0.23
1977	0.069	0.008	-0.015	-0.046	0.053	0.061	0.061	0.31
1978	0.079	0.011	-0.015	0.086	0.072	0.099	0.086	0.32

a. $DM_t \equiv \log(M_t/M_{t-1})$, where M_t is an annual average of the $M1$ definition of money.

b. $DMR \equiv DM - D\hat{M}$, where $D\hat{M}$ is an estimated value of money growth from Barro (1981c).

c. g^w is real defense purchases relative to real GNP; $g^{\overline{w}}$ is the estimated normal value of this ratio from Barro (1981a).

d. RMV is the total nominal return on a value-weighted portfolio of all NYSE stock.

e. RT is the annual average of returns to maturity on three-month Treasury Bills sold on secondary markets.

f. WPI is the seasonally unadjusted January value of the wholesale price index (1967 base); $D(\text{WPI})_t \equiv \log(\text{WPI}_{t+1}/\text{WPI}_t)$; PGNP is the seasonally adjusted first-quarter GNP deflator (1972 base).

g. $D(\text{PGNP})_t \equiv \log(\text{PGNP}_{t+1}/\text{PGNP}_t)$.

h. τ is the tax-rate variable, constructed as $\tau = 1 - (R_{\text{municipal}}/R_{\text{Aaa}})$. $R_{\text{municipal}}$ is Standard & Poors' yield on high-grade municipal bonds and R_{Aaa} is Moody's yield on A_{aa}-rated corporate bonds. Interest-rate data appear, for example, in Council of Economic Advisers, *Economic Report of the President*, January 1980, p. 278.

constructed expected long-run average value of this ratio. Because the $(g^w - g^{\bar{w}})$ variable corresponds to a gap between the current and "normal" values of the purchases ratio rather than to a spread between actual and "anticipated" amounts, it should not be surprising that this variable exhibits a substantial amount of positive serial correlation. In particular, the large number of peacetime years with small negative values of $(g^w - g^{\bar{w}})$ are offset by a smaller number of wartime years with larger excesses of g^w over $g^{\bar{w}}$. (However, war years cannot be deemed special, since they constitute 42% of the years since 1941 and 33% of those since 1946.)[12] The present analysis does not encompass any effects of war that are not proxied by the temporary-purchases variable. For example, the investigation does not deal with separate effects of patriotism, conscription, or changing probabilities of victory, which could influence future property rights.

Previous Empirical Findings on the Business-Cycle Role of Intertemporal-Substitution Variables

Sargent (1976) estimated a model from quarterly U.S. data over the period from 1951 to 1973. The analysis includes a price-surprise term, $P_t - E_{t-1}P_t$, as a key explanatory variable. (Recall that P_t represents the log of the price level, which is measured in this case by the GNP deflator.) A major finding is the minor explanatory role for the unemployment rate of this price-surprise variable, which has an estimated coefficient that is negative but has a t-value of only 2.0. When the model was reestimated by Fair (1979, pp. 703–708) with a second-order autoregressive error term and with a constraint that the expectation $E_{t-1}P_t$ be formed in an internally consistent manner, the estimated coefficient became insignificant.

It seems likely that the Sargent and Fair estimates are confounded by simultaneity problems; clearly, in an ordinary least squares (OLS) regression with the unemployment rate as a dependent variable, the sign of the estimated coefficient on the price-surprise term would depend on whether demand or supply shocks were dominant over the sample. Fair (1979, p. 704) used only the nominal money stock and population as exogenous variables for carrying out two-stage least squares, deleting

12. War years are classified as 1941–1945, 1950–1952, and 1965–1972.

Sargent's (1976, p. 234) government-purchases, employment, and surplus variables because they were absent from the structural model. (The treatment of the surplus as exogenous is surprising in any case.) Since the contemporaneous realizations of the two exogenous variables and of the long-term nominal interest rate (which was treated by Fair as predetermined) are the main bases for distinguishing supply effects of the current price level from those of the expected price level, $E_{t-1}P_t$,[13] it is unclear that the estimates can be interpreted as supply parameters. For example, one would question the independence of the interest rate from supply disturbances. These doubts are reinforced by the dramatic reversal in sign for the price-surprise coefficient that arose when Fair (1979, p. 706) added the years 1974–1977 to the sample. The natural interpretation is that adverse supply shocks have been important since 1974, with these shocks producing a positive correlation between the unemployment rate and price movements (and nominal interest rate changes).

The price-surprise term, $P_t - E_{t-1}P_t$, is also not an appropriate representation of the intertemporal-substitution variable in business-cycle models, as discussed above.[14] The relevant comparison is between current prices (or wages) and expected future values, so the $E_{t-1}P_t$ would be replaced by a variable like E_tP_{t+1}. The introduction of (partial) contemporaneous information into the expectational calculation substantially complicates any empirical analysis. In some cases (see below) it is possible to avoid the problem of explicitly constructing expectations by studying the behavior of realized real rates of return. Finally, a nominal interest rate would appear also in the intertemporal substitution variable—that is, E_tP_{t+1} would enter in discounted form for a comparison with P_t.

The empirical analyses of annual U.S. data since World War II that were summarized in Barro (1981c) deal primarily with reduced-form effects of money shocks on the unemployment rate, output, and the price level. The investigation was extended to quarterly data in Barro and Rush (1980). The major finding is the statistically significant and quantitatively important expansionary influence on real economic activity of a constructed money-shock variable. The positive response of output to a monetary disturbance is estimated to peak with a three- to four-

13. Another distinction arises from the nonlinear restrictions on the reduced form that are imposed in the calculation of $E_{t-1}P_t$.

14. However, these models would predict a positive effect of contemporaneous money shocks on the variable $P_t - E_{t-1}P_t$.

quarter lag, then gradually diminish to become insignificant after about seven quarters. The negative response of the unemployment rate is similar, although possibly it reveals a slightly longer lag relative to that of output. The empirical evidence did not indicate any periods of contractionary response following the roughly two-year interval of above-normal real activity following a money shock. Given the relatively minor role played by price surprises in the results of Sargent (1976) and Fair (1979) discussed above, it appears that these monetary influences on output and the unemployment rate involve channels that have yet to be isolated.

The results in Barro (1981a) documented positive output effects of government purchases for annual U.S. data since 1946. There is some indication that the largest expansionary influence applies to temporary movements in purchases; but, as noted above, the only temporary variations that have been isolated are parts of the defense expenditures associated with wars. Long-run changes in defense spending are estimated to have a significantly positive, but smaller, effect on output. The output effect of nondefense federal plus state and local purchases is imprecisely determined. The relatively small amount of sampling variation in this explanatory variable and the necessity of using an instrument for estimation purposes imply a large standard error for the estimated coefficient.[15] Lagged effects of government purchases on output are unimportant in the annual data. As in the case of the reduced-form monetary studies, the results on government purchases lack a description of the relative price variables that stimulate an increase in supply.

Bortz (1979) used quarterly post–World War II U.S. data to explore the reduced-form effects of money shocks on the realized real rate of return from three-month Treasury Bills. The study used the money-shock series constructed by Barro and Rush (1980) and measured real returns on Treasury Bills by netting out changes in the consumer price index. The principal finding (Bortz 1979, table 3) is a significantly negative effect of the contemporaneous and three quarterly lagged values of money shocks on the realized real return. The t-values for the estimated coefficients from lags zero to three are in a range from 2.4 to 2.7. Some statistical tests indicated a preference for a form that utilizes money-

---

15. In the theoretical model, long-run movements in government purchases would raise output, but not necessarily affect the real rate of return, if there were a direct positive influence of governmental activities on aggregate supply.

shock variables over an alternative that employs actual growth rates of the money supply. Overall, these results support the theoretical implications of business-cycle models that stress intertemporal-substitution variables.

Hall (1979, p. 16) used quarterly, post–World War II U.S. data to estimate a "labor supply" function with an intertemporal-substitution measure as a right-side variable. He found a significantly positive effect (*t*-value = 2.4) of this price variable on total employment when military purchases and military employment are used as instruments. The implied elasticity of labor supply with respect to the current real wage rate is about one-half. Hall's basic inference (p. 17) was that increases in military purchases and employment induce an increase in aggregate employment via a rise in the intertemporal-substitution variable. This finding accords with Hall's theoretical arguments and with the analysis of government purchases that was presented above. However, there is some difference between Hall's intertemporal-substitution variable and the previously discussed real rate of return variables. Hall's variable (pp. 15, 16) is the real rate of return—measured as a one-year commercial paper rate net of the annual inflation rate as indicated by changes in the GNP deflator—plus the log of the current real wage rate. This price variable can be viewed as governing the substitution between today's leisure and future consumption of commodities. If current leisure is an especially close substitute for future leisure, then it may be preferable to rewrite the substitution variable in terms of current nominal wage rates relative to discounted expected future nominal wage rates; that is, as an expected real rate of return with the rate of nominal wage rate change substituting for the rate of price change. However, if cyclical movements in real wage rates are relatively unimportant, then the distinction between this form of the intertemporal-substitution variable and Hall's construct will be minor.

New Reduced-Form Evidence on Realized Rates of Return

This section presents some evidence from annual, post–World War II U.S. data on the effects of monetary and government-purchases variables on realized real rates of return. The focus on realized returns avoids a serious empirical problem concerning the formation of price expectations. As the theoretical section makes clear, for the interval where movements in monetary aggregates are not directly observed, the sign of the effect of monetary disturbances on anticipated real returns depends on whether conditioning is done on partial or complete current information. Perceived real returns based on partial information rise with money shocks, while those that could have been calculated based on full information decline. Not surprisingly, the empirical results are highly sensitive to the choice of which current information to use in forming expectations. Some of these problems are avoided by completely neglecting current observations in these calculations, but issues are then raised concerning the timing of receipt of lagged information. Further, this procedure incorrectly ignores some contemporaneous information, such as war prospects, that should be included in determining expectations of future prices.

The theory does have several clear implications concerning the behavior of realized returns, as is clear from the earlier discussion. These propositions can be tested in a reasonably straightforward manner. A drawback of this procedure is that it fails to test directly a key hypothesis that is associated with equilibrium business-cycle theory—namely, the positive effect of monetary disturbances on contemporaneously (and incorrectly) perceived real returns. The concluding section contains some additional discussion of this gap in the analysis.

Nominal rates of return are measured empirically in two ways: first, as the annualized return to maturity on three-month Treasury Bills sold on secondary markets; and second, as the total return on a value-weighted portfolio of all NYSE stocks. The latter series is reported by the Center for Research in Security Prices of the University of Chicago. In interpreting the results it should be recalled that the theory applies to a setting of an economy-wide nominal bond market. The implications posed by the existence of equity shares has not been examined in the theoretical framework.

For the Treasury Bill series, the return for year t, $(RT)_t$, is the annual average of the three-month bill returns. For the NYSE, the return $(RMV)_t$ applies to the period from January 1 to December 31 of year t. Realized real returns have been constructed by subtracting either the annual rate of change of the seasonally unadjusted wholesale price index (WPI) measured from January of year t to January of year $t + 1$, or the change of the seasonally adjusted GNP deflator (PGNP) measured from the first quarter of year t to the first quarter of year $t + 1$.[16] There is a minor discrepancy in the timing between the inflation rates and the nominal returns, but the results were insensitive to some alterations in this dating.[17]

I have examined also the behavior of constructed "after-tax," real-returns variables. The tax rate applied to the nominal returns is the one implicit in the relation between the nominal yield to maturity on Moody's A_{aa}-rated corporate bonds and that on Standard & Poor's high-grade municipal bonds. The tax rate is determined in Table 6.1 from the formula, $\tau = 1 - (R_{municipal}/R_{Aaa})$, where the R variables represent nominal yields. This calculation assumes that corporate and municipal bonds are equivalent except for the (federal) income tax exemption on municipals. I have used the same tax-rate variable to adjust Treasury Bill and equity returns, although this procedure neglects various differences in the tax treatment of these two types of returns. Because of this and other problems, the constructed after-tax returns series should be regarded as subject to considerable measurement error. However, the tax-rate variable that was used may capture the major secular changes in the true average marginal tax rates on the two forms of asset returns.

For the case of monetary shocks, I focus on the current and lagged effects of the annual money-shock variable DMR (Table 6.1), which was derived from the analysis in Barro (1981c). Essentially, the values for annual average M_1 growth appear relative to the growth that is associated typically with current real federal spending relative to "normal," the lagged unemployment rate, and two annual lag values of money growth. The series for g_t^w, the ratio of real defense purchases to real GNP, expressed relative to its "normal" value, $g_t^{\bar{w}}$, was discussed above and also is contained in Table 6.1.

The Treasury Bill variables correspond roughly to the average annual real spot returns. Therefore these returns should exhibit the theoretical

16. The January-to-January consumer price index (CPI) yields results that are very close to those obtained with the GNP deflator. The CPI's treatment of housing costs seems to impart meaningless sensitivity of the index to variations in nominal interest rates, which I had thought might particularly be a problem in the present context. However, the CPI probably provides a better measure than the WPI of true transactions prices. The WPI may be less sensitive than the other indexes to problems of measuring quality change, which are likely to be most serious for services.

17. For example, a shift to December-to-December or February-to-February values for the WPI had negligible effects on the results.

relationships, which predict a negative effect of contemporaneous and lagged money shocks and a positive effect of the contemporaneous value of government purchases relative to normal.

The NYSE returns reflect both average spot discount rates and the effects of innovations on asset values. For example—with the expected time path of real-share earnings held fixed—an inverse effect of a money shock on real discount rates would imply an upward adjustment to contemporaneous real asset prices. Realized returns up to the date that includes the shock would be moved upward, while subsequent returns would be pushed downward. The "contemporaneous" effects revealed by the present time-aggregated annual data would be ambiguous, since they involve the offset of these two forces. The analysis of contemporaneous effects is complicated further if the shocks alter projections of real share earnings. These difficulties do not pertain to the analysis of lagged effects, which would presumably be incorporated into asset prices before the start of year t. Therefore lagged monetary shocks would be expected to exert a negative effect on realized real NYSE returns.[18]

The current value of the temporary government-purchases variable would be expected to have a positive effect on realized NYSE returns if the principal movements in the $(g^w - g^{\bar{w}})_t$ variable, which are almost exclusively war-related, were anticipated by the start of year t. I examine also the effect of the lagged value $(g^w - g^{\bar{w}})_{t-1}$, which is presumably fully understood during year t.[19]

The basic empirical results appear in Table 6.2. All regressions apply to annual data for the 1949–1977 period. The starting date was dictated by the strong effect of World War II controls on the reported price data from 1943 to 1947. Some of the data after 1977 were unavailable at the time of this study. I consider first the behavior of the stock returns, RMV. The findings are similar for these returns whether inflation rates

18. This conclusion could be altered by two effects that I believe to be minor. First, there is a lag in obtaining initial reports on the money stock (which is now less than two weeks); and second, there are subsequent revisions to the M_1 data. (Only "final" reports are used in the present analysis.) A detailed study of money stock revisions in Barro and Hercowitz (1980) indicated only trivial implications for analyses of output and the unemployment rate.

19. As constructed (Barro 1981a), the $g_t^{\bar{w}}$ variable incorporates some information about future war conditions. However, this element does not have a substantial effect on the $(g^w - g^{\bar{w}})_t$ series for the post–World War II period.

Table 6.2. Equations for realized real returns—sample period: 1949–1977[a]

Dependent variable (line)		Constant	DMR_t	DMR_{t-1}	DM_t	DM_{t-1}	$(g^w - g^{\bar{w}})_t$	R^2	D.W.[b]	$\hat{\sigma}^c$
RMV − D(WPI)	(1)	0.12 (0.04)		−8.2 (2.6)			5.1 (2.6)	0.27	2.1	0.17
	(2)	0.12 (0.04)	−1.4 (2.7)	−8.3 (2.8)			5.8 (2.9)	0.27	2.1	0.18
	(3)	0.29 (0.06)				−5.3 (1.5)	3.0 (2.2)	0.34	2.3	0.16
	(4)	0.29 (0.07)			−0.4 (2.0)	−5.0 (2.0)	3.1 (2.3)	0.34	2.3	0.17
RMV(1 − τ) − D(WPI)	(5)	0.085 (0.031)		−6.6 (2.2)			3.8 (2.1)	0.25	2.1	0.14
	(6)	0.090 (0.032)	−1.5 (2.2)	−6.8 (2.3)			4.5 (2.4)	0.27	2.1	0.15
	(7)	0.23 (0.05)				−4.4 (1.2)	2.2 (1.8)	0.34	2.4	0.14
	(8)	0.24 (0.06)			−0.6 (1.6)	−4.0 (1.6)	2.3 (1.9)	0.35	2.3	0.14
RT − D(WPI)	(9)	0.011 (0.010)		−0.3 (0.7)			0.6 (0.7)	0.03	1.9	0.046
	(10)	0.015 (0.010)	−1.4 (0.6)	−0.5 (0.7)			1.3 (0.7)	0.17	1.9	0.043
	(11)	0.020 (0.018)				−0.3 (0.4)	0.5 (0.6)	0.04	1.9	0.045
	(12)	0.034 (0.019)			−0.8 (0.5)	0.3 (0.5)	0.7 (0.6)	0.13	1.9	0.044

Table 6.2 (continued)

Dependent variable (line)		Constant	DMR_t	DMR_{t-1}	DM_t	DM_{t-1}	$(g^w - g^{\overline{w}})_t$	R^2	D.W.[b]	$\hat{\sigma}^c$
$RT(1 - \tau) - D(\text{WPI})$	(13)	0.003 (0.010)		-0.5 (0.7)			0.7 (0.7)	0.03	1.8	0.048
	(14)	0.008 (0.010)	-1.5 (0.7)	-0.6 (0.7)			1.4 (0.7)	0.19	1.8	0.044
	(15)	0.020 (0.018)				-0.5 (0.4)	0.6 (0.6)	0.07	1.9	0.047
	(16)	0.036 (0.020)			-1.0 (0.5)	0.1 (0.5)	0.9 (0.6)	0.18	1.9	0.045
$RMV - D(\text{PGNP})$	(17)	0.10 (0.03)		-7.2 (2.5)			3.7 (2.4)	0.25	2.2	0.16
	(18)	0.11 (0.04)	-0.6 (2.5)	-7.7 (2.6)			4.6 (2.7)	0.27	2.1	0.16
	(19)	0.26 (0.06)				-4.9 (1.4)	2.3 (2.0)	0.34	2.4	0.15
	(20)	0.26 (0.07)			0.1 (1.8)	-4.9 (1.8)	2.3 (2.1)	0.34	2.4	0.16
$RMV(1 - \tau) - D(\text{PGNP})$	(21)	0.075 (0.028)		-6.1 (2.0)			3.0 (1.9)	0.26	2.1	0.13
	(22)	0.077 (0.030)	-0.6 (2.0)	-6.1 (2.1)			3.3 (2.2)	0.26	2.1	0.13

							R^2	D.W.	$\hat{\sigma}$
(23)	0.21 (0.05)				−4.0 (1.1)	1.5 (1.6)	0.34	2.4	0.12
(24)	0.21 (0.05)		−0.2 (1.5)		−3.9 (1.5)	1.5 (1.7)	0.34	2.4	0.12
RT − D(PGNP)									
(25)	0.000 (0.004)	0.3 (0.3)				−0.2 (0.3)	0.03	1.9	0.019
(26)	0.002 (0.004)	0.2 (0.3)	−0.5 (0.3)			0.1 (0.3)	0.16	1.8	0.018
(27)	−0.003 (0.007)				0.1 (0.2)	−0.1 (0.3)	0.02	1.9	0.019
(28)	0.003 (0.008)		−0.4 (0.2)		0.3 (0.2)	0.0 (0.3)	0.12	1.9	0.018
RT(1 − τ) − D(PGNP)									
(29)	−0.008 (0.004)	0.1 (0.3)				−0.1 (0.3)	0.01	1.7	0.021
(30)	−0.005 (0.004)	0.0 (0.3)	−0.7 (0.3)			0.2 (0.3)	0.17	1.7	0.019
(31)	−0.003 (0.008)				−0.1 (0.2)	0.0 (0.3)	0.02	1.9	0.021
(32)	0.005 (0.008)		−0.5 (0.2)		0.2 (0.2)	0.1 (0.3)	0.17	1.9	0.019

a. All data are annual. See notes for Tables 6.1 and 6.3 for definitions and tabulations of variables. Standard errors of coefficients are shown in parentheses.

b. D.W. is the Durbin–Watson statistic.

c. $\hat{\sigma}$ is the standard error of estimate.

are measured by the WPI or by the GNP deflator. For convenience, I discuss only the results that use the WPI.

The estimated effects of the temporary government-purchases variable on realized real returns, RMV $-$ D(WPI), are positive throughout. For specifications that include also the money-shock variable, DMR, the t-values of the estimated government-purchases coefficients are in the neighborhood of 2. For example, with DMR_{t-1} as the only additional explanatory variable, the estimated coefficient on the $(g^w - g^{\bar{w}})_t$ variable is 5.1, s.e. $=$ 2.6 (line 1 of the Table 6.2), for the pre-tax real rate of return regression; and 3.8, s.e. $=$ 2.1, for the case of after-tax returns (line 5). The results are basically similar except for a small deterioration of the fit if the lagged value of the $(g^w - g^{\bar{w}})$ variable replaces the current value. With the DMR_{t-1} variable as the other explanatory variable, the estimated coefficient of the temporary government-purchases variable is then 4.7, s.e. $=$ 2.6, for the pre-tax returns case; and 3.9, s.e. $=$ 2.1, for the after-tax returns. When the contemporaneous and lagged values of the $(g^w - g^{\bar{w}})$ variable are entered simultaneously, the estimated coefficients are both positive;[20] but because of the high degree of intercorrelation between these variables, the estimated coefficients are individually insignificantly different from zero.

There is some indication that permanent movements in government purchases do not have the real rate of return influences that are produced by temporary shifts. The variables $g^{\bar{w}}_{t-1}$ and g^p_{t-1} (g^p is the ratio of real nondefense government purchases to real GNP) are insignificant in an equation that includes also the variables DMR_{t-1} and $(g^w - g^{\bar{w}})_{t-1}$. For the pre-tax returns case, the estimated coefficient on $g^{\bar{w}}_{t-1}$ is -0.1, s.e. $=$ 1.7, while that on g^p_{t-1} is -2.7, s.e. $=$ 2.7. For the after-tax returns, the corresponding estimates are -0.1, s.e. $=$ 1.4, and -2.4, s.e. $=$ 2.2.[21]

The one-year lagged monetary movements have significantly negative effects on the real stock returns. For example, the estimated effect of the DMR_{t-1} variable on the pre-tax real returns is -8.2, s.e. $=$ 2.6 (line 1); while that for the after-tax case is -6.6, s.e. $=$ 2.2 (line 5). The effect of

20. For the pre-tax real rate of return equation with the DMR_t and DMR_{t-1} variables also included, the estimated coefficients are 4.1, s.e. $=$ 4.2, for the current value of the temporary purchases variable; and 2.1, s.e. $=$ 3.8, for the lagged value.

21. The contemporaneous values of $g^{\bar{w}}$ and g^p are also insignificant, but the endogeneity of these variables (which include real GNP in the denominators) may cause some estimation problems, especially in the case of the g^p_t coefficient.

the contemporaneous variable DMR_t is insignificant (lines 2 and 6), as is also the case for a second lag value DMR_{t-2}.[22]

The negative effect of one-year lagged monetary movements appears also when actual money growth substitutes for the shock portion, DMR. The estimated coefficient of DM_{t-1} is -5.3, s.e. $= 1.5$, for the pre-tax returns (line 3); and -4.4, s.e. $= 1.2$, for the after-tax values (line 7). [The estimated coefficients of DM_t (lines 4 and 8) and DM_{t-2} turn out to be insignificant.] The fit of the equations that contain actual values of money growth are actually superior to those based on the DMR values, which differs sharply from comparisons of estimated equations for output and the unemployment rate (Barro 1981c).

Regressions were run also with sets of DMR and DM variables included simultaneously, which permitted tests for the significance of a set of DMR or DM variables, conditional on the inclusion of the other set. For example, for the case of pre-tax returns where a contemporaneous and one-year lag value of each variable is considered, the test for significance of the DMR values, given the inclusion of the DM's, corresponds to the statistic $F_{23}^2 = 0.9$. The corresponding test for the significance of the DM values, given the inclusion of the DMR's, yields the statistic $F_{23}^2 = 2.1$. Since both statistics are below the 5% critical value of 3.4, the hypothesis of zero effect for either the set of DMR variables or the set of DM values, given the inclusion of the other set, would be accepted at the 5% level. Nevertheless, the results can be viewed as suggesting (at a significance level below 95%) some negative impact on subsequent real stock returns of the perceived growth rate of money (which would be closely related to anticipated future monetary growth rates), given the values of monetary shocks. In this respect the results are reminiscent of those of Fama and Schwert (1977, pp. 135ff.), who have stressed the puzzling negative relation between anticipated inflation (as measured by the nominal interest rate on Treasury Bills with one-month maturity) and subsequently realized NYSE returns. Related results have been presented by Jaffe and Mandelker (1976) and Nelson (1976). These types of findings are elaborated and some explanations are offered in Fama (1980, pp. 21ff.).

The results for realized real returns on three-month Treasury Bills show much less explanatory power for the government purchases and

22. For the pre-tax returns equation with the DMR_{t-1} and $(g^w - g^{\bar{w}})_t$ variables included also, the estimated coefficient on DMR_{t-2} is -2.4, s.e. $= 2.5$. For the after-tax returns case, the result is -2.2, s.e. $= 2.1$.

monetary variables. A negative effect of the contemporaneous monetary shock does appear, which parallels the results from quarterly data that were reported by Bortz (1979) and discussed above. For example, for the pre-tax returns net of WPI inflation, the estimated coefficient on DMR_t is -1.4, s.e. = 0.6 (line 10 of Table 6.2); while that for the after-tax returns is -1.5, s.e. = 0.7 (line 14). The result that the contemporaneous money-shock effect is negative on the Treasury Bill returns and insignificant for the NYSE returns does accord with the theoretical discussion. The Treasury Bill regressions do not indicate a preference for the DM form of the equations, although the hypothesis of zero coefficients for either the set of DMR variables or the set of DM values would be accepted, given the inclusion of the other set. In either form of the equations, the contemporaneous (annual) value has the only significant monetary effect. One- and two-year lagged values of the DMR or DM variables are insignificant (lines 10 and 14).

For the cases where the DMR_t variable is included, the temporary government purchases variable has a positive estimated effect on the Treasury Bill returns, with t-values close to 2. The estimated coefficient for the case of pre-tax returns (line 10) is 1.3, s.e. = 0.7; while that for the after-tax case is 1.4, s.e. = 0.7 (line 14). However, the government-purchases variable becomes insignificant when the WPI is replaced by the GNP deflator to measure the inflation rate (lines 26 and 30). (The t-values for the contemporaneous monetary variables remain close to 2 in this case.)

I will consider now some details of the estimates for the equations based on the WPI that use the explanatory variables DMR_t, DMR_{t-1}, and $(g^w - g^{\bar{w}})_t$. Although this equation form is more understandable on theoretical grounds than that expressed in terms of DM values, it should be recalled that the statistical results do not reinforce this choice of form. The actual values of the pre-tax realized real returns from the NYSE and from three-month Treasury Bills are shown in Table 6.3 along with estimated values and residuals from the regressions shown in lines 2 and 10 of Table 6.2.

The estimated coefficient on DMR_{t-1} in the RMV equation (Table 6.2, line 2) of -8.3 implies that a one-percentage-point money shock reduces the mean of next year's real NYSE returns by more than 8 percentage points! Since the estimated standard error from the money growth rate equation that generates the DMR values is 0.014, the results imply that monetary fluctuations have produced large movements in ex ante real returns on the NYSE. However, this relationship should be viewed in perspective with the sample standard deviation of the realized real returns on stocks, which was 0.195 from 1949 to 1977.[23] Since the estimated coefficient on DMR_{t-1} in the Treasury Bills equation (line 10) is negligible, the effect of DMR_{t-1} on the NYSE returns represents also a differential effect on the expected real returns from stocks and short-term government securities.

The estimated coefficient for the $(g^w - g^{\bar{w}})_t$ variable of 5.8 in line 2 implies a very large positive effect of war on real NYSE returns. For example, the Korean War values for $(g^w - g^{\bar{w}})$ of 0.026 imply that the realized real returns would be higher by 0.24 than those associated with the typical peacetime value for $(g^w - g^{\bar{w}})$ of -0.015. It is clear that this magnitude of effect could not be extrapolated in a linear form to the World War II experience, where the values of $(g^w - g^{\bar{w}})$ are above 0.3.[24] These results should not be viewed as indicating that war is good for the stock market. Rather, the basic finding is that the high values of temporary government purchases associated with wartime imply an increase in the required real rate of return on equity—that is, a rise in the discount rate applied to anticipated earnings. In this context it is notable that the results remain similar if the lagged value for $(g^w - g^{\bar{w}})$, which is presumably known by the start of year t, replaces the contemporaneous value. However, the present results do not rule out a separate effect of new information about war conditions on equity prices, which could work through an effect on anticipated earnings flows.

There is, of course, no inconsistency between efficient capital markets and a predictable pattern either of overall real returns or of the return differential between stocks and Treasury Bills. The present results can be interpreted as showing a strong positive effect of war and (money-induced) recession on the return premium for stocks. It has, however, been argued (for example, in Nelson 1976, p. 482, and Fama and Schwert 1977, p. 136) that assets like common stocks should not exhibit

23. The mean real return was 0.082. With the GNP deflator used to measure inflation, the mean real return was 0.077 with a standard deviation of 0.180.

24. However, the nominal return on stocks, RMV, from 1942 to 1945 is quite high, averaging 0.24 per year (see Table 6.1). The reported inflation rates are probably meaningless for this period.

Table 6.3. Actual and estimated values for realized real rates of return[a]

Date	(1) RMV − D(WPI)	(2) RMV − D(WPI)	(3) Residual	(4) RT − D(WPI)	(5) RT − D(WPI)	(6) Residual
1941	−0.266			−0.170		
1942	0.104			−0.056		
1943	0.245			−0.011		
1944	0.183			−0.011		
1945	0.317			−0.016		
1946	−0.332			−0.278		
1947	−0.087			−0.119		
1948	0.054			0.026		
1949	0.241	0.065	0.176	0.061	0.008	0.053
1950	0.113	0.177	−0.064	−0.149	−0.012	−0.137
1951	0.217	0.067	0.149	0.032	0.020	0.012
1952	0.160	0.147	0.014	0.046	0.027	0.018
1953	−0.002	0.126	−0.128	0.010	0.048	−0.037
1954	0.434	0.249	0.185	0.016	0.024	−0.008
1955	0.219	0.031	0.188	0.002	−0.014	0.015
1956	0.049	−0.009	0.058	−0.016	0.008	−0.024
1957	−0.124	0.141	−0.265	0.016	0.017	−0.002
1958	0.368	0.132	0.237	0.013	0.004	0.009
1959	0.129	0.026	0.103	0.035	−0.016	0.052

1960	0.010	0.002	0.008	0.024	0.036	-0.012
1961	0.248	0.318	-0.070	0.026	0.013	0.013
1962	-0.075	0.059	-0.134	0.031	0.013	0.018
1963	0.194	0.138	0.056	0.026	0.003	0.024
1964	0.154	0.039	0.116	0.036	-0.011	0.046
1965	0.099	0.014	0.085	0.004	-0.006	0.011
1966	-0.104	0.094	-0.198	0.034	0.010	0.023
1967	0.238	0.176	0.062	0.033	0.032	0.001
1968	0.098	0.184	-0.086	0.022	-0.004	0.026
1969	-0.140	-0.089	-0.052	0.020	-0.007	0.027
1970	0.013	-0.013	0.026	0.042	0.015	0.027
1971	0.117	0.096	0.022	0.004	-0.023	0.027
1972	0.100	-0.141	0.240	-0.027	-0.023	-0.005
1973	-0.337	-0.060	-0.277	-0.093	-0.022	-0.071
1974	-0.443	-0.039	-0.404	-0.080	0.000	-0.080
1975	0.297	0.116	0.181	0.015	0.023	-0.008
1976	0.198	0.189	0.011	0.003	0.020	-0.018
1977	-0.107	0.132	-0.239	-0.009	-0.008	-0.001
1978	-0.013	(-0.048)	(0.035)	-0.028	(-0.022)	(-0.006)

a. Definitions for RMV, RT, and D(WPI) appear in the notes to Table 6.1. The figures shown in columns 2 and 3 are the estimated values and residuals, respectively, for the regression shown in line 2 of Table 6.2. Those in columns 5 and 6 are from the regression shown in line 10 of Table 6.2.

lower expected returns than less risky assets like Treasury Bills.[25] For the estimated values shown in Table 6.3, this situation occurs for 7 of the 29 years of the sample (1956, 1960, 1969–1970, 1972–1974). All of these years except 1960, but no other years in the sample, exhibit negative estimated real returns on stocks. These results apply to equations that include the contemporaneous values DMR_t and $(g^w - g^{\bar{w}})_t$. However, basically similar results obtain if only the lagged variables DMR_{t-1} and $(g^w - g^{\bar{w}})_{t-1}$ are used as regressors. In this case, negative expected real returns on stocks apply for 1951, 1956, 1960, 1969, and 1972–1974.

It is likely that the functional form could satisfactorily be restricted to confine the expected real NYSE returns to exceed either those on Treasury Bills or zero. For example, estimates of the functional form,

$$[RMV - D(WPI)]_t = \exp[a_0 + a_1 DMR_t + a_2 DMR_{t-1}$$
$$+ a_3(g^w - g^{\bar{w}})_t] + \text{error term,}$$

which restricts the estimated values to be positive, yields a log likelihood that is only 1.1 below that of the linear form (Table 6.2, line 2). Although the linear and nonlinear forms of the return equations have not presently been set up to allow for a test of nested hypotheses, these results suggest that the appearance of negative estimated (or expected) real NYSE returns is not an important problem.

Observations

In some respects the new empirical findings support the theoretical model—notably, in isolating realized real rate of return effects that are significantly positive for the temporary government-purchases variable and significantly negative for the monetary variables. The statistical preference for actual monetary movements over the constructed money-

---

25. Treasury Bills do not provide a riskless real rate of return—for example, the sample mean return net of WPI inflation is 0.006 with a standard deviation of 0.045. With the GNP deflator used to measure inflation, the sample mean return is 0.002 with a standard deviation of only 0.019. The relative riskiness of stocks and Treasury Bills depends also on covariances with returns from other assets, such as human capital and real estate. Conceivably, the dependence of these covariances on money shocks and other variables could account for occasional negative risk premia on stocks.

shock variable and the relatively weak effects on real Treasury Bill yields are less satisfactory features.

A different issue concerns the extent to which the present empirical analysis distinguishes hypotheses of equilibrium business-cycle theory from those of more conventional macroanalysis. The usual IS/LM model predicts a positive effect of government purchases on rates of return, which should presumably be interpreted as an effect on real, rather than nominal, returns. In this respect the predictions parallel those of the equilibrium models. The IS/LM story involves crowding out of private demands with no mention of positive supply effects, but the direction of interest-rate response would still be positive. An important difference in the "equilibrium" approach is the stress on temporary government purchases, which does receive some support from the empirical results.

With respect to monetary movements, the IS/LM framework suggests a negative response of interest rates, although the distinction between real and nominal rates is less clear in this respect. The equilibrium analysis predicts a negative effect on realized real returns and an ambiguous impact on nominal returns (which involves an effect on generally anticipated inflation). The stress on monetary shocks, rather than perceived movements in money, in the equilibrium viewpoint is not borne out in the present results, as mentioned above.

The correspondence in some respects for the rate of return implications of the equilibrium approach and other macro theories does not, of course, rule out the present statistical results as valid tests of both types of theories. Although real rate of return effects that are positive for government purchases and negative for money growth may not be surprising, I cannot find much past empirical evidence that bears on these propositions.

One hypothesis that sharply distinguishes the equilibrium model with incomplete information on monetary aggregates from more standard macroanalyses is the prediction of a positive effect of money shocks on contemporaneously (and erroneously) perceived real rates of return. As discussed before, this hypothesis cannot be tested directly from observations on realized returns, precisely because the incomplete information structure predicts that monetary disturbances move ex post returns in a direction opposite to that of ex ante (partial information) returns. Satisfactory testing of this hypothesis seems to require an explicit calculation of price expectations conditional on partial current information. I am not certain this analysis is feasible.

References

Bailey, M. L. 1971. *National Income and the Price Level*, 2nd Ed. New York: McGraw Hill.

Barro, R. J. 1976. "Rational Expectations and the Role of Monetary Policy." *Journal of Monetary Economics* 2:1–32.

———— 1977. "Long-Term Contracting, Sticky Prices, and Monetary Policy." *Journal of Monetary Economics* 3:305–316.

———— 1980. "A Capital Market in an Equilibrium Business Cycle Model." *Econometrica* 48:1393–1417.

———— 1981a. "Output Effects of Government Purchases." *Journal of Political Economy* 89(6):1086–1121.

———— 1981b. "The Equilibrium Approach to Business Cycles." In *Money, Expectations, and Business Cycles,* ed. R. J. Barro. New York: Academic Press, pp. 41–78.

———— 1981c. "Unanticipated Money Growth and Economic Activity in the United States." In *Money, Expectations, and Business Cycles,* ed. R. J. Barro. New York: Academic Press, pp. 137–169.

Barro, R. J., and Z. Hercowitz. 1980. "Money Stock Revisions and Unanticipated Money Growth." *Journal of Monetary Economics* 6:257–267.

Barro, R. J., and M. Rush. 1980. "Unanticipated Money and Economic Activity." In *Rational Expectations and Economic Policy,* ed. S. Fischer. Chicago: University of Chicago Press for the National Bureau of Economic Research, pp. 23–73.

Blinder, A. A., and S. Fischer. 1978. "Inventories, Rational Expectations, and the Business Cycle." Unpublished manuscript. Princeton, N.J.: Princeton University.

Bortz, G. A. 1979. "Effects of Forecast Errors in Monetary Growth Rates on Real Interest Rates." Unpublished manuscript. Princeton, N.J.: Princeton University.

Fair, R. C. 1979. "An Analysis of the Accuracy of Four Macroeconometric Models." *Journal of Political Economy* 87:701–718.

Fama, E. F. 1980. "Real Activity, Inflation, and Money." Unpublished manuscript. Chicago: University of Chicago.

———— and G. W. Schwert. 1977. "Asset Returns and Inflation." *Journal of Financial Economics* 5:115–146.

Fischer, S. 1977. "Long-Term Contracts, Rational Expectations and the Optimal Money Supply Rule." *Journal of Political Economy* 85:191–205.

Friedman, B. 1978. Discussion of paper by R. E. Lucas and T. J. Sargent, in Federal Reserve Bank of Boston: *After the Phillips Curve: Persistence of High Inflation and High Unemployment.*

Friedman, M. 1968. "The Role of Monetary Policy." *American Economic Review* 58:1–17.

Gray, J. A. 1976. "Wage Indexation: A Macroeconomic Approach." *Journal of Monetary Economics* 2:221–236.

Hall, R. E. 1979. "Labor Supply and Aggregate Fluctuations." Presented at the Carnegie-Rochester Conference.

Jaffe, J. F., and G. Mandelker. 1976. "The Fisher Effect for Risky Assets: An Empirical Investigation." *Journal of Finance* 31:447–458.

King, R. G. 1978. "Asset Markets and the Neutrality of Money: An Economy-Wide Bond Market." Unpublished manuscript. Rochester, N.Y.: University of Rochester.

Kydland, F. E., and E. C. Prescott. 1980. "A Competitive Theory of Fluctuations and the Feasibility and Desirability of Stabilization Policy." In *Rational Expectations and Economic Policy,* ed. S. Fischer. Chicago: University of Chicago Press for the National Bureau of Economic Research, pp. 169–198.

Lucas, R. E. 1972. "Expectations and the Neutrality of Money." *Journal of Economic Theory* 4:103–124.

––––––– 1973. "Some International Evidence on Output-Inflation Trade-offs." *American Economic Review* 63:326–334.

––––––– 1975. "An Equilibrium Model of the Business Cycle." *Journal of Political Economy* 83:1113–44.

––––––– 1977. "Understanding Business Cycles." *Carnegie-Rochester Conference Series on Public Policy* 5:7–29.

Lucas, R. E., and L. Rapping. 1969. "Real Wages, Employment, and Inflation." *Journal of Political Economy* 77:721–754.

McCallum, B. T. 1978. "Dating, Discounting, and the Robustness of the Lucas–Sargent Proposition." *Journal of Monetary Economics* 4:121–130.

Nelson, C. R. 1976. "Inflation and Rates of Return on Common Stocks." *Journal of Finance* 31:471–482.

Phelps, E. S. 1970. "The New Microeconomics in Employment and Inflation Theory." In *Microeconomic Foundations of Employment and Inflation Theory,* ed. E. Phelps. New York: Norton, pp. 1–23.

Sargent, T. J. 1973. "Rational Expectations, the Real Rate of Interest, and the Natural Rate of Unemployment." *Brookings Papers on Economic Activity* 2:429–472.

––––––– 1976. "A Classical Macroeconometric Model for the United States." *Journal of Political Economy* 84:207–237.

––––––– 1979. *Macroeconomic Theory.* New York: Academic Press.

Sargent, T. J., and N. Wallace. 1975. "Rational Expectations, the Optimal Monetary Instrument, and the Optimal Money Supply Rule." *Journal of Political Economy* 83:241–254.

7　Time-Separable Preferences and Intertemporal-Substitution Models of Business Cycles

With Robert G. King
University of Rochester
Rochester, New York

Intertemporal substitution of goods and leisure is a central component in modern equilibrium theories of the business cycle, which seek to explain macroeconomic phenomena under the twin disciplines of rational expectations and cleared markets. In such models, macroeconomic quantities at a point in time reflect (1) economic agents' intertemporal preferences for goods and leisure, (2) intertemporal production opportunities, and (3) expectations held by economic agents.

This chapter concerns a benchmark specification of preferences and production possibilities. First, we model economic agents as immortal families with time-separable preferences for goods and leisure. This specification means that the amounts of past work and consumption do not influence current or future tastes. But this form of preferences does not restrict the sizes of intertemporal-substitution effects—notably, we can still have a strong response of labor supply to temporary changes in wages or to movements in interest rates. However, there are important constraints on the relative responses of leisure and consumption to changes in relative prices and permanent income. Second, we assume that production opportunities are neoclassical, with current output de-

From *Quarterly Journal of Economics* (1984) 99:817–839; copyright © 1984 by the President and Fellows of Harvard College; reprinted by permission of John Wiley & Sons, Inc. We have benefited from many comments on this paper, especially those of Alan Stockman. The NSF supported this research.

pending on current labor services, previously accumulated capital, and exogenous technological conditions.

When the usual aggregation is permissible, time separability has some important implications for equilibrium theories of the business cycle. Neglecting investment, we see that changes in perceptions about the future—which might appear currently as income effects—have no influence on current equilibrium output. With a simple one-capital-good technology, no combination of income effects and shifts to the perceived profitability of investment will yield positive comovements of output, employment, investment, and consumption. Therefore, misperceived monetary disturbances or other sources of changed beliefs about the future cannot be used to generate empirically recognizable business cycles. In contrast, disturbances to technology, which alter the current marginal product of labor, can generate these positive comovements. Here, we find that the real wage rate must move procyclically.

Allocation of Goods and Leisure over Time

Paralleling Lucas's (1977) outline of equilibrium business-cycle models, we begin by considering a worker-entrepreneur in an environment that lacks all kinds of storable commodities. Production activities take place within a single period of the discrete time setup. The representative household's output of goods for period t, all of which is supplied to the commodity market, is

$$y_t^s = f(n_t; \alpha_t), \tag{7.1}$$

where n_t is work effort, α_t is a technological shift parameter, and $f(\cdot)$ has a nonincreasing marginal product schedule ($f_n > 0$, $f_{nn} \leq 0$).

In period t, households face current and prospective one-period real interest rates on a consumer-credit market. At date t, we let these real interest rates be $r_t, r_{t+1}, \ldots$. The implied discount factor for real expenditures at date $t + j$ is $\rho_{tj} = 1/[(1 + r_t)(1 + r_{t+1}) \ldots (1 + r_{t+j-1})]$ for $j > 0$ and $\rho_{t0} = 1$. The budget constraint for an infinitely lived[1] household is

$$b_t + \sum_{j=0}^{\infty} \rho_{tj}(y_{t+j}^s - c_{t+j}^d) = 0, \tag{7.2}$$

---

1. The length of the horizon is unimportant for present purposes, as long as the construct of a representative agent is viable.

where b_t is the real value in period t of previously accumulated financial assets ("bonds") and c_{t+j}^d is consumption demand planned for date $t + j$. For an individual, the value of initial assets b_t can be positive, negative, or zero. But because the loan market is internal, the aggregate value of these assets is zero.

Time-Separable Utility

Each household selects a time path of consumption and work (and thereby production of goods) to maximize lifetime utility, which we assume takes the strongly time-separable form,

$$U_t = \sum_{j=0}^{\infty} \beta^j u(c_{t+j}, n_{t+j}), \tag{7.3}$$

where $0 < \beta < 1$ is a fixed utility discount factor. This formulation ensures time consistency in the sense of Strotz (1956). That is, in a situation of perfect foresight, optimizing households will follow through on plans as the starting date t advances.

The form of Eq. (7.3) suggests that the interaction of goods and leisure within a period is different from their interaction across periods. Thus, for example, current consumption c_t may substitute for the contemporaneous amount of leisure, determined by n_t, in a manner different from future consumption or future leisure. Looking forward in time, one might think that there is no special rationale for this asymmetry. However, we can equally well think of time separability as restricting the manner in which past consumption and leisure influence current preferences. Equation (7.3) says that a person's rate of substitution between consumption and leisure at date t does not depend on that person's history of consumption and leisure. Accordingly, the consumption-work plan that someone formulates at the present time t can depend on previous settings for consumption and work only to the extent that these earlier choices show up in current state variables, such as wealth, knowledge, productivity, and so on. The past can matter through budget constraints, but not through shifts in "tastes."

The bulk of existing macroeconomic analyses[2] does not incorporate

---

2. Kydland and Prescott (1982) dealt with a particular form of non–time-separable preferences, which we discuss below. In their analysis a distributed lag of past work appears as a current state variable.

the history of consumption and work as state variables. In other words, most existing macroeconomic theories implicitly assume that utility functions are additively separable over time. This treatment would be satisfactory for most macroeconomic purposes if the important effects of the history of consumption and work on subsequent tastes for consumption and leisure were limited to a brief interval. Suppose, for example, that a period of currently hard work means that fatigue is a significant consideration in future allocations of work and consumption. In this case, work is like a durable good, in the sense that the level of fatigue is a current state variable. In particular, the satisfaction attached to leisure may be especially high when the accumulated amount of fatigue is great. For purposes of business-cycle analysis, we presume that such departures from separability would matter significantly only for days or weeks rather than for months or years. So, a period of unusually hard work might have little direct effect on the taste for leisure after one or two months. (Recall that we are not ruling out influences that work through the budget constraint; the discussion here concerns the effects of past choices on the form of the utility function, as specified to apply from the present date onward.)

Implications of Time-Separable Utility for Demand Functions

Consider each household's optimal choice of current consumption and work effort, derived from maximization of lifetime utility in Eq. (7.3) subject to the lifetime budget constraint in Eq. (7.2). Note that the level of work determines the current supply of goods y_t^s via the production function in Eq. (7.1). Consumption demand and goods supply are functions of the sequence of interest rates r_t, r_{t+1}, ...; the sequence of technological parameters α_t, α_{t+1}, ...; and the level of initial assets b_t. But given time-separable preferences, we can restrict the forms of these functions. For our purposes, it is convenient to write these restrictions in terms of "cross-conditions:"[3]

$$\frac{\partial c_t^d/\partial r_t}{\partial y_t^s/\partial r_t} = \frac{\partial c_t^d/\partial b_t}{\partial y_t^s/\partial b_t} = \frac{\partial c_t^d/\partial r_\tau}{\partial y_t^s/\partial r_\tau} = \frac{\partial c_t^d/\partial \alpha_\tau}{\partial y_t^s/\partial \alpha_\tau} \tag{7.4}$$

$$\text{for} \quad \tau = t + 1, t + 2, \ldots.$$

3. For general discussions of the implications of additively separable utility, see Houthakker (1960, pp. 247ff.) and Goldman and Uzawa (1964, pp. 392ff.). Powell (1974) provides a good summary of these papers and related results.

In Eq. (7.4) we evaluate the effects of a change in r_t (or r_τ), while holding fixed the interest rates in other periods and the parameters, α_t, α_{t+1}, ... Thus the effects are not income compensated (although the conditions expressed in Eq. 4 turn out still to hold if the changes in interest rates are income compensated). Similarly, the change in b_t is for fixed values of the r's and α's, whereas the change in α_τ is for fixed values of the other α's, b_t, and r's.

The cross-conditions in Eq. (7.4) derive from a property of separable preferences that has been extensively discussed in consumer theory. When preferences are separable, it is possible to write demands for each good from a separable "block"—which in our case is a time period—as a function solely of the relative prices of the goods within the block and the amount of real income allocated to expenditure on the goods in the block. In our case the relative price for period t is the "real wage rate," which is implicitly given by the marginal product of labor, $\partial f(n_t; \alpha_t)/\partial n_t$. A change in any rate of return, r_τ for $\tau = t, t + 1, \ldots$, or technological parameter, α_τ for $\tau = t + 1, \ldots$, ends up having some effect on the real income allocated to date t's expenditure. Then the responses of c_t^d and n_t—hence y_t^s—reflect only income effects. Thus the relative responses of c_t^d and y_t^s must be the same as those to pure income effects, as represented by changes in b_t. Equation (7.4) states this condition.[4]

Aggregation

We assume that the properties of individuals' demand functions—notably, the cross-conditions in Eq. (7.4)—carry over to the aggregate level.[5] This assumption permits us to do macroeconomics in the usual manner, where we focus on the behavior of a representative agent.

Equilibrium Analysis with Static Production Opportunities

Using capital letters to denote aggregates, we see that the market-clearing condition for period t is

$$Y_t^d = C_t^d(B_t, r_t, \alpha_t, \ldots) = Y_t^s(B_t, r_t, \alpha_t, \ldots), \tag{7.5}$$

4. See Barro and King (1982, pp. 11–12) for a more complete derivation along these lines.

5. Lucas (1972) constructed a model where simple aggregation does not work. The distribution of income between young and old is important in Lucas's setup, as it is generally in overlapping-generation models that neglect private intergenerational transfers.

where the dots indicate omitted future interest rates (r_{t+1}, ...) and technological parameters (α_{t+1}, ...). Although the aggregate stock of initial assets is zero with an internal loan market, it still is useful to consider hypothetical variations in B_t. These variations provide a convenient method of analyzing aggregate income effects.

The Basic Result

To apply our analysis to some equilibrium business-cycle models, we consider the responses to a pure aggregate income effect. Studying changes in B_t provides information about other disturbances with aggregate income effects, for example, shifts in the position of future production functions that leave the associated marginal product schedule unchanged.

Equation (7.5) permits us to calculate the effects of this type of disturbance on current aggregate output and the interest rate. The omitted arguments of the functions in Eq. (7.5) are viewed as given, including future values of α and r.[6] The key result is that aggregate output is invariant to pure income effects under time-separable preferences. Specifically, we get

$$\frac{dr_t}{dB_t} = \left[\frac{\partial C_t^d}{\partial B_t} - \frac{\partial Y_t^s}{\partial B_t}\right] \bigg/ \left[\frac{\partial Y_t^s}{\partial r_t} - \frac{\partial C_t^d}{\partial r_t}\right] > 0 \tag{7.6}$$

$$\frac{dY_t}{dB_t} = \left[\frac{\partial C_t^d}{\partial B_t}\frac{\partial Y_t^s}{\partial r_t} - \frac{\partial Y_t^s}{\partial B_t}\frac{\partial C_t^d}{\partial r_t}\right] \bigg/ \left[\frac{\partial Y_t^s}{\partial r_t} - \frac{\partial C_t^d}{\partial r_t}\right] = 0. \tag{7.7}$$

The positive impact on the real rate of return and the zero effect on aggregate output are readily explained. If current consumption and leisure are superior goods, the rise in perceived aggregate income raises C_t^d and lowers Y_t^s (reduces work effort). Because currently desired saving

6. More generally, we would substitute the future market-clearing values of these interest rates, as perceived by the representative individual. The prospective values of r_{t+1}, r_{t+2}, ... will not change if the typical person does not expect the disturbance to have aggregate consequences in future periods. In the present context, variations in these future interest rates are, in any case, inconsequential for current output. This result follows from Eq. (7.4), which implies that changes in any future interest rate (r_τ for $\tau = t + 1, \ldots$) will alter the current rate r_t, to leave current output unchanged. The calculated effect of the disturbance on the current interest rate, which appears in Eq. (7.6), will be inexact for this reason.

declines, the current real rate of return r_t rises. The increase in the interest rate r_t achieves commodity-market clearing, partly by stimulating current output supply (by inducing more work today) and partly by lowering current consumption demand.

The effects on current output are offsetting. The positive forces are the income effect on demand, $\partial C_t^d / \partial B_t$, and the intertemporal-substitution effect on supply, $\partial Y_t^s / \partial r_t$. Offsetting these elements are the negative income effect on supply, $\partial Y_t^s / \partial B_t$, and the negative intertemporal-substitution effect on demand, $\partial C_t^d / \partial r_t$. The net impact on output depends on the composite term,

$$[(\partial C_t^d / \partial B_t)(\partial Y_t^s / \partial r_t) - (\partial C_t^d / \partial r_t)(\partial Y_t^s / \partial B_t)],$$

which is zero as the result of the cross-conditions (7.4).

It is worth stressing that the invariance of output to an aggregate income effect does not require any limitations on the sizes of any individual substitution or income effects. For example, the substitution effect on supply $\partial Y_t^s / \partial r_t$ can be arbitrarily large. The outcome reflects the cross-condition in Eq. (7.4), which limits the relative magnitude of the various sensitivities. We derive this result from an alternative perspective in the following section.

Defoe's "Island" Model

Consider the situation of an isolated individual, Robinson Crusoe.[7] A positive income effect arises if Crusoe anticipates the arrival of some free goods in a future period. But, with static production opportunities and time-separable utility, Crusoe's behavior today is divorced entirely from that at other times. In particular, changes in this period's work and production have no implications for any state variables that will be relevant to later periods. Hence today's optimal choices of consumption and leisure are invariant with any shifts in future prospects. The invariance of current output from income effects holds immediately for Robinson Crusoe. (However, the shadow discount rate that connects tomorrow's

7. Long and Plosser (1983) similarly described a representative-agent equilibrium as the optimal choices of a Robinson Crusoe with time-separable preferences. They used a "real business-cycle" model that incorporates many consumption and capital goods.

consumption or leisure with today's r_t does tend to rise when future prospects improve.)[8]

General Implications

The invariance of current output applies in our model to any change in prospective conditions. These include any shifts in future technologies, as represented by the parameters $\alpha_{t+1}, \alpha_{t+2}, \ldots$, or changes in prospective rates of return $r_{t+1}, r_{t+2}, \ldots$. This general invariance result may be demonstrated using the cross-conditions that involve α_τ and r_τ for $\tau > t$ in Eq. (7.4).

Nonseparable Utility and Fatigue

A specific form of nonseparable preferences proposed by Kydland and Prescott (1982) would alter the previous results. Suppose that today's utility from leisure depends on "fatigue"—namely, the greater the amount of past work (possibly expressed as a distributed lag of prior work levels), the higher the marginal utility of today's leisure relative to today's consumption. Under such a specification, past work becomes a pertinent state variable for the current period. Equivalently, current effort alters future utility flows and future marginal rates of substitution between goods and leisure.

Again working from the perspective of Robinson Crusoe, we can think of the prospect of more goods—but not a higher marginal product of labor—in some future period. In this situation people expect to take more leisure in the future period where goods have become more abundant. Accordingly, there is less cost attached to being fatigued at this future date. Therefore, people become more willing to work during periods—including the present—that precede this time of abundance. In contrast to our previous discussion, equilibrium quantities will not be invariant; instead, current work and production will be higher in response to a positive income effect. (In our market context the positive

---

8. Shadow prices can be read off the derivatives of Crusoe's maximized utility function. Note that the announcement of a receipt of goods $k > 1$ periods in the future would not alter Crusoe's implicit one-period real rate of return, $(1 + r_t) = (\partial u_t/\partial c_t)/[\beta(\partial u_{t+1}/\partial c_{t+1})]$. In this sense the calculated effect on the current interest rate in Eq. (7.7) is inexact in ways that can be economically important (see note 6).

effect of the higher rate of return r_t on Y_t^s in Eq. 7.5 will end up dominating the negative effect of greater lifetime resources.)

Similarly, suppose that improvements in future labor productivity (as represented by appropriate changes in α_τ, for $\tau > t$) imply increases in future work levels. In this case it becomes more important to rest at earlier dates in order to prepare for the subsequent strenuous activity. Therefore current work and production will be reduced in this case.

In our main analysis we assume that cumulated fatigue is not an important consideration over time intervals that are interesting for macroeconomics. Therefore we abstract in our principal discussion from the types of effects considered in this section.

Monetary Theories of Business Fluctuations

If nominal disturbances are mistakenly perceived as representing shifts in intertemporal relative prices, then such shocks can be nonneutral toward aggregate output. Suppose that each economic agent produces and consumes in only one of many decentralized markets, and no one observes directly nominal aggregates or general price indexes. Lucas (1973) and Barro (1976, 1980) demonstrated that this setting can generate a positive correlation of money, aggregate output, and the price level.

In Barro's models a positive monetary disturbance (arising as a surprise transfer from the government) causes the average household to overestimate its income position, which can be represented by an increase in B_t in the present setup. However, under time-separable preferences, monetary disturbances—even if imperfectly perceived—will have no impact on current output.[9]

Government Purchases

Some recent equilibrium analyses (Hall 1980; Barro 1981) considered the effects of government purchases on aggregate output and rates of return. These studies stress the distinction between permanent and temporary changes in government purchases. The argument is that the

---

9. The "normal" positive response of output to a monetary disturbance obtains in the models of Barro (1976, 1980) only if the parameter H, which is analogous to $[(\partial C_t^d/\partial B_t)(\partial Y_t^s/\partial r_t) - (\partial Y_t^s/\partial B_t)(\partial C_t^d/\partial r_t)]$, is positive. Our analysis implies that $H = 0$ if preferences are time separable.

output effects of temporary government spending (such as the major wartime expansions of purchases) will be larger than that of permanent movements in spending of a similar magnitude, because the former will induce intertemporal substitutions of work effort and production. Time-separable preferences also have strong implications for this type of macro disturbance.

Suppose that the government demands commodities in the per capita amount g_t in period t. Assume for the moment that these expenditures are financed by lump-sum taxes, which are equal for each household. The government uses its purchases of goods to provide some services to the private sector. These services may appear in households' functions for utility or production. With respect to utility, we assume that the effects of g_t appear only in period t's flow, that is, as $u(c_t, n_t, g_t)$.[10] Hence there is still time separability in the utilities derived from goods, which now include public services as well as private consumption and leisure. Similarly, the productive-input effect of g_t is purely contemporaneous— that is, we write the production function for period t as

$$y_t = f(n_t, g_t; \alpha_t). \tag{7.8}$$

The present value of taxes appears as a negative item in each household's budget constraint. Neglecting transfers and public debt, we see that the present value of each household's taxes equals the per capita value of government purchases, $\Sigma_{j=0}^{\infty} \rho_{tj} g_{t+j}$. The household's intertemporal-budget constraint now has the form,

$$b_t - \sum_{j=0}^{\infty} \rho_{tj} g_{t+j} + \sum_{j=0}^{\infty} \rho_{tj}(y_{t+j}^s - c_{t+j}^d) = 0. \tag{7.9}$$

Changes in government purchases affect households' choices for two reasons. First, the discounted value of these purchases enters negatively into households' wealth. Second, because of the role of public services in utility and production, the value g_t interacts directly with the choices of c_t^d and y_t^s. However, for present purposes, the important point is that a cross-preference relation holds that involves prospective government

10. For present purposes, it is not central whether the government's services are "public goods," in which case the aggregate amount of purchases would matter for individuals.

purchases—namely,

$$\frac{\partial c_t^d / \partial r_t}{\partial y_t^s \, \partial r_t} = \frac{\partial c_t^d / \partial g_\tau}{\partial y_t^s \, \partial g_\tau} \qquad \text{for } \tau = t + 1, t + 2, \ldots. \qquad (7.10)$$

Again, we assume that Eq. (7.10) holds also for the aggregates C_t^d, Y_t^s, and G_t.

The introduction of the government means that the condition for clearing the commodity market must be modified to accommodate public purchases of final product—that is,

$$C_t^d(B_t, r_t, \alpha_t, G_t, \ldots) + G_t = Y_t^s(B_t, r_t, \alpha_t, G_t, \ldots). \qquad (7.11)$$

The omitted terms in Eq. (7.11) now also include effects of the prospective values of government purchases, G_{t+1}, G_{t+2}, ...

Consider a rise in current government purchases G_t when all future levels of purchases are held fixed. There is first the direct expansion of current aggregate demand. Then the change in G_t may have effects on the households' choices of work effort, production, and consumption. As one possibility (see Bailey 1971, chap. 9 and Barro 1981, pp. 1090–93), the public services substitute for some contemporaneous private consumption—so C_t^d declines—and enhance private production—so Y_t^s expands. (Because the change in purchases is temporary, there will not be a large income effect, but there might be substitution effects on desired work effort.) If the sum of the magnitudes of the responses of C_t^d and Y_t^s is less than one-to-one with the change in G_t, then an increase in current government purchases causes current aggregate demand to rise by more than supply. Therefore, a rise in r_t is typically required to clear the commodity market. The equilibrium is likely to entail higher current work effort and output but lower consumption. (These results depend on the precise manner in which public services enter the utility and production functions.)

In contrast to the suggestions of Hall (1980) and Barro (1981), permanent and temporary movements in government purchases have identical effects on current (date t) quantities of work, production, and consumption when preferences are time separable. In our setup, the previously discussed increase in spending is made more permanent by raising the levels of G_{t+1}, G_{t+2}, . . . and tracing out the impacts. But the cross-condition in Eq. (7.10) implies that changes in prospective government purchases have no significance for current output. However, the distinction between permanent and temporary government purchases does matter for the effects on the current real interest rate, r_t.[11]

Again, Robinson Crusoe tells us that his optimization problem for today is isolated from events at other dates. That is, it makes no difference to Crusoe's current work effort whether his "defense" expenditures are temporary or permanent.

Distorting Taxes and Public Debt

Suppose that taxes are levied on effort rather than being lump sum. Then an increase in government purchases implies more taxes, which motivate substitutions away from market activity and toward leisure. However, the output-effect of permanent and temporary shifts in government purchases would still be identical if the government were not permitted to issue public debt. That is, if date t expenditures were financed solely by date t taxes, then an analogue to our previous argument would demonstrate that permanent and temporary shifts in government purchases have equal effects on current work effort, production, and consumption.

If the government is permitted to borrow or lend on the economy's credit market, then a potential difference arises between permanent and temporary shifts in purchases. Suppose, as in Barro (1979), that the government uses debt issue to smooth the behavior of (income) tax rates over time. Then a permanent change in government purchases necessitates a larger adjustment of current tax rates than does a temporary one. Hence the effect on current output tends to be greater if the change in government purchases is temporary. Because of the smaller increase in tax rates, the induced substitutions away from market activities will be smaller in the case of a temporary change.

11. The current one-period interest rate r_t can depend only on quantities of consumption and work for periods t and $t + 1$. These quantities are insensitive to changes in government purchases after period $t + 1$—that is, to $G_{t+2}, \ldots$. Therefore prospective purchases after date $t + 1$ cannot affect r_t in the present model; the current, one-period rate of return r_t depends only on G_t and G_{t+1}. Basically, r_t rises when G_t increases relative to G_{t+1}, while r_{t+1} rises when G_{t+1} increases relative to G_{t+2}, and so on. Hence prospective variations in government purchases affect the term structure of real interest rates. (See Benjamin and Kochin 1985 in this context.) When investment is added to the model (below), the prospective path of purchases, $G_{t+2}, \ldots$, will also influence the current one-period rate r_t.

Intertemporal Production Opportunities

Previously, production opportunities in each period were separated from economic actions taken in other periods. The most natural way to connect different time periods on the production side is to permit economic agents to accumulate physical stocks of goods (or of human capital or knowledge). The key point is that the potential for accumulation–decumulation at the aggregate level permits a representative agent to behave, in equilibrium, more like an individual who faces a given interest rate on the credit market. That is, the economy as a whole may respond to a temporary change in income or the marginal product of labor by altering the stocks of goods carried over to the future.

Here we sketch out the simplest possible model of capital accumulation and draw out some of its implications. To a certain extent, the discussion is meant to be suggestive rather than definitive. The linkages across time that are introduced by capital accumulation substantially complicate the full dynamic equilibrium analysis.

Suppose now that the production function for period t is

$$y_t = f(n_t, k_{t-1}; \alpha_t), \tag{7.12}$$

where k_{t-1} is the stock of capital available to a household at the start of period t. Capital and consumption goods are perfect substitutes on the supply side, investment is reversible, and there are no adjustment costs—that is, k is just the accumulation of past outputs that have been designated as capital goods. The stock k_{t-1} excludes any investment during period t. Consequently, the household always equates the marginal product of capital to the one-period real rate of return,

$$\frac{\partial f}{\partial k_t} = r_t \qquad \text{for all } t, \tag{7.13}$$

which implicitly gives a demand function for capital.

Investment demand, $i_t^d \equiv k_t^d - k_{t-1}$, depends inversely on r_t, given the position of the schedule (versus k_t) for the marginal product of capital. The technological shift parameter, α_{t+1}, and any elements that affect the level of future work effort can influence the position of this marginal product schedule and, hence, affect investment demand. For our purposes, we write the aggregate investment-demand function as

$$I_t^d = I^d(r_t, K_{t-1}, \ldots),$$
(7.14)

where $\partial I_t^d / \partial r_t < 0$ and $\partial I_t^d / \partial K_{t-1} < 0$. Omitted components of Eq. (7.14) include technological parameters α_{t+1} and forces that affect aggregate work effort.

Next, we augment the goods-market equilibrium condition to incorporate aggregate investment demand. Neglecting government purchases, we see that the revised condition is

$$Y_t = C^d(B_t, r_t, \alpha_t, \ldots) + I^d(r_t, K_{t-1}, \alpha_t, \ldots)$$
(7.15)

$$= Y^s(B_t, r_t, \alpha_t, \ldots).$$

When considering some economic disturbances, we hold fixed the omitted elements in Eq. (7.15), which include future interest rates. Then it is straightforward to calculate effects on the current rate of return, r_t, and on current quantities. This procedure is suggestive but cannot give the exact change in current output because we are dealing with a nontrivial model of general equilibrium over time. That is, changes in current capital accumulation (arising from a particular disturbance) will cause variations in the future rates of return, $r_{t+1}, r_{t+2}, \ldots$, and future marginal product schedules, which are suppressed in Eq. (7.15). In turn, these variables will feed back into the commodity-market equilibrium condition and thereby alter current levels of capital accumulation, and so on.

Consider again the effects of a change in aggregate income B_t:

$$\frac{dr_t}{dB_t} = \left[\frac{\partial C_t^d}{\partial B_t} - \frac{\partial Y_t^s}{\partial B_t} \right] \Big/ \Delta > 0$$
(7.16)

$$\frac{dY_t}{dB_t} = \left[\frac{\partial C_t^d}{\partial B_t} \frac{\partial Y_t^s}{\partial r_t} - \frac{\partial Y_t^s}{\partial B_t} \frac{\partial C_t^d}{\partial r_t} - \frac{\partial Y_t^s}{\partial B_t} \frac{\partial I_t^d}{\partial r_t} \right] \Big/ \Delta < 0,$$
(7.17)

where

$$\Delta \equiv \left[\frac{\partial Y_t^s}{\partial r_t} - \frac{\partial C_t^d}{\partial r_t} - \frac{\partial I_t^d}{\partial r_t} \right] > 0.$$

As before, the rise in B_t increases C_t^d and lowers Y_t^s (assuming that consumption and leisure are superior goods), which drives up the current interest rate, r_t. Because the increase in this interest rate reduces investment demand, the necessary increase in r_t is less than that calculated before in Eq. (7.6), assuming that the income and substitution effects on Y_t^s and C_t^d are the same as previously. Earlier, current work and consumption ended up unchanged on net. Therefore, with a smaller rise in the interest rate, current work now declines on net, while current consumption rises. The fall in work implies a reduction in current production (since K_{t-1} and the aggregate production function in period t are fixed), as is shown in Eq. (7.17), which uses the cross-condition in Eq. (7.4). Given the decline in output, the increase in current consumption is made possible by a decline in current investment.

We can again explain the findings from the perspective of Robinson Crusoe. A positive income effect signals the prospect of better times ahead. Given this expectation, Crusoe has less incentive to work and suppress consumption today in order to accumulate capital. In fact, Crusoe wants to use up previous stores of goods (capital) to raise present consumption and leisure. Cutbacks in investment effectively enable Crusoe to use future abundance in order to provide for current consumption and leisure. Therefore, when we include a variable amount of investment—which ties different time periods together—we find that a positive income effect tends to lower current work, production, and investment, while raising current consumption and leisure.

We should stress the result that consumption and leisure end up moving in the same direction. We always get this result if (i) utility is separable over time, (ii) consumption and leisure are superior goods, and (iii) the current schedule for labor's marginal product does not shift. Changes in prospective conditions end up affecting households' total current real expenditure on consumption and leisure. Given time-separable utility, this change amounts solely to an income effect, which moves consumption and leisure in the same direction if both goods are superior. Thus the two goods can move in opposite directions only if there is a shift in the (schedule for the) current relative price, which is the real wage rate. But we rule this out by assuming no shift in the schedule for labor's current marginal product.

We assume that initial phases of business fluctuations—which match up to the point-in-time responses to shocks we are studying here—involve positive comovements of aggregate production, employment, investment, and consumption.[12] This typical pattern cannot be generated from pure income effects in our present model, when we impose time-separable utility and the requirement that consumption and leisure in all periods are superior goods. This observation is significant, because some equilibrium models of business cycles treat monetary shocks as operating initially through an income effect on consumer demand.[13]

Shocks to Investment Demand

Shocks to investment demand have long been viewed as a possible source of business fluctuations. King (1982) shows that monetary surprises can alter perceptions about the prospective marginal revenue product of capital, which then lead to shifts in desired investment. In any equilibrium framework, shifts to aggregate investment demand raise interest rates and output but lower consumption demand, so the "typical pattern" of business cycles does not arise.

Going further, one might conjecture that the addition of an aggregate income effect could provide the requisite boost to current consumption demand. (In King 1982, monetary surprises create positive income effects—through mistaken asset valuations—as well as boosts to the perceived marginal value product of capital.) But under the maintained hypothesis that preferences are time-separable, this route turns out to be unsatisfactory. The basic problem is that, as mentioned before, consumption and leisure end up moving in the same direction. Hence, if we introduce an income effect that is sufficiently strong to generate an

---

12. We do not mean that all aggregate business fluctuations exhibit these characteristics. For example, expansions associated with major wars tend to show declines in private investment and in at least the durable-goods component of consumer spending. This pattern is especially evident during World War II.

13. The inclusion of investment means that temporary and permanent changes in government purchases no longer have identical effects on current output (even ignoring the effects of distorting taxes). Current investment tends to decline more when the change in purchases is temporary. (This finding is consistent with the tendency of the current interest rate, r_t, to rise in response to temporary changes in purchases.) In effect, society (or Robinson Crusoe) can meet emergencies partly by working off the existing stock of capital or, at least, by investing less than otherwise. This channel reduces people's incentives to work hard and consume little during periods where government purchases are temporarily high. Because of the reduced motivation to work hard, the overall effect on current output now tends to be greater when the change in purchases is permanent rather than temporary. The effects of distorting taxation, which were described earlier, have the opposite implications. Therefore, we cannot say whether temporary or permanent changes in government purchases have a greater effect overall on current output.

increase in consumption, then we find that work effort, and therefore production, end up declining. If utility is separable over time and consumption and leisure are superior goods, then there is no package of shocks to investment demand and perceived aggregate income that can lead simultaneously to increases in current consumption and work effort.[14]

Shifts to Current Productivity and the Real Wage Rate

If utility is separable over time and all goods are superior, we can generate an increase in today's consumption and work effort—hence a decline in today's leisure—only if there is a change in the current technological parameter, α_t, that generates an upward shift in today's schedule for the marginal product of labor.[15] This change implies a substitution effect, which favors today's consumption and deters today's leisure. Therefore, when we add this effect to those discussed previously, it becomes possible for today's consumption and leisure to move in opposite directions. In particular, it becomes possible to generate the typical pattern of business cycles, which features positive comovements of current output, work effort, investment, and consumption. But notice that the real wage rate, which equals the marginal product of labor, must rise along with the increases in output and work effort. In other words, a procyclical pattern for the real wage rate is central to our theoretical analysis.

Suppose, as in some equilibrium business-cycle theories, that we introduce separate markets for commodities and labor services. A central feature of these theories is that people have incomplete information about current prices. But we stick to the plausible story that individuals buy today's leisure and consumption at prices that are observed simultaneously. That is, while people may not observe the prices of all goods at

14. Grossman (1973, p. 1367) pointed out that market-clearing macroeconomic models predict a negative association between consumption and employment, if the primary disturbances are variations in "autonomous" expenditures, such as shifts to investment demand. Without restrictions implied by time separability, however, King (1982, pp. 12–15) demonstrates that positive comovements of consumption, investment, and employment may arise if factors that raise investment demand also increase a representative economic agent's perceived wealth. The conclusion that no package of shocks can lead to the desired positive comovements is a consequence of time-separable preferences.

15. We neglect shifts in the forms of the representative household's preferences for consumption and leisure—that is, we rule out shifts in tastes as significant sources of aggregate business fluctuations.

once, they at least know the prices of those goods that they actually buy or sell. Then it will not be possible for monetary surprises or aggregate disturbances to generate misperceptions about the ratio of the current nominal wage to the prices of consumer goods that someone buys currently. Then, in order for today's consumption to rise while today's leisure falls, it is still necessary that the (observed) price of today's consumption fall relative to the (observed) price of today's leisure. Thus a procyclical pattern of the actual real wage rate arises even when we introduce elements of incomplete information about current prices.

The real wage rate in our theory refers to the marginal product of labor, which dictates the typical person's shadow price for current leisure relative to current consumption. There are at least two difficulties in using reported series on average wages to measure this concept. First, efficient long-term contracts are consistent with a discrepancy between reported wage rates and the true shadow value of current time. (See, for example, Barro 1977.) Second, because wage rates vary cross-sectionally, average wage data (for employed persons) may be misleading when the composition of the employed labor force varies. Notably, if workers with relatively low productivity tend to be laid off first, then a spurious element of countercyclical wage movement will be present in data on average wages (of employed persons). Results of Stockman (1983) indicate that movements in real wage rates are procyclical, although this relation tends to be obscured when data on average wage rates are used.

Sources of Shifts

Exogenous changes in productivity are central driving variables in the real-business-cycle theories of Kydland and Prescott (1982) and Long and Plosser (1983). Consequently, given shifts to current labor productivity, these models can generate positive comovements of consumption, work effort, and production. However, in the absence of direct shocks to current labor productivity, these positive comovements cannot arise.[16] This result is disturbing, because the real-world significance of these types of shocks, at the aggregate level, is not apparent.

---

16. For example, variations in expectations about future productivity, as explored by King and Plosser (1984), cannot generate the desired pattern unless there are accompanying changes in current productivity.

In the models considered so far, there are no current period actions that can affect the current quantity of capital services, which could then influence the schedule for the current marginal product of labor. If changes in expectations about some future variables altered the current amount of capital services used by producers, then we might be able to generate the desired pattern of positive comovements without requiring a direct shock to current labor productivity. For example, King (1980) and Merrick (1983) showed how variations in the utilization of existing capital goods, in response to changes in intertemporal relative prices, can work this way if capital and labor services are complementary.

Unfortunately, variable capacity utilization is not sufficient to generate the cyclical comovements that we seek. In the simplest formulation of the utilization decision, it is impossible to get current investment and the current utilization rate to move in the same direction, because more intense utilization is essentially a choice of less investment. However, our hunch is that production structures that mix variable utilization with "time-to-build" requirements for capital will ultimately deliver the desired positive comovements of investment, capacity utilization, employment, output, and consumption. Further, it should be possible to generate these movements in response to shifts in expectations about the future. These possibilities will be explored in future research.

Observations

Time separability of utility means that past work and consumption do not influence current and future tastes. This type of separations may be a reasonable approximation over time periods, such as quarters or years, that are of primary interest for macroeconomic analysis.

The assumption that preferences are time separable is implicit in most macroeconomic models. For example, Friedman's (1957) linkage of consumption to permanent income derives much of its attractive empirical content from the treatment of past consumptions as bygones, which are unimportant for current decisions. This preference condition, made explicit by Hall (1978), generates strong testable restrictions that are not implied by other theories, such as the habit-persistence model, which implicitly incorporate non–time-separable preferences.

In our analysis of dynamic labor supply and consumption decisions, time-separable preferences do not restrict the size of intertemporal-substitution effects: notably, we can still have a strong response of current labor supply to temporary changes in real wages or to the real interest rate. Rather, separability constrains the relative size of various responses, such as those of leisure and consumption to relative-price and income effects.

When the usual aggregation is permissible, time separability has some important implications for equilibrium theories of the business cycle. We find that some existing versions of these models cannot generate the typical cyclical pattern of aggregate quantities. Specifically, combinations of income effects and shifts to the perceived profitability of investment do not yield positive comovements of output, employment, investment, and consumption. Therefore we are unable to use misperceived monetary disturbances or other sources of changed beliefs about the future in order to generate empirically recognizable business cycles.

Given time-separable utility, we find that the typical pattern of quantity variation during business cycles requires the real wage rate to move procyclically. Some real-business-cycle models generate this pattern by postulating direct shocks to labor's current productivity. But the real-world significance of these types of shocks is unclear.

The troublesome aspect of our results is the reliance on direct shocks to labor's current productivity; changes in expectations about future variables (which might be induced by monetary fluctuations) are insufficient to generate the typical pattern of business fluctuations. However, our analysis does point to modifications in existing theories that may yield a richer pattern of responses to shifts in expectations about the future. The key element is an enrichment of the intertemporal structure of production to include elements of capacity utilization along with the dynamics of capital accumulation.

Appendix: Extensions to Uncertainty

As is common in macroeconomics, we derived our theoretical restrictions under certainty and then applied these results to a business cycle context, which involves stochastic elements, as though a "certainty equivalence" held. However, systematic incorporation of uncertainty would not alter either of the principal results of the chapter: (i) the derivation of cross-conditions or (ii) the implications for market-clearing values of real quantities. Basically, we can determine the efficient values of current leisure and consumption as conditional demands, given a level of gross saving, when preferences are separable. Then we can derive the cross-conditions. We can also show the consumption and work effort cannot respond in the same direction to any disturbance affecting the future. We illustrate this point by considering the following two-period model.

Let the agent have the utility function,

$$U = u(c_1, n_1) + \beta u(c_2, n_2), \tag{7.A1}$$

and act to maximize the expected value of U under uncertainty; c_1, c_2 are amounts of consumption in the two periods, and n_1, n_2 are amounts of effort in the two periods. Let us work backward in the standard dynamic programming fashion. First, we consider maximizing $u(c_2, n_2)$ subject to $c_2 = w_2 n_2 + a_2$, where w_2 is the wage at date 2 and a_2 is wealth in period 2. The outputs of this maximization are an indirect utility function v and two decision functions, which depend on the wage (w_2) and wealth (a_2):

$$v(a_2, w_2) = \max_{c_2, n_2} u(c_2, n_2) \tag{7.A2a}$$

subject to

$$c_2 = w_2 n_2 + a_2$$

$$c_2^*(a_2, w_2) \tag{7.A2b}$$

$$n_2^*(a_2, w_2). \tag{7.A2c}$$

The assumption that consumption and leisure are normal goods implies that $\partial c_2^*/\partial a_2 > 0$ and $\partial n_2^*/\partial a_2 < 0$.

Time separability of preferences implies that, at date 1, we can view agents as making decisions in two parts. First, at a given level of gross saving (s), agents obtain an optimal mix of consumption and leisure in a manner exactly as described for period 2. (These, in turn, imply a level of indirect utility.) That is, given that agents have $a_1 - s$ available for expenditure on period 1 goods and leisure, the decisions are $c_1^*(a_1 - s, w_1)$ and $n_1^*(a_1 - s, w_1)$. The period 1 indirect utility function is $v(a_1 - s, w_1)$. (It is not essential that there be identical conditional decision functions and indirect utility functions in each period, but it simplifies the discussion.) Second, optimal saving is selected in order to maximize

$$v(a_1 - s, w_1) + \beta E v(\tilde{a}_2, \tilde{w}_2), \tag{7.A3}$$

subject to $\tilde{a}_2 = (1 + \tilde{r}_1)s$. (A tilde over a variable indicates that it is uncertain as of period 1.) The efficiency condition for optimal saving is

$$D_1 v(a_1 - s_1, w_1) = \beta E[D_1 v(\tilde{a}_2, \tilde{w}_2)(1 + \tilde{r}_1)], \tag{7.A4}$$

where $D_1 v$ indicates the partial derivative of the indirect utility function with respect to its first argument (wealth allocated to the period under study). Along with $\tilde{a}_2 = (1 + \tilde{r}_1)s$, this condition implicitly determines an optimal level of saving s_1^* as a function of a_1, w_1 and the probability distributions of $\tilde{w}_2$ and $(1 + \tilde{r}_1)$.

Changes in any of the moments of $\tilde{w}_2$ or $(1 + \tilde{r}_1)$ are pertinent to period 1 actions only as long as they affect saving. Thus it follows that the current impact of any change affecting the right-hand side of (7.A4) can be decomposed into

$$\frac{\partial c_1}{\partial x} = -\frac{\partial c_1^*}{\partial(a_1 - s)}\frac{\partial s^*}{\partial x} \quad \text{and} \quad \frac{\partial n_1}{\partial x} = -\frac{\partial n_1^*}{\partial(a_1 - s)}\frac{\partial s^*}{\partial x}, \tag{7.A5}$$

where c_1^*, n_1^* are the conditional demand functions evaluated at $a_1 - s_1^*$, w_1 and where x is some change in the probability distribution of $\tilde{w}_2$ and $(1 + \tilde{r}_1)$.

Similarly, the influence of initial wealth on period 1 actions can be written as

$$\frac{\partial c_1}{\partial a_1} = \frac{\partial c_1^*}{\partial(a_1 - s_1)}\left(1 - \frac{\partial s^*}{\partial a_1}\right) \quad \text{and} \tag{7.A6}$$

$$\frac{\partial n_1}{\partial x} = \frac{\partial n_1^*}{\partial(a_1 - s_1)}\left(1 - \frac{\partial s^*}{\partial a_1}\right).$$

Thus it follows directly that cross-conditions hold for any change in the distribution of $\tilde{w}_2$ and $\tilde{r}_1$:

$$\frac{\partial c_1/\partial x}{\partial n_1/\partial x} = \frac{\partial c_1/\partial a_1}{\partial n_1/\partial a_1}. \tag{7.A7}$$

Further, any package of changes in future variables must ultimately result in some particular level of saving. Whatever that change is, expressions (7.A5) tell us that consumption and effort must be moving in opposite directions implies $\partial c_1^*/\partial(a_1 - s_1^*) > 0$ and $\partial n_1^*/\partial(a_1 - s_1^*) < 0$.

Extensions to life spans longer than two periods do not alter these results because it would be possible to repeat the argument with a multi-period indirect utility function—a value function in dynamic programming terminology—replacing $v(\tilde{a}_2, \tilde{w}_2)$ in (7.A3).

References

Bailey, M. J. 1971. *National Income and the Price Level,* 2nd Ed. New York: McGraw-Hill.

Barro, R. J. 1976. "Rational Expectations and the Role of Monetary Policy." *Journal of Monetary Economics* 2:1–32.

—— 1977. "Long-Term Contracting, Sticky Prices, and Monetary Policy." *Journal of Monetary Economics* 3:101–115.

—— 1979. "On the Determination of the Public Debt." *Journal of Political Economy* 87:940–971.

—— 1980. "A Capital Market in an Equilibrium Business Cycle Model." *Econometrica* 48:1393–1417.

—— 1981. "Output Effects of Government Purchases." *Journal of Political Economy* 89:1086–1121.

Barro, R. J., and R. G. King. 1982. "Time-Separable Preferences and Intertemporal-Substitution Models of Business Cycles." National Bureau of Economic Research Working Paper No. 888.

Benjamin, D., and L. A. Kochin. 1985. "War, Prices, and Interest Rates: Gibson's Paradox Revisited." In *A Retrospective on the Classical Gold Standard, 1821–1931,* ed. M. Bordo and A. J. Schwartz. Chicago: University of Chicago for the National Bureau of Economic Research, pp. 587–604.

Friedman, M. 1957. *A Theory of the Consumption Function.* Princeton, N.J.: Princeton University Press.

Goldman, S. M., and H. Uzawa. 1964. "A Note on Separability in Demand Analysis." *Econometrica* 32:387–398.

Grossman, H. I. 1973. "Aggregate Demand, Job Search, and Employment." *Journal of Political Economy* 81:1353–69.

Hall, R. E. 1978. "Stochastic Implications of the Life Cycle–Permanent Income Hypothesis: Theory and Evidence." *Journal of Political Economy* 86:971–987.

———— 1980. "Labor Supply and Aggregate Fluctuations." *Carnegie-Rochester Conference Series on Public Policy* 12:7–33.

Houthakker, H. S. 1960. "Additive Preferences." *Econometrica* 28:244–257.

King, R. G. 1980. "Money, Real Wages and the Business Cycle." Unpublished manuscript. Rochester, N.Y.: University of Rochester.

———— 1982. "Investment, Imperfect Information and Equilibrium Business-Cycle Theory." Unpublished manuscript. Rochester, N.Y.: University of Rochester.

King, R. G., and C. I. Plosser. 1984. "The Behavior of Money, Credit and Prices in a Real Business Cycle." *American Economic Review* 74:363–380.

Kydland, F., and E. C. Prescott. 1982. "Time-to-Build and Aggregate Fluctuations." *Econometrica* 50:1345–70.

Long, J. B., and C. I. Plosser. 1983. "Real Business Cycles." *Journal of Political Economy* 81:36–69.

Lucas, R. E. 1972. "Expectations and the Neutrality of Money." *Journal of Economic Theory* 4:103–124.

———— 1973. "Some International Evidence on Output-Inflation Trade-offs." *American Economic Review* 63:326–334.

———— 1977. "Understanding Business Cycles." *Carnegie-Rochester Conference Series on Public Policy* 5:7–29.

Merrick, J. E. 1983. "The Anticipated Real Interest Rate, Capital Utilization and the Cyclical Pattern of Real Wages." *Journal of Monetary Economics* 13:17–30.

Powell, A. 1974. *Empirical Analysis of Demand Systems.* Lexington, Mass.: Lexington, Bowles.

Stockman, A. C. 1983. "Aggregation Bias and the Cyclical Behavior of Real Wages." Unpublished manuscript. Rochester, N.Y.: University of Rochester.

Strotz, R. H. 1956. "Myopia and Inconsistency in Dynamic Utility Maximization." *Review of Economic Studies* 23:165–180.

8   Interest-Rate Targeting

Central bankers, including those at the Federal Reserve, seem to talk mainly in terms of controlling or targeting interest rates. Given the pervasiveness of this outlook, it would probably be useful for economists to assign interest rates a major role in a positive theory of monetary policy. Nevertheless, many monetary theorists—especially those of an equilibrium persuasion (and sometimes called monetarists)—have viewed monetary policy mainly in terms of the behavior of monetary aggregates. In this view the targeting of interest rates is either impossible or undesirable (see, for example, Friedman 1968 and Brunner 1968). One aspect of modern versions of this skepticism concerns price-level determinism under an interest-rate rule (see Sargent and Wallace 1975 and McCallum 1981). A major result here is that an interest-rate target requires some additional mechanism to pin down the levels of nominal variables. However, this observation does not distinguish an interest-rate rule from rules related to monetary growth or inflation, which may also be incomplete with respect to the levels of money and prices. In any event, because any of these rules can be extended to achieve price-level determinism, this criticism does not constitute a serious attack on the logic or desirability of this class of policies.

Part of the difficulty in thinking of monetary policy in terms of interest rates concerns the familiar distinction between real and nominal rates. It may be that systematically and significantly influencing expected real interest rates—which is what many macroeconomists imagine when

From *Journal of Monetary Economics* (1989) 23:3–30. The data from this project will be available from the Inter-University Consortium at the University of Michigan. I have benefited from comments by Marvin Goodfriend, Bob King, Greg Mankiw, Allan Meltzer, Ben McCallum, and Bill Schwert. This research was supported by the National Science Foundation.

they view monetary policy in terms of interest rates—is beyond the power of monetary authorities over periods of interesting length. In fact, my assumption throughout this chapter is that expected real interest rates are exogenous with respect to monetary policy. But even with this extreme assumption about real rates, the nominal interest rate is a perfectly fine nominal variable that the monetary authority ought to be able to control—at least if it does not try simultaneously to regulate some other nominal rate of change, such as the inflation rate, the growth rate of a monetary aggregate, or the rate of change of the exchange rate. Moreover, because interest rates can be observed rapidly and with great accuracy, they are good candidates for variables that the monetary authority could monitor and react to in a feedback manner. In this respect, feedback from nominal interest rates to monetary instruments seems more attractive than some alternative suggestions that involve the inflation rate or the growth rate of nominal GNP.

In this chapter I explore the behavior of monetary policy that is consistent with an objective of interest-rate targeting. I argue that such an objective appears reasonable and leads in a theoretical model to well-defined behavior for the monetary base and the price level. Furthermore, this behavior for money and prices provides testable hypotheses about these variables under a regime where the monetary authority targets nominal interest rates. The empirical results suggest that this regime is a good approximation to reality in the United States in the post–World War II period, and perhaps also in the interwar period. The sample before World War I reveals very different behavior for the nominal interest rate and therefore provides an interesting contrast to the recent experience.

The Basic Theoretical Model

I use a simple stochastic model of money supply and demand, which builds on models of Goodfriend (1987), McCallum (1986), and Hetzel (1987). The private economy is described by two equations, the first pertaining to interest-rate determination and the second to the real demand for money:

$$R_t = E_t p_{t+1} - p_t + r_t + v_t, \tag{8.1}$$

$$m_t - p_t = \alpha_t - \beta R_t + \eta_t, \tag{8.2}$$

where

R_t = nominal interest rate;

p_t = log of price level;

$E_t p_{t+1}$ = expectation of next period's log of price level, based on information available at date t;

m_t = log of quantity of money (measured empirically as the monetary base);

r_t = "permanent" part of the expected real interest rate;

v_t = temporary shock to the expected real interest rate, distributed independently as white noise (mean 0, variance σ_v^2);

α_t = permanent part of level of real demand for money;

η_t = temporary shock to real demand for money, distributed independently as white noise (mean 0, variance σ_η^2);

$\beta > 0$ = coefficient of the nominal interest rate in the money-demand function.

The permanent components of the expected real interest rate and money demand follow random walks,

$$r_t = r_{t-1} + w_t, \qquad \alpha_t = \alpha_{t-1} + a_t, \qquad (8.3)$$

where w_t and a_t are distributed independently as white noise (mean 0, variances σ_w^2 and σ_a^2, respectively). If the expected real interest rate is stationary, then $\sigma_w^2 = 0$.

Equation (8.1) says that the expected real interest rate, $r_t + v_t$, is the sum of a random-walk and a white-noise component. The main restriction in this specification is that movements in the expected real rate are independent of monetary disturbances, that is, of shifts in the demand for money, a_t and η_t, or in the supply of nominal money. It is straightforward to allow for nonzero covariances between the shocks to the expected real interest rate and the shocks to money demand. However, it is more important that "monetary policy" cannot affect the expected real interest rate in this model.

The specification of money demand in Eq. (8.2) is similar in spirit. The shifts to money demand, a_t and η_t, include effects from changes in output (permanent and transitory, respectively). But these changes— and other shifts to the level of the money-demand function—are treated as independent of the behavior of the nominal money stock. However, monetary policy can influence the nominal interest rate, R_t, and thereby affect the quantity of real money demanded. The particular functional form, with the constant semi-elasticity $-\beta$, is solely for analytical convenience.

There are, of course, models in which monetary shocks can affect the expected real interest rate and output. These include equilibrium-style approaches with incomplete information about monetary aggregates and price levels, models where expected inflation influences transaction costs and the demand for money, and frameworks with sticky prices. It is unclear, however, whether any of these approaches have isolated quantitatively important effects of money on real variables. Therefore my reason for treating the expected real interest rate and output as exogenous with respect to money is that I lacked an alternative specification that I regarded as theoretically or empirically superior. However, even if this assumption is wrong, it may still be satisfactory in the present context if money matters mostly for nominal variables—such as the price level and the nominal interest rate—and only secondarily for real variables.

The monetary authority controls the quantity of nominal money (the monetary base), m_t, in each period. Given the assumed dichotomy between money and real variables, it is difficult to motivate a meaningful objective for the monetary authority. For example, any concern about output and expected real interest rates would not matter for the choice of monetary policy. I assume that the monetary authority cares about two things: (1) the departure of the nominal interest rate, R_t, from a target value, $\overline{R}_t$, and (2) the spread between the price level, p_t, and people's prior expectation, $E_{t-1}p_t$. In particular, I assume (as detailed below) that the authority wants to hold down the magnitudes of the two gaps, $|R_t - \overline{R}_t|$ and $|p_t - E_{t-1}p_t|$. (For a related discussion of central-bank objectives, see Goodfriend 1987, p. 339.) Fundamentally, these concerns must reflect some real consequences from the two types of gaps—that is, monetary policy must not be fully neutral. My basic assumption is that these nonneutralities are important enough to motivate an interest in monetary policy but not important enough to generate significant effects on the time pattern of expected real interest rates and outputs. In particular, the real effects can be neglected for the purpose of using Eqs. (8.1) and (8.2) to determine the time path of the price level and the nominal interest rate.

It turns out in this model that the monetary authority can keep the nominal interest rate, R_t, arbitrarily close to its target, $\overline{R}_t$, in each period. Therefore, if $\overline{R}_t$ were constant, then the model would predict little variation in nominal interest rates. But it is well known that, especially in recent years, nominal interest rates move around a good deal and in a largely unpredictable manner. In fact, even for short-term rates, a random walk is a pretty good description of the recent data. To accommodate this observation, the model incorporates a time-varying target for the nominal interest rate that follows a random walk,

$$\overline{R}_t = \overline{R}_{t-1} + u_t, \tag{8.4}$$

where u_t is an independent, white-noise process with mean 0 and variance σ_u^2.

The subsequent results would change little if Eq. (8.4) were modified to $\overline{R}_t = \rho \overline{R}_{t-1} + u_t$, where ρ is close to but below unity. The interest-rate target would then have a long-run tendency to revert to a stationary mean. But this change would matter little for the high-frequency properties of the nominal interest rate, monetary growth, and inflation, which are the main concerns of this study. In addition, it would be straightforward to allow for nonzero covariances between u_t and the other disturbance terms.

One motivation for Eq. (8.4) is that the nominal interest rate is the tax rate on money, and the government sets this tax rate as part of an overall problem of optimal public finance. The desire to smooth taxes intertemporally, as stressed in Barro (1979) and Mankiw (1987), tends also to motivate smoothness in individual components of the tax package, such as the tax rate on money.[1] In this context smoothness means that the government avoids predictable movements, up and down, of the tax rates. Consequently, tax rates—here the target nominal interest rate, $\overline{R}_t$—would follow a Martingale process, as implied by the random-walk model in Eq. (8.4).

1. Lucas (1984) viewed the tax rate on money as a determinant of the relative cost of cash and credit goods. Therefore, if the tax rate on final output is set optimally, it is unclear whether the tax rate on money should be positive—that is, that money-using goods should be taxed more heavily than credit-(or barter-)using goods. (For a similar argument, see Kimbrough 1986.) However, a positive tax rate on money does allow the government to tax some black-market activities where final product is not taxed. Also, if the main existing taxes are on some of the factor inputs, especially labor, then it may be desirable to tax other inputs, such as monetary services.

Many economists are skeptical that this optimal-tax argument is a major element in the conduct of monetary policy in the United States or many other countries. However, for subsequent purposes, the only significant consideration is that policy involve an interest-rate target, $\overline{R}_t$, that shifts unpredictably over time. This behavior could be motivated by models of monetary policy that have nothing to do with fiscal concerns.

Because of the lower bound of zero on the nominal interest rate, Eq. (8.4) cannot apply universally. However, a random walk may be a satisfactory approximation for a broad range of nominal interest rates, even if not for samples—such as that for the 1940s and early 1950s in the United States—where the rates get close to zero.

I assume that the monetary authority and the private agents have symmetric information, with each observing m_t, R_t, and $\overline{R}_t$ during period t. In contrast, observations on the price level arise with a lag—say, one to two months for accurate indexes. I model this information lag by assuming that data on p_{t-1} become available during period t.[2] Therefore the lag in obtaining data on the general price level essentially defines the length of the period in the model. This setup accords with the notion that interest rates are observable more rapidly—and with greater accuracy—than are price indexes. Also, the approach embodies the idea that the lag in publishing figures on the money stock—say, the monetary base—is short enough to neglect.

A number of economists (such as Brunner, Cukierman, and Meltzer 1980) stress that the monetary authority cannot readily distinguish permanent shifts to money demand from temporary shifts. I model this problem by assuming that information about the permanent shock arrives with a one-period lag—that is, α_{t-1} is known at date t. More realistically, the α's would never be observed directly, and estimates of α_{t-1} (formed at date t) would utilize the observed time series of real cash balances, $m_{t-1} - p_{t-1}$, $m_{t-2} - p_{t-2}$, and so on. The inclusion of α_{t-1} in date t's information set is a tractable approximation to this specification. Similarly, I assume that people observe the permanent component of the expected real interest rate with a one-period lag—that is, r_{t-1} is known at date t.

2. Given that p_t is not observed at date t, it is possible that p_t should be replaced by $E_t p_t$ in Eq. (8.1). However, in a setting such as Barro (1976), Eq. (8.1) can arise as the aggregation over local markets, each of which observes the current local price, $p_t(z)$.

Given this informational setup, the monetary authority's optimal choice of m_t can be expressed as a function of the state of the economy at date t. Because the model is linear and the monetary authority's objective is assumed (below) to be quadratic, the optimal rule would be a linear function of the state of the economy. In particular, monetary growth can be written in the form[3]

$$m_t - m_{t-1} = \lambda_0 + \lambda_1 R_t + \lambda_2 \overline{R}_t + \lambda_3 R_{t-1} + \lambda_4 \overline{R}_{t-1} \qquad (8.5)$$

$$+ \lambda_5 \alpha_{t-1} + \lambda_6 \alpha_{t-2} + \lambda_7 r_{t-1}.$$

The coefficients λ will be determined by the policymaker's optimization problem.

Many macroeconomic models can be thought of in terms of the sign of λ_1—starting from $R_t = \overline{R}_t$ and for given $\overline{R}_t$, if R_t rises do you print more money ($\lambda_1 > 0$) or less money ($\lambda_1 < 0$) to get R_t back down to target? The condition $\lambda_1 > 0$ (which central bankers know is right and which in fact applies in this model) tends to arise in Keynesian models where monetary expansion has an inverse effect on the expected real interest rate. But in the present model, the expected real interest rate is exogenous. Therefore a positive response of $m_t - m_{t-1}$ to an increase in R_t ($\lambda_1 > 0$) can work to reduce R_t in this model only if expected inflation, $E_t p_{t+1} - p_t$, declines.[4] This reduction in expected inflation tends to occur if expected future monetary growth, $E_t m_{t+1} - m_t$, falls. In other words, an increase in R_t must create a tendency for some of today's infusion of money to be taken back in the future—for example, in the next period. This effect follows from the term $\lambda_3 R_{t-1}$ in Eq. (8.5), if $\lambda_3 < 0$. In fact, it is the negative value of λ_3, and not the value of λ_1, that matters for interest-rate targeting. The value of λ_1 is irrelevant in this context because it turns out to affect equally the levels of money (and prices) for periods t and $t + 1$. However, the choice of λ_1 matters if the monetary authority

3. Because α_{t-1} is observable at date t, the lagged price level, p_{t-1}, turns out not to enter into Eq. (8.5).

4. Shiller (1980, p. 130) recognized this possibility but regarded it as implausible: "We usually think that increasing high-powered money is, if anything, a signal of higher inflation. It would seem implausible, then, that these lower interest rates are due to lower inflationary expectations. It is conceivable that exogenous increases in the money stock might be a sign of lower inflation over a certain time horizon if the parameters of our model were just right." In the present model the parameters turn out to be "just right" as a consequence of the monetary authority's optimizing behavior.

cares not only about targeting nominal interest rates but also—as I assume—about the predictability of the price level. This last consideration will pin down the desired response of today's money to today's interest rate, which then determines the value of λ_1 and thereby makes determinate the levels of money and prices at each date. For this reason, the problem of price-level indeterminism (as discussed in Sargent and Wallace 1975 and McCallum 1981) will not arise here.

The linear model described by Eqs. (8.1)–(8.5) can be solved (after doing a lot of algebra) in the usual way by the method of undetermined coefficients (see Lucas 1973, Barro 1976, McCallum 1983, 1986, and Goodfriend 1987). The main complication is that the expected price level, $E_t p_{t+1}$ in Eq. (8.1), depends on the expectations $E_t a_t$ and $E_t w_t$. That is, lacking full current information about this period's permanent shocks to money demand and the expected real interest rate—a_t and w_t—people form expectations conditioned on limited current information. This information is conveyed by observing today's nominal interest rate, R_t, and money stock, m_t. (Recall that p_t is not observable at date t.)

In any event, the result from this exercise is an equilibrium solution for R_t, p_t, and m_t as linear functions of current shocks, $(a_t, \eta_t, w_t, v_t, u_t)$, and lagged variables.[5] The results involve the eight λ coefficients that characterize monetary policy in Eq. (8.5).

Monetary Policy

Given the equilibrium solution described in the preceding section, the monetary authority chooses its policy coefficients, $\lambda_0, \ldots, \lambda_7$, to minimize the expression,

$$A \cdot E(R_t - \bar{R}_t)^2 + B \cdot E(p_t - E_{t-1}p_t)^2, \tag{8.6}$$

where A and B are positive constants. The objective penalizes interest-rate gaps and price-level surprises in the typical future period, which is well defined because the two expectations of squared gaps in expression (8.6) end up being the same for all dates t. (The results would not change if the objective involved an expected present value of the terms shown in Eq. 8.6.)

---

5. I use McCallum's (1983, 1986) procedure for selecting the unique bubble-free solution.

Instead of examining the solution to the model for arbitrary choices of the λ coefficients, I begin with the optimizing conditions that are intuitive and then use these restrictions to collapse the equilibrium solution to a manageable form. Recall that Eq. (8.5) is

$$m_t - m_{t-1} = \lambda_0 + \lambda_1 R_t + \lambda_2 \bar{R}_t + \lambda_3 R_{t-1} + \lambda_4 \bar{R}_{t-1}$$
$$+ \lambda_5 \alpha_{t-1} + \lambda_6 \alpha_{t-2} + \lambda_7 r_{t-1}.$$

The policymaker's optimization implies the following conditions:

1. $\lambda_1 + \lambda_2 + \lambda_3 + \lambda_4 = 1$; in the long run, a higher value of nominal interest rates and nominal-interest-rate targets must, for a given expected real rate, correspond one-to-one to a higher monetary growth rate [if not, then the term, $E(R_t - \bar{R}_t)^2$, is unbounded as $t \to \infty$].

2. $\lambda_7 = -1$; given the long-term behavior of nominal interest rates, an increase in the permanent component of the expected real rate implies a one-to-one reduction of the inflation rate and, hence, of the monetary growth rate [again needed to keep $E(R_t - \bar{R}_t)^2$ bounded].

3. $\lambda_0 = 0$; without sustained real growth, monetary growth corresponds in the long run to the inflation rate and, hence, to the difference between the nominal and expected real interest rates; more generally, λ_0 equals the long-term growth rate of real money demanded [this condition keeps down $E(R_t - \bar{R}_t)^2$ with no implications for $p_t - E_{t-1}p_t$].

4. $\lambda_5 = -\lambda_6 = 1$; the first part, $\lambda_5 = -\lambda_6$, is necessary to keep $E(R_t - \bar{R}_t)^2$ bounded as $t \to \infty$; the second part says that permanent shifts to money demand, $a_{t-1} = \alpha_{t-1} - \alpha_{t-2}$, are fully accommodated once they are recognized as permanent. This response holds down $E(p_t - E_{t-1}p_t)$ without affecting $R_t - \bar{R}_t$.

Given conditions 1–4, the form for the monetary growth rate can be written as

$$m_t - m_{t-1} = \lambda_1(R_t - \bar{R}_t) + \lambda_3(R_{t-1} - \bar{R}_{t-1}) + \bar{R}_{t-1}$$
$$+ (\lambda_1 + \lambda_2)(\bar{R}_t - \bar{R}_{t-1}) + a_{t-1} - r_{t-1}.$$

The next optimizing condition is

5. $\lambda_1 + \lambda_2 = -\beta$; a (permanent) shift in the target, $u_t = \overline{R}_t - \overline{R}_{t-1}$ (and hence, in actual nominal interest rates, which are being targeted), depresses real money demanded by the amount $-\beta$. The reduction in monetary growth by this amount avoids a price level response and, therefore, holds down $E(p_t - E_{t-1}p_t)$ (without affecting $R_t - \overline{R}_t$).

Given conditions 1–5, the monetary growth rate is given by

$$m_t - m_{t-1} = \lambda_1(R_t - \overline{R}_t) + \lambda_3(R_{t-1} - \overline{R}_{t-1}) \tag{8.7}$$
$$+ \overline{R}_{t-1} - \beta u_t + a_{t-1} - r_{t-1}.$$

This form highlights the role of the coefficients λ_1 and λ_3, which describe monetary reactions to current and lagged interest-rate gaps. Corresponding to Eq. (8.7), the model's equilibrium solution can be used to derive the following results:

$$R_t - \overline{R}_t = \frac{\eta_t + a_t + v_t + w_t}{1 - \lambda_3 + \beta}, \tag{8.8}$$

$$p_t - E_{t-1}p_t = -\frac{(\eta_t + a_t)(1 - \lambda_1 - \lambda_3)}{1 - \lambda_3 + \beta} + \frac{(v_t + w_t)(\lambda_1 + \beta)}{1 - \lambda_3 + \beta}. \tag{8.9}$$

Because the economy cannot distinguish in the current period between temporary and permanent shocks, the two money-demand disturbances enter as the sum $\eta_t + a_t$ and the two real-interest-rate disturbances enter as the sum $v_t + w_t$.

In the absence of a monetary response, a positive shock to money demand, $\eta_t + a_t$, lowers $p_t - E_{t-1}p_t$. To the extent that the economy views the shock as temporary, $E_t p_{t+1} - p_t$ rises (that is, the temporary disturbance would not affect $E_t p_{t+1}$), so $R_t - \overline{R}_t$ increases. The reaction, λ_1, of $m_t - m_{t-1}$ to $R_t - \overline{R}_t$ offsets the tendency of $p_t - E_{t-1}p_t$ to fall in Eq. (8.9). If $\lambda_3 < 0$, the negative reaction of $m_{t+1} - m_t$ lowers $E_t p_{t+1} - p_t$ and, thereby, reduces $R_t - \overline{R}_t$ in Eq. (8.8).

A positive shock to the expected real interest rate, $v_t + w_t$, raises $R_t - \overline{R}_t$ directly in Eq. (8.8). The reaction of monetary growth, λ_1, and the reduction in money demand, β, lead to increases in $p_t - E_{t-1}p_t$ in Eq. (8.9). To the extent that $m_{t+1} - m_t$ declines (with $\lambda_3 < 0$), the response of $R_t - \bar{R}_t$ to $v_t + w_t$ gets smaller in Eq. (8.8).

Define the overall variance of money-demand and real-interest-rate shocks as

$$\sigma^2 \equiv \sigma_\eta^2 + \sigma_a^2 + \sigma_v^2 + \sigma_w^2. \tag{8.10}$$

The results in Eqs. (8.8) and (8.9) imply that the terms appearing in the policymaker's objective in Eq. (8.6) are given by

$$E(R_t - \bar{R}_t)^2 = \frac{\sigma^2}{(1 - \lambda_3 + \beta)^2}, \tag{8.11}$$

$$E(p_t - E_{t-1}p_t)^2 = \frac{(\sigma_\eta^2 + \sigma_a^2)(1 - \lambda_1 - \lambda_3)^2}{(1 - \lambda_3 + \beta)^2} \tag{8.12}$$

$$+ \frac{(\sigma_v^2 + \sigma_w^2)(\lambda_1 + \beta)^2}{(1 - \lambda_3 + \beta)^2}.$$

Note that $E(R_t - \bar{R}_t)^2$ in Eq. (8.11) is independent of λ_1. (The contemporaneous reaction, λ_1, of money to the interest rate affects the levels of money and prices but not the rates of change that matter for the nominal interest rate.) Hence λ_1 can be chosen to minimize $E(p_t - E_{t-1}p_t)^2$ for a given value of λ_3. In particular, the solution for λ_1 as a function of λ_3 does not depend on the weights, A and B, in expression (8.6). The resulting condition is

$$\lambda_1 = \frac{(1 - \lambda_3)(\sigma_\eta^2 + \sigma_a^2) - \beta(\sigma_v^2 + \sigma_w^2)}{\sigma^2}. \tag{8.13}$$

Given this choice for λ_1 as a function of λ_3, $E(p_t - E_{t-1}p_t)^2$ in Eq. (8.12) becomes

$$E(p_t - E_{t-1}p_t)^2 = \frac{(\sigma_\eta^2 + \sigma_a^2)(\sigma_v^2 + \sigma_w^2)}{\sigma^2}, \tag{8.14}$$

which is independent of λ_3. As long as the current and prospective reactions of money to interest-rate gaps, λ_1 and λ_3, maintain the correct relationship—dictated by Eq. (8.13)—the overall level of the reaction does not matter for the determination of p_t. Therefore λ_3 can now be chosen [independently of the weights A and B in expression (8.6)] to minimize $E(R_t - \bar{R}_t)^2$. It follows immediately from Eq. (8.11) that the best choice is $\lambda_3 \to -\infty$.[6] Equation (8.13) then implies $\lambda_1 \to \infty$, but the ratio λ_1/λ_3 remains finite and is given by

$$\frac{\lambda_1}{\lambda_3} = -\frac{\sigma_\eta^2 + \sigma_a^2}{\sigma^2}, \tag{8.15}$$

that is, as the ratio of money-demand variance to the sum of money-demand and expected-real-interest-rate variance. Hence $0 \le |\lambda_1/\lambda_3| \le 1$: the current reaction of money to the nominal interest rate is smaller in magnitude and opposite in sign to the prospective reaction. However, in the limit, each reaction becomes infinite in order to keep the nominal interest rate, R_t, arbitrarily close to its target, $\bar{R}_t$, in each period.

The form of the monetary rule from Eq. (8.7) and the optimal choices for λ_1 and λ_3 lead to the equilibrium solutions for R_t, p_t, and m_t:

$$R_t = \bar{R}_t = R_{t-1} + u_t, \tag{8.16}$$

$$p_t = m_{t-1} - \left(\frac{\sigma_v^2 + \sigma_w^2}{\sigma^2}\right)(\eta_t + a_t) + \left(\frac{\sigma_\eta^2 + \sigma_a^2}{\sigma^2}\right)(v_t + w_t) \tag{8.17}$$
$$+ (1 + \beta)\bar{R}_{t-1} - (\eta_{t-1} + v_{t-1}) - \alpha_{t-1} - r_{t-1},$$

$$m_t = m_{t-1} + \left(\frac{\sigma_\eta^2 + \sigma_a^2}{\sigma^2}\right)(\eta_t + a_t + v_t + w_t) - \beta u_t + \bar{R}_{t-1} \tag{8.18}$$
$$- (\eta_{t-1} + v_{t-1}) - r_{t-1}.$$

Equation (8.18) shows that monetary growth partially accommodates the current shocks to money demand and the expected real interest rate, $\eta_t + a_t + v_t + w_t$—that is, the coefficient is $(\sigma_\eta^2 + \sigma_a^2)/\sigma^2$ (where σ^2 is the total variance). The result says that contemporaneous monetary accommodation is greater the larger the variance of money demand $(\sigma_\eta^2 + \sigma_a^2)$

---

6. The choice $\lambda_3 \to \infty$ also seems to work. However, $\lambda_3 \ge (1 + \beta)$ can be ruled out on grounds discussed by McCallum (1986, p. 140, n. 7). In particular, if $\lambda_3 \ge (1 + \beta)$, then the realization of a shock—say, η_t—causes an unstable dynamic response of the price level.

relative to that of the expected real interest rate ($\sigma_v^2 + \sigma_w^2$). Interpreting $\sigma_\eta^2 + \sigma_a^2$ as the variance of the LM curve and $\sigma_v^2 + \sigma_w^2$ as the variance of the IS curve, the results are reminiscent of those found by Poole (1970). However, in the present model, the trade-off is not between targeting nominal interest rates and targeting monetary aggregates. The targeting of the nominal interest rate is complete here, independent of the variances of money demand and the expected interest rate—that is, of the relative volatility of the LM and IS curves. In the present model, the trade-off that determines the extent of current accommodation comes, in Eq. (8.17), from the negative response of p_t to the money-demand shock, $\eta_t + a_t$, and the positive response to the real-interest-rate shock, $v_t + w_t$. (The former reflects the negative effect on prices from an increase in money demand less the positive effect from the monetary response. The latter reflects only the monetary reaction.) The extent of monetary accommodation is the one that makes the overall variance of p_t from these two sources of disturbances as small as possible.

With a one-period lag, monetary growth exhibits an inverse, one-to-one reaction to the temporary shocks ($\eta_{t-1} + v_{t-1}$ in Eq. 8.18). This response generates the reduction in expected inflation that allows the monetary authority to offset an incipient excess of R_t over $\overline{R}_t$. In particular, although the temporary shock, $\eta_t + v_t$, induces an increase in today's monetary growth, it also generates a reversal pattern where next period's monetary growth falls by more than today's increase.

A permanent shock to money demand, $a_t = \alpha_t - \alpha_{t-1}$, is accommodated partially (since it cannot be disentangled from a temporary shock), but there is no adjustment of monetary growth at date $t + 1$ when the value of a_t is revealed. Hence the reversal pattern for monetary growth does not arise for permanent shifts to money demand. (If a_t were observable at date t, then money growth would react one-to-one immediately and subsequent growth rates of money would be unchanged.)

Finally, a shock to the interest-rate target, $u_t = \overline{R}_t - \overline{R}_{t-1}$—which I assume is observable at date t—affects monetary growth by the amount $-\beta$ and thereby leaves p_t unchanged. (If any of the other disturbances—η_t, a_t, v_t, w_t—were observable, then the policymaker could similarly insulate the price level from these shocks.)

One of the prime sources of shifts to money demand, $\eta_t + a_t$, would be movements in output. The results in Eqs. (8.17) and (8.18) imply (for a given expected real interest rate) that these exogenous shifts in output would be contemporaneously negatively correlated with the price level and contemporaneously positively correlated with the money supply. Thus the results are consistent with Fair's (1979) findings about the relation between shocks to output and prices for the United States in the post–World War II period. Also, the results accord with many analyses that report a positive correlation between money and output, although the relation in this model reflects only the endogenous response of the money supply [which has been stressed by King and Plosser (1984)]. On the other hand, lagged output—that is, η_{t-1}—would be negatively correlated with current money (and prices). This result means that monetary growth would exhibit a countercyclical reaction to lagged output. This type of relation has been found for M1 growth in the post–World War II United States in Barro (1981).

Implications of the Theory for Monetary-Base Growth and Inflation

Let $\Delta R_t = R_t - R_{t-1}$, $\Delta m_t = m_t - m_{t-1}$ (the growth rate of the monetary base), and $\Delta p_t = p_t - p_{t-1}$ (the inflation rate). Equation (8.16) implies that ΔR_t is white noise. (If $\overline{R}_t$ were not a random walk but instead had a mean-reverting tendency in the long run, then the process for R_t would change accordingly.) Equations (8.17) and (8.18) prescribe the patterns for Δp_t and Δm_t that are consistent with this process for ΔR_t. These predictions about inflation and monetary-base growth are the principal empirical content of the theory.

Taking first differences of Eq. (8.18) leads to

$$\Delta m_t = \Delta m_{t-1} + \left(\frac{\sigma_\eta^2 + \sigma_a^2}{\sigma^2}\right)(\eta_t + a_t + v_t + w_t) - \beta u_t \qquad (8.19)$$

$$- \left(\frac{\sigma_\eta^2 + \sigma_a^2}{\sigma^2}\right) a_{t-1} - \left(1 + \frac{\sigma_\eta^2 + \sigma_a^2}{\sigma^2}\right)(\eta_{t-1} + v_{t-1} + w_{t-1})$$

$$+ (1 + \beta)u_{t-1} + (\eta_{t-2} + v_{t-2})$$

$$= \Delta m_{t-1} + E_t = \Delta m_{t-1} + e_t + a_1 e_{t-1} + a_2 e_{t-1},$$

where E_t is a composite error term and e_t is a white-noise disturbance. In other words, the model implies that Δm_t is an ARIMA (0, 1, 2) process. Furthermore, the theory imposes restrictions on the coefficients of this process. The unitary coefficient on Δm_{t-1} reflects the nonstationarity in monetary growth that is induced by the nonstationarity of the nominal-interest-rate target in Eq. (8.4) [and also by any nonstationarity of the expected real interest rate in Eq. (8.3)].

The two MA coefficients must satisfy the conditions

$$a_1(1 + a_2)\sigma_e^2 = \text{cov}(E_t, E_{t-1}) \tag{8.20}$$

$$= -\left(\frac{\sigma_\eta^2 + \sigma_a^2}{\sigma^2}\right)^2 \sigma_a^2 - \left(1 + \frac{\sigma_\eta^2 + \sigma_a^2}{\sigma^2}\right)^2 (\sigma_\eta^2 + \sigma_v^2)$$

$$- \left(\frac{\sigma_a^2 + \sigma_\eta^2}{\sigma^2}\right)\left(1 + \frac{\sigma_a^2 + \sigma_\eta^2}{\sigma^2}\right)\sigma_w^2 - \beta(1 + \beta)\sigma_u^2 \leq 0,$$

$$a_2\sigma_e^2 = \text{cov}(E_t, E_{t-2}) = \frac{(\sigma_\eta^2 + \sigma_a^2)(\sigma_\eta^2 + \sigma_v^2)}{\sigma^2} \geq 0, \tag{8.21}$$

where σ_e^2 is the variance of e_t. Hence, $a_1 \leq 0$ and $a_2 \geq 0$. Moreover, the magnitude of a_1 is much greater than that of a_2—one inequality that holds is $|a_1| \geq 4a_2/(1 + a_2)$ or, equivalently, $a_2 \leq |a_1|/(4 - |a_1|)$. As σ_u^2 and σ_w^2 become small, the solution approaches stationarity for $\bar{R}_t$ and r_t, and hence for monetary growth and inflation. In particular, as σ_u^2 and σ_w^2 approach zero, the solution tends toward $a_1 + a_2 = -1$.

The equation for the inflation rate comes from first-differencing of Eq. (8.17). After substituting for Δm_{t-1} on the right side [using Eq. (8.18)] and simplifying, we find that

$$\Delta p_t = \Delta p_{t-1} - \left(\frac{\sigma_v^2 + \sigma_w^2}{\sigma^2}\right)(\eta_t + a_t) \tag{8.22}$$

$$+ \left(\frac{\sigma_\eta^2 + \sigma_a^2}{\sigma^2}\right)(v_t + w_t) + \left(\frac{\sigma_v^2 + \sigma_w^2}{\sigma^2}\right)(\eta_{t-1} + a_{t-1})$$

$$- \left(1 + \frac{\sigma_\eta^2 + \sigma_a^2}{\sigma^2}\right)(v_{t-1} + w_{t-1}) + u_{t-1} + v_{t-2}$$

$$= \Delta p_{t-1} + F_t = \Delta p_{t-1} + f_t + b_1 f_{t-1} + b_2 f_{t-2},$$

where F_t is a composite error term and f_t is a white-noise disturbance (which is not generally independent of e_t). As before, Δp_t is an ARIMA $(0, 1, 2)$ process; the unitary coefficient on Δp_{t-1} again reflects mainly the nonstationarity of the nominal-interest-rate target. The two MA coefficients satisfy

$$b_1(1 + b_2)\sigma_f^2 = \text{cov}(F_t, F_{t-1}) \tag{8.23}$$

$$= -\left(\frac{\sigma_v^2 + \sigma_w^2}{\sigma^2}\right)^2 (\sigma_\eta^2 + \sigma_a^2)$$

$$- \left(\frac{\sigma_\eta^2 + \sigma_a^2}{\sigma^2}\right)\left(1 + \frac{\sigma_\eta^2 + \sigma_a^2}{\sigma^2}\right)(\sigma_v^2 + \sigma_w^2)$$

$$- \left(1 + \frac{\sigma_\eta^2 + \sigma_a^2}{\sigma^2}\right)\sigma_v^2 \le 0,$$

$$b_2\sigma_f^2 = \text{cov}(F_t, F_{t-2}) = \left(\frac{\sigma_\eta^2 + \sigma_a^2}{\sigma^2}\right)\sigma_v^2 \ge 0, \tag{8.24}$$

where σ_f^2 is the variance of f_t. Hence $b_1 \le 0$ and $b_2 \ge 0$. The magnitude of b_1 tends to be much greater than that of b_2, with $|b_1| \ge 4b_2/(1 + b_2)$ applying. Again, $\sigma_u^2 = \sigma_w^2 = 0$ implies $b_1 + b_2 = -1$.

The precise forms of the time-series processes for Δm_t and Δp_t depend on the distributional specifications for the underlying stochastic shocks. Furthermore, the results are sensitive to discrepancies between the period in the theory and that in a data set. However, the general nature of the results should be robust to these problems. Namely, first, monetary growth and inflation have a unit root if there is a unit root in the nominal interest rate; second, monetary growth and inflation each have a reversal pattern, which shows up with a short lag as a negative and substantial moving-average term; and third, a weaker but positive moving average term appears at a longer lag.

One other result involves a comparison of the variance of $R_t - R_{t-1}$—given in Eq. (8.16) as σ_u^2—with the one-period variances of monetary growth and inflation. Inspection of Eq. (8.22) shows that the variance of $\Delta p_t - \Delta p_{t-1}$ involves σ_u^2 plus other positive terms—therefore, this variance $[\text{var}(F_t)]$ exceeds that of $R_t - R_{t-1}$. Similarly, Eq. (8.19) implies that the variance of $\Delta m_t - \Delta m_{t-1}[\text{var}(E_t)]$ exceeds σ_u^2. Hence the model predicts that inflation and monetary growth are each more volatile than the nominal interest rate. This result seems to conflict with the common view that inflation moves relatively little in the short run. However, the prediction turns out to accord with the data.

Seasonals

So far, the model contains no systematic seasonals, but these are known to be important for money in the post–World War II period and for nominal interest rates before the founding of the Federal Reserve (see, for example, Kemmerer 1910, chap. 2; Macaulay 1938, chart 20; Shiller 1980, pp. 136–137; Clark 1986; Miron 1986; and Mankiw, Miron, and Weil 1987). I consider briefly here the implications of systematic seasonals in money demand and in the real interest rate. For simplicity, I now neglect the various stochastic terms considered before. Given the linearity of the model, the new effects would be additive to those from the stochastic terms.

The model with deterministic seasonals and no stochastic shocks is

$$R_t = r + p_{t+1} - p_t + T_t, \tag{8.25}$$

$$m_t - p_t = \alpha - \beta R_t + S_t, \tag{8.26}$$

$$m_t - m_{t-1} = \mu + \Sigma_t, \tag{8.27}$$

where T_t, S_t, and Σ_t are seasonal factors, μ is the mean growth rate of money, and $E_t p_{t+1} = p_{t+1}$ applies in this deterministic model. Suppose, as some have argued is true of the Federal Reserve, that the monetary authority sets Σ_t to offset the effects of T_t and S_t on the nominal interest rate. Then, with $R_t = \bar{R}$, Eq. (8.25) implies

$$p_{t+1} - p_t = \bar{R} - r - T_t.$$

Using $R_t = \bar{R}$, we find that Eq. (8.26) implies

$$m_t - m_{t-1} = p_t - p_{t-1} + S_t - S_{t-1}.$$

Substituting into this last relation for $p_t - p_{t-1}$ from above (with a one-period lag) and for $m_t - m_{t-1}$ from Eq. (8.27) yields (after setting $\mu = \bar{R} - r$)

$$\Sigma_t = -T_{t-1} + S_t - S_{t-1}.$$

This seasonal pattern for monetary growth eliminates the seasonal in the nominal interest rate—that is, achieves $R_t = \bar{R}$.

The implied relations for monetary growth and inflation are

$$\Delta m_t = \mu - T_{t-1} + S_t - S_{t-1}, \tag{8.28}$$

$$\Delta p_t = \mu - T_{t-1}. \tag{8.29}$$

Note that, if the seasonal applied to money demand (S_t) but not to the real interest rate (T_t), then the seasonal in monetary growth would eliminate the seasonal in inflation along with that in the nominal interest rate. But, if there is a seasonal in the real interest rate, then a seasonal in inflation remains.

Because the seasonals in money demand and the real interest rate were assumed to be deterministic and understood by the monetary authority, the seasonal in the nominal interest rate could be eliminated by introducing a deterministic seasonal into monetary growth. More generally, the seasonals in money demand and the real interest rate could evolve stochastically and also be unknown to the monetary authority. But, even in this case, the policymaker could remove the seasonal in the nominal interest rate by pursuing the type of feedback reaction to the nominal interest rate that was considered before. Hence, if the elimination of seasonals in nominal interest rates is deemed to be desirable (on public-finance grounds?), then the possibility of removing them in this way strengthens the case for interest-rate targeting.

Empirical Findings

The empirical results involve seasonally unadjusted data since 1890 on nominal interest rates (four- to six-month prime commercial paper),[7] the monetary base (unadjusted for changes in reserve requirements), the consumer price index (CPI-U, available since 1913, except that the index without the shelter component was used since 1970), and the producer price index (PPI, all commodities). All variables are monthly but observed at the quarterly intervals of January, April, July, and October. The identification of the period in the theory with quarters is, of course, arbitrary. (Recall that the period in the theory relates especially to the flow of information about the price level.)

7. Results for the nominal interest rate are similar with the three-month loan rate used by Mankiw, Miron, and Weil (1987).

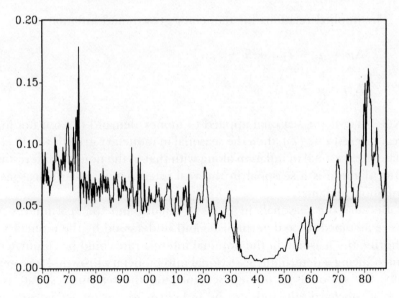

Figure 8.1. Interest rate on commercial paper, 1860–1987

The underlying data are monthly averages of daily figures for interest rates and the monetary base (except that before August 1917 the figures on the monetary base are at the end of each month). The price indexes are an average of observations during each month, although for the CPI some of the components are sampled less frequently than once per month. The three-month spacing between each observation should minimize the problems related to time-averaged data. That is, the formulation approximates point-in-time data observed once per quarter.

Figures 8.1–8.4 depict the four time series under study.[8] All variables

8. The nominal interest rate applies to four- to six-month commercial paper (six-month paper in recent years), as reported since 1890 in U.S. Board of Governors of the Federal Reserve System, *Banking and Monetary Statistics; Banking and Monetary Statistics, 1941–1970; Annual Statistical Digest, 1970–1979,* and later issues; and the *Federal Reserve Bulletin.* Earlier data, from Macaulay (1938, app. table 10), refer to sixty- to ninety-day commercial paper. (These were adjusted upward by 0.014 to merge with the other series in 1890.) The monetary base since 1914 comes from the Federal Reserve sources noted above. Earlier data come from the National Bureau of Economic Research. The CPI since 1913 is from the Bureau of Labor Statistics (CPI-U, with the CPI less shelter used since 1970 to avoid problems with mortgage interest costs). The PPI (all commodities) since 1913 comes from the Bureau of Labor Statistics. Data from 1890 to 1912 are from U.S. Department of Labor, 1928 (kindly provided by Jeff Miron). Data before 1890 are from Warren and Pearson (1933, table 1).

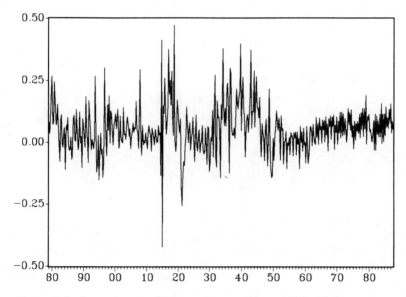

Figure 8.2. Growth rate of the monetary base, 1879–1987

are measured at annual rates. Figure 8.1 shows the nominal interest rate from 1860 to 1987, Fig. 8.2 the growth rate of the monetary base from 1879 to 1987, Fig. 8.3 the growth rate of the consumer price index from 1913 to 1987, and Fig. 8.4 the growth rate of the producer price index from 1860 to 1987.

Table 8.1 contains regression results for the recent period, 1954:1 to 1987:4. Starting in 1954 avoids the extremely low nominal interest rates through the early 1950s, for which the lower bound of zero would be significant (so nominal interest rates could not be approximated as a random walk). Also, this sample excludes any effects on measured price indexes from the controls during World War II and the Korean War.

The basic format of the empirical results consists of estimated equations for an ARMA representation with systematic seasonals,

$$Y_t = q_1 S_{1t} + q_2 S_{2t} + q_3 S_{3t} + q_4 S_{4t} + \rho Y_{t-1} + e_t \tag{8.30}$$
$$+ c_1 e_{t-1} + c_2 e_{t-2} + c_3 e_{t-3} + c_4 e_{t-4},$$

where e_t is a white-noise error and Y_t represents R_t, Δm_t, Δp_t, or $\Delta(\text{PPI})_t$. [R is the commercial paper rate, Δm is the growth rate of the monetary base, Δp is the growth rate of the CPI, and $\Delta(\text{PPI})$ is the growth rate of

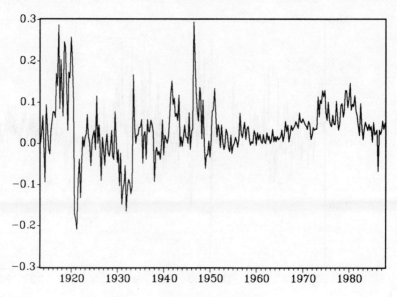

Figure 8.3. Inflation rate (CPI), 1913–1987

the producer price index.][9] The variable S_{1t} is a seasonal dummy for the first quarter (1 for January, 0 otherwise), and similarly for S_{2t} (for April), S_{3t} (for July), and S_{4t} (for October). For R_t as the dependent variable, the hypothesis under a regime of interest-rate targeting is $q_1 = q_2 = q_3 = q_4 = 0$ (or possibly a constant), $\rho = 1$, $c_1 = c_2 = c_3 = c_4 = 0$. For Δm_t, Δp_t, and $\Delta(\text{PPI})_t$, the model under interest-rate targeting suggests nonzero values for q_1, q_2, q_3, and q_4, $\rho = 1$, $c_1 \leq 0$, and $c_2 \geq 0$, with $|c_1|$ much greater than c_2 and $c_1 + c_2 \geq -1$. More generally, the theory suggests that the moving-average coefficients will be negative and of substantial magnitude over the near term (such as c_1), and positive but of much smaller size later on.

Aside from the estimated coefficients and (asymptotic) standard errors, Table 8.1 reports the following statistics:

$Q(10)$ Box–Pierce Q-statistic for serial correlation of residuals with 10 lags, with degrees of freedom and asymptotic significance level (based on the χ^2 distribution) shown in parentheses.

9. Schwert (1987b, table 9) showed that an ARIMA(0, 1, 4) process works well on seasonally adjusted monthly data for the growth rate of the monetary base, CPI inflation, and PPI inflation.

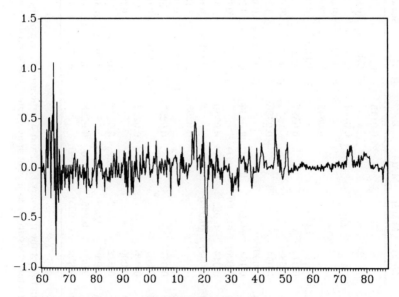

Figure 8.4. Inflation rate (PPI), 1860–1987

seasonals   Likelihood-ratio statistic (equal to $-2 \cdot \log$ of likelihood
             ratio) for the equation with seasonals against the null
             hypothesis of the same equation except for no seasonal-
             ity ($q_1 = q_2 = q_3 = q_4$), with the asymptotic significance
             level (based on the χ^2 distribution with three degrees of
             freedom) shown in parentheses.

The random-walk model, $R_t = R_{t-1}$ + constant (where the constant
could be set to zero here), is satisfactory for the nominal interest rate in
the post-1954 period. Notably, $Q(10)$ from line 1 of Table 8.1 has a
significance level of 0.18, and the likelihood-ratio statistic for seasonals
has a significance level of 0.67.[10] The unrestricted estimate of R_{t-1} is
0.934, s.e. = 0.030. The implied "t-value" relative to unity is 2.2, which is
below the 0.10 critical value of 2.6 from the Dickey–Fuller test (Fuller
1976, table 8.5.2, the section for $\hat{\tau}_\mu$). Given the random-walk-like behav-

10. Weak evidence of seasonality in the nominal interest rate appears in some subsamples of the post-1954 period—for example, for 1954:1–1959:4 and the 1970s. However,
the seasonals look very different for these two periods. The seasonal found for the 1954–
1959 period seems to be consistent with the results of Diller (1969, chap. 3).

Table 8.1. Regression results for 1954:1–1987:4

Dependent variable Y_t [a]	Seasonal constants[b]					Y_{t-1}	Estimated MA coefficients				σ^c	$Q(10)^d$	Seasonals[e]
	C	S_1	S_2	S_3	S_4		MA(1)	MA(2)	MA(3)	MA(4)			
(1) R	0.000 (0.001)					1					0.0115	14.0 (10, 0.18)	1.6 (0.67)
(2)	0.005 (0.002)					0.934 (0.030)					0.0114	12.0 (9, 0.22)	1.7 (0.65)
(3) Δm	0.000 (0.007)					1					0.0845	631 (10, 0.000)	195 (0.000)
(4)		0.045 (0.006)	−0.082 (0.006)	0.097 (0.006)	−0.058 (0.006)	1	−0.791 (0.088)	−0.074 (0.088)			0.0327	9.2 (8, 0.33)	109 (0.000)
(5)		0.845 (0.006)	−0.081 (0.009)	0.097 (0.006)	−0.056 (0.011)	0.990 (0.098)	−0.796 (0.128)	−0.054 (0.090)			0.0326	9.3 (7, 0.24)	129 (0.000)
(6)		0.045 (0.006)	−0.082 (0.006)	0.097 (0.006)	−0.057 (0.006)	1	−0.754 (0.089)	−0.163 (0.090)	−0.063 (0.090)	0.148 (0.091)	0.0334	11.3 (6, 0.08)	119 (0.000)
(7)		0.047 (0.007)	−0.079 (0.010)	0.097 (0.006)	−0.053 (0.012)	0.952 (0.114)	−0.733 (0.144)	−0.014 (0.093)	−0.093 (0.093)	0.132 (0.091)	0.0330	9.0 (5, 0.11)	83 (0.000)
(8) Δp	0.000 (0.003)					1					0.0298	41 (10, 0.000)	18.1 (0.001)
(9)		−0.005 (0.004)	0.015 (0.004)	0.004 (0.004)	−0.013 (0.004)	1	−0.665 (0.088)	0.087 (0.087)			0.0235	14.6 (8, 0.07)	22.5 (0.000)
(10)		−0.003 (0.005)	0.017 (0.005)	0.007 (0.005)	−0.010 (0.005)	0.944 (0.074)	−0.647 (0.115)	0.096 (0.090)			0.0232	12.5 (7, 0.09)	23.4 (0.001)
(11)		−0.005 (0.004)	0.015 (0.004)	0.004 (0.004)	−0.013 (0.004)	1	−0.666 (0.088)	0.072 (0.088)	0.262 (0.089)	−0.022 (0.091)	0.0233	10.9 (6, 0.09)	14.1 (0.005)
(12)		0.000 (0.005)	0.019 (0.005)	0.010 (0.006)	−0.006 (0.006)	0.870 (0.088)	−0.592 (0.126)	0.089 (0.092)	0.245 (0.095)	0.020 (0.104)	0.0228	6.7 (5, 0.25)	11.5 (0.01)

Source: See note 8.

a. The dependent variables are R, the commercial paper rate; Δm, the growth rate of the monetary base; and Δp, the growth rate of the CPI. The underlying data are for January, April, July, and October of each year. Interest rates are measured at annual rates. The standard error (s.e.) appears in parens.

b. S_1, S_2, S_3, and S_4 are seasonal constants for each of the four quarters.

c. σ is the standard error (s.e.) of estimate.

d. $Q(10)$ is the Q-statistic for serial correlation of residuals, based on 10 lags of the residuals. Degrees of freedom and significance level for the statistic are in parentheses.

e. Seasonals is a likelihood-ratio test for significance of seasonal dummies, versus the alternative of a single constant. This statistic is ior of the nominal interest rate, the theory's other predictions should apply to monetary-base growth and inflation.

The estimated equation in the ARIMA(0, 1, 2) form for the growth rate of the monetary base appears in line 4 of the table. The equation exhibits strong seasonality, with a likelihood-ratio statistic of 109. The Q-statistic for serial correlation of residuals is 9.2, which is significant at only the 0.33 level. The estimated MA(1) coefficient is highly significant, -0.79, s.e. $= 0.09$, and conforms in sign and rough magnitude with the model's predictions. Corresponding to an MA(1) value of -0.79, the model implies $0 \le MA(2) \le 0.25$. The estimated MA(2) coefficient on line 4 is -0.07, s.e. $= 0.09$, which is insignificantly below zero, but significantly less than 0.25.

Line 6 of the table shows that the inclusion of more moving-average terms leads to an estimated MA(4) coefficient of 0.15, s.e. $= 0.09$. Thus the results accord with the prediction that the moving-average terms will be negative and large in magnitude over the near term (lag 1), and positive but small in size later on (in this case at lag 4, but not at lags 2 or 3). Lines 5 and 7 show that freely estimated coefficients of Δm_{t-1} (0.990, s.e. $= 0.098$; 0.952, s.e. $= 0.114$, respectively) differ insignificantly from one according to the Dickey–Fuller test.[11]

The ARIMA(0, 1, 2) form for the CPI inflation rate appears on line 9 of Table 8.1. The seasonals are again significant, although less dramatically than for the monetary base. The Q-statistic is now significant at the 0.07 level. The estimated MA(1) coefficient, -0.66, s.e. $= 0.09$, again accords with the theory. Corresponding to MA(1) $= -0.66$, the theory predicts $0 \le MA(2) \le 0.20$, which is consistent with the estimated value for MA(2) of 0.09, s.e. $= 0.09$. The inclusion of more moving-average terms on line 11 leads to MA(3) $= 0.26$, s.e. $= 0.09$. Finally, lines 10 and 12 show that freely estimated coefficients for Δp_{t-1} are insignificantly different from one (0.944, s.e. $= 0.074$; 0.870, s.e. $= 0.088$, respectively).

The underlying theory regarded the nominal interest rate as controllable by the monetary authority but treated the expected real interest rate as exogenous with respect to monetary variables. Hence monetary policy affected the nominal interest rate only by influencing the expected rate of inflation. Many economists are skeptical about this model because they think of nominal interest rates as highly flexible and of

---

11. Schwert's (1987a, table 3) Monte Carlo results indicate that the Dickey–Fuller test for a unit root works well if the underlying process is ARIMA(0, 1, 1). Therefore this test should be appropriate in the present context.

actual and expected inflation rates as sticky in the short run. The results in Table 8.1 conflict with this view in that the residual standard deviation for quarterly CPI inflation—2.4% per year on line 9—is about double that of the nominal interest rate—1.2% per year on line 1. Similarly, as the theory predicts, the residual standard deviation for monetary base growth—3.3% per year on line 4—exceeds that for the nominal interest rate.[12]

Table 8.2 shows comparable results for the interwar period, 1922:1–1940:4. There is now some indication of predictable movements in the nominal interest rate. For example, in line 2 of the table, the estimated MA(1) coefficient is 0.24, s.e. = 0.12, and the likelihood-ratio statistic for the seasonals has a significance level of 0.04. However, the seasonal coefficients are small in magnitude. The unrestricted estimate of R_{t-1} on line 3 (0.949, s.e. = 0.029) again differs insignificantly from one. Overall, these results for the interest rate turn out to be a middle ground between those shown in Table 8.1 for the post-1954 period and those examined below for the pre-1914 period, which reveal substantial predictable movements in the nominal interest rate.

The ARIMA(0, 1, 2) process for monetary-base growth, shown in line 5 of Table 8.2, again exhibits pronounced seasonality, although the pattern differs from that for the post-1954 period. The MA(1) coefficient is substantially negative (−0.66, s.e. = 0.12), but the new element is the significantly negative MA(2) value (−0.28, s.e. = 0.12). Even with the inclusion of more moving-average terms (line 7), the results do not reveal the eventually positive terms predicted by the theory. However, the coefficients of Δm_{t-1} (lines 6 and 8) still differ insignificantly from one.

For CPI inflation, the ARIMA(0, 1, 2) process on line 10 looks similar to that estimated for the post-1954 period. There is, however, no appearance of positive MA coefficients at longer lags (line 12). The estimated coefficients for Δp_{t-1} (lines 11 and 13) still differ insignificantly from one.

Table 8.3 shows results for the period 1890:1–1913:4, which applies to the gold standard and precedes the founding of the Federal Reserve. For this period the nominal interest rate may be stationary and a coeffi-

<hr>

12. The estimated residual standard errors for inflation and monetary growth correspond to σ_f and σ_e for Eqs. (8.22) and (8.19), respectively. The corresponding standard errors for F_t and E_t are 0.028 and 0.042, respectively. These values each exceed the residual standard error for the nominal interest rate, 0.012, as predicted by the theory.

Table 8.2. Regression results for 1922:1–1940:4[a]

Dependent variable Y_t	C	S_1	S_2	S_3	S_4	Y_{t-1}	MA(1)	MA(2)	MA(3)	MA(4)	$\hat\sigma$	Q(10)	Seasonals
(1) R	-0.0007 (0.0005)					1					0.0047	16.6 (10, 0.09)	6.0 (0.12)
(2)		-0.0014 (0.0010)	0.0001 (0.0010)	-0.0024 (0.0010)	0.0009 (0.0010)	1	0.235 (0.119)				0.0045	10.7 (9, 0.30)	8.7 (0.04)
(3)		0.0001 (0.0014)	0.0016 (0.0013)	-0.0010 (0.0013)	0.0022 (0.0013)	0.949 (0.029)	0.259 (0.123)				0.0045	9.1 (8, 0.32)	8.7 (0.04)
(4) Δm	0.003 (0.015)					1					0.1346	21.3 (10, 0.02)	19.4 (0.000)
(5)		-0.090 (0.022)	-0.011 (0.022)	0.075 (0.022)	0.039 (0.022)	1	-0.659 (0.122)	-0.276 (0.122)			0.0957	10.4 (8, 0.25)	16.4 (0.001)
(6)		-0.086 (0.038)	-0.010 (0.023)	0.076 (0.022)	0.045 (0.032)	0.946 (0.250)	-0.740 (0.282)	-0.125 (0.132)			0.0959	10.1 (7, 0.19)	23 (0.000)
(7)		-0.091 (0.023)	-0.011 (0.023)	0.076 (0.023)	0.040 (0.023)	1	-0.576 (0.125)	-0.216 (0.127)	0.043 (0.127)	-0.183 (0.128)	0.0986	13.2 (6, 0.04)	9.6 (0.02)
(8)		-0.061 (0.047)	-0.005 (0.025)	0.079 (0.023)	0.063 (0.039)	0.754 (0.343)	-0.491 (0.370)	-0.088 (0.153)	0.134 (0.130)	-0.085 (0.147)	0.0986	13.9 (5, 0.02)	8.7 (0.04)
(9) Δp	0.000 (0.008)					1					0.0669	18.8 (10, 0.04)	12.1 (0.009)
(10)		-0.036 (0.012)	0.007 (0.012)	0.034 (0.012)	-0.001 (0.012)	1	-0.640 (0.120)	0.136 (0.120)			0.0536	3.5 (8, 0.90)	12.8 (0.007)
(11)		-0.035 (0.012)	-0.002 (0.014)	0.027 (0.013)	0.001 (0.012)	0.745 (0.202)	-0.509 (0.233)	0.188 (0.129)			0.0506	2.3 (7, 0.94)	15.8 (0.002)
(12)		-0.037 (0.012)	0.006 (0.012)	0.033 (0.012)	-0.001 (0.012)	1	-0.658 (0.121)	0.105 (0.122)	0.030 (0.122)	-0.229 (0.122)	0.0531	2.5 (6, 0.87)	15.0 (0.003)
(13)		-0.035 (0.012)	-0.002 (0.019)	0.027 (0.017)	0.001 (0.012)	0.749 (0.443)	-0.494 (0.458)	0.167 (0.167)	0.096 (0.199)	-0.145 (0.201)	0.0513	2.4 (5, 0.79)	12.4 (0.008)

a. See notes to Table 8.1.

Table 8.3. Regression results for 1890:1–1913:4[a]

Dependent variable Y_t	C	S_1	S_2	S_3	S_4	Y_{t-1}	MA(1)	MA(2)	MA(3)	MA(4)	$\hat{\sigma}$	Q(10)	Seasonals
(1) R	0.000 (0.001)					1					0.0109	23.8 (10, 0.009)	18.6 (0.001)
(2)		0.057 (0.002)	0.056 (0.002)	0.056 (0.002)	0.062 (0.002)	0	0.499 (0.106)	0.220 (0.106)	0.264 (0.107)		0.0087	11.7 (7, 0.11)	17.9 (0.001)
(3)		0.046 (0.023)	0.046 (0.021)	0.046 (0.021)	0.053 (0.021)	0.165 (0.372)	0.342 (0.387)	0.133 (0.220)	0.232 (0.135)		0.0087	10.9 (6, 0.09)	17.1 (0.001)
(4) Δm	0.000 (0.011)					1					0.1059	42 (10, 0.000)	49 (0.000)
(5)		0.049 (0.013)	0.011 (0.013)	-0.009 (0.013)	0.104 (0.013)	0	0.279 (0.105)				0.0658	7.2 (9, 0.62)	39 (0.000)
(6)		0.070 (0.040)	0.021 (0.022)	-0.007 (0.014)	0.102 (0.014)	-0.206[b] (0.364)	0.491 (0.379)				0.0660	6.6 (8, 0.58)	39 (0.000)
(7) Δ(PPI)	0.000 (0.016)					1					0.160	27 (10, 0.005)	25 (0.000)
(8)		-0.038 (0.023)	0.004 (0.022)	-0.024 (0.022)	0.088 (0.022)	0.229[b] (0.097)				-0.349 (0.106)	0.106	7.2 (8, 0.52)	26 (0.000)

a. PPI is the producer price index. See Table 8.1 for additional notes.
b. Estimated coefficient is significantly below 1.0 at less than 0.05 level according to the Dickey–Fuller test (Fuller 1976, table 8.5.2, section for $\hat{\tau}_\mu$).

cient of zero for R_{t-1} is satisfactory (lines 2 and 3 of the table). However, the estimated coefficient of R_{t-1} on line 3 (0.16, s.e. = 0.37) also differs insignificantly from one according to the 0.10 critical value of the Dickey–Fuller test. There is now substantial short-run predictability of movements in the nominal interest rate; in line 2 the likelihood-ratio statistic for seasonality has a significance level of 0.001. In addition, the first three MA coefficients are positive and significant (0.50, s.e. = 0.11; 0.22, s.e. = 0.11; 0.26, s.e. = 0.11).

Given the absence of interest-rate targeting, the behavior of the monetary base and the price level before 1914 should differ from that found in the later periods. The results suggest that the growth rate of the monetary base before 1914 (which coincides in this period with currency in circulation) is stationary, and a coefficient of zero for Δm_{t-1} is satisfactory (lines 5 and 6 of Table 8.3). (The estimated coefficient of Δm_{t-1} is −0.21, s.e. = 0.36, which differs significantly from 1 at about the 0.01 level according to the Dickey–Fuller test.) There are significant seasonals in monetary-base growth, as shown on line 5 by the significance level of 0.000 for the likelihood-ratio statistic.[13] However, this seasonal in the monetary base did not eliminate the seasonal in the nominal interest rate. In fact, because the United States was on the gold standard, the behavior of the monetary base (and the U.S. price level) would have been largely constrained to be consistent with the world price level, including its seasonal pattern if it had one. Therefore it would not generally be possible under this type of monetary system to choose a seasonal in the monetary base that removed the seasonal in the nominal interest rate.

Aside from the seasonals, the results for the growth rate of the monetary base on line 5 indicate a positive MA(1) coefficient, 0.28, s.e. = 0.11. The simple specification that monetary-base growth is an MA(1) with seasonals appears satisfactory according to the Q-statistic.

Viewed jointly, the results for the nominal interest rate and the monetary base in Tables 8.1–8.3 are consistent with the viewpoint (expressed recently by Shiller 1980, Miron 1986, and Mankiw, Miron, and Weil 1987 that shifts in monetary policy after the founding of the Federal Reserve in 1914 were responsible for the elimination of predictable tem-

---

13. The finding of significant seasonals in monetary-base growth before 1914 accords in a general way with Kemmerer (1910, chap. 6) but seems to conflict with results reported by Clark (1986, pp. 106ff.).

porary movements, including seasonals, in the nominal interest rate. The present analysis identifies these shifts in monetary policy with specific changes in the process for monetary-base growth. Namely, the growth rate became nonstationary, a substantially negative MA(1) coefficient appeared, and the seasonal patterns changed. Moreover, the results for the interwar period suggest that the Federal Reserve did not get the monetary process right immediately. Only in the post-1954 period does all the short-term predictability of nominal interest rate movements seem to disappear. On the other hand, the results are consistent with the idea that the elimination of the international gold standard—also occurring in 1914—was responsible for the changed behavior of nominal interest rates. The elimination of the gold standard may have been a prerequisite for the implementation of a monetary policy that successfully targeted nominal interest rates (see Clark 1986, pp. 85ff., but also Goodfriend 1988).

Results for the PPI inflation rate from 1890 to 1913 appear on lines 7 and 8 of Table 8.3. This inflation rate exhibits significant seasonality and appears to be stationary (the estimated coefficient of Δp_{t-1} on line 8 of Table 8.3 is 0.23, s.e. = 0.10, which is significantly below 1). The estimated MA coefficients are insignificant, except for a negative MA(4) (-0.35, s.e. = 0.11), which might reflect stochastic variation in seasonals. The CPI is unavailable for this period, except for rough estimates on an annual basis. (For the later samples, the time-series parameters estimated for PPI inflation accord in a rough way with those for CPI inflation.)

Observations

Theoretical reasoning suggests that interest-rate targeting is a reasonable guide for monetary policy. In a model where expected real interest rates and output are exogenous with respect to monetary variables, the central bank influences nominal interest rates by altering expected rates of inflation. It turns out that the monetary authority can come arbitrarily close to meeting its (time-varying) target for the nominal interest rate, even while holding down the forecast variance of the price level. The latter objective pins down the extent of accommodation of the money supply to shifts in the demand for money. The greater the variance of shocks to money demand (that is, of the LM curve) relative to that of the expected real interest rate (that is, the IS curve), the greater the degree of accommodation.

Incipient increases in the nominal interest rate (caused by shocks to money demand or the expected real interest rate) lead in the usual way to monetary expansion—for example, to open-market purchases of bonds. This response lowers expected inflation because the influx of money is temporary. That is, the central bank plans to take back later some of today's infusion of money, and the expectation of this behavior lowers anticipated growth rates of money and prices. Therefore, the nominal interest rate falls back toward its target value even though the expected real interest rate does not change.

If the target nominal interest rate moves as a random walk, the successful targeting by the central bank implies that the nominal interest rate also follows this pattern. Given this policy of interest-rate targeting—and the assumed specification for money demand and the expected real interest rate—the growth rate of the monetary base and the price level must follow ARIMA(0, 1, 2) processes. The unit roots in these processes reflect mainly the nonstationarity of the nominal interest rate. The moving-average terms correspond to the responses to temporary shocks—in particular, the tendency for infusions of money (in response to incipient rises in the nominal interest rate) to be followed by removal of money in the future.

Empirical evidence for the United States since 1890 accords in the main with the theoretical propositions. In particular, the results indicate that shifts in monetary policy after the founding of the Fed in 1914 led to the elimination of predictable temporary movements, including seasonals, in the nominal interest rate (on short-term commercial paper). The results identify the changes in monetary policy with specific changes in the process for monetary-base growth. Namely, the growth rate became nonstationary, a substantially negative moving-average term appeared (indicating the tendency for reversals in monetary growth), and the seasonal patterns changed. The results suggest that it was not until the post-1954 period that the Fed smoothed the nominal interest rate in the sense of achieving nearly random-walk-like behavior in this rate.

The empirical work could be usefully extended to consider in more detail the joint determination of the nominal interest rate, monetary base, and the price level. Such a joint treatment would allow testing of the model's detailed predictions about the cross-relations among the time-series processes. However, these predictions tend to be sensitive to parts of the specification—such as the independence of the underlying shocks—that were not crucial for the results obtained so far. Thus it will probably be necessary to make the model less restrictive in this respect. With these extensions, it would be possible to estimate parameters, such as the interest sensitivity of money demand and the relative variances of the different disturbances.

References

Barro, R. J. 1976. "Rational Expectations and the Role of Monetary Policy." *Journal of Monetary Economics* 2:1–32.

——— 1979. "On the Determination of the Public Debt." *Journal of Political Economy* 87:940–971.

——— 1981. "Unanticipated Money Growth and Economic Activity in the United States." In *Money, Expectations, and Business Cycles,* ed. R. J. Barro. New York: Academic Press, pp. 137–169.

Brunner, K. 1968. "The Role of Money and Monetary Policy." *Federal Reserve Bank of St. Louis Review* 9–24.

Brunner, K., A. Cukierman, and A. H. Meltzer. 1980. "Stagflation, Persistent Unemployment, and the Permanence of Economic Shocks." *Journal of Monetary Economics* 6:467–492.

Clark, T. A. 1986. "Interest Rate Seasonals and the Federal Reserve." *Journal of Political Economy* 94:76–125.

Diller, S. 1969. *The Seasonal Variation of Interest Rates.* New York: Columbia University Press.

Fair, R. C. 1979. "An Analysis of the Accuracy of Four Macroeconometric Models." *Journal of Political Economy* 87:701–718.

Friedman, M. 1968. "The Role of Monetary Policy." *American Economic Review* 58:1–17.

Fuller, W. A. 1976. *Introduction to Statistical Time Series.* New York: Wiley.

Goodfriend, M. 1987. "Interest Rate Smoothing and Price Level Trend-Stationarity." *Journal of Monetary Economics* 19:335–348.

——— 1988. "Central Banking under the Gold Standard." *Carnegie-Rochester Conference Series on Public Policy* 29:85–124.

Hetzel, R. L. 1987. "A Critique of Theories of Money Stock Determination." Unpublished manuscript. Federal Reserve Bank of Richmond.

Kemmerer, E. W. 1910. "Seasonal Variations in the Relative Demand for

Money and Capital in the United States." Washington, D.C.: U.S. Government Printing Office.

Kimbrough, K. P. 1986. "The Optimum Quantity of Money Rule in the Theory of Public Finance." *Journal of Monetary Economics* 18:277–284.

King, R. G., and C. I. Plosser. 1984. "Money, Credit and Prices in a Real Business Cycle." *American Economic Review* 74:363–380.

Lucas, R. E. 1973. "Some International Evidence on Output-Inflation Tradeoffs." *American Economic Review* 63:326–334.

———— 1984. "Money in a Theory of Finance." *Carnegie-Rochester Conference Series on Public Policy* 21:9–45.

Macaulay, F. R. 1938. *The Movements of Interest Rates, Bond Yields and Stock Prices in the United States since 1856.* New York: National Bureau of Economic Research.

Mankiw, N. G. 1987. "The Optimal Collection of Seigniorage: Theory and Evidence." *Journal of Monetary Economics* 20:327–341.

Mankiw, N. G., J. A. Miron, and D. N. Weil. 1987. "The Adjustment of Expectations to a Change in Regime: A Study of the Founding of the Federal Reserve." *American Economic Review* 77:358–374.

McCallum, B. T. 1981. "Price Level Determinacy with an Interest Rate Policy Rule and Rational Expectations." *Journal of Monetary Economics* 8:319–329.

———— 1983. "On Non-Uniqueness in Rational Expectations Models: An Attempt at Perspective." *Journal of Monetary Economics* 11:139–168.

———— 1986. "Some Issues Concerning Interest Rate Pegging, Price Level Determinacy, and the Real Bills Doctrine." *Journal of Monetary Economics* 17:135–160.

Miron, J. A. 1986. "Financial Panics, the Seasonality of the Nominal Interest Rate, and the Founding of the Fed." *American Economic Review* 76:125–140.

Poole, W. 1970. "Optimal Choice of Monetary Policy Instruments in a Simple Stochastic Macro Model." *Quarterly Journal of Economics* 84:197–216.

Sargent, T. J., and N. Wallace. 1975. "Rational Expectations, the Optimal Monetary instrument, and the Optimal Money Supply Rule." *Journal of Political Economy* 83:241–254.

Schwert, G. W. 1987a. "Tests for Unit Roots: A Monte Carlo Investigation." Unpublished manuscript. Rochester, N.Y.: University of Rochester.

———— 1987b. "Effects of Model Specification on Tests for Unit Roots in Macroeconomic Data." Unpublished manuscript. Rochester, N.Y.: University of Rochester.

Shiller, R. J. 1980. "Can the Fed Control Real Interest Rates?" In *Rational*

Expectations and Economic Policy, ed. S. Fischer. Chicago: University of Chicago Press.

U.S. Department of Labor. 1928. *Index of Wholesale Prices on Pre-War Basis.* Washington, D.C.: U.S. Government Printing Office.

Warren, G. F., and F. A. Pearson. 1933. *Prices.* New York: Wiley.

PART III

Fiscal Policy

9 The Ricardian Approach to Budget Deficits

In recent years there has been much discussion about U.S. budget deficits. Many economists and other observers have viewed these deficits as harmful to the U.S. and world economies. The supposed harmful effects include high real interest rates, low saving, low rates of economic growth, large current-account deficits in the United States and other countries with large budget deficits, and either a high or low dollar (depending apparently on the time period). But the crisis scenario has been hard to maintain along with the robust performance of the U.S. economy since late 1982. This performance features high average growth rates of real GNP, declining unemployment, much lower inflation, a sharp decrease in nominal interest rates and some decline in expected real interest rates, high values of real investment expenditures, and (until October 1987) a dramatic boom in the stock market.

Persistent budget deficits have increased economists' interest in theories and evidence about fiscal policy. At the same time, the conflict between standard predictions and actual outcomes in the U.S. economy has, I think, increased economists' willingness to consider approaches that depart from the standard paradigm. In this chapter I focus on the alternative theory that is associated with the name of David Ricardo.

The Standard Model of Budget Deficits

Before examining the Ricardian approach, consider the standard model. The starting point is the assumption that the substitution of a

From *Journal of Economic Perspectives* (1989) 3(2):37–54. I am grateful for support of research from the National Science Foundation. Also, I appreciate the high-quality comments provided by the editors.

budget deficit for current taxation leads to an expansion of aggregate consumer demand. In other words, desired private saving rises by less than the tax cut, so that desired national saving declines. It follows for a closed economy that the expected real interest rate would have to rise to restore equality between desired national saving and investment demand. The higher real interest rate crowds out investment, which shows up in the long run as a smaller stock of productive capital. Therefore, in the language of Modigliani (1961), the public debt is an intergenerational burden in that it leads to a smaller stock of capital for future generations. Similar reasoning applies to pay-as-you-go social security programs, as has been stressed by Feldstein (1974). An increase in the scope of these programs raises the aggregate demand for goods, and thereby leads to a higher real interest rate and a smaller stock of productive capital.

In an open economy, a small country's budget deficits or social security programs would have negligible effects on the real interest rate in international capital markets. Therefore, in the standard analysis, the home country's decision to substitute a budget deficit for current taxes leads mainly to increased borrowing from abroad rather than to a higher real interest rate. That is, budget deficits lead to current-account deficits. Expected real interest rates rise for the home country only if it is large enough to influence world markets or if the increased national debt induces foreign lenders to demand higher expected returns on this country's obligations. In any event, there is a weaker tendency for a country's budget deficits to crowd out its domestic investment in the short run and its stock of capital in the long run. However, the current-account deficits show up in the long run as a lower stock of national wealth—and correspondingly higher claims by foreigners.

If the whole world runs budget deficits or expands the scale of its social insurance programs, then real interest rates rise on international capital markets, and crowding out of investment occurs in each country. Correspondingly, the world's stock of capital is lower in the long run. These effects for the world parallel those for a single closed economy, as discussed before.

The Ricardian Alternative

The Ricardian modification to the standard analysis begins with the observation that, for a given path of government spending, a deficit-financed cut in current taxes leads to higher future taxes that have the same present value as the initial cut. This result follows from the government's budget constraint, which equates total expenditures for each period (including interest payments) to revenues from taxation or other sources and the net issue of interest-bearing public debt. Abstracting from chain-letter cases where the public debt can grow forever at the rate of interest or higher, the present value of taxes (and other revenues) cannot change unless the government changes the present value of its expenditures. This point amounts to economists' standard notion of the absence of a free lunch—government spending must be paid for now or later, with the total present value of receipts fixed by the total present value of spending. Hence, holding fixed the path of government expenditures and nontax revenues, a cut in today's taxes must be matched by a corresponding increase in the present value of future taxes.[1]

Suppose now that households' demands for goods depend on the expected present value of taxes—that is, each household subtracts its share of this present value from the expected present value of income to determine a net wealth position. Then fiscal policy would affect aggregate consumer demand only if it altered the expected present value of taxes. But the preceding argument was that the present value of taxes would not change as long as the present value of spending did not change. Therefore the substitution of a budget deficit for current taxes (or any other rearrangement of the timing of taxes) has no impact on the aggregate demand for goods. In this sense, budget deficits and taxation have equivalent effects on the economy—hence the term *Ricardian equivalence theorem*.[2] To put the equivalence result another way, a decrease in

1. The calculations use the government's interest rate in each period to calculate present values, and assume perfect foresight with respect to future government expenditures and taxes. For further discussion see McCallum (1984) and Barro (1989).

2. The term, Ricardian equivalence theorem, was introduced to macroeconomists by Buchanan (1976). After O'Driscoll (1977) documented Ricardo's reservations about this result, some economists have referred to the equivalence finding as being non-Ricardian. But, as far as I have been able to discover, Ricardo (1951) was the first to articulate this theory. Therefore, the attribution of the equivalence theorem to Ricardo is appropriate even if he had doubts about some of the theorem's assumptions. As to whether the presence of this idea in Ricardo's writings is important for scientific progress, I would refer to Rosenberg's (1976, p. 79) general views on innovations in the social sciences: "what often happens in economics is that, as concern mounts over a particular problem . . . an increasing number of professionals commit their time and energies to it. We then eventually realize that there were all sorts of treatments of the subject in the earlier literature . . . We then proceed to read much of our more sophisticated present-day understanding back into the work of earlier writers whose analysis was inevitably more fragmentary and incomplete

the government's saving (that is, a current budget deficit) leads to an offsetting increase in desired private saving and hence to no change in desired national saving.

Because desired national saving does not change, the real interest rate does not have to rise in a closed economy to maintain balance between desired national saving and investment demand. Hence there is no effect on investment and no burden of the public debt or social security in the sense of Modigliani (1961) and Feldstein (1974). In a setting of an open economy there would also be no effect on the current-account balance, because desired private saving rises by enough to avoid having to borrow from abroad. Therefore budget deficits would not cause current-account deficits.

Theoretical Objections to Ricardian Equivalence

At least five major theoretical objections have been raised against the Ricardian conclusions. The first is that people do not live forever and hence do not care about taxes that are levied after their death. The second is that private capital markets are "imperfect," with the typical person's real discount rate exceeding that of the government. The third is that future taxes and incomes are uncertain. The fourth is that taxes are not lump sum, because they depend typically on income, spending, wealth, and so on. The fifth is that the Ricardian result hinges on full employment. I assume throughout that the path of government spending is given. The Ricardian analysis applies to shifts in budget deficits and taxes for a given pattern of government expenditures; in particular, the approach is consistent with real effects from changes in the level or timing of government purchases and public services.

In many cases it turns out that budget deficits matter and are in that sense non-Ricardian. It is important, however, to consider not only whether the Ricardian view remains intact, but also what alternative conclusions emerge. Many economists raise points that invalidate strict Ricardian equivalence and then simply assume that the points support a

---

than the later achievement. It was this retrospective view which doubtless inspired White-head to say somewhere that everything of importance has been said before—but by some-one who did not discover it." (This last point relates to "Stigler's Law," which states that nothing is named after the person who discovered it.)

specific alternative—usually the standard view that a budget deficit lowers desired national saving and thereby drives up real interest rates or leads to a current-account deficit. Many criticisms of the Ricardian position are also inconsistent with this standard view.

Finite Horizons and Related Issues

The idea of finite horizons, motivated by the finiteness of life, is central to life-cycle models—see, for example, Modigliani and Brumberg (1954) and Ando and Modigliani (1963). In these models individuals capitalize only the taxes that they expect to face before dying. Consider a deficit-financed tax cut, and assume that the higher future taxes occur partly during the typical person's expected lifetime and partly thereafter. Then the present value of the first portion must fall short of the initial tax cut, because a full balance results only if the second portion is included. Hence the net wealth of persons currently alive rises, and households react by increasing consumption demand. Thus, as in the standard approach sketched above, desired private saving does not rise by enough to offset fully the decline in government saving.

A finite horizon seems to generate the standard result that a budget deficit reduces desired national saving. The argument works, however, only if the typical person feels better off when the government shifts a tax burden to his or her dependents. The argument fails if the typical person is already giving to his or her children out of altruism. In this case people react to the government's imposed intergenerational transfers, which are implied by budget deficits or social security, with a compensating increase in voluntary transfers (Barro 1974). For example, parents adjust their bequests or the amounts given to children while the parents are still living. Alternatively, if children provide support to aged parents, then the amounts given can respond (negatively) to budget deficits or social security.

The main idea is that a network of intergenerational transfers makes the typical person a part of an extended family that goes on indefinitely. In this setting, households capitalize the entire array of expected future taxes and thereby plan effectively with an infinite horizon. In other words, the Ricardian results, which seemed to depend on infinite horizons, can remain valid in a model with finite lifetimes.

Two important points should be stressed. First, intergenerational ransfers do not have to be "large"; what is necessary is that transfers based on altruism be operative at the margin for most people.[3] Specifically, most people must be away from the corner solution of zero transfers, where they would, if permitted, opt for negative payments to their children. (The results also go through, however, if children typically support their aged parents.) Second, the transfers do not have to show up as bequests at death. Other forms of intergenerational transfers, such as *inter vivos* gifts to children, support of children's education, and so on, can work in a similar manner. Therefore, the Ricardian results can hold even if many persons leave little in the way of formal bequests.

One objection to Ricardian equivalence is that some persons, such as those without children, are not connected to future generations (see Tobin and Buiter 1980, pp. 86ff.). Persons in this situation tend to be made wealthier when the government substitutes a budget deficit for taxes. At least this conclusion obtains to the extent that the interest and principal payments on the extra public debt are not financed by higher taxes during the remaining lifetimes of people currently alive. However, the quantitative effects on consumption tend to be small. For example, if the typical person has 30 years of remaining life and consumes at a constant rate, then a one-time budget deficit of $100 per person would increase each person's real consumption demand by $1.50 per year if the annual real interest rate is 5% and by $2.10 per year if the real interest rate is 3%.[4]

The aggregate effect from the existence of childless persons is even smaller, because people with more than the average number of descendants experience a decrease in wealth when taxes are replaced by budget deficits. (In effect, although some people have no children, all children must have parents.) In a world of different family sizes, the presumption for a net effect of budget deficits on aggregate consumer demand depends on different propensities to consume out of wealth for people with and without children. Because the propensity for those without children tends to be larger (because of the shorter horizon), a positive net effect on aggregate consumer demand would be predicted. However, the quantitative effect is likely to be trivial. Making the same as-

3. Weil (1987) and Kimball (1987) analyzed conditions that ensure an interior solution for intergenerational transfers. Bernheim and Bagwell (1988) argued that difficulties arise if altruistic transfers are pervasive. See Barro (1989) for a discussion of their analysis.

4. The assumption is the real debt remains permanently higher by the amount of the initial deficit. For some related calculations, see Miller and Upton (1974, Chapter 8) and Poterba and Summers (1987, sec. 1).

sumptions as in the previous example, one finds that a budget deficit of $100 per capita would raise real consumption demand per capita by 30 cents per year if the real interest rate is 5% and by 90 cents if the real interest rate is 3%.

A variety of evidence supports the proposition that intergenerational transfers—defined broadly to go beyond formal bequests—are operative for most people. Darby (1979, chap. 3) and Kotlikoff and Summers (1981) calculated that the accumulation of households' assets in the United States for the purpose of intergenerational transfers is far more important than that associated with the life cycle. This observation suggests that most people give or receive intergenerational transfers—a conclusion that supports the Ricardian position. Modigliani (1988) contested this conclusion, but Kotlikoff (1988) showed that Modigliani's findings derive from an extremely narrow view of intergenerational transfers. Modigliani focused on bequests at death, and he also did not treat interest earnings on prior bequests as income attributable to intergenerational transfers.

Some authors accepted the idea that intergenerational transfers are important but argued that the motivation for the transfers matters for the results. Bernheim, Shleifer, and Summers (1985) considered the possibility that bequests, instead of being driven by altruism, are a strategic device whereby parents induce their children to behave properly. Some imaginative evidence was presented (involving how often children visit and communicate with their parents) to document the importance of strategic bequests. In this strategic model, if the government redistributes income from young to old (by running a deficit or raising social security benefits), then the old have no reason to raise transfers to offset fully the government's actions. Instead, the old end up better off at the expense of the young, and aggregate consumer demand rises. Then, as in the standard approach, real interest rates increase or domestic residents borrow more from abroad.

One shortcoming of this approach is that it treats the interaction between parents and children as equivalent to the purchases of services on markets. In this setting parents would tend to pay wages to children, rather than using bequests or other forms of intergenerational transfers. These features—as well as the observation that most parents seem to care about their children's welfare—can be better explained by introducing altruism along with a desire to influence children's behavior. In this case Ricardian equivalence may or may not obtain. Consider the utility that a parent would allocate to his or her child if there were no difficulty in motivating the child to perform properly. Suppose that the parent can design a credible threat involving bequests that entails the loss of some part of this utility for the child. (Note that if no threats are credible, then the whole basis for strategic bequests disappears.) If the threat is already large enough to induce the behavior that the parent desires, then Ricardian equivalence still holds. For example, if the government runs a budget deficit, the parent provides offsetting transfers to the child and thereby preserves the child's level of utility, as well as the behavior sought by the parent. On the other hand, the parent may have to allow excess utility to the child to secure a sufficient threat against bad performance. Then a budget deficit enables the parent to reduce the child's utility (as desired) while maintaining or even enhancing the threat that influences behavior. In this case Ricardian equivalence would not hold.

Other economists argue that the uncertainty of the time of death makes many bequests unintended and that such bequests would not respond very much to budget deficits. The imperfection of private annuity markets is usually mentioned to explain why unintended bequests are significant. But this reasoning is backward, because annuities do not entail greater adverse selection problems than many other types of insurance. The small amount of private annuities outstanding, other than the substantial amount in the form of pensions, reflects primarily a lack of demand, which itself is an indication that people desire to make the most of the bequests that occur. In any event, because the Ricardian results involve a broad concept of intergenerational transfers rather than especially bequests at death, a focus on formal bequests is misplaced.

Imperfect Loan Markets

Many economists argue that the imperfection of private credit markets is central to an analysis of the public debt (see, for example, Mundell 1971). To consider this argument, assume that a closed economy consists of two types of infinite-lived economic agents: those of group A who have the same discount rate, r, as the government (and are therefore willing to hold the government's debt), and those of group B who have the higher discount rate, $\bar{r} > r$. The constituents of group A would include large businesses, pension funds, and some individuals. The members of group B, such as small businesses and many households, possess poor collateral; therefore, loans to these people imply large costs of evaluation and enforcement. It follows that the members of group B face higher borrowing rates (even after an allowance for default risk) than the government. Whether or not they are actually borrowing, the high discount rate $\tilde{r}$ for group B corresponds to a high rate of time preference for consumption and a high marginal return on investment.

Suppose that the government cuts current taxes and runs a budget deficit. Further, assume that the division of the tax cut between groups A and B—say, fifty–fifty—is the same as the division of the higher future taxes needed to service the extra debt. Because those from group A experience no net change in wealth, they willingly hold their share of the extra public debt. For group B, where the discount rate $\tilde{r}$ exceeds r, the present value of the extra future taxes falls short of the tax cut. The members of this group are better off because the tax cut effectively enables them to borrow at the lower interest rate, r. This cut in the effective borrowing rate motivates the members of group B to raise current consumption and investment.

In the aggregate a budget deficit now raises aggregate demand, or equivalently, the aggregate of desired private saving increases by less than one-to-one with the government's deficit. It follows that the real interest rate r, which applies to group A and the government, must rise to induce people to hold the extra public debt. Hence there is crowding out of consumption and investment by members of group A. For group B, the opportunity to raise current consumption and investment means that the rate of time preference for consumption and the marginal return to investment would decline. That is, the discount rate $\tilde{r}$ falls. Thus the main effects are a narrowing of the spread between the two discount rates, r and $\tilde{r}$, and a diversion of current expenditures from group A to group B. In the aggregate investment may either rise or fall, and the long-term effect on the capital stock is uncertain. The major change, however, is a better channeling of resources to their ultimate uses. Namely, the persons from group B—who have relatively high values for rates of time preference and for marginal returns to investment—command a greater share of current output. In any event the outcomes are nonneutral, and in that sense non-Ricardian.

The important finding from the inclusion of imperfect loan markets is that the government's issue of public debt can amount to a useful form of financial intermediation. The government induces people with good access to credit markets (group A) to hold more than their share of the extra public debt. Those with poor access (group B) hold less than their share and thereby effectively receive loans from the first group. This process works because the government implicitly guarantees the repayment of loans through its tax collections and debt payments. Thus loans between A and B take place even though such loans were not viable (because of "transaction costs") on the imperfect private credit market.

This much of the argument may be valid, although it credits the government with a lot of skill in the collection of taxes from people with poor collateral (which is the underlying source of the problem for private lenders). Even if the government possesses this skill, the conclusions do not resemble those from the standard analysis. As discussed before, budget deficits can amount to more financial intermediation and are in that sense equivalent to a technological advance that improves the functioning of loan markets. From this perspective, it is reasonable to find a reduced spread between various discount rates and an improvement in the allocation of resources. If the government really is better at the process of intermediating, then more of this activity—that is, more public debt—raises perceived wealth because it actually improves the workings of the economy.

In the preceding analysis, the imperfection of credit markets reflected costs of enforcing the collection of loans. A different approach, followed by Yotsuzuka (1987) in his extension of the models of King (1986) and Hayashi (1987), allows for adverse selection among borrowers with different risk characteristics. Individuals know their probabilities of default, but the lenders' only possibility for learning these probabilities comes from observing the chosen levels of borrowing at going interest rates. In this setting the government's borrowing amounts to a loan to a group that pools the various risk classes. Such borrowing matters if the private equilibrium does not involve similar pooling. However, by considering the incentives of lenders to exchange or not exchange information about their customers, Yotsuzuka argues that the private equilibrium typically involves a pooled loan of limited quantity at a relatively low interest rate. Then the high-risk types may borrow additional amounts at a high interest rate. (The assumption is that this additional borrowing is not observable by other lenders.) In this case the government's borrowing replaces the private pooled lending and leads to no real effects. That is, Ricardian equivalence holds despite the imperfect private loan market where high-risk people face high marginal borrowing rates. The general lesson again is that Ricardian equivalence fails because of imperfect credit markets only if the government does things in the loan market that are different from, and perhaps better than, those carried out privately.

Uncertainty about Future Taxes and Incomes

Some economists have argued that the uncertainty about individuals' future taxes—or the complexity in estimating them—implies a high rate of discount in capitalizing these future liabilities (Bailey 1971, pp. 157–158; Buchanan and Wagner 1977, pp. 17, 101, 130; Feldstein 1976, p. 335). In this case, a substitution of a budget deficit for current taxes raises net wealth because the present value of the higher expected future taxes falls short of the current tax cut. It then follows that budget deficits raise aggregate consumer demand and reduce desired national saving.

A proper treatment of uncertainty leads to different conclusions. Chan (1983) considered first the case of lump-sum taxes that have a known distribution across households. However, the aggregate of future taxes and the real value of future payments on public debt are subject to uncertainty. In this case a deficit-financed tax cut has no real effects. Individuals hold their share of the extra debt because the debt is a perfect hedge against the uncertainty of the future taxes. (This analysis assumes that private credit markets have no "imperfections" of the sort discussed earlier.)

Suppose now that future taxes are still lump sum but have an uncertain incidence across individuals. Furthermore, assume that there are no insurance markets for relative tax risks. Then a budget deficit tends to increase the uncertainty about each individual's future disposable income. Chan (1983, p. 363) showed for the "usual case" (of nonincreasing absolute risk aversion) that people react by reducing current consumption and, hence, by raising current private saving by more than the tax cut. Consequently, the effects on real interest rates, investment, the current account, and so on are the opposites of the standard ones.

The results are different for an income tax (Chan 1983, pp. 364–366; Barsky, Mankiw, and Zeldes 1986). Suppose that each person pays the tax τy_i, where y_i is the person's uncertain future income. Suppose that there are no insurance markets for individual income risks and that τ is known. (The analysis thus abstracts from uncertainties in relative tax rates across individuals.) In this case a budget deficit raises the future value of τ and thereby reduces the uncertainty about each individual's future disposable income. In effect, the government shares the risks about individual disposable income to a greater extent. It follows that the results are opposite to those found before—namely, a budget deficit tends to raise current consumption and, hence, to raise private saving by less than the tax cut.

Overall, the conclusions depend on the net effect of higher mean future tax collections on the uncertainty associated with individuals' future disposable incomes. Desired national saving tends to rise with a budget deficit if this uncertainty increases, and vice versa.

The Timing of Taxes

Departures from Ricardian equivalence arise also if taxes are not lump sum—for example, with an income tax. In this situation, budget deficits change the timing of income taxes and thereby affect people's incentives to work and produce in different periods. It follows that variations in deficits are nonneutral, although the results tend also to be inconsistent with the standard view.

Suppose, for example, that the current tax rate on labor income, τ_1, declines, and the expected rate for the next period, τ_2, rises. To simplify matters, assume that today's budget deficit is matched by enough of a surplus next period that the public debt does not change in later periods. Because the tax rate applies to labor income, households are motivated to work more than usual in period 1 and less than usual in period 2. Because the tax rate does not apply to expenditures (and because wealth effects are negligible here), desired national saving rises in period 1 and falls in period 2. Therefore, in a closed economy, after-tax real interest rates tend to be relatively low in period 1—along with the budget deficit—and relatively high in period 2—along with the surplus. In an open economy, a current-account surplus accompanies the budget deficit, and vice versa. Hence the results are non-Ricardian but also are counter to the standard view. (Temporary variations in consumption taxes tend to generate the standard pattern where real interest rates, current-account deficits, and budget deficits are positively correlated.)

In a world of distorting taxes, unlike the Ricardian case where debt and deficits do not matter, it is possible to determine the optimal path of the budget deficit, which corresponds to the optimal time pattern of taxes. In effect, the theory of debt management becomes a branch of public finance—specifically, an application of the theory of optimal taxation.

One result is that budget deficits can be used to smooth tax rates over time, despite fluctuations in government expenditures and the tax base.[5] For example, if time periods are identical except for the quantity of government purchases—which are assumed not to interact directly with labor supply decisions—then optimality dictates uniform taxation of labor income over time. This constancy of tax rates requires budget deficits when government spending is unusually high, such as in wartime, and surpluses when spending is unusually low.

Constant tax rates over time will not be optimal in general—for example, optimal tax rates on labor income may vary over the business cycle. To the extent that some smoothing is called for, budget deficits would occur in recessions and surpluses in booms. If optimal tax rates are lower than normal in recessions and higher than normal in booms, then the countercyclical pattern of budget deficits is even more vigorous. The well-known concept of the full-employment deficit, as discussed in Brown (1956) and Council of Economic Advisers (1962, pp. 78–82), adjusts for this cyclical behavior of budget deficits.

The tax-smoothing view has implications for the interaction between inflation and budget deficits if the public debt is denominated in nominal terms. Basically, the fiscal authority's objective involves the path of tax rates and other real variables. Therefore, other things equal, a higher rate of expected inflation (presumably reflecting a higher rate of monetary growth) motivates a correspondingly higher growth rate of the nominal, interest-bearing debt. This response keeps the planned path of the real public debt invariant with expected inflation. This behavior means that differences in expected rates of inflation can account for substantial variations in budget deficits if deficits are measured in the conventional way to correspond to the change in the government's nominal liabilities. This element is, however, less important for an inflation-adjusted budget deficit, which corresponds to the change in the government's real obligations (Siegel 1979; Eisner and Pieper 1984).

With perfect foresight, the strict tax-smoothing model implies constant tax rates. More realistically, new information about the path of government spending, national income, and so on would lead to revisions of tax rates. However, the sign of these revisions would not be predictable. Thus, in the presence of uncertainty, tax smoothing implies that tax rates would behave roughly like random walks.

---

5. For discussions of the tax-smoothing model of budget deficits, see Pigou (1928, chap. 6) and Barro (1979, 1986).

It is possible to use the tax-smoothing approach as a positive theory of how the government operates rather than as a normative model of how it should act.[6] Barro (1979, 1986) showed that this framework explains much of the behavior of U.S. federal deficits from 1916 to 1983, although the deficits since 1984 turn out to be substantially higher than predicted. Over the full sample, the major departures from the theory are an excessive reaction of budget deficits to the business cycle (consequently, tax rates fall below "normal" during recessions) and an insufficient reaction to temporary military spending (consequently, tax rates rise above normal in wartime). These departures were found also by Sahasakul (1986), who looked directly at the behavior of average marginal tax rates. Barro (1987, sec. 3) found for the British data from the early 1700s through 1918 that temporary military spending was the major determinant of budget deficits. Also, unlike the results for the U.S. case, the results for the British data indicated a one-to-one response of budget deficits to temporary spending.

Full Employment and Keynesian Models

A common argument is that the Ricardian results depend on "full employment" and surely do not hold in Keynesian models. In standard Keynesian analysis (which still appears in many textbooks), if everyone thinks that a budget deficit makes them wealthier, the resulting expansion of aggregate demand raises output and employment and thereby actually makes people wealthier. (This result holds if the economy begins in a state of "involuntary unemployment.") There may even be multiple, rational expectations equilibria, where the change in actual wealth coincides with the change in perceived wealth.

This result does not mean that budget deficits increase aggregate demand and wealth in Keynesian models. If we had conjectured that budget deficits made people feel poorer, the resulting contractions in output and employment would have made them poorer. Similarly, if we had started with the Ricardian notion that budget deficits did not affect wealth, the Keynesian results would have verified that conjecture. The odd feature of the standard Keynesian model is that *anything* that makes people feel wealthier actually makes them wealthier (although the per-

6. A colleague of mine argues that a "normative" model should be defined as a model that fits the data badly.

ception and actuality need not correspond quantitatively). This observation raises doubts about the formulation of Keynesian models, but says little about the effect of budget deficits. Moreover, in equilibrium models that include unemployment (such as models with incomplete information and search), there is no clear interplay between the presence of unemployment and the validity of the Ricardian approach.

Empirical Evidence on the Economic Effects of Budget Deficits

It is easy on theoretical grounds to raise points that invalidate strict Ricardian equivalence. Nevertheless, it may still be that the Ricardian view provides a useful framework for assessing the first-order effects of fiscal policy. Furthermore, it is not clear that the standard analysis offers a more accurate guide. For these reasons it is especially important to examine empirical evidence.

The Ricardian and standard views have different predictions about the effects of fiscal policy on a number of economic variables. The next three sections summarize the empirical evidence on interest rates, saving, and the current-account balance.

Interest Rates

The Ricardian view predicts no effect of budget deficits on real interest rates, whereas the standard view predicts a positive effect, at least in the context of a closed economy. Many economists have tested these propositions empirically (for a summary, see U.S. Treasury Department 1984). Typical results show little relationship between budget deficits and interest rates. For example, Plosser (1982, p. 339) found for quarterly U.S. data from 1954 to 1978 that unexpected movements in privately held federal debt do not raise the nominal yield on government securities of various maturities. In fact, there is a weak tendency for yields to decline with innovations in federal debt. In Plosser's (1987, tables 8 and 11) later study, which included data through 1985, he reached similar conclusions for nominal and expected real yields. Evans (1987) obtained similar results for nominal yields with quarterly data from 1974 to 1985 for Canada, France, Germany, Japan, the United Kingdom, and the United States.

Evans (1987a, tables 4–6) found for annual U.S. data from 1931 to 1979 that current and past real federal deficits have no significant association with nominal interest rates on commercial paper or corporate bonds or with realized real interest rates on commercial paper. Over the longer period from 1908 to 1984, an analysis of monthly data indicates a negative relation between deficits and nominal or real interest rates (Evans, 1987a, tables 1–3). Evans also explored the effects of expected future budget deficits or surpluses. He assumed that people would have expected future deficits in advance of tax cuts, such as those in 1981, and future surpluses in advance of tax hikes. But interest rates turned out typically not to rise in advance of tax cuts and not to fall in advance of tax hikes.

Overall, the empirical results on interest rates support the Ricardian view. Given these findings, it is remarkable that most macroeconomists remain confident that budget deficits raise interest rates.

Consumption and Saving

Many empirical studies have searched for effects of budget deficits or social security on consumption and saving. Most of these studies—exemplified by Kochin (1974) and the papers surveyed in Esposito (1978)—relied on estimates of coefficients in consumption functions. Basically, the results are all over the map, with some favoring Ricardian equivalence and others not.

The inconclusive nature of these results probably reflects well-known identification problems. The analysis does not deal satisfactorily with the simultaneity between consumption and income and also has problems with the endogeneity of budget deficits. For example, deficits and saving (or investment) have strong cyclical elements, and it is difficult to sort out the causation in these patterns. Because of these problems, I regard as more reliable some results that exploit situations that look more like natural experiments.

One such study, a comparison of saving in Canada and the United States, was carried out by Chris Carroll and Lawrence Summers (1987). They noted that the private saving rates in the two countries were similar until the early 1970s but have since diverged; for 1983–1985, the Canadian rate was higher by about six percentage points. After holding fixed some macroeconomic variables and aspects of the tax systems that influence saving, the authors isolated a roughly one-to-one, positive effect of government budget deficits on private saving. That is, the rise in the private saving rate in Canada, relative to that in the United States, reflected the greater increase in the Canadian budget deficit as a ratio to GNP. Thus, as implied by the Ricardian view, the relative values of the net national saving rates in the two countries appeared to be invariant with the relative values of the budget deficits. These results are particularly interesting because the focus on relative performance in Canada and the United States holds constant the many forces that have common influences on the two countries. It may be that this procedure lessens the problems of identification that hamper most studies of consumption functions.

Recent fiscal policy in Israel comes close to a natural experiment for studying the interplay between budget deficits and saving.[7] In 1983 the gross national saving rate of 13% corresponded to a private saving rate of 17% and a public saving rate of −4%. In 1984 the dramatic rise in the budget deficit led to a public saving rate of −11%. (A principal reason for the deficit was the adverse effect of the increase in the inflation rate on the collection of real tax revenues.) For present purposes, the interesting observation is that the private saving rate rose from 17 to 26%, so the national saving rate changed little actually rising from 13 to 15%. Then the stabilization program in 1985 eliminated the budget deficit, along with most of the inflation; consequently, the public saving rate increased from −11% in 1984 to 0 in 1985–86 and −2% in 1987. The private saving rate decreased dramatically at the same time—from 26% in 1984 to 19% in 1985 and 14% in 1986–87. Therefore, the national saving rates were relatively stable, going from 15% in 1984 to 18% in 1985, 14% in 1986, and 12% in 1987. The main point is that this evidence reveals the roughly one-to-one offset between public and private saving that the Ricardian view predicts.

Finally, I should note the "Reagan experiment," which featured large U.S. budget deficits from 1984 to 1987 during a peacetime boom. (While an interesting experiment—applauded on scientific grounds even by opponents of Reagan—the magnitudes are much less dramatic than those in Israel.) Unfortunately, the effects of recent U.S. budget deficits on U.S. investment and saving are controversial, especially because it is unclear whether recent investment and saving rates are high or low.

7. I am grateful to Ed Offenbacher for calling my attention to the Israeli experience. The data, all expressed in U.S. dollars, are from Bank of Israel (1987).

National accounts measures of rates of net investment and net national saving are low and have often been cited. But the ratio of real gross investment (broadly defined to include purchases of consumer durables) to real GNP averaged 27.9% from 1984 to 1987, higher than the average of 23.8% from 1947 to 1987. In fact, the recent investment ratios represent a post–World War II high. If saving is measured (as I would argue is appropriate) by the change in the real market value of assets, then recent saving rates have not been low. For example, the change in real household net worth as a ratio to real GNP averaged 11.2% from 1984 to 1987, higher than the mean of 10.1% from 1949 to 1987.[8] Thus, even though a good portion of recent U.S. budget deficits may qualify as exogenous, it is not yet clear how these deficits affected U.S. investment and saving.

Current-Account Deficits

Popular opinion attributes the large current-account deficits in the United States since 1983 to the effects of budget deficits. Figure 9.1 shows the values since 1948 of the ratio of the total government budget surplus (national accounts' version) to GNP (solid line) and the ratio of net foreign investment to GNP (dotted line).[9] Through 1982 there is no association between these two variables (correlation = $-.02$). However, including the data since 1983 raises the correlation to .37. In effect, the U.S. data since World War II reveal a single incident—the period since 1983—when budget and current-account deficits have been high at the same time. Although this recent comovement is interesting, it does not by itself provide strong support for the view that budget deficits cause current-account deficits.

8. Household net worth comes from Board of Governors of the Federal Reserve System (1988). The nominal year-end figures were divided by the fourth-quarter GNP deflator. The Federal Reserve numbers include stocks, housing, and consumer durables at estimated market value, but bonds at par value. I made no adjustments for households' liabilities for future taxes associated with the government's debt net of assets. There is a conceptual problem here because some of this liability is already reflected in the market values of households' stocks, housing, and so on. Also, the Federal Reserve's measures of government liabilities and assets are not well developed.

9. The data are quarterly, seasonally adjusted values from Citibase. The results are similar if the federal surplus is used instead of the total government surplus.

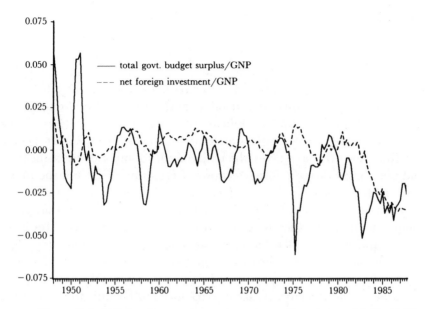

Figure 9.1. U.S. budget and current-account surpluses, 1948–1987; data are seasonally adjusted, quarterly values from Citibase

Evans (1988, tables 1–5) carried out a cross-country empirical investigation of the relation between budget and current-account deficits. He looked first at annual, post–World War II data for Canada, with the United States used as a proxy for the rest of the world. (In a model where budget deficits matter, the current-account deficit responds to the home country's budget deficit relative to the budget deficit in the rest of the world.) Then he looked at quarterly data since 1973 on the United States, Canada, France, Germany, and the United Kingdom, with the aggregate of the major industrialized countries (other than the country under study) used to represent the rest of the world. Evans's overall finding is that the results are consistent with the Ricardian hypothesis that current-account balances are independent of budget deficits. (Only the estimates for Germany suggest a positive relation between budget and current-account deficits, but the results in this case are not statistically significant.) Evans (1988, p. 31) reacts to his findings with the question, "If large U.S. budget deficits did not produce the large U.S. current-account deficits of the 1980s, what did?" and concludes that this question is an interesting topic for future research.

Observations

The Ricardian approach to budget deficits amounts to the statement that the government's fiscal impact is summarized by the present value of its expenditures. Given this present value, rearrangements of the timing of taxes—as implied by budget deficits—have no first-order effect on the economy. Second-order effects arise for various reasons, which include the distorting effects of taxes, the uncertainties about individual incomes and tax obligations, the imperfections of credit markets, and the finiteness of life. To say that these effects are second order is not to say that they are uninteresting; in fact, the analysis of differential taxation in the theory of public finance is second order in the same sense. However, careful analysis of these effects tends to deliver predictions about budget deficits that differ from those of standard macroeconomic models.

I have argued that empirical findings on interest rates, consumption and saving, and the current-account balance tend mainly to support the Ricardian viewpoint. However, this empirical analysis involves substantial problems about data and identification, and the results are sometimes inconclusive. It would be useful to assemble additional evidence, especially in an international context.

Although the majority of economists still lean toward standard macroeconomic models of fiscal policy, it is remarkable how respectable the Ricardian approach has become in the last decade. Most macroeconomists now feel obligated to state the Ricardian position, even if they then go on to argue that it is either theoretically or empirically in error. I predict that this trend will continue and that the Ricardian approach will become the benchmark model for assessing fiscal policy.

There is a parallel between the Ricardian equivalence theorem on intertemporal government finance and the Modigliani–Miller (1958) theorem on corporate finance. Everyone knows that the Modigliani–Miller theorem is literally incorrect in saying that the structure of corporate finance does not matter. But the theorem rules out numerous sloppy reasons for why this structure might have mattered and thereby forces theoretical and empirical analyses into a disciplined, productive mode. Similarly, I would not predict that most analysts will embrace Ricardian equivalence in the sense of concluding that fiscal policy is irrelevant. But satisfactory analyses will feature explicit modeling of elements that lead to departures from Ricardian equivalence, and the predicted consequences of fiscal policies will flow directly from these elements.

References

Ando, A., and F. Modigliani. 1963. "The 'Life Cycle' Hypothesis of Saving: Aggregate Implications and Tests." *American Economic Review* 53:55–84.

Bailey, M. J. 1971. *National Income and the Price Level,* 2nd Ed. New York: McGraw-Hill.

Bank of Israel. 1987. *Annual Report.* Jerusalem.

Barro, R. J. 1974. "Are Government Bonds Net Wealth?" *Journal of Political Economy* 82:1095–1117.

——— 1979. "On the Determination of the Public Debt." *Journal of Political Economy* 87:940–971.

——— 1986. "U.S. Deficits since World War I." *Scandinavian Journal of Economics* 88(1):195–222.

——— 1987. "Government Spending, Interest Rates, Prices, and Budget Deficits in the United Kingdom, 1701–1918." *Journal of Monetary Economics* 20:221–247.

——— 1989. "The Neoclassical Approach to Fiscal Policy." In *Modern Business Cycle Theory,* ed. R. J. Barro. Cambridge, Mass.: Harvard University Press, pp. 178–235.

Barsky, R. B., N. Mankiw, and P. Zeldes. 1986. "Ricardian Consumers with Keynesian Propensities." *American Economic Review* 76:676–691.

Bernheim, B. D., and K. Bagwell. 1988. "Is Everything Neutral?" *Journal of Political Economy* 96:308–338.

Bernheim, B. D., A. Shleifer, and L. H. Summers. 1985. "The Strategic Bequest Motive." *Journal of Political Economy* 93:1045–76.

Board of Governors of the Federal Reserve System. 1988. *Balance Sheets for the U.S. Economy, 1948–87.* Washington, D.C.

Brown, E. C. 1956. "Fiscal Policy in the 'Thirties: A Reappraisal." *Journal of Political Economy* 46:857–879.

Buchanan, J. M. 1976. "Barro on the Ricardian Equivalence Theorem." *Journal of Political Economy* 84:337–342.

Buchanan, J. M., and R. E. Wagner. 1977. *Democracy in Deficit.* New York: Academic Press.

Carroll, C., and L. H. Summers. 1987. "Why Have Private Savings Rates in the United States and Canada Diverged?" *Journal of Monetary Economics* 20:249–279.

Chan, L. K. C. 1983. "Uncertainty and the Neutrality of Government Financing Policy." *Journal of Monetary Economics* 11:351–372.

Council of Economic Advisers. 1962. *Annual Report*. Washington, D.C.: U.S. Government Printing Office.

Darby, M. R. 1979. *The Effects of Social Security on Income and the Capital Stock.* Washington, D.C.: American Enterprise Institute.

Eisner, R., and P. Pieper. 1984. "A New View of the Federal Debt and Budget Deficits." *American Economic Review* 74:11–29.

Esposito, L. 1978. "Effect of Social Security on Saving: Review of Studies Using U.S. Time-Series Data." *Social Security Bulletin* 41:9–17.

Evans, P. 1987a. "Interest Rates and Expected Future Budget Deficits in the United States." *Journal of Political Economy* 95:34–58.

———— 1987b. "Do Budget Deficits Raise Nominal Interest Rates? Evidence from Six Industrial Countries." *Journal of Monetary Economics* 20:281–300.

———— 1988. "Do Budget Deficits Affect the Current Account?" Unpublished manuscript. Columbus: Ohio State University.

Feldstein, M. S. 1974. "Social Security, Induced Retirement, and Aggregate Capital Accumulation." *Journal of Political Economy* 82:905–926.

———— 1976. "Perceived Wealth in Bonds and Social Security: A Comment." *Journal of Political Economy* 84:331–336.

Hayashi, F. 1987. "Tests for Liquidity Constraints: A Critical Survey and Some New Observations." In *Advances in Econometrics, Fifth World Congress,* ed. T. F. Bewley. Cambridge: Cambridge University Press, pp. 91–120.

Kimball, M. S. 1987. "Making Sense of Two-Sided Altruism." *Journal of Monetary Economics* 20:301–326.

King, M. A. 1986. "Tax Policy and Consumption Smoothing." Unpublished manuscript. London: London School of Economics.

Kochin, L. A. 1974. "Are Future Taxes Anticipated by Consumers?" *Journal of Money, Credit and Banking* 6:385–394.

Kotlikoff, L. J. 1988. "Intergenerational Transfers and Savings." *Journal of Economic Perspectives* 2:41–58.

Kotlikoff, L. J., and L. H. Summers. 1981. "The Role of Intergenerational Transfers in Aggregate Capital Accumulation." *Journal of Political Economy* 89:706–732.

McCallum, B. T. 1984. "Are Bond-Financed Deficits Inflationary? A Ricardian Analysis." *Journal of Political Economy* 92:123–135.

Miller, M. H., and W. Upton. 1974. *Macroeconomics, a Neoclassical Introduction.* Homewood, Ill.: Irwin.

Modigliani, F. 1961. "Long-Run Implications of Alternative Fiscal Policies and the Burden of the National Debt." *Economic Journal* 71:730–755.

—— 1988. "The Role of Intergenerational Transfers and Life Cycle Saving in the Accumulation of Wealth." *Journal of Economic Perspectives* 2:15–40.

Modigliani, F., and R. Brumberg. 1954. "Utility Analysis and the Consumption Function: An Interpretation of Cross-Section Data." In *Post-Keynesian Economics,* ed. K. K. Kurihara. New Brunswick, N.J.: Rutgers University Press, pp. 388–436.

Modigliani, F., and M. H. Miller. 1958. "The Cost of Capital, Corporation Finance and the Theory of Investment." *American Economic Review* 48:261–297.

Mundell, R. A. 1971. "Money, Debt, and the Rate of Interest." In *Monetary Theory,* ed. R. A. Mundell. Pacific Palisades: Goodyear, pp. 5–13.

O'Driscoll, G. P. 1977. "The Ricardian Nonequivalence Theorem." *Journal of Political Economy* 85:207–210.

Pigou, A. C. 1928. *A Study in Public Finance.* London: Macmillan.

Plosser, C. I. 1982. "Government Financing Decisions and Asset Returns." *Journal of Monetary Economics* 9:325–352.

—— 1987. "Further Evidence on the Relation between Fiscal Policy and the Term Structure." *Journal of Monetary Economics* 20:343–367.

Poterba, J. M., and L. H. Summers. 1987. "Finite Lifetimes and the Savings Effects of Budget Deficits." *Journal of Monetary Economics* 20:369–391.

Ricardo, D. 1951. "Funding System." In *The Works and Correspondence of David Ricardo,* Vol. 4, *Pamphlets and Papers, 1815–1823,* ed. P. Sraffa. Cambridge: Cambridge University Press, pp. 184–189.

Rosenberg, N. 1976. *Perspectives on Technology.* Cambridge: Cambridge University Press.

Sahasakul, C. 1986. "The U.S. Evidence on Optimal Taxation over Time." *Journal of Monetary Economics* 18:251–275.

Siegel, J. J. 1979. "Inflation-Induced Distortions in Government and Private Saving Statistics." *Review of Economics and Statistics* 61:83–90.

Tobin, J., and W. Buiter. 1980. "Fiscal and Monetary Policies, Capital Formation, and Economic Activity." In *The Government and Capital Formation,* ed. G. M. von Furstenberg. Cambridge: Ballinger, pp. 73–151.

U.S. Treasury Department. 1984. *The Effect of Deficits on Prices of Financial Assets: Theory and Evidence.* Washington, D.C.: U.S. Government Printing Office.

Weil, P. 1987. "Love Thy Children: Reflections on the Barro Debt Neutrality Theorem." *Journal of Monetary Economics* 19:377–391.

Yotsuzuka, T. 1987. "Ricardian Equivalence in the Presence of Capital Market Imperfections." *Journal of Monetary Economics* 20:411–436.

10   U.S. Deficits since World War I

Much recent attention has focused on the large values of actual and projected federal deficits in the United States. To evaluate this discussion, we have to know whether these deficits represent a shift in the structure of the government's fiscal policy or just the usual reaction to other influences, such as recession, inflation, and government spending. A related, but broader, question is whether the process that generates deficits in recent years differs from that in place earlier—say, during the interwar period of 1920–1940. For example, has there been a change in the average deficit or in the magnitude of the countercyclical response of deficits?

I begin by summarizing the tax-smoothing theory of deficits, which I developed earlier. Then I estimate this model on U.S. data for 1916–1983. Basically, the results are consistent with an unchanged structure of deficits over this period. Specifically, the large deficits for 1981–1983 reflect mainly the usual response to recession (interacting with big government) and to anticipated inflation.

The Tax-Smoothing Model of Deficits

I analyze the determination of deficits within the framework of the tax-smoothing model that I developed before (see Barro 1979, 1986).[1] In this approach the government faces the exogenous, deterministic stream

From *Scandinavian Journal of Economics* (1986) 88(1):195–222. This research was supported by the National Science Foundation.
    1. Some related work is presented in Kydland and Prescott (1980) and Lucas and Stokey (1983). The general idea of the implications of tax smoothing for the behavior of deficits also appears in Pigou (1928, chap. 6).

of real expenditures, other than interest payments, as given by $g(t)$. The base of real taxable income is the deterministic amount $y(t)$, which generally depends on the path of tax rates. I think of $y(t)$ as a fixed fraction of the economy's real GNP for period t. Let $\tau(t)$ be the average tax rate at date t, so that the amount of real income-tax revenue is $\tau(t)y(t)$. If the real interest rate is the constant r and the initial real public debt is $b(0)$, then the government's budget constraint in terms of present values is[2]

$$\int_0^\infty \tau(t)y(t)e^{-rt}\,dt = \int_0^\infty g(t)e^{-rt}\,dt + b(0). \tag{10.1}$$

This formulation does not separate out the revenue from money creation from the government's other revenues. Rather, I think of inflationary finance as a tax on holdings of money. Then, in order to focus on taxes in one period versus those in another, I combine the inflation tax with the variety of other levies (on income, sales, property, and so on) that apply at the same date. In particular, there seems to be no reason to give special treatment to the inflation tax.[3]

Suppose that the allocative effects from taxation depend on the "average marginal tax rate," $\tau^m(t)$, for each period. That is, the time path of average marginal tax rates, $\tau^m(1)$, $\tau^m(2)$, . . . , influences people's incentives to work, produce, and consume in the various periods. Here I take a Ramsey-like optimal-taxation perspective in order to formulate a testable positive theory of the government's choices of tax rates over time.[4] In particular, if each period is similar in terms of elasticities of labor supply, and so on, then the Ramsey formulation dictates roughly equal tax rates, $\tau^m(t)$, for each period.[5] More generally, this approach would allow the tax rate to depend on time-varying features of the economy, such as war or peace, boom or recession. But to bring out the main

---

2. This analysis assumes that the real interest rate exceeds the economy's steady-state growth rate. For a discussion, see McCallum (1984).

3. Anticipated inflation amounts to a form of excise tax. But unanticipated inflation entails a capital levy, which has different implications for the excess burden of taxation; see, for example, Barro (1983). However, changes in other kinds of taxes can also imply capital levies.

4. For discussions of Ramsey taxation, See Atkinson and Stiglitz (1980, chap. 12) and Ramsey (1927).

5. Kydland and Prescott (1980, pp. 185–186) argued that this rule will be close to optimal if intertemporal-substitution effects are strong.

implications of the approach, I focus on the hypothesis that the government plans for equal average marginal tax rates, $\tau^m(t)$, in each period.

I assume that the average marginal tax rate for any period bears a stable relation to that period's average tax rate, $\tau(t)$—that is,

$$\tau^m(t) = f[\tau(t)], \tag{10.2}$$

where the function f is invariant over time. In this case, the stabilization of average marginal tax rates entails stabilization of average tax rates. If τ denotes the constant value of the average tax rate, then the government's intertemporal budget constraint in Eq. (10.1) implies that this tax rate is

$$\tau = \frac{\int_0^\infty g(t)e^{-rt}\,dt + b(0)}{\int_0^\infty y(t)e^{-rt}\,dt}. \tag{10.3}$$

Suppose that real government spending, $g(t)$, and the real tax base (real GNP), $y(t)$, are fluctuating around trend values that grow at the common rate n. That is, the time paths, $g^*(t) = g^*(0)e^{nt}$ and $y^*(t) = y^*(0)e^{nt}$, have the same present values as the respective actual time paths, $g(t)$ and $y(t)$.[6] Then the current "normal" values, $g^*(0)$ and $y^*(0)$, satisfy the conditions,

$$g^*(0) = (r - n)\int_0^\infty g(t)e^{-rt}\,dt, \tag{10.4}$$

$$y^*(0) = (r - n)\int_0^\infty y(t)e^{-rt}\,dt.$$

Dropping the time subscripts and substituting back into Eq. (10.3) yields the formula for the (stabilized) average tax rate,

$$\tau = \frac{g^* + (r - n)b}{y}. \tag{10.5}$$

Hence, the tax rate equals the ratio of normal real spending to normal real income, where normal real spending includes the real interest pay-

6. These assumptions rule out any drift in the ratio, g/y. In the long run, this drift would be subject to the bounds, $0 < g/y < 1$.

ments on the outstanding public debt, rb, less the amount financed by the usual growth of the real debt, nb. I discuss this last item further below.

The current deficit—which I define to be the change in the real quantity of interest-bearing public debt, db/dt—is given at any date by

$$\frac{db}{dt} = g + rb - \tau y = g + rb - \frac{y[g^* + (r - n)b]}{y^*}.$$

Rearranging terms yields

$$\frac{db}{dt} = \left(1 - \frac{y}{y^*}\right)[g^* + (r - n)b] + (g - g^*) + nb. \tag{10.6}$$

The first term on the r.h.s. of Eq. (10.6) indicates that the real debt rises when output is below "normal"—that is, when $y/y^* < 1$. Effectively, tax revenues fall in proportion to the fall in output (in order for the average tax rate not to change). Hence the amount of revenue lost is the proportional shortfall of output, $(1 - y/y^*)$, multiplied by the normal amount of real government spending (and revenues), $g^* + (r - n)b$. Note that, when tax rates are stabilized over time, the coefficient of the cyclical variable, $(1 - y/y^*)[g^* + (r - n)b]$, is unity in Eq. (10.6). Alternatively, if the government were to set relatively low tax rates during recessions, then it would have to engineer a more dramatic countercyclical response of deficits. In this case, the coefficient of the cyclical variable would exceed one.

Empirically, the term $(r - n)b$ in Eq. (10.6) is small relative to g^*. That is, normal real spending g^* is large relative to real interest payments, rb, less the growth term, nb. Hence I neglect the term, $(r - n)b$, in the subsequent analysis. Then it is appropriate to measure g^* as the normal amount of real government expenditures exclusive of interest payments.

The second term on the r.h.s. of Eq. (10.6), $g - g^*$, indicates that the real debt rises by the amount of temporary real government spending. Thereby, the government avoids abnormally high tax rates during periods when its expenditures are unusually high. Empirically, the dominant parts of temporary spending are the unusually high military outlays in wartime. Thus the unitary coefficient on the $(g - g^*)$ variable in Eq. (10.6) reflects especially the government's desire to equalize tax rates during wartime and peacetime periods. Alternatively, if tax rates were, say, above normal during wars, then the coefficient on the $(g - g^*)$ variable would be less than one.

Finally, other things equal, the last term in Eq. (10.6) says that the real debt grows at the rate n, which is the trend growth rate of the economy. If the debt did not grow along with the economy, then interest payments would fall over time relative to GNP, which would be inconsistent with stabilizing the average tax rate.

When the time paths $g(t)$ and $y(t)$ are uncertain, the values g^* and y^* are also uncertain. I interpret these magnitudes in Eq. (10.6) as corresponding to anticipated present values of real government spending and GNP, assuming a known value of the real interest rate r. Possibly, some further results could be obtained by modeling explicitly the uncertainty for future government spending and private endowments.[7]

The main point is that new information about the long-run values of spending, g^*, and income, y^*, lead to corresponding changes in the average tax rate, τ, as shown in Eq. (10.5). Thus the tax rate adjusts for surprise changes in spending and income, but the sign or magnitude of the necessary adjustments cannot be predicted in advance. In other words, the tax rate follows a Martingale. However, some predictable changes in tax rates may appear if, as mentioned before, the tax rate depends on the state of the economy. For example, if tax rates were lower than normal during recessions, then predictable increases in tax rates would occur along with the (predictable) ends of recessions. Similarly, if tax rates were higher than normal during wars, then predictable declines in tax rates would show up at the (predictable) ends of wars. Thus the Martingale property for tax rates is not central to the approach followed in this chapter.[8]

Another property of the theory is that it prescribes no target value for the level of public debt or for the ratio of debt to income. A higher initial value of debt is "undesirable" in the sense that it requires a higher tax rate at each date—Eq. (10.5)—which then entails a larger excess burden from taxation. But (with default ruled out), it is not worthwhile for the

---

7. See Lucas and Stokey (1983) for a treatment of uncertainty in a related context.

8. In a previous study (Barro 1981a), I accepted the random-walk hypothesis for average tax rates, although the statistical tests were not very powerful. Subsequently, I have rejected the random-walk hypothesis for some revised systems. Sahasakul (1984) found evidence that average marginal tax rates are lower than normal during recessions and higher than normal during wars.

government systematically to run surpluses to pay off the debt.[9] Such a policy implies temporarily high tax rates, which violates the tax-smoothing criterion. Thus, given the right-side variables in Eq. (10.6), there is no independent effect on the deficit (net of the term, nb) from the starting value of the debt–income ratio. (This conclusion would still follow even if the government varied the tax rate with the business cycle or with conditions of war and peace.)

The above argument is consistent with the marked tendency of the ratio of public debt to GNP to fall in peacetime, nonrecession years; see Barro (1984, chap. 15) for the long-term evidence on this behavior for the United States and the United Kingdom. The variable g^* incorporates a country's propensity to experience infrequent but possibly large wars. Therefore, temporary spending, $g - g^*$, is negative rather than zero in the typical peacetime year. Hence, the debt–income ratio tends to fall in peacetime and to rise sharply during the infrequent large wars.

If the price level follows a know path, then Eq. (10.6) describes the time path of the real debt. Hence, the nominal debt—denoted by B— grows at the rate of inflation, π, plus the amount implied by the r.h.s. of Equation (10.6). That is, neglecting the term, $(r - n)b$, in Eq. (10.6),

$$\frac{dB}{dt} = (n + \pi)B + \left(1 - \frac{y}{y^*}\right) Pg^* + P(g - g^*). \tag{10.7}$$

The main point is that the behavior of the real debt depends only on real variables. Hence the government's deficit policy is specified in real terms, rather than being subject to some form of money illusion.

A one-time surprise jump in the price level would shift the real debt, b, by a discrete amount in the opposite direction. Then, except for the shift in b on the r.h.s. of Eq. (10.6), there would be no alteration to the subsequent path of the real debt—in particular, there is no tendency to adjust the nominal debt to compensate for unexpected inflation (and thereby to restore some target value of the real debt). It follows in Eq. (10.7) that the variable π should be replaced by the expected rate of inflation, π^e. (In the presence of indexed public debt, the actual rate of inflation would be appropriate.)

9. If an increase in the debt–income ratio raises the required real interest rate payable on public debt (perhaps because of an increasing probability of the government's default), there would be a force that deters the government from amassing very high debt–income ratios.

Given the expected real interest rate, r, a higher value of anticipated inflation shows up as a higher nominal interest rate. Hence the previous result says that the government finances the (expected) inflation part of its nominal interest payments by issuing new nominal debt rather than by levying taxes. Although this interpretation is suggestive, it turns out that the results do not depend on a one-to-one relation between expected inflation and nominal interest rates. Any discrepancy here appears as a different value for the expected real interest rate. But a different level of the real interest rate does not affect the behavior of the debt in Eq. (10.7), assuming a given real growth rate, n, and neglecting the effect from the $(r - n)b$ term in Eq. (10.6). A permanently higher real interest rate induces a once-and-for-all adjustment of the tax rate— Eq. (10.5)—but no response of the deficit. On the other hand, if the expected real interest were temporarily high or low, the deficit would adjust accordingly. Thus far, I have not investigated this possibility empirically.

When the debt is long term, there are also changes in the real market value from changes in long-term nominal interest rates. A one-time jump in the nominal interest rate shifts the current market value of the debt by a discrete amount in the opposite direction. For example, Butkiewicz (1983) shows that the market value of the debt (B^m) can be well approximated empirically from the par value (B^p) by using the formula,

$$B^m \approx \frac{B^p(1 + hc)}{1 + hR},\tag{10.8}$$

where c is the average coupon rate on the outstanding bonds, R is the overall market yield, and h is the average maturity of the bonds. For given values of c and h, the effect of a change in market yield on the market value of debt is approximately

$$dB^m \approx - dR \left(\frac{hB^m}{1 + hR}\right).\tag{10.9}$$

Equations (10.6) and (10.7) describe the paths of the market value of the real and nominal debt, respectively, subsequent to the initial discrete shift in market value at the moment of the one-time shift in yield. In particular, this discrete shift affects the subsequent path of the debt only through the change in b on the right side of the equations (and by any change in expected inflation that accompanies the shift in the long-term nominal interest rate). As with a surprise change in the price level, there is no tendency to return to a normal real market value of the debt. But to explain the overall movements in the market value of the debt, it is necessary to include an additional variable—namely, that shown in Eq. (10.9)—to measure the effect of surprise changes in interest rates. In practice, I assume that all changes in the yield on government bonds, R, are unanticipated.

When considering the public debt, most researchers deal with the par value rather than the market value. (However, some reliable estimates of market value are now available for the post–World War II period, as discussed below.) A surprise jump in nominal interest rates has no immediate effect on the debt when measured at par value. But as the old debt matures, the government effectively replaces it with new debt, which bears, say, a higher coupon. (I assume that all debt is issued at par.) Thus, if nothing else changes, then the government would face a rising path of real interest payments—that is, current real payments would be low relative to the average of anticipated future real payments. Like any path of rising real expenditures, the government's policy of tax-smoothing requires a rise in the current tax rate, which means a smaller current deficit. In other words, a surprise increase in nominal interest rates leads to a gradual reduction over time in the real debt when measured at par value. In fact, if there are no further surprises in interest rates (and the debt has finite maturity), then the real par value gradually approaches the real market value, which fell in a discrete fashion at the moment of the one-time shift in interest rates.

Eq. (10.8) implies that the effect on the par value of the debt from a change in the average coupon rate is

$$dB^p \approx - \, dc \left(\frac{hB^p}{1 + hc} \right). \tag{10.10}$$

Suppose that the retirement of old debt means that the coupon rate, c, gradually approaches the market yield, R, with the speed of adjustment depending inversely on the average maturity, h—that is,

$$\frac{dc}{dt} \approx \left(\frac{1}{h} \right) (R - c).$$

Then Eq. (10.10) implies that the effect on the par value of the debt is

$$\frac{dB^p}{dt} \approx \frac{-(R - c)B^p}{1 + hc}. \tag{10.11}$$

I add the r.h.s. variable (unsuccessfully) to some of the equations that I estimate below. (I have data on the variables R, c, and h only for the period since 1946.)

Setup of the Empirical Analysis

The equation that I estimate with annual U.S. data over the period 1916–1982 takes the form

$$\frac{B_t - B_{t-1}}{P_t y_t} = a_0 \left(\frac{B_{t-1}}{P_t y_t}\right) + a_1 \pi_t^e \left(\frac{B_{t-1}}{P_t y_t}\right) + a_2 \text{YVAR}_t \tag{10.12}$$

$$+ a_3 \text{GVAR}_t + a_4 \text{RVAR}_t + u_t.$$

I divided through by nominal GNP, $P_t y_t$, in order to scale the error term, u_t (and thus make it closer to being homoscedastic). In this case the dependent variable is the ratio of the nominal deficit to GNP (where the "deficit" includes only the amount financed by sales of interest-bearing debt to the private sector).

The independent variables in Eq. (10.12) are as follows:

B　　End-of-calendar year (par or market) value of the U.S. government's interest-bearing public debt, exclusive of holdings at federal agencies and trust funds or the Federal Reserve. Market-value figures are based on Seater (1981) and Butkiewicz (1983).

π_t^e　　Expected rate of inflation (for the CPI), generated as a forecasting relation using two annual lags of inflation, π_{t-1} and π_{t-2}, and one annual lag of monetary growth (based on annual averages of $M1$), μ_{t-1}. I found that including additional lags or adding an interest rate variable did not add much explanatory power for inflation. Thus the equation for inflation is[10]

$$\pi_t = b_0 + b_t\pi_{t-1} + b_2\pi_{t-2} + b_3\mu_{t-1} + \varepsilon_t, \tag{10.13}$$

where ε_t is an error term. Equation (10.13) is estimated jointly with the debt equation (10.12).

The behavior of inflation in recent years differs markedly from that before World War II. First, the recent period exhibits positive persistence in inflation rates from year to year, whereas the earlier period shows some negative persistence; second, lagged monetary growth is now a positive predictor of inflation, which is not the case before; and third, the variance of the inflation rate—conditioned on information from the previous year—is much smaller in recent years. I have found it satisfactory to treat the earlier sample as consisting of 1920–1940, 1946–1949. For these years there is "gold-standard-like" behavior of the inflation rate—in particular, higher inflation today generates a prediction of lower inflation later on. The other sample period for inflation consists of the period after the Treasury–Federal Reserve Accords that ended the pegging of interest rates, 1954–1982, plus the years associated with World War I, 1916–1919, World War II, 1941–1945, and the Korean War, 1950–1953. That is, I get reasonable results by treating the period of managed money, 1954–1982, as exhibiting coefficients in Eq. (10.13) that are the same as those in World Wars I and II and the Korean War. Notably, with the constraints of the gold standard effectively relaxed during the wars, it is unsatisfactory to group these observations with those from the earlier sample.

I model the error term, ε_t, in Eq. (10.13) as having one variance for the period 1916–1942 and another (lower) variance for the period 1948–1982. Because of the price controls for 1943–1947, the observa-

10. The inflation rates are January-to-January values, using the CPI less shelter since 1947. For 1943–1947, the data are strongly affected by price controls. Instead of using the reported price levels, I substituted values based on the extrapolation of an estimated price-level equation from some previous research; see Barro (1981c, p. 157). This adjustment shifts the inflation rates as follows: from 2.9 to 25.8% for 1943, from 2.3 to 13.0% for 1944, from 2.2 to 3.2% for 1945, from 16.7 to −4.8% for 1946, and from 10.2 to −2.9% for 1947. Because I excluded the years 1943–1947 from the estimation of the inflation equation, this procedure matters directly only for the measures of lagged inflation in 1948–1949. See, however, note 14.

tions from these years are not used to estimate the coefficients of Eq. (10.13). Finally, note that the coefficient of the expected inflation variable, $\pi_t^e B_{t-1}/P_t y_t$, in Eq. (10.12) is $a_1 = 1$.

Returning to the specification of variables in Eq. (10.12), I define

$$YVAR_t \equiv \left(1 - \frac{y_t}{y_t^*}\right)\left(\frac{g_t^*}{y_t}\right)$$

and

$$GVAR_t \equiv \frac{g_t - g_t^*}{y_t}.$$

I base the measurement of temporary real federal spending, $g_t - g_t^*$, on the analysis of Sahasakul (1984, tables 1 and 2). He began with the variable that I constructed previously (Barro 1981b) to measure the temporary parts of military spending that accompany wars. It turned out that shifts during peacetime in the ratio of military spending to GNP were best treated as predominantly permanent (in the sense that the ratios followed random walks). Sahasakul found additional components of temporary real federal spending from the following: (1) a drift since the 1930s in the ratio of federal transfers to GNP; (2) the tendency since the 1930s of real federal transfers to move countercyclically; and (3) the tendency of wars to crowd out the nonmilitary components of federal spending. Thus his measure of temporary spending added these items to my previous construct for the military component.

For the cyclical variable YVAR in Eq. (10.12), I need a measure of the temporary shortfall of output, $(1 - y_t/y_t^*)$. In a previous study (Barro 1979), I used the deviation of current real GNP, which measured y_t, from trend real GNP, which measured y_t^*.[11] I again report some results with this construct, although it deals incorrectly with permanent shifts to the level of output. In these cases the variable indicates a permanent departure of output from normal. The results improve if I use instead the unemployment rate, U_t, to proxy for the shortfall in output, $(1 - y_t/y_t^*)$. As long as the unemployment rate is stationary in levels, this

---

11. For trend real GNP, the growth rate was 3.4% per year since 1946 and before 1914. For 1915–1945, the connection of the two trend lines implied an average growth rate of 2.5% per year.

variable will work satisfactorily even when there are permanent shifts to the level of output.

My main results use the total employment rate (including the military in the labor force).[12] Then I assume a stable relation between percentage shortfalls in output and the departure of the unemployment rate from a fixed natural rate:

$$1 - \frac{y_t}{y_t^*} = \lambda(U_t - 0.054). \tag{10.14}$$

I take the natural unemployment rate in this formulation to be 5.4%, which is the median rate over the sample 1890–1982. (The value 5.4% is also close to the median and mean over the period 1948–1982.) For the post–World War II period (for which data are available), I obtain similar results if I use instead the prime-age male unemployment rate, U_t^m. Some people argue that, because of demographic shifts, this variable is more stable over long periods than the overall unemployment rate. Note that in Eq. (10.14) the parameter λ is an Okun's law–type coefficient, which is likely to lie between 2 and 3.

As a general statement, it would be preferable to construct normal output, y_t^*, as an explicit time-series representation for "permanent income." (The measure for $g_t - g_t^*$ does take this approach.) But I have thus far been unsuccessful along these lines in the construction of the variable y_t^*.

The variable YVAR$_t$ depends also on normal real federal spending g_t^*, which comes from Sahasakul's (1984) analysis, as discussed above. Note that the effect of cyclical fluctuations, $(1 - y_t/y_t^*)$, on the ratio of deficits to GNP depends on the ratio, g_t^*/y_t. Although this ratio is typically fairly stable in the short run, it can change a great deal in the long run. For example, in 1982 the variable g_t^*/y_t is 0.21 whereas in 1933 it is 0.06. Hence—because of the high value of normal real federal spending in recent years—a one percentage point shortfall in output has over three times as much effect on the deficit–GNP ratio as it would have in 1933 (where the percentage shortfall in output was much larger).

The tax-smoothing model suggests that the coefficient of YVAR$_t$ in Eq. (10.12) would be $a_2 = 1$. However, any tendency to lower tax rates

---

12. I also adjusted the values from 1933 to 1943 as suggested by Darby (1976) to include New Deal workers as employed.

during recessions leads to $a_2 > 1$. When the unemployment rate proxies for the shortfall in output Eq. (10.14), the estimated coefficient on $YVAR_t$ is also multiplied by the Okun's law coefficient, λ.

The variable $RVAR_t$ in Eq. (10.12) accounts for the effects of changes in interest rates. With the debt measured at par value, the interest-rate variable (available since 1946) is $RVAR_t = (B_{t-1}/P_t y_t) \cdot (\bar{R}_t - \bar{c}_t)/(1 + \bar{h}_t \bar{c}_t)$, where R is the yield, h is average maturity, c is the average coupon rate, and overbars signify averages over the year. When the debt is measured at market value (available accurately since 1941), the interest-rate variable is $RVAR_t = (B_{t-1}/P_t y_t) \cdot \bar{h}_t(R_t - R_{t-1})/(1 + \bar{h}_t \bar{R}_t)$. In both cases the hypothesized coefficient in Eq. (10.12) is $a_4 = -1$.

Finally, some preliminary results indicated that the magnitude of the error term, u_t, in Eq. (10.12) was typically higher during the years associated with the major wars—that is, World Wars I and II. Partly this outcome could reflect the difficulty in obtaining accurate proxies for temporary government spending during wartime. In any case, I partially account for this problem by allowing the variance of the error term, σ^2, to depend on the magnitude of the temporary spending variable. Specifically, I assume a linear relation between the log of the variance and a three-year moving average of the square of the spending variable:

$$\log (\sigma_t^2) = \alpha_0 + \alpha_1[(GVAR_{t-1})^2 + (GVAR_t)^2 \qquad (10.15)$$
$$+ (GVAR_{t-1})^2].$$

The α coefficients are estimated along with those in Eq. (10.12) and (10.13),[13] with the observations in Eq. (10.12) weighted by the estimated value of $1/\sigma_t$.

Empirical Results

Table 10.1 shows joint, maximum-likelihood estimates for the deficit equation (10.12) and the inflation equation (10.13) over the period 1916–1982. For the deficit equations in this table, the RVAR variable is

13. The residuals $\hat{u}_t$ from an unweighted form of Eq. (10.12) were regressed on the spending values to obtain $\log[(\hat{u}_t)^2] = \alpha_0 + \alpha_1[(GVAR_{t-1})^2 + (GVAR_t)^2 + (GVAR_{t+1})^2]$. Then the estimated values for the α coefficients were used to obtain second-stage, weighted estimates of Eq. (10.12).

omitted and the YVAR variable is based on the overall unemployment rate. The inflation equations report separate coefficients for the two subperiods, 1920–1940, 1948–1949; and 1916–1919, 1941–1942, 1950–1982. Also, the observations in the inflation equation for the period 1916–1942 are weighted by 0.40 to correct for heteroscedasticity (that is, for a higher error variance in the earlier period).

For set 1 in Table 10.1, the inflation equation in the earlier subperiod (1920–1940, 1948–1949) shows a positive effect of the first lag of inflation (0.28, s.e. = 0.14) and a negative effect from the second lag (−0.44, s.e. = 11). The coefficient of lagged monetary growth (0.10, s.e. = 0.12) differs insignificantly from zero. Thus the main effect is a tendency for higher than normal inflation to be followed eventually by lower than normal inflation. This behavior is consistent with a gold standard-type mechanism. By contrast, the subperiod that includes wars and the recent peacetime years (1916–1919, 1941–1942, 1950–1982) shows positive persistence of inflation (0.23, s.e. = 0.12, on the first lag; 0.07, s.e. = 0.11, on the second). Further, lagged monetary growth has important explanatory value (0.72, s.e. = 0.14). These findings are broadly similar for all of the cases that I consider later on.

Expected inflation, π_t^e, is calculated from the coefficients of the inflation equation.[14] In set 1 of Table 10.1, the coefficient of the π_t^e variable [that is, of $\pi_t^e \cdot (B_{t-1}/P_t y_t)$] in the deficit equation is constrained to equal one, whereas in set 2 it is left free. (Similarly, the other cases in the table alternate between restricted and unrestricted values of this coefficient.) Note that the unconstrained estimate is 1.00, s.e. = 0.17. Because the results in other cases are also consistent with the hypothesized value of unity, I focus subsequently on the results in which the coefficient is set to one.

In set 1 the estimated coefficient of the temporary spending variable, GVAR, is 0.59, s.e. = 0.07. Thus the estimated value differs significantly from zero but also differs significantly from the value of one that is suggested by the tax-smoothing model. I discuss this result further below.

14. As noted before, the years 1943–1947 were omitted from the estimation of the inflation equation. To calculate π_t^e for the years 1944–1949, I used estimated values of lagged inflation (as discussed in note 10) rather than the reported numbers. For the years 1946–1947, the coefficients were those applicable to the earlier subperiod (1920–1940, 1948–1949), whereas for 1943–1945, the coefficients were those estimated from the other subperiod (1916–1919, 1941–1942, 1950–1982).

Table 10.1. Basic regression results for deficits and inflation: 1916–1982

| | Equation for $(B_t - B_{t-1})/P_t y_t$ [a] | | | | | Equation for π_t [b] | | | | |
Set	Con-stant	$\pi_t^e(B_{t-1}/P_t y_t)$ [c]	GVAR [d]	YVAR [e]	σ and D.W. [f]	Sub-samples for π_t [g]	Con-stant	π_{t-1} [h]	π_{t-2} [h]	μ_{t-1} [i]	σ and D.W. [f]
(1)	0.0134 (0.0053)	1	0.59 (0.07)	3.73 (0.35)	0.0110 1.97	(a)	−0.0136 (0.0088)	0.28 (0.14)	−0.44 (0.11)	0.10 (0.12)	0.0216 1.71
						(b)	−0.0010 (0.0060)	0.23 (0.12)	0.07 (0.11)	0.72 (0.14)	
(2)	0.0135 (0.0065)	1.00 (0.17)	0.59 (0.07)	3.73 (0.36)	0.0110 1.97	(a)	−0.0136 (0.0094)	0.28 (0.16)	−0.44 (0.12)	0.10 (0.12)	0.0216 1.71
						(b)	−0.0009 (0.0061)	0.23 (0.12)	0.07 (0.11)	0.72 (0.15)	
(3)	0.0025 (0.0063)	1	0.58 (0.08)	1.54 [j] (0.19)	0.0127 1.57	(a)	−0.0155 (0.0093)	0.25 (0.16)	−0.40 (0.12)	0.02 (0.13)	0.0217 1.67
						(b)	−0.0014 (0.0061)	0.26 (0.12)	0.06 (0.11)	0.73 (0.15)	
(4)	−0.0031 (0.0085)	1.25 (0.22)	0.55 (0.08)	1.61 [j] (0.20)	0.0125 1.70	(a)	−0.0109 (0.0090)	0.18 (0.14)	−0.33 (0.11)	0.01 (0.11)	0.0219 1.60
						(b)	−0.0014 (0.0061)	0.21 (0.11)	0.09 (0.10)	0.73 (0.14)	
(5a) [k]	0.0035 (0.0057)	1	0.22 (0.11)	4.29 (0.35)	0.0097 2.20	(a)	−0.0147 (0.0081)	0.29 (0.15)	−0.45 (0.10)	0.10 (0.12)	0.0216 1.65
(5b) [k]	0.0294 (0.0180)	1	0.79 (0.11)	5.81 (4.23)		(b)	0.0018 (0.0058)	0.21 (0.11)	0.09 (0.10)	0.68 (0.14)	

(6a)[k]	0.0053	0.92	0.22	4.28	0.0097	(a)	−0.0164	0.34	−0.47	0.09	0.0216
	(0.0065)	(0.17)	(0.11)	(0.35)			(0.0091)	(0.17)	(0.12)	(0.12)	
(6b)[k]	0.0289	0.73	0.86	7.12	2.18	(b)	0.0011	0.22	0.09	0.69	1.68
	(0.0177)	(0.34)	(0.14)	(4.50)			(0.0060)	(0.11)	(0.10)	(0.14)	

a. The dependent variable in the deficit equation is $(B_t - B_{t-1})/P_t y_t$, where $P_t y_t$ is nominal GNP and B_t is the end-of-December value of privately held, interest-bearing public debt. The figures are par values except for sets 13 and 14, which use market values.

There are separate coefficients for the deficit equation over the two subperiods, 1920–1940, 1948–1982 and 1916–1919, 1941–1947, in sets 5 and 6. Otherwise a single set of coefficients applies for the full sample. The observations are weighted as described in the text.

Values in parentheses below values for coefficients are standard errors.

b. The dependent variable in the inflation equation is π_t, which is the January-to-January growth rate of the CPI (measured without the shelter component since 1947).

The inflation equation in sets 1–6 allows for separate coefficients for the early subperiod, 1920–1940, 1948–1949, and the other subperiod, 1916–1919, 1941–1942, 1950–1982. The earlier observations are weighted by 0.40 (the maximum-likelihood estimate from set 1) to correct for heteroscedasticity. The observations for 1943–1947 are deleted from the inflation equation (in sets 1–6).

Values in parentheses below values for coefficients are standard errors.

c. The values for π_t^e are calculated as forecasts of π_t from the coefficients of the inflation equation. The value 1 indicates that the coefficient of the variable, $\pi_t^e B_{t-1}/P_t y_t$, is constrained to unity.

d. The variable GVAR, based on temporary federal spending, is discussed in the text.

e. The cyclical variable YVAR, described in the text, is based on the overall unemployment rate, $U_t - 0.054$, for sets 1–2 and 5–6. Sets 3 and 4 use real GNP relative to trend.

f. $\hat{\sigma}$ is the standard error of estimate. D.W. (shown below $\hat{\sigma}$) is the Durbin–Watson statistic.

g. (a) is the early subperiod, 1920–1940, 1948–1949; (b) is the other subperiod, 1916–1919, 1941–1942, 1950–1982.

h. Lagged values of the dependent variable.

i. Lagged value of monetary growth (based on annual averages of M1).

j. Uses real GNP relative to trend rather than overall unemployment rate.

k. (a) is the subperiod 1920–1940, 1948–1982; (b) is the subperiod 1916–1919, 1941–1947.

The estimated coefficient of the cyclical variable YVAR (3.73, s.e. = 0.35) is positive and highly significant, a result that shows the strong countercyclical behavior of deficits. Dividing by an Okun's law coefficient of 2½ implies that the reaction of deficits to shortfalls in output involves a coefficient of about 1½; see Eq. (10.14). The excess of this coefficient above one reflects the tendency during recessions for tax rates to be below normal, rather than merely being stabilized.

To see the quantitative effect of unemployment on the deficit, recall that the pertinent variable is $YVAR_t = (U_t - 0.054) \cdot (g_t^*/y_t)$, which has an estimated coefficient of 3.7. In 1982 the variable g_t^*/y_t equals 0.21, which means that a one percentage point increase in the unemployment rate raises the estimated ratio of the deficit to GNP by $3.7 \cdot (0.21) = 0.8$ percentage points per year. For a nominal GNP of $3073 billion (1982), the corresponding increase in the deficit is by $0.8\% \cdot 3073 = \$27$ billion.

The standard error of estimate for the deficit equation—that is, for the ratio of the deficit to GNP—is $\hat{\sigma} = 0.011$ (see, however, the results below for different subperiods). Because the deficit regression was weighted in accordance with the value of GVAR (see above), this number for $\hat{\sigma}$ applies as the magnitude of GVAR approaches zero. But it turns out (see Table 10.3) that the value $\hat{\sigma} = 0.011$ applies as a close approximation to all observations except those associated with World Wars I and II. The Durbin–Watson statistic of 2.0 indicates that serial correlation of residuals is not a problem. (The R^2 for the regression is 0.8.)

Sets 3 and 4 of Table 10.1 show how the results change when real GNP relative to trend is used instead of the unemployment rate to measure the cyclical variable, YVAR. Although the fit is somewhat poorer, the general results are close to those found before. Note that the estimated coefficient of the YVAR variable (1.54, s.e. = 0.19 in set 3) now shows directly the response of the deficit to shortfalls in output. That is, a decline by 1% in real GNP tends to lower real federal receipts by about 1.5%. Correspondingly, tax rates are below normal during recessions and above normal in booms.

Sets 5 and 6 of Table 10.1 check whether the deficit equation is stable over the years influenced by major war, 1916–1919, 1941–1947, and the remainder of the sample. The hypothesis of stable coefficients is rejected at the 1% level. (For set 5, the value of $-2 \cdot \log(\text{likelihood ratio})$ is 15.8, as compared with the 1% χ^2 value with three degrees of freedom of 11.3.) It is clear from the estimated coefficients shown in set 5 that the main element behind this instability is the different estimates for the GVAR variable 0.22, s.e. = 0.11, for the sample 1920–1940, 1948–1982, versus 0.79, s.e. = 0.11, for the sample 1916–1919, 1941–1947. In fact, it may be that the principal information about the effects of temporary spending comes from the major wars; so an estimated coefficient of about 0.8 is the most reliable figure. In particular, the main movements in the GVAR variable over the remaining sample, 1920–1940, 1948–1982, may be primarily measurement error, which would account for the low value of the estimated coefficient. Note also that the estimated value for the war sample, 0.79, s.e. = 0.11, does not differ greatly from the hypothesized value of unity. That is, temporary spending of $1 leads to almost $1 of additional deficit.[15]

After excluding the years associated with the major wars (1916–1919, 1941–1947), I also checked whether the deficit equation was consistent with the same coefficients for the interwar period, 1920–1940, and the post–World War II sample, 1948–1982. In this case the hypothesis of stability is accepted. (The value of $-2 \cdot \log$(likelihood ratio) is only 1.2, compared with a 5% critical value from the χ^2 distribution with 3 degrees of freedom of 7.8.) This finding is important, because it indicates that the process for generating deficits in the interwar years, 1920–1940, is broadly similar to that in the recent period, 1948–1982. In particular, the statistical evidence does not support the idea that there has been a shift toward a fiscal policy that generates more real public debt on average or that generates larger deficits in response to recessions.[16]

Sets 7 and 8 of Table 10.2 show separate estimates for the subperiod 1920–1940; sets 9 and 10 show those for 1950–1982. These results are basically consistent with those discussed earlier. Note in set 9 that the standard error of estimate, $\hat{\sigma}$, from the deficit equation for the 1950–1982 sample is only 0.006 (compared with 0.011 for the overall sample, 1916–1982). Thus, with a GNP of about $3 trillion, the value $\hat{\sigma} = 0.006$ means that a one-standard-error estimation interval for the deficit in recent years is about ±$18 billion.

Sets 11 and 12 of Table 10.2 change the YVAR variable to use the prime-age male unemployment rate, $U_t^m - 0.041$, where 0.041 is the

15. During World War II the constructed series for $g*/y$ does show a sharp increase (see Table 10.3). Thus a substantial portion of the extra spending was financed by higher taxes (and the creation of high-powered money).

16. The estimated coefficient of YVAR is 4.43, s.e. = 0.84, for 1920–1940, and 4.15, s.e. = 0.49, for 1948–1982.

Table 10.2. Regression results for subsamples

Set	Sample	Equation for $(B_t - B_{t-1})/P_t y_t$ [a]						Equation for π_t [b]				
		Constant	$\pi^e(B_{t-1}/P_t y_t)$ [c]	GVAR [d]	YVAR [e]	RVAR [f]	$\hat{\sigma}$ and D.W. [g]	Constant	π_{t-1} [h]	π_{t-2} [h]	μ_{t-1} [i]	$\hat{\sigma}$ and D.W.
(7)	1920–1940	−0.0162	1	0.13	5.31	—	0.0092	−0.0214	0.20	−0.38	0.24	0.0402
		(0.0123)		(0.15)	(0.61)		2.24	(0.0099)	(0.20)	(0.12)	(0.15)	2.01
(8)		−0.0172	0.86	0.14	5.24	—	0.0092	−0.0206	0.26	−0.44	0.23	0.0398
		(0.0120)	(0.19)	(0.15)	(0.59)		2.20	(0.0103)	(0.22)	(0.15)	(0.18)	2.12
(9)	1950–1982	−0.0027	1	0.05	3.68	—	0.0061	0.0033	0.15	0.33	0.49	0.0269
		(0.0066)		(0.10)	(0.40)		2.01	(0.0064)	(0.09)	(0.09)	(0.15)	1.01
(10)		−0.0181	1.41	0.05	3.57	—	0.0059	0.0112	0.12	0.30	0.36	0.269
		(0.0174)	(0.39)	(0.10)	(0.40)		2.12	(0.0087)	(0.07)	(0.09)	(0.15)	0.95
(11)		−0.0113	1	−0.03	3.49[j]	—	0.0068	0.0000	0.20	0.33	0.53	0.0269
		(0.0066)		(0.11)	(0.43)		1.61	(0.0067)	(0.10)	(0.10)	(0.17)	1.02
(12)		−0.0329	1.61	−0.02	3.35[j]	—	0.0065	0.0109	0.15	0.29	0.34	0.0266
		(0.0186)	(0.42)	(0.10)	(0.43)		1.79	(0.0087)	(0.07)	(0.09)	(0.15)	0.96
(13)		0.0033	1	0.06	3.98	−0.73	0.0071	0.0043	0.06	0.41	0.48	0.0278
		(0.0068)		(0.12)	(0.47)	(0.14)	2.09	(0.0070)	(0.11)	(0.11)	(0.19)	1.02
(14)		−0.0197	1.61	0.05	3.72	−0.75	0.0068	0.0150	0.05	0.35	0.28	0.0280
		(0.0212)	(0.48)	(0.12)	(0.49)	(0.14)	2.16	(0.0090)	(0.08)	(0.11)	(0.17)	0.93

(15)	−0.0046 (0.0065)	1	0.16 (0.11)	3.72 (0.38)	0.92 (0.56)	0.0058 1.92	0.0056 (0.0067)	0.12 (0.09)	0.32 (0.09)	0.47 (0.15)	0.268 0.99
(16)	−0.0152 (0.0161)	1.29 (0.38)	0.13 (0.11)	3.36 (0.39)	0.76 (0.60)	0.0057 2.00	0.0111 (0.0088)	0.10 (0.08)	0.30 (0.09)	0.37 (0.16)	0.0268 0.95
(17)	−0.0028 (0.0068)	1	0.06 (0.10)	3.66 (0.41)	0.08 (0.54)	0.0060 2.04	0.0035 (0.0066)	0.15 (0.09)	0.34 (0.09)	0.49 (0.16)	0.0269 1.01
(18)	−0.0182 (0.0177)	1.42 (0.40)	0.05 (0.10)	3.57 (0.42)	−0.04 (0.55)	0.0059 2.11	0.0112 (0.0087)	0.12 (0.07)	0.30 (0.09)	0.36 (0.15)	0.0267 0.95

a. See footnote a for Table 10.1.

b. The dependent variable is π_t, which is the January-to-January growth rate of the CPI (measured without the shelter component since 1947). Values in parentheses below the values for the coefficients are standard errors.

c–e. See footnotes c–e for Table 10.1.

f. Sets 13 and 14 use the market value of debt; the variable $\mathrm{RVAR}_t = (B_{t-1}/P_t y_t) \cdot \bar{h}_t (R_t - R_{t-1})/(1 + \bar{h}_t R_t)$, where R is the average yield on government debt and h is the average maturity. Overbars indicate estimates of averages over the year. For sets 15 and 16, the variable is $\mathrm{RVAR}_t = (B_{t-1}/P_t y_t) \cdot (\bar{R}_t - \bar{C}_t)/(1 + \bar{h}_t C_t)$, where C is the average coupon rate on government debt. Sets 17 and 18 use the lagged value of this last measure of RVAR.

g. $\hat{\sigma}$ is the standard error of estimate. D.W. (shown below $\hat{\sigma}$) is the Durbin–Watson statistic.

h.–i. See footnotes h and i for Table 10.1.

j. Based on the prime-age male unemployment rate, $U_t^m - 0.041$, rather than the overall unemployment rate.

Table 10.3. Values of explanatory variables

Date	GVAR^a	YVAR^b	g^*/y^c	$B_{t-1}/P_t y_t^d$	Weight^e
1916	−0.012	0.0001	0.040	0.020	0.88
1917	0.100	−0.0002	0.046	0.015	0.53
1918	0.199	−0.0051	0.128	0.084	0.48
1919	0.089	−0.0039	0.102	0.256	0.54
1920	−0.022	0.0003	0.086	0.284	0.90
1921	0.012	0.0041	0.055	0.343	0.99
1922	−0.020	0.0013	0.060	0.303	0.99
1923	−0.024	−0.0016	0.060	0.258	0.98
1924	−0.019	0.0001	0.054	0.249	0.98
1925	−0.022	−0.0099	0.055	0.216	0.98
1926	−0.024	−0.0018	0.054	0.204	0.98
1927	−0.020	−0.0019	0.052	0.186	0.98
1928	−0.019	−0.0004	0.053	0.171	0.99
1929	−0.019	−0.0009	0.050	0.153	0.99
1930	−0.012	0.0002	0.051	0.164	0.99
1931	−0.002	0.0078	0.062	0.194	1.00
1932	0.008	0.0106	0.050	0.276	1.00
1933	0.015	0.0126	0.058	0.326	0.99
1934	0.012	0.0122	0.090	0.328	0.99
1935	0.014	0.0096	0.083	0.349	1.00
1936	0.002	0.0065	0.114	0.365	1.00
1937	−0.002	0.0043	0.090	0.369	1.00
1938	0.018	0.0077	0.091	0.405	0.99
1939	0.001	0.0067	0.094	0.396	0.99
1940	0.014	0.0050	0.096	0.385	0.97
1941	0.047	0.0013	0.130	0.332	0.63
1942	0.182	−0.0035	0.183	0.335	0.20
1943	0.303	−0.0061	0.166	0.495	0.05
1944	0.341	−0.0062	0.147	0.677	0.02
1945	0.302	−0.0049	0.141	0.907	0.07
1946	0.037	−0.0018	0.152	1.087	0.30
1947	−0.024	−0.0025	0.155	0.888	0.96

Table 10.3 (continued)

Date	GVAR[a]	YVAR[b]	g^*/y^c	$B_{t-1}/P_t y_t^d$	Weight[e]
1948	−0.029	−0.0028	0.166	0.774	0.97
1949	−0.024	0.0008	0.188	0.749	0.98
1950	−0.012	−0.0005	0.160	0.699	0.99
1951	0.010	−0.0039	0.176	0.597	0.99
1952	0.017	−0.0050	0.201	0.558	0.99
1953	0.007	−0.0056	0.216	0.539	1.00
1954	0.006	−0.0002	0.196	0.549	0.99
1955	−0.017	−0.0024	0.198	0.511	0.99
1956	−0.020	−0.0038	0.197	0.511	0.99
1957	−0.019	−0.0027	0.204	0.446	0.99
1958	−0.007	0.0023	0.209	0.436	0.99
1959	−0.017	−0.0002	0.204	0.415	0.99
1960	−0.018	−0.0002	0.203	0.414	0.99
1961	−0.001	0.0023	0.207	0.394	0.99
1962	−0.016	−0.0002	0.214	0.374	0.99
1963	−0.017	0.0002	0.207	0.361	0.99
1964	−0.021	−0.0008	0.202	0.339	0.99
1965	−0.021	−0.0020	0.196	0.315	0.99
1966	−0.013	−0.0036	0.200	0.286	0.99
1967	−0.001	−0.0034	0.202	0.269	1.00
1968	0.000	−0.0040	0.199	0.251	1.00
1969	−0.004	−0.0040	0.200	0.239	1.00
1970	−0.009	−0.0012	0.206	0.222	1.00
1971	−0.011	0.0006	0.206	0.212	0.99
1972	−0.015	0.0000	0.209	0.208	0.99
1973	−0.023	−0.0015	0.208	0.181	0.99
1974	−0.019	0.0000	0.214	0.181	0.99
1975	−0.003	0.0063	0.218	0.174	0.99
1976	−0.008	0.0045	0.216	0.203	1.00
1977	−0.011	0.0032	0.214	0.213	0.99
1978	−0.016	0.0011	0.212	0.211	0.99
1979	−0.016	0.0006	0.209	0.208	0.99

Table 10.3 (continued)

Date	GVAR[a]	YVAR[b]	$g*/y^c$	$B_{t-1}/P_t y_t^d$	Weight[e]
1980	−0.007	0.0034	0.214	0.205	1.00
1981	−0.004	0.0044	0.208	0.229	1.00
1982	0.008	0.0085	0.207	0.227	1.00
1983	0.008	0.008	0.205	0.257	—
1984	(−0.003)	(0.004)	(0.205)	(0.278)	—
1985	(−0.003)	(0.005)	(0.205)	(0.301)	—

a. GVAR $= (g_t - g_t^*)/y_t$, where y_t is real GNP and $(g_t - g_t^*)$ is an estimate of temporary real federal spending from Sahasakul (1984, tables 10.1 and 10.2).

b. YVAR $= (U_t - 0.054) \cdot g_t^*/y_t$, where U_t is the unemployment rate in the total labor force (adjusted as suggested by Darby (1976) for 1933–1943) and g_t^* is normal real federal spending from Sahasakul.

c. $g*/y$ is the ratio of normal federal spending to GNP.

d. $B_{t-1}/P_t y_t$ is the ratio to nominal GNP of the stock of privately held, interest bearing public debt at the end of the previous year (see the notes to Table 10.4.

e. The weight applicable to the estimated equation for the deficit-GNP ratio is $1/\sigma_t$, where $\log(\sigma_t^2) = \text{constant} + 13.2[(\text{GVAR}_{t-1})^2 + (\text{GVAR})^2 + (\text{GVAR}_{t+1})^2]$. The weight is normalized to equal one when the value of GVAR $= 0$.

mean value of U^m since 1950. Although the fit of the deficit equation is slightly worse than that in sets 9 and 10 (which use the overall unemployment rate), the general nature of the results is similar.

Sets 13 and 14 of Table 10.2 use the estimated market value of the public debt, rather than the par value, in the construction of the dependent variable. The equation for the deficit now includes an interest-rate variable, RVAR$_t$, which picks up the effect on the market value of debt from changes in interest rates. For set 13 (where the coefficient of the π^e variable is fixed at one), the estimated coefficient of RVAR$_t$ is −0.73, s.e. = 0.14, which differs significantly from the hypothesized value of −1 at the 5% level but not at the 1% level. The other results are broadly similar to those found in sets 9 and 10, which are based on the par value of public debt.

In sets 15–18 of Table 10.2, I attempt to find an effect from changes in interest rates on the deficit when measured at par value. (The variable RVAR$_t$ is now based on the difference between the yield and the coupon rate—see the notes to Tables 10.1 and 10.2.) Although the hypothesized coefficient of RVAR$_t$ is −1, the estimated values in sets 15 and 16 are positive, but with high standard errors. Because the RVAR$_t$ variable may be proxying for within-period revisions of expected inflation, I used instead the lagged value, $RVAR_{t-1}$, in sets 17 and 18. The estimated coefficients do decrease—for example, to 0.08, s.e. = 0.54, in set 17. Here the estimated coefficient differs significantly from -1 at the 5% level but not at the 1% level. Clearly the effects of interest rates on the deficit require further investigation.

The Behavior of U.S. Deficits since 1916

Table 10.4 shows actual and estimated values for the deficit–GNP ratio, $(B_t - B_{t-1})/P_t y_t$, and the inflation rate, π_t, since 1916. The estimated values come from the regressions shown in set 1 of Table 10.1 (where the coefficient of the π^e variable is constrained to unity). Table 10.3 shows the values of the explanatory variables, GVAR and YVAR (based on the overall unemployment rate), as well as the ratio of normal spending to GNP, g^*/y, and the ratio of debt to GNP, $B_{t-1}/P_t y_t$.

Note first the positive deficits associated with World War I (1917–1919). At the peak in 1918 the deficit is 16% of GNP, although the estimated value is only 11%. Naturally, the main element behind these deficits is temporary federal spending, which equaled almost 20% of GNP in 1918.

Throughout the 1920s there are surpluses. These derive, first, from negative values of anticipated inflation, especially for 1921–1922; second, from the economic boom (negative values of the cyclical variable, YVAR) for most of 1923–1929; and third, from relatively low values of the GVAR variable. From 1931 to 1940, the deficits are all positive, amounting to about 6% of GNP in 1933–1935. This behavior reflects primarily the countercyclical response to the Depression.

Temporary federal spending accounts for the bulk of the huge deficits during World War II. From 1943 to 1945, temporary spending averaged over 30% of GNP. Correspondingly, deficits are about 25% of GNP for 1943–1944, although only 17% for 1945.

For the post–World War II period, note first that neither the actual nor estimated values of the deficit–GNP ratios are very high during the Korean War, say, 1950–1953. (However, for 1951, the actual value is -1.1% while the estimate is $+2.0\%$.) The values of GVAR are positive for 1951–1953, but those for the cyclical variable, YVAR, are low. The regular response of deficits to recessions shows up, for example, in 1949, 1954, 1958, and 1961. The Kennedy–Johnson tax cuts for 1964–1965

Table 10.4. Values of deficits and inflation

Date	$(B_t - B_{t-1})/P_t y_t$ [a]	$\widehat{(B_t - B_{t-1})/P_t y_t}$ [b]	Residual[c]	π_t	$\hat{\pi}_t$ [d]	$\pi_t - \hat{\pi}_t$
1916	−0.001	−0.005	0.004	0.112	0.060	0.052
1917	0.098	0.061	0.038	0.178	0.142	0.052
1918	0.162	0.111	0.051	0.169	0.130	0.039
1919	0.046	0.070	−0.024	0.155	0.112	0.043
1920	−0.011	−0.015	0.005	−0.014	−0.025	0.011
1921	−0.013	0.000	−0.014	−0.117	−0.078	−0.039
1922	−0.011	−0.019	0.008	−0.008	−0.051	0.043
1923	−0.010	−0.007	−0.002	0.027	0.038	−0.010
1924	−0.012	−0.007	−0.005	0.002	0.003	−0.001
1925	0.000	−0.019	0.019	0.036	−0.022	0.058
1926	−0.022	−0.018	−0.004	−0.023	0.004	−0.027
1927	−0.012	−0.019	0.007	−0.015	−0.034	0.019
1928	−0.008	−0.012	0.004	−0.010	−0.008	−0.001
1929	−0.009	−0.014	0.005	0.000	−0.008	0.008
1930	−0.001	0.002	−0.003	−0.073	−0.009	−0.064
1931	0.017	0.023	−0.006	−0.106	−0.038	−0.069
1932	0.036	0.043	−0.007	−0.103	−0.018	−0.085
1933	0.057	0.058	0.000	0.026	−0.009	0.034
1934	0.060	0.069	−0.009	0.030	0.037	−0.008
1935	0.068	0.046	0.022	0.015	−0.009	0.024
1936	0.040	0.027	0.013	0.019	−0.006	0.025
1937	0.011	0.019	−0.008	0.009	−0.002	0.011
1938	0.018	0.038	−0.021	−0.019	−0.016	−0.003
1939	0.029	0.027	0.001	−0.002	−0.024	0.021
1940	0.029	0.034	−0.005	0.012	0.006	0.006

Year						
1941	0.092	0.074	0.018	0.106	0.110	−0.005
1942	0.265	0.146	0.119	0.078	0.139	−0.063
1943	0.249	0.239	0.010	(0.258)	0.153	0.105
1944	0.237	0.360	−0.122	(0.130)	0.254	−0.124
1945	0.168	0.321	−0.153	(0.032)	0.168	−0.131
1946	−0.100	−0.021	−0.079	(−0.048)	−0.047	−0.001
1947	−0.027	−0.042	0.016	(−0.029)	−0.034	0.005
1948	−0.029	−0.015	−0.013	0.008	0.003	0.005
1949	0.026	0.000	0.026	−0.030	0.002	−0.032
1950	−0.010	−0.010	0.000	0.082	−0.014	0.096
1951	−0.011	0.020	−0.031	0.041	0.034	0.007
1952	0.011	0.024	−0.014	0.002	0.046	−0.043
1953	0.010	0.011	0.000	0.007	0.038	−0.030
1954	0.007	0.020	−0.013	−0.012	0.018	−0.031
1955	0.000	−0.008	0.008	0.000	0.008	−0.008
1956	−0.014	−0.006	−0.008	0.033	0.020	0.013
1957	−0.005	−0.008	0.004	0.034	0.015	0.019
1958	0.014	0.016	−0.001	0.013	0.013	0.000
1959	0.015	0.000	0.015	0.011	0.013	−0.002
1960	−0.006	0.006	−0.012	0.016	0.029	−0.013
1961	0.009	0.009	0.000	0.007	0.004	0.003
1962	0.007	0.001	0.006	0.014	0.016	−0.002
1963	0.002	0.003	−0.001	0.015	0.020	−0.005
1964	0.003	−0.002	0.005	0.010	0.025	−0.015
1965	−0.003	−0.005	0.003	0.020	0.032	−0.012
1966	−0.002	−0.007	0.006	0.030	0.034	−0.005
1967	0.005	0.001	0.004	0.035	0.040	−0.005
1968	0.008	−0.002	0.010	0.040	0.037	0.004
1969	−0.006	0.000	−0.006	0.053	0.059	−0.006

Table 10.4 (continued)

Date	$(B_t - B_{t-1})/P_t y_t$ [a]	$\widehat{(B_t - B_{t-1})/P_t y_t}$ [b]	Residual [c]	π_t	$\hat{\pi}_t$ [d]	$\pi_t - \hat{\pi}_t$
1970	0.008	0.005	0.003	0.044	0.055	−0.011
1971	0.017	0.007	0.010	0.033	0.040	−0.007
1972	0.012	0.006	0.006	0.036	0.057	−0.021
1973	−0.001	−0.005	0.004	0.095	0.059	0.036
1974	0.007	0.005	0.003	0.112	0.074	0.038
1975	0.051	0.036	0.015	0.065	0.066	−0.002
1976	0.035	0.026	0.009	0.052	0.055	−0.003
1977	0.026	0.020	0.006	0.060	0.055	0.005
1978	0.020	0.012	0.008	0.082	0.069	0.013
1979	0.016	0.012	0.004	0.113	0.079	0.034
1980	0.029	0.029	0.000	0.103	0.084	0.019
1981	0.027	0.032	−0.006	0.077	0.074	0.003
1982	0.051	0.056	−0.006	0.041	0.074	−0.033
1983	0.052	0.055	−0.003	0.040	0.059	−0.019
1984	—	0.042	—	(0.039)	0.085	(−0.046)
1985	—	0.039	—	—	(0.060)	—

a. B_t is the value from the end of December of the privately held part of the interest-bearing public debt—that is, the gross public debt less holdings by federal agencies and trust funds and the Federal Reserve and less any non-interest-bearing debt; see Barro (1979) for details. $(B_t - B_{t-1})/P_t y_t$ is the ratio to nominal GNP of the change in this concept of the public debt—hence, it is a measure of the deficit–GNP ratio.

b. Estimated value of the deficit–GNP ratio from the equation in set 1 of Table 10.1.

c. The residual from the equation, $\pi_t \equiv \log(P_{t+1}/P_t)$, where P_t is the January value of the seasonally adjusted CPI (less shelter since 1947). See n. 10 for a discussion of the values for 1943–1947.

d. $\hat{\pi}_t$ is the estimated value from set 1 of Table 10.1. These values are used to measure expected inflation, π_t^e.

do not correspond to notable residuals in the equation for deficits. For 1964, the residual is 0.5%; and for 1965, it is 0.3%.

For the Vietnam War—say, 1966–1968—the positive residuals for deficits support the common view that taxes were raised insufficiently at this time. But, perhaps because of the surcharge on the income tax, a substantial negative residual does show up for 1969.

Since 1969, expected inflation has become an important influence on the deficit. Specifically, the values of π_t^e are between 4 and 6% for 1969–1973, increase to 7% for 1974–1975, fall to between 5 and 7% for 1976–1979, reach 8% in 1979–1980, and then decline to 7% for 1981–1982.

The deficit equation underpredicts the deficits during the recession years, 1975–1976. In particular, for 1975, the actual ratio of the deficit to GNP is 5.1% (the same as in 1982), but the estimated value is only 3.6%. However, the deficit equation is on track for the 1980–1982 recession. For 1982, the actual deficit–GNP ratio is 5.1% although the estimated value is even higher: 5.6%. This estimate breaks down into 3.2 percentage points from the recession (YVAR), 1.7 percentage points from expected inflation ($\pi_t^e \cdot B_{t-1}/P_t y_t$), 0.5 percentage points from temporary government spending (GVAR),[17] and 0.3 percentage points from the constant term. Thus, the main elements are the recession and expected inflation—given these factors, the deficit for 1982 accords with prior experience.

I also used the estimated equation (Table 10.1, set 1)—together with data available in mid-1984—to forecast deficits for 1983–1985. For 1983, the inflation equation implies the value $\pi_t^e = 5.9\%$. (The actual inflation rate for 1983 is 4.0%.) The main element in the decline of expected inflation from 1982 (where $\pi_t^e = 7.4\%$) is the low actual inflation for 1982 ($\pi_t = 4.1\%$). Using the actual values for 1983 of the unemployment rate ($U_t = 9.5\%$), nominal GNP ($3305 billion), and the ratio of normal federal spending to GNP (0.205) yields an estimated value for the deficit–GNP ratio of 5.5%. This figure corresponds closely to the actual value of 5.2%. In terms of deficits (that is, changes in privately held, interest-bearing federal debt), the estimated value of $181 billion is close to the actual value of $170 billion. Thus, if anything, the deficit for 1983 is slightly lower than would be expected.

---

17. This temporary spending reflects the countercyclical response of federal transfers. Hence this effect derives also from the recession.

For 1984, the calculated value of expected inflation is $\pi_t^e = 8.5\%$. The increase from 1983 reflects primarily the high value of monetary growth in 1983 (10.3%). I then assume for 1984 an unemployment rate of 7.5%, a nominal GNP of $3660 billion (10% above the 1983 value),[18] and—as in 1983—a ratio of normal federal spending to GNP of 20.5%. Then it turns out that the forecast for 1984's ratio of the deficit to GNP is 4.2%. This figure breaks down into 1.6 percentage points from the continuing effect of the recession (YVAR) and 2.4 percentage points from expected inflation ($\pi_t^e \cdot B_{t-1}/P_t y_t$). This projected value of the deficit–GNP ratio implies a deficit for 1984 of $152 billion. This figure seems to be roughly in line with other near-term projections (available in mid-1984). (However, one should add about $15 billion to my number to incorporate the creation of high-powered money—also my value applies to the calendar year rather than to the fiscal year.)

Finally, for 1985, I calculate that expected inflation is $\pi_t^e = 6.9\%$.[19] Using an unemployment rate of 7.8%, a value for nominal GNP of $3886 billion (see note 18), and a ratio of normal federal spending to GNP of 20.5%, I project a ratio of the deficit to GNP for 1985 of 3.9%. (This value breaks down into 1.9 percentage points from the YVAR variable and 1.8 points from expected inflation.) The implied deficit is $152 billion, the same nominal amount as in 1984. Again, this figure (supplemented to include about $15 billion for money creation) seems not out of line with some popular near-term forecasts.[20]

The main point is that the actual behavior of deficits through 1983— as well as popular forecasts for 1984–1985—are reasonably in line with prior experience since at least World War I. The main things that are out of line with the previous structure are projections of longer-term deficits on the order of $300 billion, conditioned on relatively low values of the unemployment rate and expected inflation. Because there is nothing in the data to suggest this type of structural break, I view these

18. These values and those for 1985 are from Litterman (1984).

19. I assume here, using the data available through August 1984, that inflation for 1984 is 3.9% and the growth rate of money is 6.8%.

20. The actual budget deficits for 1984 and 1985—measured by the changes in privately held U.S. government bonds—were $190 billion and $205 billion, respectively. These amounts were well above the projected value of $152 billion for each year. These results, and those for 1986 and 1987, indicate that the Reagan fiscal policy really was significantly different from the policy in place from 1916 to 1983—a verdict that was not apparent to me in mid-1984 when I wrote the original version of this chapter.

forecasts of deficits as amounting to predictions that either taxes will be increased or spending decreased. Standard projections of deficits should not be regarded as forecasts, once the endogeneity of taxes and spending is taken into account.

For recent years, where the effects of the constant term and the GVAR variable are relatively minor, the forecasts of deficits emerge from a simple equation. Namely,

$$\left(\frac{B_t - B_{t-1}}{P_t y_t}\right) \approx \pi_t^e \left(\frac{B_{t-1}}{P_t y_t}\right) + 3.73(U_t - 0.054)\left(\frac{g_t^*}{y_t}\right). \tag{10.16}$$

The values for g_t^*/y_t—the ratio of normal federal spending to GNP—appear in Table 10.3. Using the recent value of 0.205 in Eq. (10.16) yields the forecasting equation

$$\left(\frac{B_t - B_{t-1}}{P_t y_t}\right) \approx -0.041 + \pi_t^e \left(\frac{B_{t-1}}{P_t y_t}\right) + 0.76 U_t. \tag{10.17}$$

Equation (10.17) provides a close approximation to the previously mentioned forecasts of deficits for 1983–1985.

Note from Eq. (10.17) that each percentage point increase in expected inflation, π_t^e, raises the deficit–GNP ratio in accordance with the ratio of the stock of debt to GNP, $B_{t-1}/P_t y_t$. Thereby, the nominal debt grows, other things equal, at the expected rate of inflation. The debt–GNP ratio was about 26% in 1983. Hence, in recent years a one percentage point increase in expected inflation meant about a one-quarter percentage point increase in the deficit–GNP ratio.

Equation (10.17) implies also that each percentage point increase in the unemployment rate raises the deficit–GNP ratio by about three-quarters of a percentage point. However, it is important to recall that the magnitude of this effect depends on the size of government as measured by the ratio g_t^*/y_t in Eq. (10.16). That is, the effect of a given percentage shortfall in taxable income on the level of government revenue depends on the normal share of the government in the economy. For example, if one plugs the 1933 value of the ratio g^*/y (0.059 rather than 0.205) into Eq. (10.16), then the coefficient on the unemployment rate in Eq. (10.17) falls from 0.76 to 0.22. Thus the condition that generates particularly large cyclical deficits is high unemployment interacting with big government.[21]

Finally, notice from Eq. (10.16) that, if the unemployment rate were to decline to 5.4%, significant deficits would arise only because of nonzero expected inflation. In fact, these nominal deficits would just maintain the (planned) real value of the public debt over time. In this case an appropriate concept of the real deficit—namely, the change in the real debt— would be near zero. Further, if expected inflation were to decline toward zero, the conventional measure of the nominal (and real) deficit would also approach zero. The point is that there is nothing in the experience of deficits through 1983 that conflicts in any major way with these propositions.

References

Atkinson, A. B., and J. E. Stiglitz. 1980. *Lectures on Public Economics.* New York: McGraw-Hill.

Barro, R. J. 1979. "Determination of the Public Debt." *Journal of Political Economy* 87(5):940–971.

——— 1981a. "On the Predictability of Tax-Rate Changes." Chapter 11 of this book.

——— 1981b. "Output Effects of Government Purchases." *Journal of Political Economy* 89(6):1086–1121.

——— 1981c. "Unanticipated Money Growth and Economic Activity in the United States." In *Money Expectations and Business Cycles,* ed. R. J. Barro. New York: Academic Press, pp. 137–169.

——— 1983. "Inflationary Finance under Discretion and Rules." *Canadian Journal of Economics* 16(1):1–16.

——— 1984. *Macroeconomics.* New York: Wiley.

——— 1986. "The Behavior of U.S. Deficits." In *The American Business Cycle: Continuity and Change,* ed. R. J. Gordon. Chicago: University of Chicago Press for the National Bureau of Economic Research, pp. 361–394.

21. If one plugs in the 1933 unemployment rate of 27% in Equation (10.17), then (with $\pi_t^e = 0$) the estimated ratio of the deficit to GNP is a remarkable 16%. The actual ratio for 1933 was only 6% which I attribute primarily to the smaller size of the federal government, as measured by the ratio, g^*/y. My assessment is that, if the United States encounters a much more serious recession than that in 1982, the deficits will dwarf those experienced recently.

Butkiewicz, J. 1983. "The Market Value of Outstanding Government Debt, Comment." *Journal of Monetary Economics* 11:373–379.

Darby, M. R. 1976. "Three-and-a-Half Million U.S. Employees Have Been Mislaid; or, an Explanation of Unemployment, 1934–41." *Journal of Political Economy* 84:1–16.

Kydland, F., and E. Prescott. 1980. "A Competitive Theory of Fluctuations and the Feasibility and Desirability of Stabilization Policy." In *Rational Expectations and Economic Policy.* ed. S. Fischer. Chicago: University of Chicago Press for the National Bureau of Economic Research, pp. 169–198.

Litterman, R. 1984. "Economic Forecasts from a Vector Autoregression." Federal Reserve Bank of Minneapolis.

Lucas, R., and N. Stokey. 1983. "Optimal Fiscal and Monetary Policy in an Economy without Capital." *Journal of Monetary Economics* 12(1):55–93.

McCallum, B. 1984. "Bond-Financed Deficits and Inflation: A Ricardian Analysis." *Journal of Political Economy* 92:123–135.

Pigou, A. C. 1928. *A Study in Public Finance.* London: Macmillan.

Ramsey, F. P. 1927. "A Contribution to the Theory of Taxation." *Economic Journal* 37:47–61.

Sahasakul, C. 1984. "The U.S. Evidence on Optimal Taxation." Unpublished manuscript. Rochester, N.Y.: University of Rochester.

Seater, J. 1981. "The Market Value of Outstanding Government Debt, 1919–75." *Journal of Monetary Economics* 8:85–101.

11   On the Predictability of Tax-Rate Changes

Some previous papers (Barro 1979, 1980; Kydland and Prescott 1980) suggested that the smoothing of tax rates over time would be a desirable guide for debt-management policy. For example, the large temporary outlays by government in wartime would be primarily debt financed to avoid a substantial increase in wartime tax rates relative to rates that would be expected for later years. Similarly, assuming that real government spending is not strongly procyclical, a countercyclical response of the public debt allows for smoothing of tax rates over the business cycle.

Heuristically, the case for intertemporal uniformity of tax rates—say, on factor incomes—emerges if the (own- and cross-) responsiveness of factor supplies to after-tax rewards is similar at different dates. For example, the Ramsey-like rule for taxation in inverse relation to own supply elasticities yields this answer in the context of a uniform intertemporal pattern of elasticities.[1]

Departures from uniform taxation over time would be suggested if factor supply elasticities interact, for example, with the contemporaneous level of government spending or with the state of the business cycle. The signs or magnitudes of these effects are not apparent on theoretical grounds—conceivably, the uniformity of tax rates over time may remain as a satisfactory approximation to optimal policy.

The basic approach in this chapter is, first, to adopt the criterion of

Unpublished manuscript (1981).

1. Atkinson and Stiglitz (1980, chap. 12) discuss the limitations of the analysis that focuses on own elasticities. They also present some more general treatments of the optimal tax problem. Conditions for the optimality of uniform taxation are presented in Sandmo (1974) and Sadka (1977). The theory has not yet been developed for the context of uncertainty about future values of government spending, aggregate real income, and so on.

constant expected overall tax rates as an approximate guide to optimal public finance and, second, to regard this proposition as a positive theory about government behavior. The properties of tax collections over time are examined empirically to test whether actual behavior departs significantly from that dictated by this simple rule for intertemporal public finance.

A previous empirical investigation (Barro 1979) considered the implications of tax smoothing at the level of the federal government for the determination of U.S. public debt. The present analysis looks directly at the behavior of taxes—specifically, at propositions that concern the unpredictability of changes in future tax rates.

Suppose that τ_t represents the (average marginal) tax rate applying to incomes that accrue during period t. (The restriction to income taxes is not central to the analysis.) The basic hypothesis is that τ_t is set in accordance with a rule that generates equality between τ_t and all expected future tax rates, as perceived at date t. In particular, constancy of tax rates emerges if the realizations for all future values of real government spending, real GNP, and so on equal their mean values as conditioned on date t information.

The level of τ_t is determined from the government's intertemporal budget constraint, taking account of tax effects on the scale of economic activity—that is, on the tax base. Departures of real government spending, real GNP, and so on from their prior expectations generate revisions in tax rates. In a simple setting where taxes are proportional to income, the change in the tax rate depends on a weighted sum of changes in expected future values of government spending relative to aggregate income. For present purposes, the important point is that τ_t is set at each date so that

$$E(\tau_{t+i}|I_t) = \tau_t \qquad \text{for} \quad i = 1, 2, \ldots. \tag{11.1}$$

applies, where I_t represents date t information. In other words, tax rates follow a Martingale process. Alternatively, in first-difference form, all future changes in tax rates are unpredictable:

$$E(\tau_{t+i} - \tau_{t+i-1})|I_t = 0 \qquad \text{for} \quad i = 1, 2, \ldots. \tag{11.2}$$

Equation (11.2) is the main proposition that is tested in this chapter. The full distribution of tax-rate changes need not be time invariant to satisfy

Eqs. (11.1) and (11.2), but the empirical analysis embodies this additional restriction. In this form, tax rates are generated from a random walk.

The random-walk model for tax rates is reminiscent of similar propositions for some asset prices, which have been the subject of considerable empirical investigation. See Fama (1970) for a survey of this area. The approach is also analogous to the study of consumption that has been carried out by Hall (1978).

Suppose that real government spending, aside from interest payments, and real GNP are not themselves generated from random-walk processes. In this case the unpredictability of changes in future values, as shown for tax rates in Eq. (11.2), would not apply for these other variables. The essence of the tax-rate-smoothing policy implied by Eqs. (11.1) and (11.2) is that any foreseeable behavior for real government spending,[2] real GNP, and so on is incorporated in the setting of the current tax rate to avoid a pattern whereby tax rates would vary with the predictable changes in the other variables. Tests for the unpredictability of tax-rate changes are most interesting in an environment where some future changes in real government spending, real GNP, and so on are forecastable. In particular, it would be less interesting to find that tax-rate shifts were unpredictable if changes in the government spending–GNP ratio were also unpredictable. Accordingly, the empirical analysis includes tests in the form of Eq. (11.2) for other variables—notably, for the government spending–GNP ratio—along with the tests for tax rates. A comparison across the various equations is of substantial interest from the perspective of assessing the tax-rate-smoothing model.

Empirical Counterparts of Tax Rates

Although average marginal tax rates matter in the theoretical analysis, data considerations limit the empirical investigation to aggregate average tax rates. The implicit assumption is the absence of substantial changes over time in the relation of these average rates to the underlying average marginal tax rates.

2. The theory applies to government spending net of interest payments. The interest payments are determined from the initial debt and the time path of deficits, given the time path of interest rates.

The spirit of the theory pertains to an overall package of taxes at each date rather than to individual components. Specifically, the finding of predictability of tax-rate changes for particular categories of taxation would not invalidate the central thesis. Therefore, the analysis deals with the overall tax (and so-called nontax) receipts for a specified governmental entity. The primary results deal with the U.S. federal government, although findings are indicated also for the U.S. total government sector.[3] An attempt was made to consolidate the Federal Reserve with the federal government by excluding from receipts the transfers made by the Federal Reserve to the U.S. Treasury. (Curiously, this item appears under corporate tax liabilities.) Values of the tax variables and detailed definitions appear in Table 11.1.

One issue concerns the treatment of inflationary finance, which is excluded in conventional measures of tax collections. The current tax rate on holdings of high-powered (government-issue) money, H, is determined by a short-term nominal interest rate, R. The flow, $R \cdot H$, represents the expected costs per period that are imposed on holders of money. In a perfect-foresight setting, the present value of these flows (back to some "initial" date) corresponds also to the present value of government revenue from money creation. Departures of the actual present value of revenues from this magnitude are associated with unexpected capital gains or losses on cash holdings—see Auernheimer (1974) for a discussion of this matter. Because the calculated tax on high-powered money (see Table 11.1) is small and not highly variable, the inclusion of this element has a negligible impact on the empirical results. The analysis that is reported here excludes the tax on money from the measures of total tax rates.

Many transfer programs—such as welfare and social security—contain income-test provisions. The allocative effects in these cases parallel those that are generated by an income tax. Conceptually, it would be appropriate to include the effective tax that is implied by transfer programs into the measure of date t's overall tax rate. Some governmental regulations could also be considered as contributing to the effective tax rate on economic activity during period t. Because it was unclear how to

3. Mobility across governmental jurisdictions may limit the possibilities for a tax-rate-smoothing debt policy—see Benjamin and Kochin (1978). Therefore the model may fit better for the federal government than for state and local governments. The federal government can, however, set a debt policy to smooth total tax rates rather than federal rates. In this case, the model would apply to total government tax rates.

Table 11.1. Variables used in regressions

Date	TAXF[a]	GF[b]	TAXT[c]	GT[d]	CAS[e]	DY[f]	r[g]	R·H/GNP[h]
1879	0.029	0.019	—	—	0	0.099	—	—
1880	0.028	0.013	—	—	0	0.139	—	—
1881	0.029	0.015	—	—	0	0.016	—	—
1882	0.028	0.015	—	—	0	0.048	—	—
1883	0.027	0.017	—	—	0	−0.021	—	—
1884	0.025	0.017	—	—	0	0.021	—	—
1885	0.027	0.018	—	—	0	−0.004	—	—
1886	0.028	0.018	—	—	0	0.054	—	—
1887	0.030	0.018	—	—	0	0.022	—	—
1888	0.030	0.019	—	—	0	−0.034	—	—
1889	0.029	0.020	—	—	0	0.044	—	—
1890	0.030	0.020	—	—	0	0.072	—	—
1891	0.025	0.021	—	—	0	0.044	—	—
1892	0.024	0.023	—	—	0	0.092	—	—
1893	0.023	0.024	—	—	0	−0.049	—	—
1894	0.022	0.025	—	—	0	−0.029	—	—
1895	0.021	0.021	—	—	0	0.111	—	—
1896	0.022	0.023	—	—	0	−0.020	—	—
1897	0.025	0.021	—	—	0	0.095	—	—
1898	0.027	0.032	—	—	0.005	0.017	—	—
1899	0.030	0.027	—	—	0	0.089	—	—
1900	0.029	0.023	—	—	0	0.025	—	—
1901	0.026	0.021	—	—	0	0.111	—	—
1902	0.025	0.020	—	—	0	0.009	—	—
1903	0.023	0.020	—	—	0	0.049	—	—
1904	0.022	0.024	—	—	0	−0.013	—	—
1905	0.021	0.021	—	—	0	0.072	—	—
1906	0.021	0.018	—	—	0	0.110	—	—
1907	0.020	0.018	—	—	0	0.016	—	—
1908	0.020	0.023	—	—	0	−0.086	—	—
1909	0.019	0.020	—	—	0	0.116	—	—
1910	0.019	0.019	—	—	0	0.028	—	—
1911	0.019	0.018	—	—	0	0.026	—	—
1912	0.018	0.017	—	—	0	0.055	—	—
1913	0.018	0.018	—	—	0	0.009	—	—
1914	0.018	0.018	—	—	0	−0.045	—	—

Table 11.1 (continued)

Date	TAXF[a]	GF[b]	TAXT[c]	GT[d]	CAS[e]	DY[f]	r[g]	R·H/GNP[h]
1915	0.017	0.018	—	—	0	−0.009	—	—
1916	0.017	0.017	—	—	0	0.076	—	—
1917	0.021	0.108	—	—	0.23	0.007	—	—
1918	0.056	0.220	—	—	0.28	0.116	—	—
1919	0.083	0.137	—	—	0	−0.036	—	—
1920	0.074	0.047	—	—	0	−0.045	—	—
1921	0.073	0.051	—	—	0	−0.091	—	—
1922	0.048	0.030	—	—	0	0.147	—	—
1923	0.046	0.026	—	—	0	0.114	—	—
1924	0.045	0.025	—	—	0	−0.002	—	—
1925	0.040	0.024	—	—	0	0.081	—	0.003
1926	0.040	0.022	—	—	0	0.062	0.113	0.003
1927	0.041	0.023	—	—	0	−0.005	0.316	0.003
1928	0.039	0.026	—	—	0	0.006	0.355	0.004
1929	0.037	0.023	0.109	0.093	0	0.064	−0.118	0.004
1930	0.034	0.029	0.119	0.115	0	−0.098	−0.236	0.003
1931	0.027	0.051	0.125	0.152	0	−0.080	−0.385	0.003
1932	0.029	0.049	0.152	0.166	0	−0.149	0.176	0.004
1933	0.048	0.064	0.167	0.173	0	−0.021	0.577	0.003
1934	0.054	0.090	0.160	0.181	0	0.075	0.037	0.001
1935	0.055	0.083	0.157	0.171	0	0.086	0.355	0.001
1936	0.061	0.100	0.156	0.183	0	0.127	0.286	0.001
1937	0.078	0.075	0.170	0.154	0	0.045	−0.422	0.001
1938	0.076	0.094	0.176	0.185	0	−0.042	0.347	0.001
1939	0.074	0.091	0.170	0.182	0	0.073	0.060	0.001
1940	0.086	0.093	0.177	0.172	0	0.072	−0.056	0.001
1941	0.123	0.158	0.200	0.221	0.004	0.143	−0.187	0.001
1942	0.145	0.348	0.206	0.396	0.162	0.136	0.074	0.001
1943	0.205	0.439	0.256	0.476	0.205	0.148	0.229	0.001
1944	0.195	0.444	0.243	0.478	1.09	0.073	0.177	0.001
1945	0.200	0.385	0.251	0.422	0.603	−0.014	0.315	0.001
1946	0.187	0.151	0.243	0.198	0	−0.157	−0.216	0.002
1947	0.185	0.110	0.244	0.165	0	−0.020	−0.049	0.002
1948	0.166	0.119	0.227	0.179	0	0.041	0.013	0.003
1949	0.149	0.143	0.216	0.213	0	0.006	0.219	0.003

Table 11.1 (continued)

Date	TAXF[a]	GF[b]	TAXT[c]	GT[d]	CAS[e]	DY[f]	r^g	$R \cdot H/GNP^h$
1950	0.174	0.127	0.240	0.197	0.071	0.084	0.215	0.002
1951	0.194	0.162	0.257	0.227	0.097	0.078	0.143	0.003
1952	0.193	0.192	0.259	0.257	0.030	0.037	0.127	0.003
1953	0.190	0.198	0.258	0.265	0.021	0.038	0.004	0.003
1954	0.173	0.178	0.245	0.252	0	−0.013	0.438	0.002
1955	0.181	0.159	0.252	0.234	0	0.065	0.233	0.003
1956	0.184	0.159	0.260	0.236	0	0.021	0.064	0.004
1957	0.184	0.167	0.261	0.248	0	0.018	−0.136	0.004
1958	0.174	0.186	0.255	0.272	0	−0.002	0.354	0.003
1959	0.183	0.174	0.264	0.256	0	0.058	0.116	0.004
1960	0.188	0.171	0.274	0.256	0	0.023	−0.001	0.004
1961	0.186	0.183	0.275	0.273	0	0.025	0.240	0.003
1962	0.187	0.184	0.277	0.272	0	0.056	−0.092	0.003
1963	0.191	0.180	0.282	0.270	0	0.039	0.183	0.003
1964	0.178	0.173	0.271	0.265	0.001	0.051	0.145	0.003
1965	0.179	0.168	0.272	0.261	0.007	0.057	0.114	0.004
1966	0.186	0.178	0.280	0.272	0.025	0.058	−0.120	0.005
1967	0.187	0.193	0.284	0.293	0.047	0.027	0.218	0.004
1968	0.198	0.195	0.300	0.298	0.073	0.043	0.088	0.005
1969	0.207	0.188	0.314	0.293	0.046	0.025	−0.147	0.006
1970	0.192	0.193	0.304	0.305	0.021	−0.003	−0.009	0.006
1971	0.184	0.194	0.300	0.309	0.007	0.030	0.122	0.004
1972	0.192	0.196	0.311	0.306	0.001	0.056	0.136	0.004
1973	0.194	0.189	0.311	0.298	0	0.053	−0.263	0.006
1974	0.200	0.197	0.318	0.313	0	−0.014	−0.401	0.007
1975	0.184	0.218	0.303	0.336	0	−0.013	0.274	0.004
1976	0.191	0.210	0.313	0.324	0	0.057	0.197	0.004
1977	0.195	0.207	0.316	0.317	0	0.052	−0.107	0.004
1978	0.200	0.200	0.319	0.309	0	0.043	0.008	0.005
1979	0.206	0.197	0.322	0.306	0	0.023	0.097	0.006

make these ideas operational, I have not incorporated either transfers or regulations into the measures of effective tax rates.

Appropriate empirical counterparts for the overall tax base are not straightforward. Net and gross national product come immediately to mind—the latter concept might be preferable because reported depreciation is largely arbitrary from an economic standpoint and because the (true) depreciation component of GNP is potentially subject to taxation.

Table 11.1 (continued)

Sources: Data since 1929 for government receipts and expenditures, GNP, net interest payments, and transfers from the Federal Reserve to the U.S. Treasury are from the *National Income and Product Accounts of the U.S., 1929–1974* and issues of *U.S. Survey of Current Business.*

Earlier data on federal receipts and expenditures are from Firestone (1960, Table A–3). Data before 1929 on interest paid and received by the federal government are from issues of the *Annual Report of the Secretary of the Treasury,* Washington, D.C., U.S. Government Printing Office. Federal Reserve transfers were zero before 1929. Earlier figures for real and nominal GNP are from *Long-Term Economic Growth, 1860–1970,* Series A1, A7. Values before 1889 are based on Gallman's data, which were obtained from Anna Schwartz.

CPI data, compiled by the Bureau of Labor Statistics, were obtained from the Chase Data Bank. *R* is from *Banking and Monetary Statistics, 1941–1970,* and issues of the *Federal Reserve Bulletin. H* is from Friedman and Schwartz (1963, Table B–3), *Banking and Monetary Statistics, 1941–1970,* and issues of the *Federal Reserve Bulletin.*

a. TAXF is total federal government receipts less transfers from the Federal Reserve, divided by nominal GNP. Before 1929 an estimate of interest received by the federal government was also deducted. (The original data included this interest as a component of revenue.)

b. GF is total federal expenditures less net interest payments, divided by nominal GNP. Before 1929 an estimate of gross interest paid was deducted. (Interest received appears on the receipt side of the accounts.)

c. TAXT is total government receipts (intergovernmental transfers are netted out) less transfers from the Federal Reserve, divided by nominal GNP. Data were obtained since 1929.

d. GT is total government expenditures (intergovernmental transfers are netted out) less net interest payments, divided by GNP. Data were obtained since 1929.

e. CAS is battle deaths per 1,000 total population, as discussed in Barro (1981, Table 11.1).

f. $DY \equiv \log(Y_t/Y_{t-1})$, where Y is real GNP, 1972 base.

g. r is the total nominal return over the year for a value-weighted portfolio of all New York Stock Exchange issues (as compiled by the University of Chicago's Center for Research on Security Prices) less an inflation rate. The inflation rate from 1948 to 1979 is $\log(P_t/P_{t-1})$, where P_t is the December value of the seasonally unadjusted CPI for an urban consumer, exclusive of shelter. (See n. 7.) For 1926–1947, the inflation rate is based on the overall CPI for an urban consumer.

h. R is the annual average interest rate on four- to six-month maturity prime Commercial Paper. H is the annual average of seasonally adjusted high-powered money (total currency outside the U.S. Treasury plus reserves of member banks at the Federal Reserve). $R \cdot H/GNP$ is the ratio of $R \cdot H$—the cost per year of holding the stock of high-powered money—to nominal GNP.

In any event, tax assessments are not necessarily limited to final product or net income—levies can be based on intermediate flows, including governmental transfer payments, and on various stock variables, such as overall wealth or estates. Some experimentation indicated that the results were insensitive to the choice of tax base among GNP, NNP, or either of these concepts augmented by governmental transfers. The results discussed in this chapter use GNP as the proxy for the tax base. Hence tax-rate variables are measured as federal or total government tax (and nontax) receipts relative to GNP. The hypothesis of unpredictability for changes in future average marginal tax rates translates empirically into a proposition of unpredictability for changes in future values of tax receipts relative to GNP.

The analysis is limited to annual observations on tax receipts. Within-year data do not seem meaningful because of discrepancies between the time of tax accrual (which is pertinent for allocative effects) and the time of payment to the government.

Government-expenditure ratios are measured analogously—as either federal or total annual government spending relative to GNP. The total government figures exclude intergovernmental transfers. Net interest payments are determined endogenously, given an initial debt stock, by the tax/deficit policy in conjunction with the time path of other government spending. From the standpoint of tax-rate smoothing, the pertinent matter is the predictability of changes in government spending aside from interest payments. Therefore, net interest payments have been excluded from the government expenditure variables. (However, the results are little changed if this adjustment is not made.) Before 1929 an estimate of federal interest paid is excluded from spending and an estimate of interest received by the federal government is deducted from total receipts. See the notes to Table 11.1 for details.

Time-Aggregation Problems

Working (1960) discussed a difficulty in testing random-walk hypotheses with time-averaged data on commodity or stock prices. The same problem arises in the present context where annual averages of tax rates are used.[4] If the random-walk model applies at some interval that is shorter than a year (and that might be infinitesimal), then a random walk would not appear in the time-averaged annual data. Suppose, for example, that a positive innovation to the tax rate (reflecting, say, a change in information about future real government spending) occurs during year t. This change affects period t's average annual tax rate by less than one-to-

4. It also affects Hall's (1978) analysis of consumption, although the problem was not considered there.

one—depending on the timing of the informational shift during the year—but alters expected future tax rates on a one-to-one basis. Therefore, future time-averaged tax rates, $\bar{\tau}_{t+i}$, would not be related to $\bar{\tau}_t$ by a unitary coefficient. In terms of first differences from one year to the next, the serial independence of tax-rate changes would be replaced by a pattern of positive association.

Using first differences of time-averaged observations, $D\bar{\tau}_t \equiv \bar{\tau}_t - \bar{\tau}_{t-1}$, Working's analysis shows—for the case where the interval for the fundamental random-walk model is infinitesimal and where the underlying distribution of the disturbances is time invariant—that the simple correlation between $D\bar{\tau}_t$ and $D\bar{\tau}_{t-1}$ equals 0.25. Note that the simple correlations of $D\bar{\tau}_t$ with earlier lag values remain equal to zero. With the inclusion of four lagged values, $D\bar{\tau}_{t-i}$, it can be shown (see Appendix) that the *partial* correlations of $D\bar{\tau}_t$ with each lagged value are given by (0.268, $-0.072, 0.019, -0.005$). Subsequent partial correlations would be negligible. Generally, $D\bar{\tau}_t$ can be written as a moving-average process that involves a pattern of weights on the underlying innovations applicable to periods t and $t - 1$. For testing purposes, it is convenient to approximate this process in terms of the time-averaged variables as an autoregression with a finite number of lags. Assuming normality for the underlying disturbances, the approximation is

$$D\bar{\tau}_t = 0.268D\bar{\tau}_{t-1} - 0.072D\bar{\tau}_{t-2} + 0.019D\bar{\tau}_{t-3} \qquad (11.3)$$

$$- 0.005D\bar{\tau}_{t-4} + \text{white noise.}$$

This equation replicates the pattern of partial correlations that was just described.

For a case where current information, I_t, is limited to current and past tax rates, Eq. (11.3) suggests that the random-walk model can be tested via univariate autoregressions in which the coefficients are constrained to equal the hypothesized values. (Note that the constant equals zero—that is, a drift in the tax rate violates the underlying theory.) Although this procedure is carried out empirically, it has the shortcoming of ignoring the predictive content of other variables, such as real government spending and real GNP. Unfortunately, simple results that are analogous to Eq. (11.3) do not generally obtain when additional variables are introduced.

Suppose that an array of variables, X_t, is added to the analysis. These variables may be correlated with contemporaneous or lagged innovations to the tax rate. However, the theory implies independence of X_t from future innovations. Because $D\bar{\tau}_t$ involves underlying disturbances from periods t and $t - 1$, $D\bar{\tau}_t$ would not be independent of X_{t-1}, but would be independent of all variables dated from $t - 2$ and earlier. Therefore consider equations for $D\bar{\tau}_t$ in which all right-side variables (including lagged values of $D\bar{\tau}$) are dated only up to $t - 2$. The theory implies that all coefficients in this form would be zero.[5]

The form for the multivariate analysis is

$$D\bar{\tau}_t = a_0 + a_2 X_{t-2} + a_3 X_{t-3} + \cdots + u_t, \tag{11.4}$$

where the X's represent an array of informational variables, which are dated from $t - 2$ and earlier. The lagged dependent variables, $D\bar{\tau}_{t-2}$, ..., are included with the set of X's. The error term, u_t, is a moving average of tax-rate innovations that apply to periods t and $t - 1$. Therefore, as mentioned earlier, the model implies independence of u_t from the regressors in Eq. (11.4). We want to estimate Eq. (11.4) to test the hypothesis that all the coefficients—including the constant, a_0—are zero. Ordinary least squares estimation of Eq. (11.4) yields consistent estimates for the coefficients. However, because u_t is a moving average of white-noise errors, the usual test statistics would be invalid (asymptotically). Appropriate tests can be carried out by using a filtering method proposed by Hayashi and Sims (1981).

Suppose that we write u_t as the first-order moving average,

$$u_t = v_t + \lambda v_{t-1}, \tag{11.5}$$

where v_t is white noise and $|\lambda| < 1$. The value, $\lambda = 0.268$, replicates the pattern of serial correlation for the case of a time-averaged random walk with an infinitesimal length of time between innovations. However, because of time averaging, the underlying process cannot be written in the present case precisely as shown in Eq. (11.5) (see Appendix.) If Eq.

---

5. If the variable, $D\bar{\tau}_{t-1}$, were added, its coefficient need no longer correspond to the value 0.268, which is shown in Eq. (11.3). See the Appendix.

(11.4) is filtered by $(1 - \lambda L + \lambda^2 L^2 - \cdots)$, where L is the lag operator, then a serially independent error emerges. That is,

$$u_t - \lambda u_{t-1} + \lambda^2 u_{t-2} - \cdots = (v_t + \lambda v_{t-1}) - \lambda(v_{t-1} + \lambda v_{t-2})$$
$$+ \lambda^2(v_{t-2} + \lambda v_{t-3}) - \cdots = v_t,$$

if we neglect the final term, which involves a high power of λ. Because u_t reflects time averaging, this type of backward filtering would create contemporaneous correlation between the transformed error and the transformed regressors. The earlier values of the X's will generally be correlated with the filtered residuals. Therefore, this procedure would yield inconsistent estimates of coefficients.

A serially independent error can also be generated by using the forward filter, $(1 - \lambda L^{-1} + \lambda^2 L^{-2} - \cdots)$. The application of this filter to Eq. (11.4) brings in only future values of the u_t's. Therefore, the original X's (not the transformed X's) are independent of these error terms. Hence, the X's can be used as instruments for estimation purposes. The general procedure entails, first, forward-filtering Eq. (11.4) (using the known value $\lambda = 0.268$) to create serially independent errors; and, second, using the original X's as instruments to estimate the equation in filtered form. The resulting statistics allow for asymptotically valid tests of the random-walk hypothesis, $a_0 = a_2 = a_3 = \cdots = 0$.

With the tax-rate change, $D\bar{\tau}_t$, examined only in relation to variables that are dated two or more years previously, there are questions about the power of statistical tests. The comparison with parallel relationships for real government spending and other variables is important in this respect—that is, the presence of predictive power in these other equations would suggest that the tests for tax-rate changes were meaningful. Also, the presence of drift in the tax rate—that is, a test for a nonzero constant in the $D\bar{\tau}_t$ equation—is not sensitive to the exclusion of explanatory variables from date $t - 1$. Despite questions about statistical power in annual equations with first lags omitted, it is unclear how else to proceed in the multivariate case. The possibility for a direct analysis—as shown in Eq. (11.3) for the univariate setting—depends on the statistical properties of the additional variables, X, which are not the focus of the theory. Further, with respect to aggregate tax rates, it does not seem feasible to use data at an interval finer than one year.

Table 11.2. Estimated drift coefficients and sample standard deviations for changes in tax and spending ratios

Sample	Dependent variable[a]	Estimated drift coefficient[b]
1884–1979	D(TAXF)	0.0019(0.0015), $t = 1.3$
	D(GF)	0.0019(0.0048), $t = 0.4$
1884–1929	D(TAXF)	0.0002(0.0014), $t = 0.2$
	D(GF)	0.0001(0.0050), $t = 0.0$
1930–1979	D(TAXF)	0.0034(0.0025), $t = 1.4$
	D(GF)	0.0035(0.0079), $t = 0.4$
1934–1979	D(TAXT)	0.0033(0.0024), $t = 1.4$
	D(GT)	0.0028(0.0082), $t = 0.3$
1948–1979	D(TAXF)	0.0007(0.0024), $t = 0.3$
	D(GF)	0.0025(0.0030), $t = 0.8$
1948–1979	D(TAXT)	0.0024(0.0022), $t = 1.1$
	D(GT)	0.0042(0.0033), $t = 1.3$

a. Dependent variables are the first differences of tax and spending ratios, as defined in Table 11.1.

b. The estimates are calculated after the dependent variable is filtered by $(1 - \lambda L + \lambda^2 L^2 - \lambda^3 L^3 + \lambda^4 L^4)$, where $\lambda = 0.268$. The estimated values from this form are multiplied by 1/0.79 to calculate the estimated constant and standard error for the original form of the equation. The 5% critical level of 2.0 applies for the t-ratios that are shown in the table.

Drift in the Tax and Spending Ratios

Table 11.2 reports the estimated coefficients and standard errors for equations that include only the constant term. For the federal government, the dependent variable is either the change in the ratio of federal tax receipts to GNP, $D(\text{TAXF})_t \equiv (\text{TAXF})_t - (\text{TAXF})_{t-1}$, or the change in the ratio of federal spending to GNP, $D(\text{GF})_t \equiv \text{GF}_t - \text{GF}_{t-1}$. The periods considered are 1884–1979, 1884–1929, 1930–1979, and 1948–1979. Comparable variables are considered for the total government sector for 1934–1979 and 1948–1979 samples. Data and definitions of variables appear in Table 11.1. Graphs of the tax and spending ratios are shown in Figures 11.1 and 11.2.

The estimated constants correspond, of course, to the means of the dependent variables over each sample. The error term is a moving-

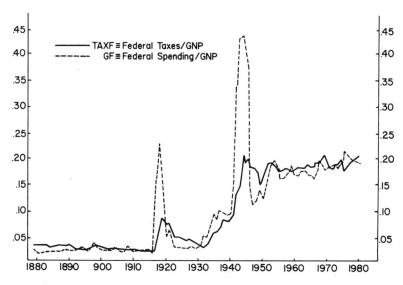

Figure 11.1. Federal tax and expenditure ratios, 1879–1979

average process under the specification of a time-averaged random walk. Therefore, an appropriate filter can be applied to the dependent variable to obtain an estimate for the standard error of the constant term. For the time-averaged random-walk model, the appropriate filter is $(1 - \lambda L + \lambda^2 L^2 - \cdots)$, where $\lambda = 0.268$.[6]

Consider first the results for the federal government. Because the federal tax and spending ratios rose over all samples that were considered, the estimated constants in the first-difference specification—that is, the estimated drift for each ratio in level form—are all positive. In all cases, however, the estimated constants differ insignificantly from zero at the 5% level. Therefore there is no evidence of systematic drift for the federal tax and spending ratios. When the total government sector is substituted for the federal government, the estimated constants are again positive but insignificantly different from zero.

Because no drift was isolated for the government spending ratios, it cannot be claimed that debt management was used to prevent a trend in spending from being reflected in systematic movements in tax rates. On

6. The backward filter is satisfactory here because the only regressor is a constant. OLS estimation is applied to the dependent variable in filtered form. The estimated constant and its standard error are then divided by $1/(1 - \lambda + \lambda^2 - \cdots) = 1/0.79$ to convert back to the original form of the equation.

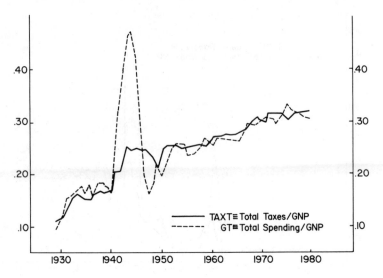

Figure 11.2. Total government tax and expenditures ratios, 1929–1979

the other hand, the findings are consistent with the absence of drift in both spending and tax ratios. The historical rises in these ratios, as shown in Figures 11.1 and 11.2, are not necessarily indications of systematic trends. Restrictions on constant terms are reconsidered below as parts of joint hypotheses with other coefficients.

Results from Univariate Autoregressions

Table 11.3 reports results for OLS regressions that include a constant and four annual lags of the dependent variable. The form of these equations is

$$DZ_t = \alpha_0 + \alpha_1 DZ_{t-1} + \alpha_2 DZ_{t-2} + \alpha_3 DZ_{t-3} \qquad (11.6)$$

$$+ \alpha_4 DZ_{t-4} + \text{error term},$$

where Z represents TAXF, GF, TAXT, or GT. The sample periods and dependent variables coincide with those just discussed.

Consider the case where the dependent variable is the change in the federal-spending ratio, $D(GF)$. Over the longer samples, 1884–1979,

Table 11.3. Univariate autoregressions

| Sample | Dependent variable[a] (Z) | $\hat{\alpha}_0$ | $\hat{\alpha}_1$ | $\hat{\alpha}_2$ | $\hat{\alpha}_3$ | $\hat{\alpha}_4$ | Test: $\alpha_1 = 0.268$, $\alpha_2 = -0.072$, $\alpha_3 = 0.019$, $\alpha_4 = -0.005$[b] | |
							α_0 unrestricted	$\alpha_0 = 0$
1884–1979	D(TAXF)	0.0017(0.0012)	0.22(0.10)	0.08(0.11)	−0.18(0.11)	−0.02(0.10)	$F_{91}^4 = 1.3(2.5)$	$F_{91}^5 = 1.3(2.3)$
	D(GF)	0.0021(0.0035)	0.44(0.10)	−0.30(0.11)	−0.03(0.11)	−0.22(0.10)	$F_{91}^4 = 4.2(2.5)$	$F_{91}^5 = 3.4(2.3)$
1884–1929	D(TAXF)	0.0002(0.0011)	0.31(0.15)	−0.04(0.16)	−0.14(0.16)	−0.21(0.15)	$F_{41}^4 = 1.2(2.6)$	$F_{41}^5 = 1.0(2.4)$
	D(GF)	0.0002(0.0034)	0.45(0.15)	−0.77(0.15)	0.29(0.15)	−0.37(0.15)	$F_{41}^5 = 5.1(2.6)$	$F_{41}^5 = 4.1(2.4)$
1930–1979	D(TAXF)	0.0031(0.0021)	0.18(0.15)	0.09(0.15)	−0.18(0.15)	0.01(0.15)	$F_{45}^4 = 0.7(2.6)$	$F_{45}^5 = 1.0(2.4)$
	D(GF)	0.0039(0.0059)	0.43(0.15)	−0.12(0.16)	−0.18(0.16)	−0.20(0.15)	$F_{45}^4 = 2.9(2.6)$	$F_{45}^5 = 2.4(2.4)$
1934–1979	D(TAXT)	0.0054(0.0022)	−0.12(0.15)	−0.05(0.14)	−0.23(0.14)	−0.10(0.15)	$F_{41}^4 = 2.3(2.6)$	$F_{41}^5 = 2.3(2.4)$
	D(GT)	0.0041(0.0063)	0.38(0.15)	−0.14(0.16)	−0.20(0.16)	−0.18(0.15)	$F_{41}^4 = 2.2(2.6)$	$F_{41}^5 = 1.8(2.4)$
1948–1979	D(TAXF)	0.0004(0.0018)	−0.07(0.19)	−0.37(0.18)	−0.24(0.18)	−0.22(0.18)	$F_{27}^4 = 1.7(2.7)$	$F_{27}^5 = 1.4(2.6)$
	D(GF)	0.0020(0.0024)	0.15(0.19)	−0.05(0.07)	−0.10(0.06)	0.07(0.06)	$F_{27}^4 = 1.3(2.7)$	$F_{27}^5 = 1.2(2.6)$
	D(TAXT)	0.0054(0.0022)	−0.12(0.15)	−0.05(0.14)	−0.23(0.14)	−0.10(0.15)	$F_{27}^4 = 1.5(2.7)$	$F_{27}^5 = 1.4(2.6)$
	D(GT)	0.0041(0.0063)	0.38(0.15)	−0.14(0.16)	−0.20(0.16)	−0.18(0.15)	$F_{27}^4 = 1.8(2.7)$	$F_{27}^5 = 1.8(2.6)$

a. OLS autoregressions use the indicated dependent variable, with a constant and four annual own lags as regressors. The form is shown in Eq. (11.6). The standard error for each estimated coefficient, $\hat{\alpha}_i$, is shown in parentheses.

b. The F-statistics apply to the set of coefficients restrictions that are indicated in the heading. 5% critical values are in parentheses.

1884–1929, and 1930–1979, the hypothesis from Eq. (11.3), $\alpha_1 = 0.268$, $\alpha_2 = -0.072$, $\alpha_3 = 0.019$, $\alpha_4 = -0.005$, is rejected at the 5% level. With the constant unrestricted and 5% critical values shown in parentheses, the results are $F_{91}^4 = 4.2$ (2.5) for the 1884–1979 period, $F_{41}^4 = 5.1$ (2.6) for 1884–1929, and $F_{45}^4 = 2.9$ (2.6) for 1930–1979. With the constant set to zero, the corresponding results are $F_{91}^5 = 3.4$ (2.3), $F_{41}^5 = 4.1$ (2.4), and $F_{45}^5 = 2.4$ (2.4). Overall, the data from the longer samples indicate that the past history of changes in the federal-spending ratio has some predictive power for future changes. In terms of coefficient estimates, the first-lag values, $\hat{\alpha}_1$, range from 0.43 to 0.45, which exceed the theoretical value of 0.27 for a time-averaged random walk. Estimates of subsequent lag coefficients tend to be more negative than those implied by the random-walk model. Over the 1948–1979 sample, the random-walk hypothesis would be accepted for the federal-spending ratio—the result is $F_{27}^4 = 1.3$ (2.7) with the constant unrestricted and $F_{27}^5 = 1.2$ (2.6) with the constant set to zero.

For the tax-rate change, $D(\text{TAXF})$, the random-walk model from Eq. (11.3) is accepted over all samples. With the constant unrestricted, the hypothesis, $\alpha_1 = 0.268$, $\alpha_2 = -0.072$, $\alpha_3 = 0.019$, $\alpha_4 = -0.005$, corresponds to statistics of $F_{91}^4 = 1.3$ (2.5) for the 1884–1979 sample, $F_{41}^4 = 1.2$ (2.6) for 1884–1929, $F_{45}^4 = 0.7$ (2.6) for 1930–1979, and $F_{27}^4 = 1.7$ (2.7) for 1948–1979. With a zero constant included in the null hypothesis, the corresponding statistics are $F_{91}^5 = 1.3$ (2.3), $F_{41}^5 = 1.0$ (2.4), $F_{45}^5 = 1.0$ (2.4), and $F_{27}^5 = 1.4$ (2.6). In all cases one accepts the hypothesis that the past history of changes in the federal tax–GNP ratio has no predictive value for subsequent changes.

With $D(\text{TAXF})$ used as the dependent variable, the estimated coefficients differ insignificantly from the random-walk values in a joint sense. However, it may be worth noting the pattern of point estimates for the 1948–1979 sample. As indicated in Table 11.3, these estimates and standard errors are $\hat{\alpha}_1 = -0.07$ (0.19), $\hat{\alpha}_2 = -0.37$ (0.18), $\hat{\alpha}_3 = -0.24$ (0.18), and $\hat{\alpha}_4 = -0.22$ (0.18). This pattern of negative coefficients on past tax-rate changes would be predicted by a model that specified a target level of tax rates. In this case shifts in tax rates would tend to be reversed later. Although the pattern of estimated coefficients over the 1948–1979 period is suggestive of this mechanism, the insignificant F-values imply that the post–World War II data are also consistent with the random-walk model for tax rates.

Overall, the evidence from the longer samples supports the idea that tax rates are set to smooth out predictable movements in federal spending relative to GNP. The significant F-values for the $D(GF)$ variable in tests of Eq. (11.3) indicate that some smoothable variations in the federal-spending ratio have been isolated. For the 1948–1979 period, the lack of predictive power from the own past history is accepted for both the tax and spending ratios. This finding is consistent with the underlying theory—however, the results are less interesting in that no smoothable movements in $D(GF)$ were detected.

For the total government sector, the analysis is carried out only for the samples, 1934–1979 and 1948–1979. In this case the random-walk model is accepted over both sample periods for the spending and tax ratios.

Results from Vector Autoregressions

The variables selected for vector autoregressions were those that seemed promising a priori as predictors for tax-rate changes. The two types of variables considered were those that pertained to the evolution of government spending and those that related to aggregate output fluctuations.[7] The ratio of government spending to GNP, as discussed before, is one of the included variables. A measure of the persistence of these expenditure changes is likely to be important for tax-rate determination—in particular, tax rates should respond strongly and contemporaneously to spending changes that are viewed as largely permanent. Some previous analysis (Barro 1981) isolated a war-intensity variable as a good indicator of the temporary nature of the accompanying changes in defense spending. This variable, which is defined for war years as the concurrent U.S. casualty rate (CAS), is included in the vector autoregressions. (See Table 11.1 for a definition and tabulation.) I have found no other variables that signal the duration of changes in government spending.

The growth rate of real GNP, DY, is included as a business cycle-type variable. The real rate of return on equity, r,[8] has also been used, pri-

7. I examined also lagged values of public debt expressed relative to GNP. These variables were unimportant for explaining changes in the tax and spending ratios.

8. The dollar rate of return for each year is the value-weighted total return for all New York Stock Exchange issues, as compiled by the University of Chicago's Center for Research on Security Prices. An inflation rate is subtracted to determine the real rate of

marily because it functions as a good predictor for subsequent values of DY. Together, the DY and r variables provide some predictive value for subsequent growth rates of output. Therefore, these variables would be likely to pick up any systematic "cyclical" patterns in tax rates. See Table 11.1 for a listing of the DY and r variables.

I have not attempted to include any political variables, such as the proclamation of tax "surcharge" for 1968, the announcement of a "one-time tax rebate" for 1975, or Reagan's promise during 1980 to cut tax rates for 1981 and later years. The issue is whether these pronouncements have any information content—holding fixed the other included variables—for subsequent changes in overall tax rates. It is not clear how to quantify these types of announcement variables over the full sample in order to test for their predictive value.

Annual lagged values of each variable from two to four years back have been included in the vector autoregressions. The previous discussion of time-averaging indicates the difficulty in interpretation for first-lag values, which are not considered. With the tax-rate change used as the dependent variable, the random-walk model predicts zero coefficients for all independent variables. Clearly, the interest in these tests is heightened if some predictive power appears for changes in the government-spending ratio and output growth, even when all first lags of the independent variables are excluded.

Results appear in Table 11.4 for the federal government over 1930–1975 and 1948–1975 samples. Some further detail on these regressions appears in Table 11.A1 of the Appendix. The samples start in 1930 because the r variable was unavailable before 1926. Some satisfactory approximations for this variable could be generated from available stock-price indexes and dividend data. However, because the quality of real GNP data also deteriorates before 1929, it may not pay to extend the sample much before 1930. The forward-filtering procedure that was described earlier accounts for the termination of the samples in 1975.

---

return. From 1948 to 1979, the inflation rate is calculated from the seasonally unadjusted December value of the consumer price index for an urban consumer, measured exclusive of the shelter component. (Shelter was deleted to avoid the erroneous measures of mortgage interest costs. For the 1967–1979 period, where the CPI net of mortgage interest costs is available, there was a close correspondence between the inflation rate measured net of shelter and that measured net only of mortgage interest costs.) Before 1948, the overall CPI for an urban consumer was used.

Table 11.4. Vector autoregressions[a]

(1) Variable	(2) All variables except constant (25.0)[b]	(3) All variables including constant (26.3)[b]	(4) D(TAXF) (7.8)[b]	(5) D(GF) (7.8)[b]	(6) CAS (7.8)[b]	(7) DY (7.8)[b]	(8) r (7.8)[b]
1930–1975 sample							
D(TAXF)	21.7	23.0	0.2	5.6	6.2	5.7	11.0
D(GF)	54.4	54.7	1.9	11.3	25.0	7.9	5.0
CAS	81.9	—	9.1	48.2	48.7	3.1	0.2
DY	30.4	—	3.7	5.5	14.2	15.0	10.6
r	12.9	—	1.7	4.7	0.6	3.2	2.2
1948–1975 sample							
D(TAXF)	21.7	21.7	6.1	2.9	2.1	1.1	2.4
D(GF)	29.1	30.5	6.4	0.6	3.6	2.2	4.3
CAS	53.9	—	34.3	28.9	8.8	23.9	10.9
DY	12.0	—	3.3	0.6	2.6	0.0	6.3
r	19.6	—	3.5	11.0	5.0	0.0	5.9

a. Results apply to vector autoregressions with the sample and dependent variable as shown in the first column. In the original form, the independent variables comprise a constant and annual lags 2–4 for the five variables D(TAXF), D(GF), CAS, DY, and r. Variables are defined and tabulated in Table 11.1.

The dependent variable and the set of independent variables were filtered forward by $(1 - .268L^{-1} + .072L^{-2} - .019L^{-3} + .005L^{-4})$. The filtered dependent variable was regressed on the filtered independent variables, using the original regressors as instruments. The test statistics refer to the following restrictions. Col. 2: The coefficients of all independent variables, except the constant, equal zero. Col. 3: The coefficients of all independent variables, including the constant, equal zero. Cols. 4–8: The coefficients for all lags (2–4) of the indicated variable equal zero, but no other restrictions are imposed. The table reports the value of $-2\log(\text{likelihood ratio})$ that corresponds to each set of restrictions. If one assumes that the filtered errors are normal and serially independent, this expression equals $v\log(\widetilde{\text{SSE}}/\text{SSE})$, where n is the number of observations, $\widetilde{\text{SSE}}$ is the restricted sum of squared errors, and SSE is the unrestricted sum. Under the null hypothesis, this test statistic is distributed asymptotically as $\chi^2(\rho)$ where ρ is the number of restrictions on the coefficients.

b. 5% critical value is given in parentheses.

Table 11.4 reports likelihood-ratio test statistics for hypotheses that stem from the random-walk model. Column 2 corresponds to the restriction that all coefficients of the independent variables, except for the constant, equal zero. Column 3 adds a zero restriction for the constant. Columns 4–8 test separately for the significance of the set of lagged values (from $t - 2$ to $t - 4$) for each independent variable. In these cases the null hypothesis specifies zero values for the coefficients of the three lags of one variable but imposes no constraints on the coefficients of the other variables.

Consider first the results for the federal government over the 1930–1975 period. For the tax-rate change, $D(\text{TAXF})$, the hypothesis that all coefficients of the independent variables are zero corresponds to a statistic of 21.7 (5% critical value = 25.0) when the constant is unrestricted and 23.0 (26.3) when the constant is constrained to equal zero. Therefore, the hypothesis is accepted that federal tax-rate changes are unpredictable, based on the information contained in annual lagged values up to date $t - 2$ for the five variables considered. The test statistics are also below the 5% critical level for each variable treated separately, except for the equity return, r. In that case the test statistic of 11.0 exceeds the critical value of 7.8.

The random-walk model is rejected for the federal-spending ratio over the 1930–1975 period. With $D(\text{GF})$ as the dependent variable, the restriction that the coefficients of all independent variables equal zero now generates a test statistic of 54.4 (5% critical value = 25.0) when the constant is unrestricted and 54.7 (26.3) when the constant is set to zero. Therefore, the random-walk model would be rejected at the 5% level in this case. The individual test statistics indicate separate significance for the lags of the casualty-rate variable (likelihood-ratio statistic = 25.0), changes in the federal-spending ratio (11.3), and output growth (7.9). In these cases the 5% critical value is 7.8. The results reflect especially the predictable effect of war on subsequent changes in federal spending (which is negative, because of the temporary nature of war.)[9] The insignificance for the lags of the CAS variable in the equation for $D(\text{TAXF})$ indicates that this predictable influence on spending does not carry over to a forecastable movement in tax rates. Deficit spending during wars allows for the smoothing of tax rates.

---

9. The estimated coefficient of CAS_{t-2} in the equation for $D(\text{GF})_t$ is -0.25, s.e. = 0.06. See Table 11.A1 in the Appendix.

The distinction between spending and tax behavior does not hinge entirely on the war variable. With the lags of the CAS variable deleted, the lags of the remaining four variables are jointly significant for $D(GF)$ over the 1930–1975 period—the test statistic is 29.4 with a 5% critical value of 21.0. These variables are still jointly insignificant for $D(TAXF)$, where the test statistic is 15.5.

The results for output growth, DY, indicate some explanatory power over the 1930–1975 period. The test statistic for zero coefficients on all lagged variables (with no restriction on the constant) is shown in Column 2 of Table 11.4 as 30.4 (5% critical value = 25.0). For individual variables, there is significance for the lags of DY, CAS, and r—the respective statistics, with 5% critical values of 7.8, are 15.0, 14.2, and 10.6. Therefore the equation for federal tax-rate changes over the 1930–1975 sample could have picked up a systematic response to business fluctuations—that is, to the expectation that output was currently high or low relative to "normal" (with allowance for drift in the level of output). To this extent, the findings rule out an important cyclical pattern for the federal tax–GNP ratio.[10]

The independent variables are jointly significant when CAS is used as the dependent variable—the test statistic in Table 11.4 is 81.9, which exceeds the 5% critical value of 25.0.[11] The main role is played by the lags of CAS and $D(GF)$. The variables considered lack explanatory power for future values of the real rate of return on equity, r. In this case the test statistic is 12.9, which is below the 5% critical level.

Table 11.4 also contains results for the 1948–1975 sample. The conclusions on the federal tax-rate variable, $D(TAXF)$, are similar to those just described. In particular, the hypothesis of unpredictability for tax-rate changes is again accepted. The likelihood-ratio statistics are now 21.7 (5% critical value = 25.0) with the constant unrestricted, and 21.7 (26.3) with the constant set to zero. The test statistics are also below the 5% critical level when each independent variable is considered separately.

10. My previous results on the cyclical behavior of public debt (Barro 1979, pp. 963ff.) were based on the relation of current real GNP to an estimated time trend. That analysis should be revised to utilize a measure of current real GNP relative to predicted future values. The temporary federal spending variable from that analysis should be similarly recomputed.

11. Because CAS ≥ 0 applies, the linear specification for this variable is inappropriate. However, the only purpose of this equation is to indicate the significant explanatory value of the lagged variables.

For the federal-spending ratio, $D(GF)$, the random-walk model is rejected over the 1948–1975 period. However, the rejection is less decisive than in the case of the longer sample. The likelihood-ratio statistic is now 29.1 (5% critical value = 25.0) with the constant unrestricted and 30.5 (26.3) with the constant set to zero. Despite the joint significance of the independent variables over the 1948–1975 sample, none of the (sets of) variables emerges individually as significant. The test statistics are below the 5% critical value of 7.8 for each case.

Although the evidence over the 1948–1975 period is weaker than that for 1930–1975, the overall conclusions from the two samples are consistent. Some significant predictive power was isolated for changes in the federal-spending ratio, but this systematic pattern does not appear in the federal-tax ratio. Apparently, the management of public debt avoids a predictable pattern in the federal-tax ratio.

For the post–World War II sample, there is no longer any predictable power for output growth, DY. With the five independent variables considered only up to date $t - 2$, it is not possible here to forecast growth rates of output that depart from the mean value. (When the variables are considered separately, the largest value for the likelihood-ratio statistic, 6.3, arises for the lags of the equity return, r.) Accordingly, the estimates for the 1948–1975 sample would be unable to detect predictable tax-rate changes that were associated with anticipated movements in output.

The results over the 1948–1975 period again reveal significant explanatory power for future values of the war-intensity variable, CAS. The independent variables are jointly insignificant for forecasting the real rate of return on equity, r.[12]

Results with Total Taxes and Spending

The conclusions from the vector autoregressions are not greatly modified if federal taxes and spending are replaced by total government measures. Because of data limitations, the 1930–1975 sample is now replaced by 1934–1975. The findings for 1934–1975 show no predictability for changes in tax rates—the test statistics for the joint insignificance of the independent variables are 23.4 (5% critical value = 25.0)

---

12. However, the lags of the $D(GF)$ variable are separately significant in this case.

when the constant is unrestricted, and 24.9 (26.3) with the constant set to zero. Significant predictive value is again found when the ratio of total government spending to GNP is considered. The statistics are 55.6 (25.0) when the constant is unrestricted, and 55.8 (26.3) with the constant set to zero.

The results over the 1948–1975 sample are also similar to those discussed previously for the federal government. For the case of total taxes, the likelihood-ratio statistic is now 24.6 (25.0) with the constant unrestricted and 25.1 (26.3) when the constant is restricted to be zero. For total government spending, the corresponding test statistics are 26.7 and 29.5.

The Volatility of Tax and Spending Ratios

The underlying theory implies that tax-rate movements would smooth out predictable variations in the ratio of government spending to income. In this respect the model is reminiscent of interest-rate term-structure models, where the long rate is supposed to smooth out predictable movements in short rates. Shiller (1979, 1980) has used such models to generate propositions that concern the relative volatility of variables— for example, the variance of changes in long-term interest rates should be smaller than that of short rates. The parallel proposition here would be an excess of the variance of changes in spending ratios over that for changes in tax rates.

The sample standard deviations (about sample means), $\hat{\sigma}$, for changes in spending and tax ratios are consistent with the view that tax rates would be more stable than spending ratios. Over all samples that were considered, and for either the federal government or the total government sector, the $\hat{\sigma}$ values are higher for the changes in the spending ratio than they are for the changes in the tax ratio. For the 1884–1979 sample, the results are $\hat{\sigma}_{D(GF)} = 0.0402$ and $\hat{\sigma}_{D(TAXF)} = 0.0116$. Over the 1930–1979 sample, the comparable values are 0.0487 and 0.0140. When total government measures are used, the results over the 1930–1979 period are 0.0461 versus 0.0120.

For the 1948–1979 period, the spending ratios are far more stable, and the differences in $\hat{\sigma}$ values are less dramatic. The values are 0.0134 for $D(GF)$ and 0.0106 for $D(TAXF)$. Corresponding figures for total government are 0.0145 and 0.0097.

The greater volatility in spending ratios than in tax ratios supports the underlying view of tax smoothing. However, it is clear that a smaller variance for changes in tax ratios than for changes in spending ratios does not per se rule out a pattern of predictable movements in tax rates. Therefore, the volatility tests should be viewed as supplementary to the tests that have been carried out earlier.

Observations

The present evidence is generally supportive of the tax-rate smoothing model of intertemporal public finance. Valid tests of the random-walk model for aggregate federal and total government tax rates led to acceptance at conventional significance levels. The parallel hypothesis for the ratio of government spending to GNP was rejected. A sharp distinction between the behavior of spending and taxes emerges from longer samples that start before World War II. However, some contrast remains in the post–World War II sample. The volatility tests for taxes versus government spending were also consistent with the tax-rate-smoothing viewpoint.

Given the limitation to annual data and the necessity of deleting first lags in the vector autoregressions, the approach can miss predictable patterns in overall tax rates that apply to short time intervals. For example, if a change occurs that would induce a permanent shift in tax rates, but adjustment-cost considerations dictate postponing the effective date for changes in the tax law until the following calendar year, then tax rates would be perceived for some portion of a year as high or low relative to expected long-run values. The tests that delete first lags would not pick up this relationship. However, the results from the univariate autoregressions do rule out simple, statistically significant patterns of association for overall tax-rate changes from one year to the next.

From the viewpoint of intertemporal-substitution effects, the important issue concerns current tax rates relative to anticipated future rates. For example, an expectation of rising tax rates on labor earnings would generate a positive substitution effect on current labor supply. Similarly, anticipations about future changes in the investment tax credit have been emphasized as a source of intertemporal substitution effects on investment demand (Kydland and Prescott, 1977, pp. 482–486). The present techniques and explanatory variables were incapable of identify-

ing situations where current overall tax rates for the federal or total
government sector were temporarily significantly above or below their
long-run expected values. If this finding is sustained in more general
circumstances, it suggests that existing aggregate time-series observations will not be useful in assessing how responsive the economy would
be to overall taxes that were perceived as temporarily high or low. The
necessary experiment seems not to have been carried out. Policies that
involve intertemporal manipulation of aggregate tax rates probably cannot be evaluated with the available time-series data.

Appendix: Analysis of the Time-Aggregation Problem

Suppose that observations correspond to "years" as numbered by $t = 1$,
$2, \ldots$ Each year is composed of underlying segments, $i = 1, 2, \ldots, n$.
The basic model dictates a random walk for a variable τ at these underly-
ing time units:

$$\tau_{ti} = \tau_{t,i-1} + u_{ti}, \tag{11.A1}$$

for all t and $i = 1, \ldots, n$, where $\tau_{t,0} \equiv \tau_{t-1,n}$. The disturbance u_{ti} is i.i.d.
with zero mean. The distribution of u_t is assumed to be normal in some
of the discussion.

The time-averaged observation for period t is

$$\bar{\tau}_t \equiv \frac{1}{n} \sum_{i=1}^{n} \tau_{ti}. \tag{11.A2}$$

Eq. (11.A1) implies that the first difference, $D\bar{\tau}_t \equiv \bar{\tau}_t - \bar{\tau}_{t-1}$, is given by

$$D\bar{\tau}_t = \frac{1}{n} \{ [nu_{t,1} + (n-1)u_{t,2} + \cdots + u_{t,n}] \tag{11.A3}$$

$$+ [u_{t-1,2} + 2u_{t-1,3} + \cdots + (n-1)u_{t-1,n}] \}.$$

That is, $D\bar{\tau}_t$ is a moving-average process, involving disturbances applicable to years t and $t - 1$.

From Eq. (11.A3) it follows (as in Working 1960) that the simple correlation between $D\bar{\tau}_t$ and $D\bar{\tau}_{t-1}$ is

$$\text{CORR}(D\bar{\tau}_t, D\bar{\tau}_{t-1}) = \frac{\text{COV}(D\bar{\tau}_t, D\bar{\tau}_{t-1})}{\text{VAR}(D\bar{\tau}_t)} = \frac{(n^2 - 1)}{2(2n^2 + 1)}. \qquad (11.A4)$$

As the underlying interval becomes infinitesimal, $n \to \infty$ and

$$\lim_{n \to \infty} \text{CORR}(D\bar{\tau}_t, D\bar{\tau}_{t-1}) = 1/4. \qquad (11.A5)$$

It follows from inspection of Eq. (11.A3) that the simple correlation of $D\bar{\tau}_t$ with $D\bar{\tau}_{t-i}$, where $i \geq 2$, is zero. With $D\bar{\tau}_{t-1}$ omitted, $D\bar{\tau}_t$ is independent of the set of lagged variables, $D\bar{\tau}_{t-2}, D\bar{\tau}_{t-3}, \ldots$.

Equation (11.A3) can be used also to evaluate a string of partial correlations involving $D\bar{\tau}_t$ and a set of lagged values $D\bar{\tau}_{t-i}$, where $i = 1, 2, \ldots$. With four lags included, the pattern of partial correlations turns out to be 56/193 (0.29), $-15/193$ (-0.08), 4/193 (0.02), and $-2/193$ (-0.01).

Consider another time-averaged, random-walk variable in first-difference form,

$$D\bar{X}_t = \frac{1}{n}\{(nv_{t,1} + \cdots + v_{t,n}) \qquad (11.A6)$$

$$+ [v_{t-1,2} + \cdots + (n - 1)v_{t-1,n}]\}.$$

The underlying interval length, as determined by n, coincides with that for τ. The disturbances, (u_{ti}, v_{ti}), are now treated as bivariate normal with zero mean, serial independence, and contemporaneous correlation ρ.

It can be shown that the partial correlation of $D\bar{\tau}_t$ with $D\bar{X}_{t-1}$, given $D\bar{\tau}_t$, is zero. Similarly, given the string of lagged values, $D\bar{\tau}_{t-i}$, the partial correlation of $D\bar{\tau}_t$ with $D\bar{X}_{t-i}$ is zero.

Suppose now that X is observed directly rather than in time-averaged form. The first difference is then

$$DX_t = v_{t,1} + \cdots + v_{t,n}. \qquad (11.A7)$$

Given that $(u_{t,i}, v_{t,i})$ are bivariate normal and taking the case where $n \to \infty$, one can show that the mean of $D\bar{\tau}_t$, conditioned on observations for

Table 11.A1. Multivariate autoregressions for federal taxes and spending

Dependent variable[a] and sample	D(TAXF) 1930–1975	D(TAXF) 1948–1975	D(GF) 1930–1975	D(GF) 1948–1975
Constant	0.007(0.004)	−0.003(0.009)	0.018(0.008)	−0.001(0.010)
$D(TAXF)_{t-2}$	−0.15 (0.24)	−1.09 (0.76)	0.08 (0.52)	0.08 (0.83)
$D(TAXF)_{t-3}$	0.11 (0.27)	−0.52 (0.39)	−0.72 (0.60)	−0.65 (0.43)
$D(TAXF)_{t-4}$	−0.09 (0.27)	−0.86 (0.48)	−0.37 (0.59)	−0.52 (0.52)
$D(GF)_{t-2}$	−0.14 (0.11)	0.32 (0.26)	0.13 (0.25)	0.00 (0.28)
$D(GF)_{t-3}$	0.05 (0.10)	0.05 (0.21)	−0.30 (0.21)	−0.18 (0.23)
$D(GF)_{t-4}$	0.02 (0.08)	0.00 (0.11)	0.48 (0.19)	0.00 (0.12)
CAS_{t-2}	−0.03 (0.03)	0.02 (0.18)	−0.25 (0.06)	0.18 (0.19)
CAS_{t-3}	0.03 (0.02)	0.22 (0.18)	0.12 (0.05)	−0.23 (0.20)
CAS_{t-4}	−0.04 (0.03)	−0.07 (0.09)	−0.01 (0.06)	0.08 (0.09)
DY_{t-2}	0.18 (0.18)	0.18 (0.26)	0.28 (0.17)	−0.27 (0.28)
DY_{t-3}	−0.06 (0.08)	−0.27 (0.28)	0.13 (0.17)	0.33 (0.30)
DY_{t-4}	−0.01 (0.15)	0.10 (0.12)	−0.26 (0.12)	0.09 (0.13)
r_{t-2}	−0.01 (0.01)	0.00 (0.02)	−0.06 (0.03)	−0.01 (0.02)
r_{t-3}	−0.05 (0.02)	−0.02 (0.03)	−0.05 (0.04)	0.04 (0.03)
r_{t-4}	−0.02 (0.02)	0.03 (0.04)	−0.04 (0.04)	−0.03 (0.05)
$\hat{\sigma}$	0.014	0.011	0.031	0.021
D.W.	2.2	2.8	1.5	2.1

a. The dependent variable is noted in the first row as either the first difference of TAXF or GF. Each column reports the array of estimated coefficients and standard errors for a single regression. The dependent variables are a constant and lags $t - 2$, $t - 3$, and $t - 4$ of $D(TAXF)$, $D(GF)$, CAS, DY, and r. See Table 11.4 and the text for a discussion of the estimation procedure. The definitions of variables appear in Table 11.1. $\hat{\sigma}$ is the standard error of estimate. D.W. is the Durbin–Watson statistic.

$D\bar{\tau}_{t-1}$ and DX_{t-1} (using the general formula for the conditional normal density from Graybill 1961, p. 63) is

$$E[D\bar{\tau}_t|D\bar{\tau}_{t-1}, DX_{t-1}] = \frac{1}{4}\left[\frac{1 - (3/2)\rho^2}{1 - (3/8)\rho^2}\right]D\bar{\tau}_{t-1} \qquad (11.A8)$$

$$+ \frac{3}{8}\left(\rho\frac{\sigma_u}{\sigma_v}\right)\left[\frac{1}{1 - (3/8)\rho^2}\right]DX_{t-1}.$$

Recall that ρ is the correlation between u_{ti} (the τ innovation) and v_{ti} (the X innovation). σ_u and σ_v are the standard deviations for u_{ti} and v_{ti}, respectively. When $\rho = 0$, the coefficients in Eq. (11.A8) reduce to ($\frac{1}{4}$, 0).

Generally, the coefficient of DX_{t-1} has the same sign as ρ. The coefficient of $D\bar{\tau}_{t-1}$ is positive if $\rho^2 < \frac{2}{3}$—that is, if $|\rho| < 0.82$. Otherwise, the coefficient is negative. The magnitude of this coefficient is no greater than $\frac{1}{4}$—the value approaches $-\frac{1}{5}$ as $|\rho| \to 1$.

When the "information variable," X, is not generated from a random walk, Eq. (11.A8) no longer applies. In most cases there is no reason to impose a random-walk structure on the X's. Therefore, the analysis in the text was limited to vector autoregressions in which all first lags were excluded.

References

Atkinson, A. B., and J. E. Stiglitz. 1980. *Lectures on Public Economics.* New York: McGraw-Hill.

Auernheimer, L. 1974. "The Honest Government's Guide to the Revenue from the Creation of Money." *Journal of Political Economy* 82:598–606.

Barro, R. J. 1979. "On the Determination of the Public Debt." *Journal of Political Economy* 87:940–971.

——— 1980. "Federal Deficit Policy and the Effects of Public Debt Shocks." *Journal of Money, Credit and Banking* 12:747–762.

——— 1981. "Output Effects of Government Purchases." *Journal of Political Economy* 89(6):1086–1121.

Benjamin, D. K., and L. A. Kochin. 1978. "A Theory of State and Local Finance: The Comparative Statistics of Mobility." Unpublished manuscript. Seattle: University of Washington.

Fama, E. F. 1970. "Efficient Capital Markets: A Review of Theory and Empirical Work." *Journal of Finance* 25:383–417.

Firestone, J. M. 1960. *Federal Receipts and Expenditures during Business Cycles.* Princeton, N.J.: Princeton University Press.

Friedman, M., and A. J. Schwartz. 1963. *A Monetary History of the United States.* Princeton, N.J.: Princeton University Press.

Graybill, F. A. 1961. *An Introduction to Linear Statistical Models,* Vol. 1. New York: McGraw-Hill.

Hall, R. E. 1978. "Stochastic Implications of the Life Cycle–Permanent Income Hypothesis: Theory and Evidence." *Journal of Political Economy* 86:971–987.

Hayashi, F., and C. Sims. 1981. "Efficient Estimation of Time Series Models with Predetermined, but not Exogenous, Instruments," Unpublished manuscript. Minneapolis: University of Minnesota.

Kydland, F. E., and E. C. Prescott. 1977. "Rules rather than Discretion: The Inconsistency of Optimal Plans." *Journal of Political Economy* 85:473–491.

—— 1980. "A Competitive Theory of Fluctuations and the Feasibility and Desirability of Stabilization Policy." In *Rational Expectations and Economic Policy,* ed. S. Fischer. Chicago: University of Chicago Press for the National Bureau of Economic Research, pp. 169–198.

Sadka, E. 1977. "A Theorem on Uniform Taxation." *Journal of Public Economics* 7:387–391.

Sandmo, A. 1974. "A Note on the Structure of Optimal Taxation." *American Economic Review* 64:701–706.

Shiller, R. J. 1979. "The Volatility of Long-Term Interest Rates and Expectations Models of the Term Structure." *Journal of Political Economy* 87:1190–1219.

—— 1980. "The Use of Volatility Measures in Assessing Market Efficiency." National Bureau of Economic Research Working Paper No. 565.

Working, H. 1960. "Note on the Correlation of First Differences of Averages in Random Chain." *Econometrica* 28:916–918.

12   Output Effects of Government Purchases

Macroeconomic analysis typically assigns government purchases an important role in influencing aggregate demand and thereby in affecting output and employment. Bailey (1971) points out that these expansionary effects are offset to the extent that governmentally provided goods and services are close substitutes for private consumption expenditures. Hall (1980) argues that temporary changes in government purchases can have a substantial business-cycle role, because they stimulate intertemporal substitution of work and production. These effects are most important in the case of transitory expenditures that are not close substitutes for private spending—notably for wartime spending—but would not apply to long-run changes in government purchases. Public services also play a role as an input (perhaps usually with positive marginal product) into private production processes. This characteristic provides a direct channel whereby shifts in government purchases can alter the level of total output.

The present analysis focuses on the theoretical and empirical distinction between temporary and permanent variations in government purchases. A simple theoretical framework is used to analyze the output and real-rate-of-return effects of these purchases. I argue first that movements in the real rate of interest arise mainly when government pur-

Journal of Political Economy (1981) 89(6):1086–1121; © 1981 by The University of Chicago. Earlier versions of this chapter were presented at the Charles Haywood Murphy Symposium on Government Debt, Fiscal Policy, and Expectational Theory at Tulane University, October 1979, and at seminars at Columbia, Harvard, the University of Florida, and Stanford. I have benefited especially from comments by Jeremy Bulow, Stan Engerman, Ben Friedman, Donald Hester, Bob King, Levis Kochin, Yoram Peles, and Charles Plosser and from the research assistance of Louis Chan, Gary Gorton, and Chitra Ramaswami. This research was supported by the National Science Foundation.

chases are temporarily high or low and, second, that the response of output is likely to be larger when the change in purchases is temporary rather than permanent.

The empirical section estimates the division of defense purchases into permanent and temporary components by considering the effects of war and of war expectations. Defense spending associated with wars is largely transitory, whereas other changes in defense spending turn out to be predominantly permanent. Shifts in nondefense federal plus state and local purchases are also mostly permanent in character.

Analysis of real GNP reveals a significant expansionary effect of temporary defense purchases. Permanent defense purchases have a significantly weaker, but still significantly positive, effect on real GNP. The coefficient associated with permanent nondefense purchases is imprecisely determined. Because no temporary changes in nondefense purchases were isolated, it was not possible to determine the output effects from this category of purchases. Some more detailed hypotheses that concern the generation of expected long-run average defense purchases are formulated, tested, and accepted. Finally, the determination of real GNP during World War II is analyzed and compared with relationships for the postwar period.

Theoretical Considerations

Setup of the Model

This section constructs a simple theoretical framework, which is used to study the effects of government purchases on output and the real rate of interest. The setting is designed to focus on the distinction between temporary and permanent movements in government purchases.

Suppose that the economy-wide credit market establishes an anticipated real rate of interest on loans, which is denoted by r. For simplicity, economic agents are assumed to act as if r were constant over time. The model can be extended to permit (valid) expectations in some circumstances of divergences between current and anticipated future values of r (see below).

An increase in r motivates the postponement of consumption and leisure from the present to the future. Therefore r has a negative effect on consumption demand, C^d, and a positive effect on the supply of labor services.[1] The positive effect on labor supply implies—through the equilibration of a labor market that is not considered explicitly—a positive effect of r on commodity supply, Y^s. For present purposes, it is satisfactory to ignore the intervening factor markets and view households and producers as integrated economic units. In this case, the rise in r directly boosts current supplies of goods and services. A higher value of r tends also to deter the accumulation of capital. To simplify matters, however, the discussion of investment effects is limited to footnotes in the subsequent analysis.

The Government's Budget

The government's real demand for commodities during period t is denoted by G_t. Let T_t represent the real value of date t's tax collections, net of any transfer payments. Taxes and transfers are treated initially as lump sum in nature, but this assumption is relaxed later. Inflationary finance can be viewed as a particular form of (non–lump-sum) tax, which need not be introduced separately for present purposes. The model does not deal with monetary variables or the determination of the absolute price level and the nominal interest rate. These matters do not seem central for a study of the real effects of government purchases.

Abstracting initially from interest-bearing public debt, the government's budget constraint requires an equality each period between purchases and the net amount of real taxes:

$$G_t = T_t. \tag{12.1}$$

The possibility of government borrowing relaxes this condition of budget balance each period but does not alter the principal findings that are discussed below.

In calculating its permanent income, the representative household figures in the anticipated present value of its share of taxes-net-of-transfers. For aggregate purposes, the important magnitude at some starting date 0 is the expectation of the present value, $\sum_{t=1}^{\infty} [T_t/(1 + r)^t]$. From Eq. (12.1), this magnitude coincides with the expected present value of gov-

---

1. A change in r involves pure, unambiguous substitution effects if the underlying production technology is held fixed (see Bailey 1971, chap. 6).

ernment purchases, $\Sigma_{t=1}^{\infty} [G_t/(1 + r)^t]$.[2] It is convenient to work with the uniform flow of purchases, $\overline{G}$, that would yield the same present value of purchases as the time path, G_t. This flow, which is referred to as "permanent purchases," is determined from the condition

$$\overline{G} \equiv r \sum_{t=1}^{\infty} \left[\frac{G_t}{(1 + r)^t} \right]. \tag{12.2}$$

Holding fixed any service value that the private sector attaches to the time path of G_t—which is discussed next—a rise in $\overline{G}$ impacts on households exactly as would a corresponding decrease in permanent income. In particular, an increase in permanent purchases, $\overline{G}$, tends to reduce C^d and raise the supply of labor services at all dates. (The positive response of work effort depends on the lump-sum nature of taxes. See the subsequent discussion.) The increase in work offers translates—through the equilibration of the labor market or via the direct behavior of households/producers in the present framework—into increased commodity supply, Y^s.

For a given value of r, a rise in $\overline{G}$ requires a one-to-one decline in the representative household/producer's "average" planned value over time for C^d net of Y^s. This result follows from the intertemporal budget constraint for a household/producer, where the time path of C^d and net real taxes appear on the expenditure side, and the time path of Y^s appears on the income side. If the current value of C^d net of Y^s falls by less than one-to-one with $\overline{G}$, then the typical household must be planning to reduce some future net values by greater than one-to-one. That is, the household responds in this case to the drop in effective permanent income by shifting relative expenditures (on consumption and leisure) from the future to the present. Similarly, a decline in current values by more than one-to-one with $\overline{G}$ would signify an intention to shift expenditures from the present to the future. Because a pure income effect is involved, it seems reasonable to concentrate on the intermediate case

2. With public debt included, the expected present value of net real taxes equals the expected present value of real purchases plus the initial amount of real government debt. In particular, there is still a one-to-one relation between changes in the anticipated present values of real purchases and net real taxes. This calculation assumes that the government's real interest rate equals r. The possibility of chain-letter, perpetual deficit finance has also been excluded. See Barro (1978) for a discussion of these and related matters, including the role of finite lifetimes.

where the intertemporal pattern of expenditures is unchanged. In this case, at a given value of r, the decline in current C^d net of the increase in Y^s exactly matches the rise in $\overline{G}$.[3]

The Role of Public Services

The government is viewed as utilizing its commodity purchases at each date, G_t, to provide a contemporaneous flow of public services to the private sector. These services are treated as provided free of charge to households/producers. Two types of services are considered. One form is modeled as a direct conveyer of utility to households. Examples that do not encompass the traditional roles of government include parks, libraries, school lunch programs, (subsidized) hospitals, and, possibly, highway and transportation programs. (The latter category could be viewed alternatively as an input to private production functions.) An important feature of these forms of public services is the possibility of close substitution with private consumer spending.

The second type of service is an input to private production processes, which can apply either to businesses or households. Examples include the provision of a legal system, aspects of national defense, fire and police services, education, and various regulatory activities. (The last item is likely to exhibit negative marginal product.) In some cases these services would be close substitutes for private inputs of labor and capital. However, in areas like the provision of a legal system and national defense, the public services are likely to enhance the marginal products of private factors.

In many situations a particular government activity would exhibit features of both general types of public services that are being considered. The extent to which each feature was represented would vary across a wide range of programs. Despite this real world diversity, the formal analysis proceeds as if there were a single type of governmental activity, which has service attributes that are partly of the direct-utility type and partly of the productive-input type.

3. This result does not depend on an infinite horizon for the representative household. Finite lives can alter the effects of some government actions, such as changes in public debt or social security, that involve a publicly mandated shift in incomes across generations. Government purchases that are financed contemporaneously by taxes (which are independent of age) do not involve these considerations.

Government-provided services are often modeled as "public," as opposed to private, goods in the sense of being "nonrival"—one person's enjoyment of the good does not diminish the enjoyment by another person.[4] It is doubtful that this characteristic applies to the majority of government purchases at the current time. Falling outside of this category would be the bulk of expenditures on education, hospitals, school lunch programs, and any service that is subject to congestion, such as parks, courts, libraries, transportation and highway projects, and police/fire services. Even in the case of national defense, the benefits to individuals are likely to be relative to the total amount of property that is being defended, because the level of external threat would respond to the potential prize from conquest (see Thompson 1974).

In a nonrivalry situation, individual utility or production would depend on the total of government services rather than on the quantity provided to the particular economic unit. Because nonrivalry seems atypical, the modeling assumes that individual utility and production depend on real government purchases per capita. However, the general form of the analysis would not be altered appreciably if some elements of nonrivalry were introduced.

Consider, first, the direct interplay in utility functions between government services and household choices of consumption and leisure. Suppose, as stressed by Bailey (1971, chap. 9), that the contemporaneous levels of (per capita) G_t and (individual) C_t are close substitutes in utility terms. For example, assume that each unit of G_t (per capita) is viewed as providing utility services that are equivalent to a fraction θ of a unit of contemporaneous individual consumption expenditure.[5] That is, household utility depends on the effective consumption flow at each date, $C_t^* \equiv C_t + \theta G_t$, where $0 \leq \theta \leq 1$. The formulation neglects this type of utility substitution among noncontemporaneous values for C and G or between G and leisure.[6] The provision of these types of public services means that households obtain units of effective consumption, C^*, that

4. This characteristic is embedded in the theoretical analysis of Samuelson (1954).

5. The parameter θ can be viewed in the following analysis as applying to the marginal unit of G_t.

6. The time path of G_t could also affect overall household utility in a form that was additively separable from the time paths of effective consumption and leisure. In this sense the θ parameter need not limit the utility value that households attach to public services. This possibility does not invalidate the subsequent discussion of permanent income changes that are induced by shifts in $\overline{G}$.

exceed the quantity of private real expenditures, C. The permanent flow of government purchases, $\overline{G}$, can be used to finance the uniform effective consumption flow, $\theta\overline{G}$.[7] This aspect of public services offsets the negative permanent income effect from G that was described earlier (see also note 6). The permanent income effect that is pertinent to private choices on consumption expenditure and leisure is now $(\theta - 1)\overline{G}$—the condition $0 \leq \theta \leq 1$ implies that the permanent income effect of $\overline{G}$ is still less than or equal to zero, but no larger than one in magnitude.

With $\overline{G}$ held fixed, an increase in G_t now implies some direct crowding out of contemporaneous private commodity demand. In order to maintain the level of effective consumption, C_t^*—which is appropriate when $\overline{G}$, the other determinants of permanent income, and r are held fixed—C_t^d must decline with G_t in accordance with the parameter θ. The greater the utility substitution (at the margin) between C_t and G_t—as measured here by θ—the larger the negative response of C_t^d to an increase in G_t. As long as $\theta \leq 1$ applies, aggregate commodity demand for date t—$Y_t^d \equiv C_t^d + G_t$—rises as the nonnegative fraction, $(1 - \theta)$, of increases in G_t (when $\overline{G}$ is held fixed).

Consider next the role of public services as an input to private production processes. It is assumed that public services of this type have a positive marginal product, which is denoted by MPG. The condition MPG ≤ 1, which is assumed to hold, implies that the marginal response of (aggregate) private output to an increase in (aggregate) G does not exceed the social cost of providing the extra public services input. Through its role as a productive input, an increment in G raises commodity supply, Y^s, for given levels of private factor inputs. Note that part of total output will be utilized to provide intermediate goods, which take the form of publicly supplied production inputs. Although there are good reasons in principle for deleting these intermediate goods from measures of final product, this approach is not followed in the national accounts.[8] In the theoretical analysis the output measure, Y, is also gross of this type of intermediate production.

Because the public services inputs are provided freely, a change in G alters private sector real incomes in accordance with the marginal prod-

7. The discussion assumes that the inequality constraint, $C_t \geq 0$, is never binding.

8. These matters are discussed in Kuznets (1948, pp. 156–157) and Musgrave (1959, pp. 186–188). The double-counting property for publicly provided production inputs implies that empirical counterparts of total output, like real GNP, overstate the response of final output to government purchases.

uct, MPG. The representative household receives a per capita share of this extra real income. This effect further offsets the inverse influence of $\overline{G}$ on permanent income. The net effect now depends on the term $(\theta + \text{MPG} - 1)$, which is nonpositive but no greater than one in magnitude if $0 \leq \theta + \text{MPG} \leq 1$ applies.[9]

If variations in G alter the marginal products of private productive inputs, then additional effects would arise through changes in factor demand functions. Cases where public services substitute for private inputs—such as the provision of public rather than private guards—would generate reductions in the marginal product of labor. On this count the private demand for labor would tend to fall when G rises. In some other cases the private demand for capital services would decline. However, to the extent that background services like national defense and a legal system are expanded, factor marginal products are likely to rise, which would generate the opposite responses in private factor demands. The main analysis neglects the array of possible effects of government purchases on private factor marginal products.

Commodity-Market Clearing

The equilibrium condition for the commodity market is given by

$$Y^d \equiv C^d(\ldots, r, G, \overline{G}) + G = Y^s(\ldots, r, G, \overline{G}). \qquad (12.3)$$
$$ (-)(-)(-) (+)(+)(+)$$

Recall that the analysis has neglected the investment component of demand and has, thus far, assumed lump-sum taxation. Time subscripts have been omitted for convenience. Signs beneath the independent variables refer to partial derivatives. The omitted arguments in the C^d and Y^s functions involve various fixed aspects of households' permanent incomes, the production technology, and so on. As mentioned before, the real rate of return, r, exerts intertemporal-substitution effects that are negative on C^d and positive on Y^s. A rise in G has a negative crowding-out effect on the contemporaneous choice of C^d. The impact of G on Y^s

---

9. Recall that the analysis deals with a composite government service that has attributes of the direct-utility (θ) and production-input (MPG) type. A particular category of purchases is unlikely to exhibit a high value for both parameters, θ and MPG. Therefore, if $\theta \leq 1$ and MPG ≤ 1 apply for each category of purchases, the condition $\theta + \text{MPG} \leq 1$ is likely to hold for the composite over all categories.

is nonnegative if MPG $\geq$ 0. A rise in $\overline{G}$ reduces the pertinent measure of households' permanent incomes, as discussed before, and thereby leads to a decrease in C^d and a rise in Y^s.

Effects of a Temporary Rise in Government Purchases

Consider a temporary expansion of real government purchases, where G rises while $\overline{G}$ is held fixed. The budget condition from Eq. (12.1) implies that these purchases are financed by a contemporaneous increase in real taxes-net-of-transfers, T. In fact, for the context of a temporary rise in government spending—which is most pronounced at the federal level in wartime—it is more natural that the bulk of contemporaneous finance would take the form of interest-bearing debt issue rather than tax increases. This behavior allows the government to spread the higher taxes necessitated by temporary spending over a large time interval instead of implementing exceptionally high tax collections for a few periods (see Barro 1979, 1980b for discussions). With $\overline{G}$ held fixed, it would be possible to utilize interest-bearing debt to maintain the entire initial time path of net real tax collections, T_t. In any event, for the setting of lump-sum taxes, the present value of tax obligations is not altered by shifts between public debt and taxes (see note 2). Because households' calculations of permanent incomes depend only on this present-value magnitude, the effects of increases in government purchases that are financed by debt issue would coincide with the effects of those that are financed by higher taxes.

The rise in G reduces C^d in Eq. (12.3) in accordance with the utility substitution parameter, θ. Therefore aggregate demand, Y^d, rises on net by $(1 - \theta)$ times the increase in G. If the marginal product of public services, MPG, is positive, Y^s rises with G on the right side of Eq. (12.3). Overall, the shift in "excess demand," $Y^d - Y^s$, is determined by the term $(1 - \theta - \text{MPG})$. It was already assumed that this term is nonnegative—that is, the direct, one-to-one effect of G on aggregate demand is offset only partially by the utility-substitution and productive-input aspects of government purchases.

Because an increase in G raises excess commodity demand, a rise in the real rate of return is required to restore commodity-market clearing.[10] This response in r reduces C^d and raises Y^s. The rise in Y^s reflects

10. Because the expansion of G is temporary, the rise in the equilibrium real rate of interest would also be temporary. An extension to allow divergences between current and expected future real rates of return does not alter the basic analysis.

the substitution of current work effort for planned future effort. Since Y^s was also increased directly by the rise in G, it is apparent that equilibrium output rises. This output effect is greater the smaller the value of θ, the larger the value of MPG, and the greater the real interest rate elasticity of Y^s relative to that of C^d. In the polar case where $\theta = 1$ and MPG = 0, the response of Y and r to G would be nil. In this circumstance, government purchases would amount to lump-sum transfers to households, because G_t and C_t were perfect substitutes in the utility function.

Private consumer spending, C^d, is crowded out from the rise in r and from the initial negative effect of G. Therefore, the positive response of Y to G must be less than one-to-one—that is, the model exhibits an output dampener rather than a multiplier.

The positive response of output to temporary movements in government purchases would apply especially to wartime periods.[11] The higher real rate of return can be viewed as a price signal that induces the intertemporal substitution of resources toward periods such as wars in which aggregate output is valued unusually highly. This type of substitution has been stressed by Hall (1980, sec. 2), who points out also that this behavior differs in some important respects from the responses of supply to monetary misperceptions that occur in some business-cycle theories that stress intertemporal substitution on the supply side (for example, Lucas and Rapping 1969; Lucas 1975; Barro 1980a). The effect of temporary government purchases on the time arrangement of work and production does not rely on elements of misperception with respect to the general price level or other variables.

Effects of a Permanent Rise in Government Purchases

Suppose now that G and $\overline{G}$ rise by equal amounts. The increase in G was shown already to raise excess commodity demand in accordance with the term $(1 - \theta - \text{MPG})$. A higher value of $\overline{G}$ was shown earlier to reduce effective permanent income by the same factor. It was also noted above that the typical or intermediate response of C^d net of Y^s would be one-to-one with this type of change in effective permanent income. (This re-

---

11. Wartime may also be associated with uncertainties on maintaining property rights, which would tend to reduce private investment demand. The possibly changing probability of winning or losing a conflict would enter in this context. The analysis abstracts from these effects and from controls on prices or interest rates. Also excluded are effects of patriotism or coercive behavior, such as conscription.

sponse arises when households reduce expenditures on consumption and leisure by the same amount in each period.) In this case the response of $(C^d - Y^s)$ equals $-(1 - \theta - \text{MPG})$ times the change in $\overline{G}$. Since this response exactly offsets the excess demand effect of G, the overall response in $(Y^d - Y^s)$ would be zero. It follows in this case that the real rate of interest is invariant with permanent changes in government purchases (under lump-sum taxation).[12] Although the invariance of r would not hold in general, this conclusion for an intermediate case contrasts with the presumption of a positive effect for the setting of a temporary increase in government purchases.

When r is unchanged, it follows from Eq. (12.3) that consumption falls and total output rises. The expansion of production reflects partly the direct effect of G on Y^s (which was assumed to be positive) and the negative income effect of $\overline{G}$ on leisure. (The net response of leisure becomes ambiguous when income taxation is introduced—see the subsequent analysis.) The decline in consumption means that output rises by less than one-to-one with the permanent expansion of government purchases—that is, an output dampener is again predicted.

Non–Lump-Sum Taxation

Some of the results are affected by the unrealistic assumption that government expenditures are financed by lump-sum taxation. This section explores the consequences of income taxes in a simple environment. Because the present analysis is concerned only with tax effects that are systematically related to changes in government purchases—rather than with public finance questions per se—this simplified analysis may be adequate.

Suppose that government expenditures are financed by a general income tax. Let τ_t represent the effective tax rate on incomes that accrue during period t.[13] In a nonproportional tax setup, τ_t would represent the average marginal income tax rate. Assume now that the government can borrow and lend at the real rate of interest, r—the same rate that applies to the private sector. Given the permanent flow of real government

---

12. It follows also—assuming no direct effects on the marginal product of capital schedule—that capital accumulation would be unaltered.

13. The analysis neglects the double taxation of incomes that flow through the corporate sector. Taxation in the form of inflationary finance could be included separately without affecting the main results.

spending, which includes $\overline{G}$ and the comparable measure for real transfers,[14] and the possibility for variations in public debt, there exists some income tax rate $\overline{\tau}$ that is constant over time and also just satisfies the government's intertemporal budget constraint.[15] Although many patterns of time-varying tax rates would also satisfy the government's budgetary requirements, it will be desirable in most circumstances[16]—in terms of minimizing the distortions that are imposed on the private economy—to stabilize income tax rates over time. That is, the government would adjust its public debt issues and redemptions to prevent divergences between current and expected future income tax rates. (For discussions of this type of result, see Barro 1979; Kydland and Prescott 1980, pp. 185–186.) In this setting changes in government purchases would not generate movements in current tax rates relative to expected future rates. This conclusion means that, first, variations in G with $\overline{G}$ held fixed have no effect on tax rates; second, shifts in $\overline{G}$ imply equal changes in current and expected future tax rates, $\overline{\tau}$;[17] and third, for the purpose of studying government purchases, it is unnecessary to deal with the intertemporal-substitution effects that would arise from expected time variations in income tax rates.[18]

Given this framework for tax rate determination, it is unnecessary to modify the main conclusions that were derived earlier for the case of a temporary increase in government purchases. Notably, output and the real rate of interest continue to rise when G increases, with $\overline{G}$ held fixed. The principal modification to the previous findings is that r should be interpreted as the after-tax real rate of return, as calculated with the appropriate average marginal tax rate on interest income.[19]

14. Real interest payments on an initial public debt stock would also enter.

15. Because changes in tax rates affect the tax base, Y, the solution for $\overline{\tau}$ is generally nonunique. However, the minimal possible value for $\overline{\tau}$ is the pertinent choice.

16. It may be optimal to allow tax rates to vary over the business cycle. A countercyclical pattern shows up empirically for the U.S. federal government. However, the pattern is at least less pronounced in terms of the total government sector.

17. It is assumed that increases in tax rates induce increases in real tax revenues within the relevant range.

18. For example, these types of effects are central to a study of the investment tax credit (see Kydland and Prescott 1977, pp. 482–486).

19. This result assumes that interest income is taxable and interest payments are deductible from taxable income. The conclusion neglects systematic differences between the marginal tax rates applicable to receivers of interest income versus those pertinent for payers. The result is not affected directly by the taxation of nominal, rather than real, interest payments. However, other effects of inflation on effective tax rates would matter.

For the case of a permanent increase in government purchases, the new element is the rise in the income tax rate, $\bar{\tau}$, along with the rise in $\overline{G}$ (see note 17). The higher income tax rate motivates a shift away from market work and toward leisure and other nonmarket activities. In Eq. (12.3) this change is reflected as downward shifts in the Y^s and C^d functions.[20] For given values of r (now interpreted net of tax), G, $\overline{G}$, and so on, it is plausible that the declines in C^d and Y^s would roughly balance. In other words, as in some cases that were discussed earlier, there is no reason to expect a particular direction of change for the relative amounts of consumption and leisure expenditures that are conducted at different dates.

Given this pattern of response to a higher income tax rate, it still follows that a permanent shift in government purchases has no effect on the (after-tax) real rate of return. However, the negative effect of higher income taxation on the incentive to work offsets the tendency for output to rise.[21] The net movement in output now involves three forces: first, the substitution away from work because of higher income tax rates; second, the negative income effect (associated with the higher level of $\overline{G}$) on leisure, which motivates more work; and third, the direct productive-input effect of G on Y^s. The first two influences involve the standard ambiguous net response of leisure to the substitution and income effects that are generated by either a change in the real wage rate or a shift in the income tax rate that is applicable to labor income. However, the income effect here involves the term $-(1 - \theta - \text{MPG})\overline{G}$, while the tax shift applies one-to-one to $\overline{G}$. This difference increases the likelihood that the substitution effect will outweigh the income effect. Suppose that the substitution effect were, in fact, comparable to or dominant over the income effect. In this case the overall change in output that is induced by a permanent rise in government purchases would be bounded from above by the direct positive effect of G on Y^s. This channel corresponds to only one portion of the positive output response that arose for the case of a temporary increase in government purchases—the other part involves the intertemporal substitution effect on work effort, which is associated with the increase in r. It follows that temporary rises in gov-

20. The incentive to accumulate capital would also be diminished. Through this channel, a permanent increase in government purchases tends to reduce the capital stock, even when the after-tax rate of return is unchanged.

21. A reduction in the capital stock, as mentioned in note 20, reinforces this effect.

ernment purchases would induce larger output responses than equal-size, but permanent, rises in purchases. The sign of the output response is now ambiguous for the case of a permanent expansion of government purchases—the reaction is more likely to be positive when the marginal product of public services is high.

Overall, temporary expansions of government purchases are distinguished from permanent increases in that, first, the positive effect on output of the temporary expansion is likely to be larger and, second, a positive effect on the (after-tax) real rate of interest is predicted only for the temporary case. The present empirical investigation deals only with output effects of temporary versus permanent movements in government purchases. Some preliminary analysis of real-rate-of-return effects is carried out in Barro (1981a).

Empirical Implementation

The theoretical propositions will be tested by examining the effects of government purchases in a reduced-form relationship for output, as measured by real GNP. The analysis is an extension of previous empirical research (Barro 1981b), which stressed the business-cycle influences of monetary disturbances. This earlier work included a government-purchases variable but did not distinguish temporary from permanent government spending.

It is convenient to carry out the analysis in terms of the ratio of real government purchases to real GNP, G/Y. In particular, temporary or permanent variations in G are assumed to enter relative to Y in a linear relation for the log of output—that is,

$$\log(Y_t) = \cdots + \beta_1[(G - \overline{G})/Y]_t + \beta_2(\overline{G}/Y)_t, \tag{12.4}$$

where omitted variables indicated by . . . include current and lagged monetary shocks and other deterministic and stochastic influences on output. The variable $\overline{G}_t$, which would generally be unobservable, is the permanent flow of government purchases as perceived at date t. The empirical procedure for handling this variable is discussed below. Lagged values of G/Y and $\overline{G}/Y$ might also appear in Eq. (12.4), but these effects were not found to be important empirically.

The functional form in Eq. (12.4) implies that increments in government purchases induce increments in output in accordance with

$$dY[1 + \beta_1(G - \overline{G})/Y + \beta_2\overline{G}/Y] = \beta_1 d(G - \overline{G}) + \beta_2 d\overline{G}. \qquad (12.5)$$

Therefore, in regions where $[\beta_1(G - \overline{G})/Y + \beta_2\overline{G}/Y]$ is small relative to one, the coefficients β_1 and β_2 would indicate the approximate response of Y to unit changes in $(G - \overline{G})$ and $\overline{G}$, respectively. The empirical results suggest that this approximation is satisfactory over the 1930–1978 period in the United States, except for the World War II years.

The theoretical analysis suggests testing the hypothesis, $0 \leq \beta_2 \leq \beta_1 \leq 1$. This restriction implies that temporary changes in government purchases have a larger output effect than permanent changes but that permanent changes also raise (measured) real GNP. These conditions are likely, but not inevitable, implications of the theoretical model.

A central aspect of the empirical analysis is the representation for permanent real purchases as perceived at date t, $\overline{G}_t$. Suppose for the moment that the time-series behavior of G_t implies a relationship for $(\overline{G}/Y)_t$ in terms of a set of parameters α and a vector of currently observed variables, Z_t:

$$(\overline{G}/Y)_t = F(Z_t; \alpha). \qquad (12.6)$$

In this case the unobservable construct, $\overline{G}_t$, could be substituted out from Eq. (12.4) to yield a relation for output in terms of observable variables and the vector of unknown coefficients $(\alpha, \beta_1, \beta_2)$,

$$\log(Y_t) = \cdots + \beta_1[(G/Y)_t - F(Z_t; \alpha)] + \beta_2 F(Z_t; \alpha). \qquad (12.7)$$

Some hypotheses arise that concern the role of the Z_t variables in Eqs. (12.4), (12.6), and (12.7). If these variables can be guaranteed ex ante not to appear separately in the list of omitted elements that are denoted by . . . in Eq. (12.4), then the Z_t variables would appear in Eq. (12.7) only to the extent that they serve as determinants for $(\overline{G}/Y)_t$ in the F-function of Eq. (12.6). Some cross-equation restrictions therefore emerge for the parameters of Eqs. (12.6) and (12.7).

The next sections deal with the problem of modeling a form of Eq. (12.6) for real government purchases in the United States.[22]

Government Purchases Equation

The stress on transitory movements in government purchases suggests special attention to war-related expenditures, which are likely to be viewed as largely temporary. I have proceeded empirically by separating total government (federal plus state and local) real purchases of goods and services into a "defense" component, G^w, and other purchases, G^p. The present analysis does not attempt to classify components of government purchases in accordance either with their relative substitutabilities with private spending, as reflected above in the θ parameter, or with their role as inputs to private production, as measured above by the MPG parameter. Differences between defense and nondefense items with respect to these parameters affect the interpretation of some of the empirical findings. Presumably, defense purchases are characterized by a relatively low value of θ and possibly by a relatively high value of MPG. The former implies a relatively large output effect of temporary defense purchases, whereas the latter would enhance the output effects of both temporary and permanent defense purchases. The empirical analysis would be sharpened by obtaining a division of nondefense purchases into relatively homogeneous categories with respect to the θ and MPG parameters, but the feasibility of this classification is unclear. Transfer payments have not been included in the analysis.

---

22. Levis Kochin has suggested the attractive alternative of using the current overall tax rate as a proxy for the anticipated, long-run average ratio of government purchases to GNP. The rationale for identifying the current tax rate with the anticipated government expenditure ratio was discussed in the theoretical section. Some problems with implementing Kochin's suggestion are first, the distinction between purchases and expenditures implies that a separate model would be required to predict future transfers (including interest payments), which is not obviously easier than modeling purchases directly; and, second, the use of the tax rate to proxy the permanent expenditure ratio may work better for the federal government than for total government. See Benjamin and Kochin (1978), who argue that mobility possibilities would prevent state and local governments from choosing an excess-burden-minimizing debt policy. However, this issue involves also the federal government's interaction with state and local governments—that is, the federal government may compensate for public debt/tax variations that cannot be carried out at the state and local levels.

Table 12.1. Casualty-rate variable

Date	B^a	Date	B^a	Date	B^a
1898	0.0052	1945	0.603	1966	0.025
1917	0.23[b]	1950	0.071	1967	0.047
1918	0.28[b]	1951	0.097	1968	0.073
1941	0.0044	1952	0.030	1969	0.046
1942	0.162	1953	0.021	1970	0.021
1943	0.205	1964	0.0014	1971	0.0067
1944	1.090	1965	0.0070	1972	0.0014

Sources: Vietnam (1964–1972): *Statistical Abstract of the United States,* 1977, p. 369, table 590. World War I (1917–1918) and Spanish American War (1898): *Historical Statistics of the United States,* 1975, p. 1140, line 880. Korean War (1950–1953): relative yearly data from Department of the Army, *Battle Casualties of the Army* (1954), were applied to war total from *Statistical Abstract of the United States,* 1977, p. 369, table 589. World War II (1941–1945): relative yearly data from Office of the Comptroller of the Army, *Army Battle Casualties and Nonbattle Deaths in World War II: Final report, December 1941–December 1946,* were applied to war total from *Statistical Abstract of the United States,* 1977, p. 369, table 589. Korean War and World War II data were obtained from William Strobridge, Chief, Historical Services Division, Department of the Army.

a. *B* is battle deaths per 1,000 total population. Values of zero apply to dates not listed. Orders-of-magnitude values of *B* (per year) for earlier wars are Revolution (1775–1783), 0.2; War of 1812 (1812–1815), 0.08; Mexican War (1846–1848), 0.04; Civil War (1861–1865, Union only), 1.0. Casualty figures are from Civil War: *Historical Statistics of the United States,* 1975, p. 1140, line 880; other wars: Department of the Army, *History of Military Mobilization in the United States Army,* 1955, appendix A.

b. Yearly data were unavailable. Figures are based on war total assuming equal rate of casualties per month.

DEFENSE PURCHASES

A primary determinant of G^w would be the level of current and anticipated future wartime activity, assuming that at least the timing of wars can be treated as exogenous with respect to expenditure decisions. I have quantified this influence by using a casualty-rate measure B_t, which represents battle deaths per 1,000 total population (see Table 12.1) for the wartime years since the Civil War: 1898, 1917–1918, 1941–1945, 1950–1953, 1964–1972. In effect, this variable can be viewed as an alternative to a set of wartime dummy variables. The casualty-rate measure represents an attempt homogeneously to quantify the intensities of different wars and different years within each war, without using military expenditures or personnel measures, which are the types of variables that are to be explained. In particular, the use of separate dummy variables for each war would remove any power from the statistical tests that are carried out below.

Because of improvements in the technology of caring for wounded and offsetting changes associated with the "efficiency" of weapons, it is possible that the casualty-rate variable does not consistently measure the intensity of war at different dates. I considered using a broader casualty measure that included wounded, but the ratio of this concept to battle deaths showed no trend at least since the Spanish American War.[23] Because I was unable to obtain reliable annual data on wounded for World War II, I have restricted my analysis to the narrower battle deaths concept of casualty rates.

Prospective wars would be likely also to influence current spending, with good information on forthcoming military actions existing prior to at least the U.S. entrances into World Wars I and II. Because I have been unable to construct any instruments for these war expectations, I have introduced some actual future values of B into an equation for current defense spending. This procedure introduces errors-in-variables problems into coefficient estimation, although the present analysis is concerned primarily with obtaining conditional forecasts rather than with coefficient estimation per se. A later part of the empirical analysis considers a specification where future values of the B variables are excluded from the estimation. Lagged effects of B on spending are introduced also into the equation for defense purchases. Empirically, two annual leads, the contemporaneous value, and up to a third lag of the B variable were found to be important.

Because defense expenditures involve a substantial investment component, the amount of current spending would tend to be influenced negatively by the size of existing capital stocks. Accordingly, I have included in a defense-spending equation the variable K_{t-1}^w, which measures the beginning-of-period real stock of military equipment, structures, and inventories (Table 12.2, col. K^w). The relation of capital stock to current spending is assumed to be given by

$$K_t^w = bG_t^w + (1 - \delta)K_{t-1}^w, \tag{12.8}$$

23. The ratio of total casualties (including wounded, but excluding deaths that were unrelated to combat) to battle deaths is 5.3 for the Spanish American War, 4.8 for World War I, 3.3 for World War II, 4.0 for the Korean War, and 4.3 for the Vietnamese War. See the notes to Table 12.1 for sources of casualty data.

where δ is a depreciation rate and b measures the fraction of total defense spending that constitutes investment (net of within-year depreciation on this investment). The K^w series was constructed with values of b and δ that varied over time (see the notes to Table 12.2), but I have limited the theoretical discussion below to situations where these parameters are approximated satisfactorily as constants.

The estimating equation for G^w takes the form

$$g_t^w \equiv (G^w/Y)_t \tag{12.9}$$

$$= \alpha_0 B_t + \cdots + \alpha_3 B_{t-3} + a_1 B_{t+1} + a_2 B_{t+2} - \gamma k_{t-1}^w + u_t,$$

where G_t^w is real defense purchases, Y_t is real GNP, $k_{t-1}^w \equiv K_{t-1}^w/Y_{t-1}$, and u_t is a stochastic term. Note that the dependent variable in Eq. (12.9) is g_t^w, the ratio of real defense purchases to real GNP. The main part of the subsequent analysis is carried out in terms of ratio variables of this type. The form of Eq. (12.9) implies that a doubling of Y_t, K_{t-1}^w, and Y_{t-1}, for given values of the B variables, leads to a doubling of G_t^w. The model for determining g_t^w over time will be used to determine the currently perceived permanent flow of real purchases when expressed relative to real GNP, $\bar{g}_t^w \equiv (\bar{G}^w/Y)_t$.

The error term in Eq. (12.9) was modeled satisfactorily as a random walk, so estimation can be carried out readily in first-difference form:

$$Dg_t^w = \alpha_0 DB_t + \cdots + \alpha_3 DB_{t-3} + a_1 DB_{t+1} \tag{12.10}$$

$$+ a_2 DB_{t+2} - \gamma Dk_{t-1}^w + \varepsilon_t,$$

where D is the first-difference operator and $\varepsilon_t \equiv u_t - u_{t-1}$ is a white-noise error term. A constant is insignificant when added to Eq. (12.10) in the empirical analysis—that is, there is no trend in the defense purchases ratio. Moving-average error terms or more complicated autoregressive error structures also did not add to the explanatory value of the equation.

The form of Eq. (12.10) implies that a current shock ε_t—which is not associated with wartime in the sense that the values of the DB variables are small—would have a permanent effect on the future mean level of g^w. Because of the inclusion of the k_{t-1}^w term with a negative sign in Eq. (12.10), the effect on $\bar{g}_t^w$ of ε_t—that is, of the current actual value g_t^w with values of the B variables and k_{t-1}^w held fixed—turns out to be positive, but somewhat less than one-to-one. On the other hand, if the distribution for future values of B is stationary in level form, positive values for DB tend to be followed at later dates by negative values, which lead to decreases in future values of g^w. In other words, wars and the accompanying levels of expenditures are modeled as temporary. This mechanism implies that an increase in g_t^w that is accompanied by positive values of DB will have much less effect on $\bar{g}_t^w$ than will the equivalent peacetime change in defense spending. Wartime spending has an appreciable effect on $\bar{g}_t^w$ only to the extent that military expenditures depart from the amount associated typically with the current level of war intensity. The possibility that wars have a systematically important permanent effect on the purchases ratio is ruled out by the form of Eq. (12.10). Some alternative specifications of the error process that would have admitted this type of persisting effect were not supported empirically for the United States.

As detailed in the Appendix, Eqs. (12.10) and (12.8) can be used to express expected future values of the defense purchases ratio, g_{t+i}^w, as a function of the latest observed ratio g_t^w, the value k_{t-1}^w, and actual and expected future values of the war intensity variable, B. Summation over these expressions with proper allowance for discounting yields a relation for the permanent purchases ratio, $\bar{g}_t^w$, in terms of g_t^w, k_{t-1}^w, the array of B variables, and a real discount rate ρ (which equals the difference between the real interest rate and the growth rate of real GNP). Finally, a simple specification for the stochastic structure of the B variable—based on the frequency, intensity, and duration of wars over the full history of the United States—is used to solve for the expected future values of the B variables. With this substitution, $\bar{g}_t^w$ is determined as a function of observable magnitudes, up to the setting of a discount rate. In the case where future values of the B variables are admitted into the government purchases equation (12.10), $\bar{g}_t^w$ ends up as a function of the values $B_{t+2}, \ldots, B_{t-3}$—that is, the values B_{t+1} and B_{t+2} are treated as observable at date t. In a situation where future values of B are excluded from Eq. (12.10), $\bar{g}_t^w$ is expressed in terms of the current and lagged values, $B_t, \ldots, B_{t-3}$ (as well as the values of g_t^w and k_{t-1}^w).

The main product of this exercise from the full empirical analysis is the series for temporary real defense purchases expressed relative to real GNP, $(g^w - \bar{g}^w)_t$, which is indicated over the 1930–1978 period in Table 12.2. (This series corresponds to the choice of discount rate—the difference between the real rate of interest and the growth rate of real GNP—of 0.02 per year.) As is evident from the table, this variable iden-

Table 12.2. Government-purchases variables

Date	$(g^w)^a$	$(\bar{g}^w)^b$	$g^w - \bar{g}^w$	$(k^w)^c$	$(g^p)^d$
1889	0.0060	—	—	—	0.097
1890	0.0057	—	—	—	0.094
1891	0.0057	—	—	—	0.094
1892	0.0056	—	—	—	0.089
1893	0.0062	—	—	—	0.097
1894	0.0064	—	—	—	0.102
1895	0.0053	—	—	—·	0.092
1896	0.0059	—	—	—	0.097
1897	0.0080	—	—	—	0.091
1898	0.0192	—	—	—	0.094
1899	0.0165	—	—	—	0.087
1900	0.0131	—	—	—	0.088
1901	0.0113	—	—	—	0.081
1902	0.0110	—	—	—	0.084
1903	0.0108	—	—	—	0.088
1904	0.0123	—	—	—	0.088
1905	0.0112	—	—	—	0.089
1906	0.0093	—	—	—	0.082
1907	0.0090	—	—	—	0.091
1908	0.0117	—	—	—	0.110
1909	0.0105	—	—	—	0.089
1910	0.0100	—	—	—	0.091
1911	0.0101	—	—	—	0.105
1912	0.0094	—	—	—	0.100
1913	0.0096	—	—	—	0.096
1914	0.0139	—	—	—	0.106
1915	0.0135	—	—	—	0.112
1916	0.0164	—	—	—	0.093
1917	0.076	—	—	—	0.085
1918	0.258	—	—	—	0.080
1919	0.156	—	—	—	0.049
1920	0.038	—	—	—	0.085
1921	0.033	—	—	—	0.125
1922	0.017	—	—	—	0.116
1923	0.014	—	—	—	0.105
1924	0.014	—	—	—	0.116

Table 12.2 (continued)

Date	$(g^w)^a$	$(\bar{g}^w)^b$	$g^w - \bar{g}^w$	$(k^w)^c$	$(g^p)^d$
1925	0.012	—	—	—	0.115
1926	0.011	—	—	—	0.108
1927	0.012	—	—	—	0.118
1928	0.013	—	—	—	0.121
1929	0.013	—	—	0.055	0.117
1930	0.015	0.030	−0.015	0.056	0.141
1931	0.017	0.031	−0.014	0.057	0.158
1932	0.019	0.033	−0.014	0.063	0.175
1933	0.016	0.032	−0.016	0.063	0.176
1934	0.016	0.032	−0.016	0.056	0.187
1935	0.017	0.031	−0.014	0.050	0.174
1936	0.018	0.031	−0.013	0.045	0.179
1937	0.016	0.029	−0.013	0.043	0.165
1938	0.019	0.031	−0.012	0.046	0.187
1939	0.017	0.029	−0.012	0.045	0.183
1940	0.028	0.025	0.003	0.052	0.163
1941	0.120	0.065	0.055	0.074	0.122
1942	0.317	0.104	0.213	0.164	0.092
1943	0.439	0.093	0.346	0.309	0.069
1944	0.463	0.074	0.389	0.431	0.064
1945	0.410	0.069	0.341	0.470	0.063
1946	0.103	0.063	0.040	0.483	0.092
1947	0.055	0.069	−0.014	0.414	0.106
1948	0.056	0.072	−0.017	0.337	0.117
1949	0.064	0.091	−0.026	0.290	0.132
1950	0.066	0.074	−0.008	0.239	0.117
1951	0.123	0.098	0.026	0.209	0.107
1952	0.156	0.127	0.030	0.225	0.110
1953	0.156	0.140	0.016	0.260	0.118
1954	0.133	0.132	0.001	0.291	0.119
1955	0.115	0.132	−0.017	0.284	0.116
1956	0.112	0.129	−0.017	0.283	0.115
1957	0.116	0.133	−0.017	0.286	0.119
1958	0.115	0.133	−0.018	0.296	0.134
1959	0.108	0.129	−0.022	0.286	0.129

Table 12.2 (continued)

Date	$(g^w)^a$	$(\bar{g}^w)^b$	$g^w - \bar{g}^w$	$(k^w)^c$	$(g^p)^d$
1960	0.102	0.124	−0.022	0.282	0.133
1961	0.104	0.124	−0.021	0.278	0.138
1962	0.103	0.123	−0.020	0.268	0.138
1963	0.096	0.116	−0.021	0.263	0.142
1964	0.087	0.107	−0.021	0.251	0.145
1965	0.080	0.096	−0.016	0.235	0.147
1966	0.088	0.090	−0.002	0.219	0.146
1967	0.098	0.086	0.011	0.216	0.149
1968	0.096	0.081	0.014	0.211	0.151
1969	0.088	0.080	0.009	0.206	0.150
1970	0.079	0.083	−0.004	0.201	0.154
1971	0.068	0.080	−0.012	0.173	0.157
1972	0.063	0.076	−0.014	0.169	0.153
1973	0.056	0.074	−0.017	0.153	0.148
1974	0.055	0.071	−0.017	0.147	0.157
1975	0.055	0.070	−0.016	0.141	0.164
1976	0.050	0.067	−0.016	0.128	0.156
1977	0.049	0.064	−0.015	0.118	0.152
1978	0.046	0.060	−0.014	0.111	0.150

a. $g^w \equiv G^w/Y$, where Y is real GNP (1972 base). G^w is real defense purchases (1972 base). Data since 1929 are from *National Income and Product Accounts of the United States* and recent issues of the *United States Survey of Current Business*. The fraction of nominal defense purchases in total nominal federal purchases was multiplied by figures on real federal purchases (1972 base). Data from 1889–1928 are from Kendrick (1961, table A-I, col. 5). Figures were multiplied by 4.8, based on the overlap for 1929.

b. $\bar{G}^w$ is the estimated normal defense purchases ratio, as calculated from Eq. (12.14) in the text.

c. $k^w \equiv K^w/Y$, where K^w is the end-of-year value of net real stocks of military structures, equipment, and inventories (1972 base). Data from 1929–1969 are from Kendrick (1976, table B–24) converted from a 1958 to a 1972 index by a constant multiple (1.72). Figures were extended to 1978 using data on various expenditure components: military structures, AEC structures, military equipment, AEC equipment, inventories for GSA stockpiles, and inventories for AEC stockpiles. Depreciation estimates were based on rates used by Kendrick within each category. His calculations assume a higher rate of depreciation during World War II.

d. $g^p \equiv G^p/Y$, where G^p is real nondefense purchases of the federal plus state and local government sectors (1972 base). G^p was calculated as total real government purchases G less G^w. Sources for G correspond to those above for G^w, except that Kendrick (1961, table A–11a) was used for data from 1889–1928.

tifies the years associated with wartime, 1940–1946, 1951–1953, 1966–1969, as times when the defense purchases ratio is above its perceived long-run average value. Although the underlying model allows a quantitative assessment of the gap between g_t^w and $\bar{g}_t^w$ in the context of wars with different intensities and in an environment of nonconstant values for $\bar{g}_t^w$, it is also clear that the general pattern for the $(g^w - \bar{g}^w)_t$ variable would be robust to some changes in the underlying model. Notably, the important aspect of the stochastic specification for the war intensity variable B is the temporary nature of wars, rather than the details of war probabilities. Substantial variations in the discount rate ρ also have minor effects on the results.

It should not be surprising that the $(g^w - \bar{g}^w)_t$ variable exhibits a substantial amount of positive serial correlation. In this respect a gap between current and normal values—which the $(g^w - \bar{g}^w)_t$ variable is intended to capture—should be distinguished from the spread between actual and anticipated or perceived amounts, which has been stressed in earlier analyses of monetary disturbances (Barro 1981b). The latter type of variable exhibits serial independence as a consequence of rational expectations and the assumption that information is received with, at most, a one-period lag. This type of argument does not apply to a variable that measures temporary effects. In the case of the temporary defense purchases variable, the large number of (serially correlated) peacetime years with small negative values of $(g^w - \bar{g}^w)_t$ is offset by a smaller number of (serially correlated) wartime years with excesses of g_t^w over $\bar{g}_t^w$. (However, the years that are significantly affected by war—for example, the set 1941–1946, 1950–1953, 1965–1972—should not be deemed special, since they constitute 47% of the years since 1941 and 39% of those since 1946.)

GOVERNMENT PURCHASES OF NONDEFENSE ITEMS

The nondefense portion of government purchases—$g^p \equiv G^p/Y$, where G^p is nondefense real purchases—was examined statistically over samples beginning in 1929. This study revealed little predictive value for first differences, Dg^p, except for a negative association with the contemporaneous change in the defense component, Dg^w.[24] In particular, there is no drift in the nondefense purchases ratio. The negative association of

24. Past history of the residuals, lagged values of Dg^p or Dg^w, a capital stock measure Dk^p, and a constant were all insignificant.

Dg^p with Dg^w reflects the crowding out of nondefense government spending in wartime. The dependence of Dg^p only on Dg^w means that departures of g^p from the perceived normal value $\bar{g}^p$ are determined completely by the difference between g^w and $\bar{g}^w$. With $g^w - \bar{g}^w$ held fixed, changes in g^p amount entirely to shifts in the permanent component of nondefense purchases. Accordingly, with the g^w variables entered separately, the coefficient of the g^p variable in an output equation would reveal the effects of permanent changes in nondefense purchases. It is not possible here to estimate the response of output to temporary changes in nondefense purchases, since no temporary changes were isolated over the sample.

Empirical Results

The principal empirical analysis involves joint estimation of the government purchases equation (12.10) and a relation for output that is based on the form of Eq. (12.4). With the defense and nondefense components of government purchases entered separately, the output equation becomes

$$\log(Y_t) = \cdots + \beta_1(g^w - \bar{g}^w)_t + \beta_2\bar{g}_t^w + \beta_3 g_t^p. \tag{12.11}$$

Note that the real government purchases variables all appear as ratios to real GNP. The variable $\bar{g}_t^w \equiv (\bar{G}^w/Y)_t$ is determined as a function of observables from Eq. (12.10) when used in conjunction with some relations that are derived in the Appendix (Eqs. 12.A5 and 12.A6).

The first set of hypothesis tests involves the output effects of the variables $(g^w - \bar{g}^w)_t$ and $\bar{g}_t^w$ in Eq. (12.11)—specifically, that the coefficients of these variables satisfy the restrictions, $0 \le \beta_2 \le \beta_1 \le 1$. As indicated earlier, the coefficient on the g_t^p variable, β_3, reveals the output effect of a permanent change in nondefense purchases. If nondefense purchases were characterized by closer substitutability with private consumption expenditure (the θ parameter) and by lesser impact on private production (the MPG parameter) than defense purchases, $\beta_2 > \beta_3$ would follow. However, this condition cannot be viewed as a firm implication of the theory. The model also suggests the restriction, $0 \le \beta_3 \le 1$.

The second set of hypothesis tests checks whether the explanatory variables for $\bar{g}_t^w$—in this case $B_{t+2}, \ldots, B_{t-3}$ and k_{t-1}^w—enter an unrestricted reduced form for output as determined solely by their role in determining $\bar{g}_t^w$ in accordance with the coefficients of Eq. (12.10).

The analysis is contingent on a value of the discount rate ρ—the difference between the real interest rate and the growth rate of real GNP—in the calculation of the $\bar{g}_t^w$ variable (see Eqs. 12.A5 and 12.A6 in the Appendix). However, the results turn out to be relatively insensitive to variations in the ρ parameter at least over the range from 0.01 to 0.05 per year. The reported results refer to a fixed value of $\rho = 0.02$ per year, which is a plausible magnitude ex ante and which approximates the maximum likelihood estimate for this parameter.

Jointly estimated equations for real defense purchases and real GNP were calculated by means of a nonlinear, maximum likelihood routine from the TSP regression package, which includes estimation of contemporaneous covariances for the error terms. The estimation is joint in the sense of incorporating the role of the coefficients from Eq. (12.10) in determining the series $\bar{g}_t^w$ and thereby influencing the fit for output in the form of Eq. (12.11). In particular, the coefficients in the equation for Dg_t^w are not determined solely to obtain a best fit of Eq. (12.10). I have not carried out joint estimation in the broader context of choosing the number of leads and lags of the B variable to include Eq. (12.10), in deciding to omit moving-average error terms in this equation, in analyzing the process for nondefense purchases, and so on.

Since the dependent variable, real GNP, appears also in the denominators of the ratio variables g^w and g^p, there is a possible simultaneity problem in the estimation. Accordingly, I have used as instruments for g_t^w and g_t^p the lagged values, g_{t-1}^w and g_{t-1}^p, and also the contemporaneous values, $G_t^w/\bar{Y}_t$ and $G_t^p/\bar{Y}_t$, where $\bar{Y}_t$ is the trend value of real GNP, as determined from a regression over the 1946–1978 period of log(GNP) on a constant and time. The estimates are not altered substantially if only the pair of lagged values or only the pair of contemporaneous values relative to trend are used as instruments. Empirically, the movements in g_t^w are dominated sufficiently by conditions of war or peace that the use of instruments yields estimates for the coefficients of the $(g^w - \bar{g}^w)_t$ and $\bar{g}_t^w$ variables in Eq. (12.11) that differ only in minor ways from ordinary-least-squares (OLS) values. However, the use of instruments is important in the case of the g_t^p variable—OLS estimates for the β_3 coefficient in Eq. (12.11) appear to be biased downward substantially because of the inclusion of Y_t in the denominator of the g_t^p variable.

RESULTS FOR POST–WORLD WAR II OUTPUT SAMPLE

For an output sample that begins in 1946, the results of the joint estimation of Eqs. (12.10) and (12.11) are, for the 1932–1978 sample:

$$Dg_t^w = +0.163DB_{t+2} + 0.198DB_{t+1} + 0.273DB_t \tag{12.12}$$
$$ (0.013) \quad\quad (0.012) \quad\quad (0.014)$$

$$+ 0.240DB_{t-1} - 0.022DB_{t-2} + 0.088DB_{t-3} - 0.26Dk_{t-1}^w,$$
$$(0.017) \quad\quad (0.015) \quad\quad (0.016) \quad\quad (0.08)$$

$$\hat{\sigma} = 0.0143, \text{ D.W.} = 1.7;$$

and for the 1946–1978 sample:

$$\log(Y_t) = +2.97 + 0.0343 \cdot t + 0.83DMR_t \tag{12.13}$$
$$ (0.04) \quad (0.0008) \quad\quad (0.22)$$

$$+ 1.12DMR_{t-1} + 0.99(g^w - \bar{g}^w)_t + 0.55\bar{g}_t^w$$
$$(0.22) \quad\quad\quad (0.21) \quad\quad\quad\quad (0.12)$$

$$+ 0.62g_t^p,$$
$$(0.45)$$

$$\hat{\sigma} = .0143, \text{ D.W.} = 1.5.$$

Asymptotic standard errors are shown in parentheses below the coefficient estimates. The $\hat{\sigma}$ values are asymptotic estimates of the standard errors of the disturbance terms; D.W. is the Durbin–Watson statistic. Note that the sample for the government purchases equation (12.12) begins in 1932 and thereby includes the World War II experience.

Variables included in Eqs. (12.12) and (12.13) are Y, real GNP (1972 base); t, time trend; $DMR \equiv DM - \widehat{DM}$ is "unanticipated money growth," as measured in earlier research (Barro 1981b), where $\widehat{DM}$ is an estimated value of money growth from an equation that is based on the $M1$ definition of the money stock;[25] $g^w \equiv G^w/Y$, where G^w is real defense purchases (1972 base); $g^p \equiv G^p/Y$, where G^p is real, nondefense, federal plus state and local purchases (1972 base); B, casualty rate variable as defined in

---

25. $\widehat{DM}$ is determined from an equation that is estimated over the 1941–1978 sample:
$$\widehat{DM}_t = 0.095 + 0.49DM_{t-1} + 0.16DM_{t-2} + 0.069FEDV_t + 0.030 \cdot \log[U/(1-U)]_{t-1},$$
$$(0.024) \quad (0.14) \quad\quad (0.12) \quad\quad (0.015) \quad\quad\quad (0.008)$$
where observations from 1941–1945 are weighted by 0.36. $FEDV_t$ is real federal spending relative to a distributed lag of itself, and U is the unemployment rate in the total labor force. See Barro (1981b) for a discussion of this type of equation.

Table 12.1; and $k^w \equiv K^w/Y$, where K^w is real government defense capital stocks (1972 base).

For present purposes I focus on the role of the government purchases variables in Eq. (12.13). The money shock variables have effects that are similar to those discussed in previous research, as reported in Barro (1981b).

The $\bar{g}_t^w$ variable in the output equation is based on the specification for Dg_t^w that appears in Eq. (12.12). The main result from this equation is the strong positive spending effect of wars, as measured by the casualty-rate variable B. The equation shows a two-year lead effect of the B variable and a lagged effect out to three years. (The negative effect on Dg_t^w of the DB_{t-2} variable is difficult to interpret.) The consequences of eliminating the future values of DB from this equation are discussed later. For present purposes the most important aspect of war spending is its temporary nature, although precise calculations for $\bar{g}_t^w$ involve the distributed lag pattern of DB effects on Dg_t^w and the implications of these responses for the behavior of the capital stock ratio k^w. Equation (12.12) shows also the expected negative effect of Dk_{t-1}^w on Dg_t^w.

Using Eqs. (12.A5), (12.A6), and (12.A11) from the Appendix, and the value $\rho = 0.02$ for the discount rate, the point estimates of coefficients that appear in Eq. (12.12) can be shown to imply the formula for $\bar{g}_t^w$ as follows:

$$\bar{g}_t^w = +0.011 + 0.67g_t^w + 0.15k_{t-1}^w - 0.06B_{t-3} \qquad (12.14)$$
$$+ 0.02B_{t-2} - 0.16B_{t-1} - 0.18B_t - 0.12B_{t+1}$$
$$- 0.07B_{t+2}.$$

This relation is a particular form of Eq. (12.6). Equation (12.14) shows a positive but less than one-to-one effect on $\bar{g}_t^w$ of g_t^w, a positive effect of k_{t-1}^w (for a given value of g_t^w), and a basically negative effect of the casualty rate variables (again given the value of g_t^w). Values of $\bar{g}_t^w$ that are calculated from Eq. (12.14) are shown along with values of g_t^w in Table 12.2.

The temporary defense purchases variable, $(g^w - \bar{g}^w)_t$, has a significantly expansionary effect on output. The estimated coefficient[26] in Eq.

26. Because of the negative correlation of $(g^w - \bar{g}^w)_t$ with g_t^p, the β_1 coefficient picks up an additional effect. The extra term involves the difference between the output effects of permanent and temporary nondefense purchases. The output coefficient associated with

(12.13) is $\hat{\beta}_1 = 0.99$, s.e. $= 0.21$. The "t-value" corresponding to $\beta_1 = 0$ is 4.7. The normal defense purchases variable, $\bar{g}_t^w$, is also significantly expansionary in this equation—$\hat{\beta}_2 = 0.55$, s.e. $= 0.12$, which implies a t-value of 4.6. The estimated effect for the permanent purchases variable is somewhat greater than half that of the estimated temporary effect.[27] The results permit rejection of two extreme hypotheses: first, that only the temporary part of purchases affects output (which would require $\hat{\beta}_2$, the estimated coefficient of the $\bar{g}_t^w$ variable in Eq. (12.13), to differ insignificantly from zero), and second, that temporary and permanent purchases are of equal importance for output. The latter case would correspond to equal coefficients ($\beta_1 = \beta_2$) for the $(g^w - \bar{g}^w)_t$ and $\bar{g}_t^w$ variables—that is, to the proposition that the coefficient of the $\bar{g}_t^w$ variable would be zero in an equation that held fixed the value of the actual purchases ratio, g_t^w. For convenience, the results from Eq. (12.13) can be rewritten in this form as

$$\log(Y_t) = \cdots + 0.99g_t^w - 0.44\bar{g}_t^w.$$
$$(0.21) \quad\quad (0.24)$$

The hypothesis that the coefficient of the $\bar{g}_t^w$ variable equals zero corresponds to a t-value of 1.8, which is significant at the 5% level for the case of this one-sided test. That is, the null hypothesis of equal output effects for temporary and permanent defense purchases ($\beta_1 = \beta_2$ in Eq. 12.11) is rejected in favor of the hypothesis that temporary purchases are more expansionary, $\beta_1 > \beta_2$.[28]

---

temporary nondefense purchases could not be estimated with the available data. However, since the regression coefficient of g_t^p on $(g^w - \bar{g}^w)_t$ is on the order of -0.1, it is unlikely that the overall modification is important.

27. It has been suggested that the temporary government purchases variable may be proxying for the effects of accompanying federal deficits. The analysis in Barro (1979) documented the strong positive effect of temporary federal spending, as in wartime, on public-debt issue. Some preliminary results in Barro (1980b) indicated that lagged "debt shocks" have expansionary effects on output that are statistically significant but substantially weaker than those of monetary shocks. However, this constructed debt-shock variable filters out the normal positive association between temporary government spending and the deficit. With these debt shocks held fixed, the actual lagged values of public-debt growth have no explanatory value for output. This last finding suggests that the strong expansionary influence of temporary defense purchases does not involve a proxying for the effect of correlated movements in the federal deficit.

28. I considered discriminating between temporary and permanent defense purchases by utilizing a measure of the return on the equities of defense contractors relative to that on a market portfolio of New York Stock Exchange (NYSE) stocks. (The relative-returns

The estimated coefficient on the $(g^w - \bar{g}^w)_t$ variable in Equation (12.13) implies that a temporary change in the level of real defense purchases has almost a one-to-one effect on the contemporaneous level of output. Although this finding is consistent with the restriction, $\beta_1 \leq 1$, the evidence would also be consistent with a moderate multiplier relationship between temporary government purchases and output. The relatively high estimated output effect is associated in the theoretical model with a small value of the θ coefficient, a high value of the MPG parameter, and a high real-rate-of-return elasticity of aggregate supply relative to that of demand.

The estimated coefficient on the $\bar{g}_t^w$ variable in Eq. (12.13) implies that a permanent increase by one unit in real defense purchases leads approximately to a one-half unit rise in real GNP. This result accords with the restriction $\beta_2 \leq 1$—moreover, the estimate is significantly below unity in this case.

The estimated coefficient of g_t^p, the nondefense purchases ratio, is $\hat{\beta}_3 = 0.62$, s.e. $= 0.45$, which is positive but imprecisely determined. The relatively small amount of independent sampling variation in this variable since 1946, in conjunction with the necessity of using instrumental variables, results in the high standard error. (Using OLS techniques, we find that the estimated coefficient of the g_t^p variable is negative.) In any event the hypothesis that the coefficients of the g_t^p and $\bar{g}_t^w$ variables are equal, $\beta_2 = \beta_3$, would be accepted from the present evidence. As noted earlier, the relative output effects for these two types of permanent movements in government purchases depend, in the theoretical model, on the relative values of the θ and MPG parameters. Possibly, a more precise determination of the g_t^p coefficient would be obtained by extending the analysis to the 1930s, during which major changes occurred in the nondefense purchases ratio. The main obstacle for this extension is

---

variable was constructed using data on total returns to NYSE stocks from the Center for Research in Security Prices of the University of Chicago. A list of defense contractors and the size of these contracts for 1969 from the Department of Defense was kindly supplied to me by Claire Friedland.) This relative-returns variable has no explanatory power when added to a first-difference form of the output equation with Dg_t^w, Dg_t^p, and the determinants of $D\bar{g}_t^w$ from the form of Eq. (12.12) included as independent variables. Conceptually, it is not clear whether the relative-returns variable signifies an increase in war probability and, therefore, that current defense expenditures are more likely to be temporary, or an increase in the long-run expected quantity of defense purchases, which would imply that current defense expenditures are more likely to be permanent. Therefore, the sign of the variable is ambiguous on theoretical grounds.

the isolation of monetary shocks, which seems to require a specification for the pre–World War II monetary regime that differs from that used for the post-1941 period (see footnote 25).[29]

A combination of Eq. (12.11) with an expression for $\bar{g}_t^w$ in the form of Eq. (12.14) implies a reduced-form relation for output in terms of a constant, a time trend, DMR variables, g_t^w, g_t^p, the B variables, and k_{t-1}^w. Unrestricted estimation of this reduced form affords a test of the hypothesis that the determinants of $\bar{g}_t^w$—specifically, the B variables and k_{t-1}^w—affect output only in the manner implied by the forms of Eqs. (12.11) and (12.14). The test is based on the likelihood ratio corresponding to unrestricted and restricted forms of joint estimation. The value of $-2 \cdot \log(\text{likelihood ratio})$ turns out to be 3.2, which is below the 5% critical value for the χ^2 distribution with six degrees of freedom (the number of coefficient restrictions in this case) of 12.6.[30] Therefore the hypothesis that the determinants of $\bar{g}_t^w$ enter only in this indirect manner in influencing output is accepted.

There would, of course, be many possible output effects of war that do not operate through the channels that were specified in the present model. For example, there would be responses to conscription and patriotism, and the possibility that war would threaten future property rights. Some of these effects would, however, influence output in a manner similar to that of the pecuniary intertemporal substitution variable that was stressed in the theoretical analysis (see Barro 1981a for a discussion of wartime influences on financial rates of return). In particular, the

29. It is worth noting that the point estimates for the government purchases coefficients in Eq. (13) change little if the output equation is respecified in first-difference form (see Plosser and Schwert 1978 for a discussion). The estimated equation in this case is, for the 1946–1978 sample:

$$Dlog(Y_t) = 0.036 + 0.83D(DMR_t) + 1.01D(DMR_{t-1}) + 0.91D(g^w - \bar{g}^w)_t$$
$$\quad (0.006) \quad (0.29) \qquad\qquad (0.34) \qquad\qquad\qquad (0.22)$$
$$\quad + 0.55D\bar{g}_t^w + 0.63Dg_t^p,$$
$$\qquad (0.39) \qquad (1.67)$$
$$\hat{\sigma} = 0.0176, \quad \text{D.W.} = 2.5.$$

The jointly estimated equation for Dg_t^w is similar to that shown in Eq. (12.12). Note that the constant in the equation for $Dlog(Y_t)$ corresponds to the time trend for the level equation. The main change from the previous specification is the higher standard errors for the $\bar{g}_t^w$ and g_t^p coefficients. The Durbin–Watson statistic of 2.5 suggests overdifferencing.

30. If the discount rate ρ were regarded as a freely estimated parameter, there would be only five degrees of freedom, which would imply a critical value of 11.1.

level of temporarily high demands on resources by the government, $(g^w - \bar{g}^w)_t$, may proxy satisfactorily for the full range of wartime output effects.

More generally, because the war variables are the prime basis in this work for distinguishing temporary from permanent movements in government purchases, it would be infeasible to allow unrestricted direct wartime output effects and still carry out interesting tests of the underlying hypotheses. In any event the restriction that the war variables influence output only indirectly through influences on temporary government purchases is satisfied in the present case.

Elimination of future values of the casualty rate variable from the government purchases equation (12.12) has a substantial effect on the estimation of this equation for the 1932–1978 sample. Aside from a major deterioration in fit, the residuals then show pronounced positive serial correlation. These effects are dominated by the World War II years—in particular, from the rise in military spending in 1940–1941 prior to the onset of casualties and from the major advance in spending in 1942–1943 before the peak in casualties for 1944–1945. In these cases it seems reasonable to treat the future casualty values as rough proxies for contemporaneously available information about the intensity of the war. (Another possibility would be to use a foreign casualty rate variable, but data limitations and conceptual problems concerning the perceived threat attached to foreign conflicts have prevented the implementation of this idea.)

For the post–World War II period, this type of advance information on war intensity seems less important and, in fact, the future casualty variables lack significant explanatory power for defense expenditures over this period. With these future values deleted and 1946–1978 samples used throughout, the results of the joint estimation are, for the 1946–1978 sample:

$$Dg_t^w = +0.264DB_t + 0.226DB_{t-1} - 0.027DB_{t-2} \qquad (12.15)$$
$$ (0.061) \qquad (0.043) \qquad\quad (0.021)$$

$$+ 0.079DB_{t-3} - 0.30Dk_{t-1}^w,$$
$$ (0.022) \qquad\quad (0.11)$$

$$\hat{\sigma} = 0.0128, \quad \text{D.W.} = 1.9;$$

and

$$\log(Y_t) = +2.99 + 0.0340 \cdot t + 0.88DMR_t \qquad (12.16)$$
$$ (0.06) \quad (0.0010) \quad\ \ (0.25)$$

$$+ 1.12DMR_{t-1} + 0.96(g^w - \bar{g}^w)_t + 0.52\bar{g}^w_t$$
$$ (0.26) \qquad\qquad (0.26) \qquad\qquad (0.17)$$

$$+ 0.74g^p_t,$$
$$ (0.52)$$

$$\hat{\sigma} = 0.0177, \text{D.W.} = 1.5.$$

Although the fit of the estimated output equation (12.16) is poorer than that shown in Eq. (12.13), the pattern of estimated coefficients and standard errors is similar. Therefore, the conclusions on output effects of the government purchases variables are not sensitive to, first, elimination of the World War II years from the sample for the government purchases equation and, second, removal of the future values of the casualty rate variable from this equation. The results also remain similar if the starting date for the output equation is shifted from 1946 to 1950. This shift removes some contribution of the World War II years that works through the effects of lagged B values on the constructed $\bar{g}^w_t$ variable.

Addition of World War II Output Experience

Rather than insulating the results from World War II, it is in many respects more informative to evaluate the performance of the model during this extreme experience. Clearly, the sample variation in the wartime-related variable, $(g^w - \bar{g}^w)_t$, is raised enormously by this extension of coverage. On the other side, the inclusion of the World War II years raises problems that concern the measurement of real output during a period of extensive price controls and the accuracy of linear specifications for extreme observations.

Jointly estimated equations that include the 1942–1945 observations on output are, for the 1932–1978 sample:

$$Dg^w_t = +0.163DB_{t+2} + 0.196DB_{t+1} + 0.274DB_t \qquad (12.17)$$
$$ (0.013) \qquad\ (0.013) \qquad\ (0.015)$$

$$+ 0.242DB_{t-1} - 0.022DB_{t-2} + 0.087DB_{t-3}$$
$$(0.017) \qquad\quad (0.015) \qquad\quad (0.016)$$

$$- 0.25Dk_{t-1}^{w},$$
$$(0.08)$$

$$\hat{\sigma} = 0.0143, \quad \text{D.W.} = 1.7;$$

and for the 1942–1978 sample:

$$\log(Y_t) = +2.97 + 0.0350 \cdot t + 0.76DMR_t \qquad\qquad (12.18)$$
$$(0.05) \quad (0.0009) \qquad (0.15)$$

$$+ 0.90DMR_{t-1} + 0.71(g^w - \bar{g}^w)_t + 0.42\bar{g}_t^w$$
$$(0.15) \qquad\qquad (0.06) \qquad\qquad\quad (0.12)$$

$$+ 0.14g_t^p,$$
$$(0.51)$$

$$\hat{\sigma} = 0.0154, \quad \text{D.W.} = 1.4.$$

A test that the 1942–1945 observations for output conform to the same structure as that for the other years corresponds to a value for $-2 \cdot \log(\text{likelihood ratio})$ of 37.9, which exceeds the 5% critical value of the χ^2 distribution with four degrees of freedom of 9.5.[31] It seems likely

31. I have also carried out the estimation with an allowance for heteroscedasticity in the form of a different error variance for the output equation during the World War II years, 1942–1945. Maximum likelihood estimates indicate that those years have an error variance that is 2.6 times that for the 1946–1978 period, which corresponds to multiplying the 1942–1945 observations by 0.62 in the estimation. The results with the heteroscedasticity correction applied are, for the 1942–1978 sample,
$$\log(Y_t) = +2.98 + 0.0347 \cdot t + 0.85DMR_t + 1.01DMR_{t-1} + 0.75(g^w - \bar{g}^w)_t$$
$$(0.04) \quad (0.0009) \qquad (0.17) \qquad\quad (0.17) \qquad\qquad (0.07)$$
$$+ 0.48\bar{g}_t^w + 0.34g_t^p,$$
$$(0.12) \qquad (0.53)$$
$$\hat{\sigma} = 0.0148, \quad \text{D.W.} = 1.4.$$
Note that the $\hat{\sigma}$ value applies here to the error term for the 1946–1978 period. The pattern of results does not differ greatly from that shown in Eq. (12.18). The jointly estimated government purchases equation is very close to that shown in Eq. (12.17). A test for the addition of the 1942–1945 years for output to the rest of the sample corresponds here to a value for $-2 \cdot \log(\text{likelihood ratio})$ of 30.9, compared with a 5% χ^2 value with three degrees of freedom of 7.8. (The degrees of freedom are reduced by 1 here in comparison with the test for the context of homoscedasticity because of the estimation of the heteroscedasticity parameter.)

that this appearance of structural break during World War II would not appear if the functional form were altered to allow for a nonlinear dependence of $\log(Y_t)$ on $(g^w - \bar{g}^w)_t$. Specifically, the most important change from the 1946–1978 estimates in Eq. (12.13) to the 1942–1978 values in Eq. (12.18) seems to be the drop in the estimated coefficient of the $(g^w - \bar{g}^w)_t$ variable, $\hat{\beta}_1$, from 0.99, s.e. = 0.21, to 0.71, s.e. = 0.06. A functional representation that allowed for positive, but diminishing, output effects of temporary government purchases would probably account for the overall results in a homogeneous form, but I have not experimented along these lines. As the results in Eq. (12.18) stand, they reveal the anticipated reduction in the standard error of the $(g^w - \bar{g}^w)_t$ coefficient—in fact, if this relation were viewed as well specified, the estimated output effect of temporary government purchases, $\hat{\beta}_1$, would now be measured as significantly less than one.[32]

Observations

The empirical part of this study documents the positive output effect of defense purchases. There is evidence that temporary movements in defense purchases, which are associated primarily with wartime, produce a response in output roughly double that generated by equal-sized, but permanent, shifts in defense purchases. In all cases the results are consistent with a dampened, rather than a multiplicative, response of output. The effects of nondefense purchases are imprecisely determined.

---

32. The estimated coefficient for nondefense purchases, g_t^p, is also smaller than before, but still insignificantly different from that on the $\bar{g}_t^w$ variable. With g_t^w held fixed, the implied estimated coefficient on $\bar{g}_t^w$ is now -0.29, s.e. = 0.12. That is, the hypothesis that temporary and permanent defense purchases have equal output effects—$\beta_1 = \beta_2$—corresponds here to a t-value of 2.4. This hypothesis would, therefore, again be rejected in favor of $\beta_1 > \beta_2$. A test that the determinants of $\bar{g}_t^w$ from Eq. (12.17) enter only in this indirect manner in influencing output leads to a value for $-2 \cdot \log(\text{likelihood ratio})$ of 17.4 compared with a 5% critical value for the χ^2 distribution with six degrees of freedom of 12.6. With a heteroscedasticity correction applied for 1942–1945 (see note 31), the corresponding statistic is 10.3. Therefore, with the World War II observations included in the output sample, there is greater indication of an output effect of war that operates directly and not only through the $(g^w - \bar{g}^w)_t$ variable. However, this conclusion could also be affected by inappropriate linear specification of Eq. (12.18).

The theoretical section stresses intertemporal substitution variables as the channel for the strong positive output effect of temporary shifts in government purchases. Preliminary empirical analysis of realized real rates of return (Barro 1981a) provides some support for this mechanism, but further joint consideration of output and real-rate-of-return behavior would constitute useful research.

Appendix: Derivation of the Permanent Defense Purchases Ratio, $\bar{g}^w$

Equation (12.10) can be written in the form,

$$Dg_t^w = A(\mathrm{L})DB_t - \gamma Dk_{t-1}^w + \varepsilon_t, \tag{12.A1}$$

where $A(\mathrm{L})$ is a polynomial in the lag operator L, which allows both lags and leads of DB_t to affect Dg_t^w. Equation (12.8) implies that the evolution of k^w is governed by

$$k_t^w = bg_t^w + (1 - \delta')k_{t-1}^w, \tag{12.A2}$$

where $(1 - \delta') \equiv (1 - \delta)(1 - \lambda)$ and λ is the (assumed constant) growth rate of real GNP.

Equations (12.A1) and (12.A2), together with a specification for the stochastic structure of the B variable, imply a distribution for future values of g^w, conditional on information available at date t (which is assumed in the present case to include the values of B_{t+1} and B_{t+2}). Equation (12.A1) implies that future values of the spending–GNP ratio are given by

$$g_{t+i}^w = g_t^w + A(\mathrm{L})(B_{t+i} - B_t) - \gamma(k_{t+i-1}^w - k_{t-1}^w) \tag{12.A3}$$
$$+ \text{ error term.}$$

Equation (12.A2) can be used repeatedly to eliminate future values of k^w from Eq. (12.A3), which leads eventually to the condition.

$$g_{t+i}^w = g_t^w \left[\frac{\delta' + b\gamma(1 - \delta' - b\gamma)^i}{\delta' + b\gamma} \right] \tag{12.A4}$$

$$+ b\gamma k_{t-1}^w \left[\frac{1 - (1 - \delta' - b\gamma)^i}{\delta' + b\gamma} \right] + A(L)(B_{t+i} - B_t)$$

$$- b\gamma[A(L)B_{t+i} + (1 - \delta' - b\gamma)A(L)B_{t+i-2} + \cdots$$

$$+ (1 - \delta' - b\gamma)^{i-2}A(L)B_{t+1}] + \text{error term.}$$

The bracketed expression multiplying g_t^w is positive but less than one, as indicated in the text. The coefficient on k_{t-1}^w is positive—that is, future values of g_{t+i}^w rise with k_{t-1}^w for a given value of g_t^w—because k_{t-1}^w exerted a depressing effect on g_t^w that should be filtered out in determining the "permanent component" of g_t^w. The term $A(L)(B_{t+i} - B_t)$ measures the temporary effect of the B variable on g_{t+i}^w relative to that on g_t^w (which is filtered out as above in obtaining the permanent component of g_t^w). The final bracketed term accounts for the interaction between B-induced temporary spending and the resulting negative effect of the implied accumulation of k^w on subsequent spending.

The variable of interest for output determination is

$$\bar{g}_t^w = \left(\frac{\rho}{1 + \rho} \right) \left[g_t^w + \sum_{i=1}^{\infty} \frac{E g_{t+i}^w}{(1 + \rho)^i} \right],$$

where E is the expectation operator. The discount rate is $\rho = r - \lambda$, where λ is again the growth rate of real GNP. The variable $\bar{g}_t^w$ can be determined from summation over i in Eq. (12.A4) to be

$$\bar{g}_t^w = g_t^w \left(\frac{\rho + \delta'}{\rho + \delta' + b\gamma} \right) + k_{t-1}^w \left(\frac{\delta'\lambda}{\rho + \delta' + b\gamma} \right) \tag{12.A5}$$

$$+ \Phi_t \left(\frac{\rho}{1 + \rho} \right) \left(\frac{\rho + \delta'}{\rho + \delta' + b\gamma} \right),$$

where $\Phi_t \equiv \Sigma_{i=1}^{\infty} E[A(L)(B_{t+i} - B_t)]/(1 + \rho)^i$. Again, the effect of g_t^w is positive but less than unitary, and the effect of k_{t-1}^w is also positive.

For the case where $A(L) = \alpha_0 + \alpha_1 L + \alpha_2 L^2 + \alpha_3 L^3 + a_1(1/L) + a_2(1/L)^2$, and where observations on the B variable through B_{t+2} are available at date t, the Φ_t expression in the last term of Eq. (12.A5) can be written as

$$B_{t-3}(-\alpha_3/\rho) + B_{t-2}[-\alpha_2/\rho + \alpha_3/(1 + \rho)] \qquad (12.\text{A}6)$$

$$+ B_{t-1}[-\alpha_1/\rho + \alpha_2/(1 + \rho) + \alpha_3/(1 + \rho)^2]$$

$$+ B_t[-\alpha_0/\rho + \alpha_1/(1 + \rho) + \alpha_2/(1 + \rho)^2 + \alpha_3/(1 + \rho)^3]$$

$$+ B_{t+1}[-a_1/\rho + \alpha_0/(1 + \rho) + \alpha_1/(1 + \rho)^2 + \alpha_2/(1 + \rho)^3$$

$$+ \alpha_3/(1 + \rho)^4] + B_{t+2}[-a_2/\rho + a_1/(1 + \rho) + \alpha_0/(1 + \rho)^2$$

$$+ \alpha_1/(1 + \rho)^3 + \alpha_2/(1 + \rho)^4 + \alpha_3/(1 + \rho)^5]$$

$$+ \Psi_t[a_2 + a_1/(1 + \rho) + \alpha_0/(1 + \rho)^2$$

$$+ \alpha_1/(1 + \rho)^3 + \alpha_2/(1 + \rho)^4 + \alpha_3/(1 + \rho)^5],$$

where $\Psi_t \equiv \Sigma_{i=1}^{\infty} EB_{t+i+2}/(1 + \rho)^i$ is a variable that measures the effect on expected future spending of anticipated future wars (in the present case from year $t + 3$ onward).

The variable $\bar{g}_t^w$ in Eq. (12.A5) is now related to various parameters and the variables $g_t^w, k_{t-1}^w, B_{t-3}, \ldots, B_{t+2}$, and Ψ_t. The remaining work is to relate expectations of future values of B, as entering through the Ψ_t variable, to currently observed variables, including values of B up to B_{t+2}.

Expectations of Future Wars

Calculation of expected future casualty rates is based on the following stationary probability model for wars.[33] First, a 2×2 matrix is specified for the probability of war or peace next year (or rather for year $t + 3$ when conditions at $t + 2$ are assumed known at date t), conditional on war or peace prevailing currently. It is assumed that information about

---

33. War probabilities and the distribution of sizes of wars need not be constant over time, although there is no indication of substantial structural change in the small sample of evidence afforded by the 200 years of U.S. history. (The largest value for the B variable would actually apply to the Civil War—see the notes to Table 12.1.) From the standpoint of constructing the $\bar{g}_t^w$ variable, shifts in the stochastic structure for wars would essentially be an alternative to the present specification that allows for shifts in spending for a given war structure, as represented by the stochastic variable ε_t in Eq. (12.A1). In the context of output analysis, it is not clear that there would be much empirical difference between these alternatives.

the future course of B is contained fully in the most recent observation, earlier values of B and values of other variables not having to be considered. The probability of war during at least part of next year, given peace for the latest observation, is based on data over the 1774–1978 period—namely,

$$p_1 = \text{Prob}(B_{t+1} > 0 \mid B_t = 0) = 9/162 = 0.06, \tag{12.A7}$$

where 162 is the total number of peacetime years in the sample (where $B_t = 0$), and 9 is the number of these years that were followed by the outbreak of war.[34] Correspondingly, the probability of peace continuing is given by

$$(1 - p_1) = \text{Prob}(B_{t+1} = 0 \mid B_t = 0) = 0.94.$$

The value of p_1 is slightly higher if the sample is limited to the more recent period 1889–1978 (the sample for which relatively accurate observations on G^w and B are available), for which the result is $p_1 = 5/68 = 0.07$.

The probability of the continuation of war is given for the 1774–1978 sample by

$$p_2 = \text{Prob}(B_{t+1} > 0 \mid B_t > 0) = 33/42 = 0.79, \tag{12.A8}$$

where 42 is the number of war years (where $B_t \neq 0$), and 33 is the number of these that were followed by another year of war.[35] In other words nine wars began and ended over the sample 1774–1978. For the 1889–1978 period, the result would be $p_2 = 16/21 = 0.76$. Finally, the probability of no war next year, given its existence this year,[36] is given for

---

34. The year 1978 is not included in this calculation, although it could have been if peace during 1979 were also included. War years are taken to be 1775–1783, 1812–1815, 1846–1848, 1861–1865, 1898, 1917–1918, 1941–1945, 1950–1953, and 1964–1972. There may be some objection to starting the sample just before a war (which is not independent of the start of U.S. data), but the results are not highly sensitive to this choice.

35. The probability p_2 refers to the existence of war during at least part of a year following a period of war during at least part of the previous year.

36. This calculation pertains to the existence of peace over the entire year $t + 1$, conditional on war during at least part of year t.

the 1774–1978 sample by

$$(1 - p_2) = \text{Prob}(B_{t+1} = 0 \mid B_t > 0) = 0.21.$$

The expected value of B for the first year of a war is calculated as the mean value for the five wars since 1889 (for which accurate data on B are available):

$$\tilde{B} \equiv E(B_{t+1} \mid B_{t+1} > 0, B_t = 0) \tag{12.A9}$$

$$= \frac{1}{5}(0.005 + 0.23 + 0.004 + 0.071 + 0.001)$$

$$= 0.062.$$

Since war could break out at any time during the year, the annualized value of EB_{t+1}, denoted by $\tilde{B}^A$, would be roughly twice the above figure—that is, $\tilde{B}^A \approx 0.124$.

Finally, when B_{t+1} and B_t are both positive, the conditional expectation for B_t is given by

$$E(B_{t+1} \mid B_{t+1} > 0, B_t > 0) = \theta_0 + \theta_1 B_t^A,$$

where B_t^A is the current casualty rate expressed at an annual rate if hostilities applied only to a fraction of year t. The parameter θ_1 is based on the assumption (not refuted by the small sample of U.S. data) that wars tend neither to grow nor to contract over time, except that war may end at some time during year $t + 1$ as governed by the parameter p_2. Accordingly, $\theta_1 \approx 1 - \frac{1}{2}(1 - p_2) = 0.90$. The parameter θ_0 is set so that the value of the Ψ_t variable, which appears in Eq. (12.A6), converges to the value associated with $B_{t+2} = 0$ as $B_{t+2} \rightarrow 0$ (which essentially recognizes that a new war may break out next year, even if one is already going on). The value of θ_0 turns out to be $\theta_0 \approx p_1 \tilde{B}^A = 0.007$. Accordingly, I use the relation

$$E(B_{t+1} \mid B_{t+1} > 0, B_t > 0) = 0.007 + 0.90 B_t^A. \tag{12.A10}$$

Equations (12.A7)–(12.A10) allow calculation of the relevant expectation of future casualty rates, which appears in Eq. (12.A6), $\Psi_t \equiv \Sigma_{i=1}^{\infty} EB_{t+i+2}/(1 + \rho)^i$, conditional on observation of B through B_{t+2} and

Table 12.A1. Parameter values for expected casualty rates

ρ	μ_0	μ_1
0.01	1.95	2.33
0.02	0.94	2.26
0.05	0.35	2.06
0.10	0.16	1.80
0.25	0.051	1.30

for a given value of the discount rate ρ. The result takes the form

$$\Psi_t = \mu_0 + \mu_1 B_{t+2}^A, \tag{12.A11}$$

where μ_0 and μ_1 can be determined as functions of the ρ parameter.[37] Specifically, these coefficients for selected values of ρ can be seen in Table 12.A1. Since ρ corresponds to the difference between the real rate of return and the real growth rate, the values of the μ coefficients corresponding to the lower values of ρ would seem to be most pertinent. The empirical results that are reported in the text use the value $\rho = 0.02$ per year.

The combination of Eq. (12.A11) with Eqs. (12.A5) and (12.A6) allows calculation of the perceived permanent government purchases ratio, $\bar{g}_t^w$, as a function of the variables $(g_t^w, k_{t-1}^w, B_{t-3}, \ldots, B_{t+2})$ and the parameters $(\rho, \gamma, \alpha_0, \alpha_1, \alpha_2, \alpha_3, a_1, a_2)$, where ρ is the net real discount rate, γ measures the reaction of current defense purchases to existing capital stock, and the α's and a's describe the effect of the array of B variables on defense purchases. The results are therefore expressed in terms of the general form of Eq. (12.6) in the text. Other coefficients that appear in the analysis (δ', b, p_1, p_2, $\tilde{B}$—see, for example, the expressions contained in note 37) are treated as fixed at the values: $\delta' = 0.16$ per year, $b = 0.34$, $p_1 = 0.06$, $p_2 = 0.79$, and $\tilde{B} = 0.062$.

37. The general formulae are
$$\mu_0 = \frac{\tilde{B}p_1(1 - p_2)(1 + \rho + p_2\theta_1) + p_2\theta_0(1 + \rho)(\rho + p_1)}{\rho(1 + \rho + p_1 - p_2)(1 + \rho - p_2\theta_1)} \quad \text{and}$$
$$\mu_1 = \frac{p_2\theta_1}{1 + \rho - p_2\theta_1}.$$

References

Bailey, M. J. 1971. *National Income and the Price Level: A Study in Macroeconomic Theory*, 2nd ed. New York: McGraw-Hill.

Barro, R. J. 1978. "Public Debt and Taxes." In *Federal Tax Reform: Myths and Realities*, ed. M. Boskin. San Francisco: Institute of Contemporary Studies, pp. 189–209.

———— 1979. "On the Determination of the Public Debt." *Journal of Political Economy* 87(5):940–971.

———— 1980a. "A Capital Market in an Equilibrium Business Cycle Model." *Econometrica* 48:1393–1417.

———— 1980b. "Federal Deficit Policy and the Effects of Public Debt Shocks." *Journal of Money, Credit, and Banking* 12(4):747–762.

———— 1981a. "Intertemporal Substitution and the Business Cycle." *Carnegie-Rochester Conference Series on Public Policy* 14:237–268.

———— 1981b. "Unanticipated Money Growth and Economic Activity in the United States." In *Money, Expectations, and Business Cycles: Essays in Macroeconomics*, ed. R. J. Barro. New York: Academic Press, pp. 137–169.

Benjamin, D. K., and L. A. Kochin. 1978. "A Theory of State and Local Government Debt." Unpublished manuscript. Seattle: University of Washington.

Hall, R. E. 1980. "Labor Supply and Aggregate Fluctuations." *Carnegie-Rochester Conference Series on Public Policy* 12:7–33.

Kendrick, J. W. 1961. *Productivity Trends in the United States*. Princeton, N.J.: Princeton University Press for the National Bureau of Economic Research.

———— 1976. *The Formation and Stocks of Total Capital*. New York: Columbia University Press for the National Bureau of Economic Research.

Kydland, F. E., and E. C. Prescott. 1977. "Rules rather than Discretion: The Inconsistency of Optimal Plans." *Journal of Political Economy* 85(3):473–491.

———— 1980. "A Competitive Theory of Fluctuations and the Feasibility and Desirability of Stabilization Policy." In *Rational Expectations and Economic Policy*, ed. S. Fischer. Chicago: University of Chicago Press for the National Bureau of Economic Research, pp. 169–198.

Kuznets, S. 1948. "Discussion of the New Department of Commerce Income Series: National Income: A New Version." *Review of Economics and Statistics* 30:151–179.

Lucas, R. E., Jr. 1975. "An Equilibrium Model of the Business Cycle." *Journal of Political Economy* 83(6):1113–44.

Lucas, R. E., Jr. and L. A. Rapping. 1969. "Real Wages, Employment, and Inflation." *Journal of Political Economy* 77(5):721–754.

Musgrave, R. A. 1959. *The Theory of Public Finance: Study in Public Economy.* New York: McGraw-Hill.

Plosser, C. I., and G. W. Schwert. 1978. "Money, Income, and Sunspots: Measuring Economic Relationships and the Effects of Differencing." *Journal of Monetary Economics* 4:637–660.

Samuelson, P. A. 1954. "The Pure Theory of Public Expenditure." *Review of Economics and Statistics* 36:387–389.

Thompson, E. A. 1974. "Taxation and National Defense." *Journal of Political Economy* 82(4):755–782.

13 Government Spending, Interest Rates, Prices, and Budget Deficits in the United Kingdom, 1701–1918

Fluctuations in government purchases influence the economy in numerous ways. There are effects on real interest rates and on the quantities of output, consumption, and investment. There are direct effects on the price level, as well as indirect effects through the interplay with monetary growth. There are also effects on the current-account balance and on budget deficits, which may have additional influences on the economy.

In this chapter I follow Benjamin and Kochin (1984) by using the British data from the start of the eighteenth century through World War I to study some of the economic effects of government purchases. In practice the main evidence comes from the variations in military spending that are associated with war and peace. One attraction of the sample—from a scientific viewpoint—is that it features numerous wars of various sizes. Fortunately, there are also usable data for long periods on interest rates, price levels, a narrow monetary aggregate, and budget deficits.

Government Purchases and Interest Rates

Theoretical Considerations

A number of studies (Hall 1980; Judd 1985; Barro 1986b) analyze the effect of temporary government purchases on real interest rates. I con-

From *Journal of Monetary Economics* (1987) 20:221–247. This chapter was prepared originally for the Conference on Economic Effects of Budget Deficits and Government Spending at the University of Rochester, October 1986. I am grateful for advice from Olivier Blanchard, Stan Engerman, Peter Garber, Bob King, Levis Kochin, and Larry Summers. The research was supported by the National Science Foundation.

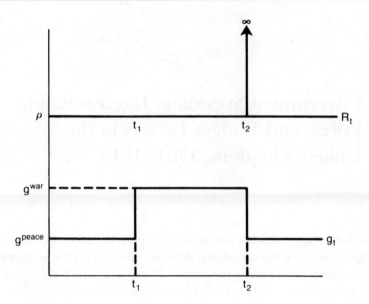

Figure 13.1. Path of government spending and the real interest rate in war and peace

sider a closed economy[1] and assume for empirical purposes that the temporary purchases represent wartime expenditures. In Fig. 13.1 a war starts unexpectedly at date t_1, and the ratio of government purchases to GNP, g_t, rises from g^{peace} to g^{war}. Suppose that the spending ratio remains constant during the war, then falls back to the value g^{peace} at date t_2 when the war ends. Finally, assume that the duration of the war—that is, the date t_2—is known as of date t_1. The main idea captured here is that the onset of a war is uncertain, but wars are known not to last forever.

Consider a model where the representative individual has an infinite horizon with the constant rate of time preference on utility equal to ρ. (For an exposition of this model as applied to variations in government purchases, see Barro 1986b.) In the steady state of this economy (with no growth in real income or population), the real interest rate equals ρ. At this point each individual is satisfied with constant consumption over time. Figure 13.1 assumes that the one-period (short-term) real interest

1. With an open economy, a temporary increase in government purchases shows up partly in borrowing from abroad instead of in a higher real interest rate. See Ahmed (1986) for this type of analysis.

rate R_t equals ρ before date t_1. If there are no storable (investment) goods, then consumption (or leisure) must fall to match the increase in g_t at date t_1. Then consumption remains constant at this depressed level during the war. Because consumption is constant—although at a lower level than before—during the war, the real interest rate R_t must still be equal to ρ. Therefore, the path shown for R_t in Fig. 13.1 shows no change at date t_1 or afterward during the war.[2]

At date t_2 the drop in g_t allows consumption to return to the higher level associated with peacetime. Because people anticipate the drop in g_t, an equilibrium requires R_t at time $t = t_2$ to exceed ρ by enough to motivate people to plan for an upward jump in consumption. Then, after date t_2, consumption is again constant and $R_t = \rho$ applies.

Looking at the situation during the war, where $t_1 < t < t_2$, short-term real interest rates are unaffected. However, long-term rates would incorporate the high short-term rate at time t_2. Hence, as Benjamin and Kochin (1984, pp. 595–596) pointed out, there would be a positive relation between g_t and real interest rates that applied to a horizon longer than $t_2 - t$. The effect on the yield to maturity would be strongest when the horizon was only slightly longer than $t_2 - t$.

The sharp distinction between short-term and long-term interest rates does not hold if there is either uncertainty about the war's duration or if there are durable (investment) goods around. In these cases temporary government purchases tend to increase short-term real interest rates, as well as longer-term rates.

Figure 13.2 illustrates the results for a standard one-sector production function with reproducible (and consumable) capital. The path for R_t shown in Fig. 13.1 is no longer an equilibrium because investors would want to liquidate their capital stocks just before date t_2. In the new equilibrium the wartime spending must crowd out some investment, as well as consumption, prior to date t_2. As the capital stock falls, the real interest rate rises to match the rising marginal product of capital. The real interest rate peaks at date t_2—thereafter, the rate falls as the capital stock is rebuilt.[3]

2. If the war were anticipated, then people would expect a fall in consumption at date t_1. In that case the real interest rate would have to be well below ρ at date t_1. More generally, the higher the probability of a war, the lower the real interest rate.

3. The level of consumption falls discretely at date t_1, then grows as long as $R_t > \rho$. If utility is isoelastic with respect to consumption (and neglecting effects on leisure), then the fastest growth rate of consumption occurs at date t_2. However, the prewar level of consumption is reattained only asymptotically as R_t approaches ρ.

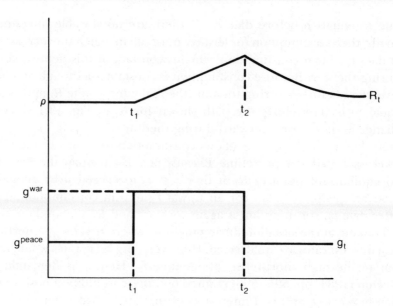

Figure 13.2. Path of government spending and the real interest rate in war and peace, allowing for investment goods

One implication from the inclusion of investment is that the short-term real interest rate, R_t, depends positively on current and lagged values of g_t. The lagged values matter because they led to reductions in the capital stock and thereby to a higher current marginal product of capital. Future values of g_t also matter—however, the effect on current short-term real interest rates is negative, whereas that on current long rates is uncertain (because future short rates rise).

This study uses wartime as an observable example of temporary government expenditure. However, there are other aspects of wars that can affect real interest rates. One is the possibility of defeat, which affects the default premium on government bonds and may also influence the security of property rights in private bonds and capital stocks. If the threat to all assets is the same, then a greater probability of defeat raises real interest rates and reduces capital intensity. Another consideration is that wartime controls in the form of rationing and production directives can substitute for movements in interest rates as devices for crowding out private spending. Then the observed response in interest rates will be weaker than otherwise. For the British case examined here, this aspect of

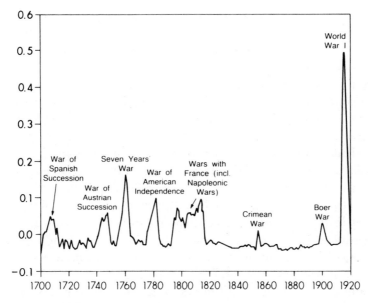

Figure 13.3. Ratio of real military spending to trend real GNP, 1701–1920, g_t, less the mean value of g_t, 0.067

a command economy would be important mainly during World War I (see Pollard 1969, chap. 2).

The Data for the United Kingdom

Thus far, there is little evidence from the U.S. time series that verifies a positive effect of temporary government purchases on real interest rates—see Barro (1981; 1987, chap. 12), Plosser (1982, 1987), and Evans (1987). But, as stressed by Benjamin and Kochin (1984), the long-term British data are promising for isolating this effect if it exists. Especially during the eighteenth century and through 1815, the United Kingdom was involved in numerous wars, which provide for substantial temporary variations in government purchases. Further, until World War I, the economy was free of most other governmental interventions, such as extensive price and interest-rate controls, which often accompany wars.

Figure 13.3 shows the ratio of real military spending to trend GNP for the United Kingdom from 1701 to 1920. Real military spending is nominal spending divided by an index of wholesale prices.[4] Trend real GNP comes from a trend line through the data on real GNP, using one growth rate (0.55% per year) from 1700 to 1770 and another (2.18% per year) from 1771 to 1938.[5]

A quick examination of Fig. 13.3 reveals the peaks associated with the eight major wars from 1701 to 1920 (treating the wars with France from 1793 to 1815 as one event). These wartime periods provide the main evidence about the effects of temporarily high government purchases. In particular, there are no comparable variations in nonmilitary spending over the sample period (except for the transfer payments in 1835, which are discussed later in the section on budget deficits).[6]

The other suggestion from Fig. 13.3 is the absence of permanent changes in the ratio of military spending to GNP, at least up to 1920. This property means that the raw movements in the spending ratio, g_t, correspond to values of the ratio that are temporarily high or low. Hence the sample will not be useful in identifying the economic effects of permanent changes in government purchases. In the next section I model the stochastic process for g_t in order to isolate the temporary part of this variable—that is, the departure of g_t from some concept of a "normal" value. It is this temporary part that has the effects on real interest rates shown in Figs. 13.1 and 13.2. However, as suggested by

4. The data on military expenditure are from Mitchell and Deane (1962, pp. 390–391, 396–399). The figures combine the items for army, navy, and ordnance and for expenditures on special expeditions and votes of credit. The dating of expenditures refers to disbursements rather than to orders (see Benjamin and Kochin 1984, p. 602, fn. 6). For 1729–1751, the fiscal-year data ended September 29 were treated as calendar year numbers. The same procedure was used for 1752–1799, where the fiscal year ended on October 10. For 1801–1854, the fiscal-year figures ended January 5 were treated as applying to the previous calendar year. For 1855–1919, the fiscal-year data ended March 31 were also viewed as covering the prior calendar year. The data on wholesale prices are from Mitchell and Deane (1962, pp. 469–470, 474, 476). The series is a linking together of the following wholesale price indexes: 1871–1920, Board of Trade total index of wholesale prices; 1850–1870, Sauerbeck–Statist overall index; 1790–1849, Gayer, Rostow, and Schwartz index of domestic and imported commodities; 1700–1789, Schumpeter–Gilboy index of consumer goods.

5. The data on real GNP are from Feinstein (1972, pp. T4, T10, T14, T18) for 1856–1918. For 1830–1855, the data are from Deane (1968, pp. 104, 106). Before 1830 there are estimates at 10-year intervals in Deane and Cole (1967, pp. 78, 282).

6. Except for 1835, nonmilitary expenditures of the central government remained between 2% and 3% of trend GNP from 1801 to 1900. See Mitchell and Deane (1962, pp. 396–398) for the data. These expenditures reached 4% of trend GNP in the early 1900s, but then fell back to 2% during World War I.

inspection of Fig. 13.3, the normal spending ratio changes little over time. Therefore, for explaining the changes in interest rates or other variables, the variable g_t turns out to do about as well as my constructed measure of temporary spending.

Table 13.1 shows the values of the military spending ratio for the eight main wars during the sample period. (This tabulation neglects a large number of small conflicts—in India, China, Afghanistan, Africa, Burma, and other countries—that peace-loving Britain pursued but that have insubstantial effects on the military spending ratio.) Note from the table that the value of the spending ratio (relative to its mean of 6.7%) ranges from a high of 49% during World War I (1916) to 16% in the Seven Years' War (1761), 10% for the American Revolution (1782), 9% during the Napoleonic Wars (1814), 6% for the War of the Austrian Succession (1748), 5% for the War of the Spanish Succession (1707), 3% for the Boer War (1901), and 1% during the Crimean War (1855). Some comparable values for the United States are 20% for World War I (1918), 34% for World War II (1944), and 2% for the Korean War (1952) (see Barro 1986b, table 3).

For the long-term interest rate I use the yield on consols (or on the comparable perpetual annuities for 1729–1752), which is available continuously since 1729.[7] These government bonds are perpetuities, except that they were redeemable at par after a stated number of years. The theory implies that temporary government spending would have a positive effect on these interest rates. Empirically, the broad nature of this relation is evident from Fig. 13.4. Note that, over the period from 1729 to 1918,[8] the interest rate (solid line) appears to rise along with the spending ratio (dotted line).

Table 13.1 reports the changes in the long-term interest rate during each of the major wars. These changes are all positive and in excess of 1 percentage point in five of the eight cases. Because the standard deviation of the annual first difference of the interest rate from 1730 to 1918

7. The data are from Homer (1977, pp. 156, 161–162, 195–197, 416). The yields apply to 3% annuities or consols until 1888 and to 2.5% consols thereafter. The possibility that the 3% consols would be redeemed at par implies that the yields on these instruments were misleadingly high after 1888.

8. The sample ends in 1918 because nonmilitary government spending begins to become important after World War I and because different accounting conventions apply thereafter to the breakdown between military and nonmilitary spending. However, it would be possible to extend the sample beyond 1918.

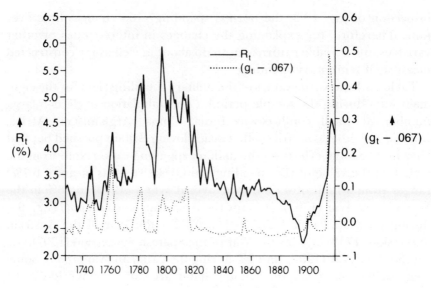

Figure 13.4. Military spending and the interest rate, 1729–1918

is 0.26 percentage points, these five cases involve increases in interest rates that are five to seven times this standard deviation. (The sample mean of the interest rate from 1729 to 1918 is 3.54%.)

A usable series on short-term interest rates is unavailable for the full sample. Most short-term interest rates, including the Bank of England's bank rate, were subject to a usury ceiling of 5% from 1714 until 1833. This ceiling was an effective constraint until at least 1817. (See Homer 1977, pp. 163–165, 205–208.) If the sample started in 1817 or later, then much of the action in the government spending variable would be lost (see Fig. 13.1). Thus I do not report results with short-term interest rates in this chapter.

The interest rate data measure nominal rates rather than the expected real rates that matter theoretically. The actual inflation rate averaged 0.4% per year from 1701 to 1918 and 0.1% per year from 1701 to 1913. It may be that the long-term expected rate of inflation was also stable and close to zero, in which case the nominal interest rates are also expected real rates. Up to now, I have been unsuccessful in generating reliable quantitative measures of long-term inflationary expectations. One problem (discussed in the section on prices and money) is that these expectations depend primarily on long-term assessments about the

Table 13.1. Behavior of temporary military spending during major wars

Period	War	Average value of g_t (%)[a]	Peak value of g_t[a]	ΔR^b (percentage points)	ΔP^b (%)
1702–1713	War of Spanish Succession	2.3	5.1 (1707)	2.7[c]	1
1740–1748	War of Austrian Succession (and other wars)	3.3	5.7 (1748)	0.6	1
1756–1763	Seven Years' War (French and Indian War)	9.6	16.1 (1761)	1.2	2
1775–1783	War of American Independence	4.9	9.8 (1782)	1.9	3
1793–1815	Wars with France (including Napoleonic Wars)	5.2	9.4 (1814)	1.6	74
1854–1856	Crimean War	0.7	0.7 (1855)	0.2	6
1899–1902	Boer War	2.5	2.7 (1901)	0.4	4
1914–1918	World War I	37.7	49.3 (1916)	1.2	109

a. g_t is the ratio of real military spending to trend real GNP (see text) less the mean value of the spending ratio (6.7%) over the period from 1701 to 1918. Periods are 1703–1712, 1741–1748, 1757–1762, 1776–1782, 1794–1815, 1855, 1900–1901, 1914–1918.

b. ΔR is the change in the consol rate in percentage points and ΔP is the percentage change in the wholesale price index. These changes apply from the year before each war to the final full year of the war. Periods are 1701–1712, 1739–1747, 1755–1762, 1775–1782, 1792–1814, 1853–1855, 1898–1901, 1913–1917.

c. Uses the rough estimate for R_t of 6.0% for 1702 and the value $R_t = 8.7\%$ for 1712—see Homer (1977, p. 156).

chances for remaining on (or in some intervals returning to) the gold standard. Possible changes in the price of gold, which did not occur to a significant extent over the sample period, might also come into play. In any event, I cannot rule out the possibility that some of the observed variations in interest rates represent changes in long-term inflationary expectations rather than movements in expected real interest rates.

Another problem is that the wartime movements in interest rates might represent changes in the default premium on British Bonds. However, this view suggests greater movements in interest rates during the wars where defeat was likely and would threaten repayment of debt. The Napoleonic Wars and World War I stand out here, but—especially for World War I—these experiences do not exhibit increases in interest rates that are obviously above those warranted by the course of expenditures. Some more information could be obtained by comparing the changes in British interest rates during British wars with the concurrent changes in interest rates in noncombatant countries. However, for the period of especial interest before 1815, the data for this comparison do not seem to exist (see Homer 1977, chap. 7).

Temporary Military Spending

In this section I model the stochastic process for the military spending ratio, g_t, and use the results to construct a measure of temporary spending. The first difference of g_t is satisfactorily modeled with second-order autoregressive and moving-average terms—that is, g_t is an ARMA(2, 1, 2) process. This process captures the temporary, but serially correlated, aspects of wartime and also allows for the possibility of permanent shifts in the spending ratio. The fitted equation from 1704 to 1918 is

$$g_t - g_{t-1} = +1.26(g_{t-1} - g_{t-2}) - 0.41(g_{t-2} - g_{t-3}) \qquad (13.1)$$
$$\phantom{g_t - g_{t-1} = +1.2}(0.25) \phantom{(g_{t-1} - g_{t-2}) - 0.}(0.12)$$

$$+ e_t - 0.72e_{t-1} - 0.27e_{t-2},$$
$$(0.26) \phantom{0.72e_{t-1} -}(0.18)$$

$$\hat{\sigma} = 0.026, \quad R^2 = 0.30,$$

where e_t is an error term. (The Q-statistic with 10 lags is 3.1, 5% critical value of 12.6.) If a constant is added to Eq. (13.1), then its estimated coefficient is 0.002, s.e. = 0.008—hence, there is no evidence of drift in the ratio of spending to GNP.

Because the coefficients of the two moving-average terms in Eq. (13.1) sum nearly to -1,[9] the results are similar in level form for g_t:

$$g_t = 0.070 + 1.27g_{t-1} - 0.43g_{t-2} + e_t + 0.25e_{t-1}, \qquad (13.2)$$
$$ (0.011) \quad (0.11) \qquad (0.11) \qquad\qquad (0.13)$$

$$\hat{\sigma} = 0.026, \quad R^2 = 0.88.$$

Thus, as suggested by inspection of Fig. 13.1, g_t may be stationary in levels. For subsequent purposes I use the first-difference specification in Eq. (13.1), although the results would be similar with Eq. (13.2).

Using Eq. (13.1) and the estimated values of the residuals, e_t, one can form "forecasts" of g_{t+i} for any date t and forecast horizon i. Thereby one can measure the "permanent" ratio of spending to GNP (analogous to permanent income) as

$$\hat{g}_t = (1 - \delta)(g_t + \delta g_{t+1}^e + \delta^2 g_{t+2}^e + \cdots), \qquad (13.3)$$

where the superscript e denotes a forecast, and δ is a constant discount factor such that $1 - \delta$ is approximately equal to the difference between the real interest rate and the growth rate of real GNP. (The constancy of δ is only an approximation.) For the British case the long-term real interest rate (from 1729 to 1913) averaged 3.5%, while the growth rate of real GNP (from 1730 to 1913) averaged 1.8%. Therefore, δ should be about 0.98. Hansen and Sargent (1981, p. 260) provided a formula that can be modified to calculate $\hat{g}_t$ for a given value of δ and for the set of ARMA coefficients estimated in Eq. (13.1).

The temporary part of the spending ratio is $\tilde{g}_t = g_t - \hat{g}_t$. This variable is plotted for the value $\delta = 0.98$ as the dotted line in Fig. 13.5. The resulting series has a pattern similar to that for the raw series g_t (net of a constant mean), which is shown as the solid line in Fig. 13.5. Further, the subsequent findings on interest rates and other variables do not differ greatly whether one uses $\tilde{g}_t$ or g_t as an explanatory variable. This result is not surprising, since the expectation from examination of Fig. 13.3 was that permanent movements in the spending ratio would be unimportant

---

9. The sum is -0.99, but with an estimated standard error of 0.39.

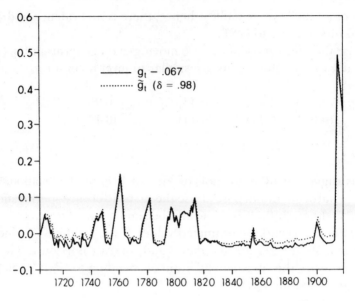

Figure 13.5. Alternative measures of temporary military spending, 1705–1918

relative to the temporary fluctuations. For this reason I have not carried out further refinements of the measurement of $\tilde{g}_t$—such as estimating Eq. (13.1) jointly with other equations.

Formal Results on Interest Rates

I model the determination of the interest rate in the form

$$r_t = a_0 + a_1 \tilde{g}_t + u_t, \tag{13.4}$$

where the coefficient a_1 is positive. If the error term u_t were stationary with an unconditional mean of zero, a_0 would be the long-run mean of the interest rate. In fact, for Britain from 1729 to 1918—where the continuous data series is available—the long-term interest rate exhibits nearly random-walk behavior, although there is some indication of stationarity. (The consol rate would have to be close to a random walk or else there would remain either very high or very low expected returns from holding these long-term bonds over short periods.) I model the error term in Eq. (13.4) by the first-order autoregressive process,

$$u_t = \lambda u_{t-1} + \varepsilon_t, \tag{13.5}$$

where ε_t is white noise, and the positive coefficient λ is close to but below unity.

Equations (13.4) and (13.5) imply that, aside from the influence of temporary military spending, the other determinants of the interest rate, u_t, are close to random walks. In the random-walk case where $\lambda = 1$, Eq. (13.4) could be estimated satisfactorily in first-difference form (with a zero constant). But if $\lambda < 1$, then it is appropriate to deal with levels of variables.

Conditional on the constructed series for $\tilde{g}_t$ (based on $\delta = 0.98$), the maximum-likelihood estimates of Eqs. (13.4) and (13.5) are

1730–1913

$$R_t = 3.54 + 6.1 \cdot \tilde{g}_t, \quad \hat{\lambda} = 0.909, \tag{13.6}$$
$$\quad\ (0.20)\ \ (1.3) \qquad\quad (0.029)$$

$$\hat{\sigma} = 0.243, \quad R^2 = 0.89, \quad R^2 \text{ (for } R_t - R_{t-1}) = 0.14,$$

$$\text{D.W.} = 2.2,$$

1730–1918

$$R_t = 3.54 + 2.6 \cdot \tilde{g}_t, \quad \hat{\lambda} = 0.931, \tag{13.7}$$
$$\quad\ (0.27)\ \ (0.7) \qquad\quad (0.027)$$

$$\hat{\sigma} = 0.248, \quad R^2 = 0.89, \quad R^2 \text{ (for } R_t - R_{t-1}) = 0.11,$$

$$\text{D.W.} = 2.1.$$

These results, and also those below, differ only slightly if g_t replaces $\tilde{g}_t$ as the explanatory variable.

Over the sample from 1730 to 1913, the estimated coefficient on $\tilde{g}_t$ is 6.1, s.e. = 1.3 ("t-value" relative to 0 of 4.9). The result implies that an increase by 1 percentage point in the temporary-spending ratio raises the long-term interest rate by 6.1 basis points.

The estimated value, $\hat{\lambda} = 0.909$, s.e. $= 0.029$, implies a "t-value" relative to the null hypothesis $\lambda = 1$ of 3.1. Considering the one-sided alternative, $\lambda < 1$, this statistic differs significantly from zero at less than the 1% level using the t distribution. It is significant at about the 2.5% level according to the distribution that is generated by Monte Carlo methods for an analogous nonstationary model in Fuller (1976, table 8.5.2, $\hat{\tau}_\mu$ sec.). Thus there is some evidence that supports the stationarity of the long-term interest rate over the period from 1730 to 1913.

Adding the World War I experience, 1914–1918, to the sample in Eq. (13.7) lowers the estimated coefficient on $\tilde{g}_t$ to 2.6, s.e. $= 0.7$.[10] Although the interest rate rises from 3.4% in 1913 to 4.6% in 1917—that is, by 1.2 percentage points—the estimated Eq. (13.6) would have predicted an increase by 2.6 points. It may be that the command economy aspects of World War I, which were mentioned previously, explain the failure of the interest rate to rise as much as predicted. For this reason, the sample that excludes World War I in Eq. (13.6) may be better than the full sample in Eq. (13.7) for estimating the response of interest rates to temporary spending in a free-market setting.

Because of the cumulative effect on capital stocks, the theory implies that the current interest rate, R_t, also reacts positively to lagged values of $\tilde{g}_t$. If five lags are included, then the results for the sample, 1730–1913, are

$$R_t = +3.54 + 7.9\tilde{g}_t - 2.9\tilde{g}_{t-1} + 3.1\tilde{g}_{t-2} + 3.9\tilde{g}_{t-2} \qquad (13.8)$$
$$\quad\;\; (0.20)\;\;\; (1.5)\quad\;\; (1.9)\qquad\; (1.9)\qquad\;\; (1.9)$$

$$\quad -5.1\tilde{g}_{t-4} + 3.3\tilde{g}_{t-5}, \qquad \hat{\lambda} = 0.917,$$
$$\qquad\;\; (1.9)\qquad (1.5)\qquad\qquad\;\; (0.030)$$

$$\hat{\sigma} = 0.234, \quad R^2 = 0.90, \quad R^2 \text{ (for } R_t - R_{t-1}) = 0.22,$$

$$\text{D.W.} = 2.2$$

Equation 13.8 shows an influence of five lagged values, although the negative effects of $\tilde{g}_{t-1}$ and $\tilde{g}_{t-4}$ are hard to explain. Additional lags are unimportant.

---

10. Using a likelihood-ratio test, one can reject at the 5% level the hypothesis that the data from 1730 to 1913 are generated from the same model as the data from 1914 to 1918.

Prices and Money

Benjamin and Kochin (1984, pp. 598–600) argued that temporary military spending has a positive effect on the general price level in the United Kingdom. In fact, they argued that the dual influence of war accounts for the celebrated positive association between the interest rate and the price level, which is known as the Gibson Paradox. However, Barsky and Summers (1985, sec. 1) observed that the Benjamin–Kochin explanation is inadequate because the Gibson Paradox applies also during nonwar periods.

The connection between military spending and the price level is straightforward under a paper standard where governments use the printing press to finance wartime expenditures. Although a common view is that governments shift readily off commodity standards and toward paper standards during wartime or other emergencies, this view does not apply to the United Kingdom during the eighteenth and nineteenth centuries. The United Kingdom was on some form of commodity standard from 1700 to 1931, except for two instances of suspension of specie payments by the Bank of England. The first was from 1797 to 1821 and was precipitated by the wars with France (see Clapham 1945, vol. 2, chap. 1). The second involved a variety of restrictions on specie payments that began in the middle of 1914 during World War I (see Sayers 1976, chap. 5). In this case the gold standard was not resumed until 1925. Although financial crises arose at other times—especially during some wars of the eighteenth century—the suspension of specie payments did not occur (see Clapham 1945, vol. 1, chap. 7). Basically, except for the years 1797–1821 and 1914–1925, the United Kingdom was on a gold standard from 1700 to 1931. (Until 1821 the system was formally bimetallic with gold overvalued at the mint—see Del Mar 1877.)

Under a gold standard the possibilities for a link between the spending ratio, g_t, and the price level, P_t, are limited. Since P_t is an index of wholesale prices, the linkage requires an effect of g_t on the price of a basket of produced, mainly tradable goods relative to the price of gold. If increased military purchases imply an increase in the demands for these goods relative to gold, then the price level would rise.

Given the value of P_t, a link between g_t and the quantity of money, M_t, amounts to a link between g_t and the real demand for money. The overall effects here are ambiguous. The real demand for money falls because the interest rate, R_t, rises. However, wartime may have a direct positive effect on the demand for money. In addition, if g_t affects real income, then the demand for money would change on this count. Empirically, I find no relation between g_t and M_t for periods where the gold standard was maintained (see below).

During periods when the gold standard is suspended, the prediction is that a higher value of g_t leads to faster rates of growth of money and prices. This prediction is based on the government's incentive to use the inflation tax under a paper standard.

Results for Money

I measure the narrow money supply, M_t, by the quantity of bank notes. The data comprise notes issued solely by the Bank of England from 1729 to 1764 and from 1775 to 1833, but include also the issues from country banks and from Scottish and Irish banks from 1834 to 1918.[11]

The empirical relation of this concept of money to military spending is illustrated by the following least-squares regressions:

SUSPENSION PERIODS: 1797–1821, 1914–1918

$$\log \left(\frac{M_t}{M_{t-1}}\right) = -0.001 + 1.12\tilde{g}_t, \tag{13.9}$$
$$(0.020) \quad (0.13)$$

$$\hat{\sigma} = 0.092, \quad R^2 = 0.73, \quad \text{D.W.} = 1.9;$$

GOLD-STANDARD PERIODS: 1731–1764, 1777–1796, 1822–1913

$$\log \left(\frac{M_t}{M_{t-1}}\right) = +0.004 + 0.02\tilde{g}_t, \tag{13.10}$$
$$(0.006) \quad (0.18)$$

$$\hat{\sigma} = 0.076, \quad R^2 = 0.00, \quad \text{D.W.} = 2.2;$$

11. The data are from Mitchell and Deane (1962, pp. 441–443, 450–451). Values for 1729 to 1764 refer to August 31 of each year. Those from 1775 to 1833 are averages of figures from the end of February and the end of August. Values from 1834 onward are annual averages of monthly or weekly figures. The available data prior to 1729 are rough estimates. The figures that I found from 1765 to 1774 are not comparable to those for the other years.

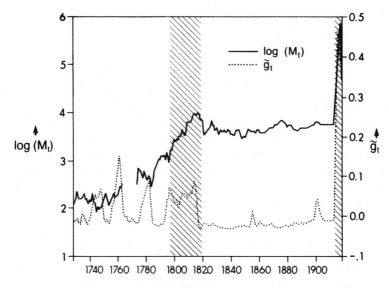

Figure 13.6. Money supply and temporary military spending, 1729–1764 and 1775–1918; shaded areas are periods of suspension

There is a strong positive relation between $\tilde{g}_t$ and monetary growth during the periods of suspension (1797–1821, 1914–1918), but no significant relation during the gold-standard years.[12] This finding also appears in Fig. 13.6, which plots the values of $\log(M_t)$ and $\tilde{g}_t$.

The conclusion is that military spending during wars led to money creation only if it first led to suspension of the gold standard. Furthermore, this pressure to suspend was successful only in two cases—the Napoleonic period and World War I—although the sample includes six other major wars (see Table 13.1). It is interesting to conjecture why suspension occurred when it did—in 1797 and effectively in 1914—and not at other times. For World War I, the magnitude of military spending is probably a sufficient explanation (see Table 13.1). However, through 1797, the ratio of military spending to GNP—which averaged 10.8% from 1794 to 1797—was less than that of the Seven Years' War (average of 16.3% from 1757 to 1762) and similar to that of some other wars (9.0% from 1703 to 1712, 10.0% from 1741 to 1748, and 11.6% from

12. A likelihood-ratio test rejects at less than the 1% level the hypothesis that the coefficients of the equations for monetary growth are the same for the two subsamples.

1776 to 1782). The main distinction of the wars with France after 1793 was the duration—22 years with only brief interruptions—although it is unclear that this length would have been foreseen in 1797. However, it may be that the French Revolution and Napoleon made the conflicts after 1793 more threatening than the earlier wars. One other fact indicating that these conflicts were taken more seriously than the prior wars was the introduction of taxes on income and property in 1799. On the other hand, Clapham's (1945, vol. 1, chap. 7) discussion of the earlier periods indicated that the Bank of England's reserve of specie was nearly exhausted in several cases—in 1710, 1745, 1763, and 1783. Therefore it may be mainly a matter of luck that suspension occurred in 1797 and not at these other times.

Results for the Price Level

Estimated equations for inflation rates (based on indexes of wholesale prices) that parallel the equations for monetary growth are as follows:[13]

SUSPENSION PERIODS: 1797–1821, 1914–1918

$$\log \left(\frac{P_t}{P_{t-1}}\right) = -0.031 + 0.62 \tilde{g}_t, \tag{13.11}$$
$$\qquad\qquad\quad (0.021)\quad (0.14)$$

$\hat{\sigma} = 0.099, \quad R^2 = 0.37, \quad \text{D.W.} = 1.5,$

GOLD-STANDARD PERIODS: 1705–1796, 1822–1913

$$\log \left(\frac{P_t}{P_{t-1}}\right) = +0.003 + 0.31 \tilde{g}_t, \tag{13.12}$$
$$\qquad\qquad\quad (0.005)\quad (0.15)$$

$\hat{\sigma} = 0.062, \quad R^2 = -0.01 \text{ (see footnote 13)}, \quad \text{D.W.} = 1.9.$

The results show that the effect of $\tilde{g}_t$ on $\log(P_t/P_{t-1})$ is significantly positive for the suspension period and just significantly positive for the gold-standard period. However, the effect is substantially larger for the

13. The variable $\tilde{g}_t$ involves the current value of real spending, $g_t = G_t/P_t$, where G_t is nominal spending. Therefore, measurement error in P_t (which is likely to be serious here) tends to generate a downward bias in a regression of $\log(P_t/P_{t-1})$ on $\tilde{g}_t$. The results shown in Eqs. (13.11) and (13.12) are instrumental estimates using as an instrument for $\tilde{g}_t$ the value that would be calculated if G_t/P_t were replaced by G_t/P_{t-1}.

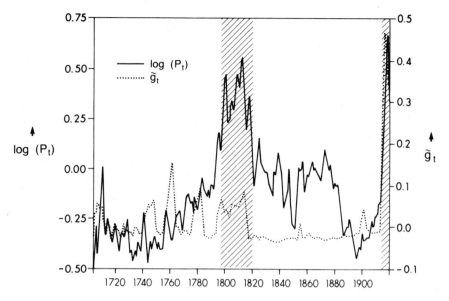

Figure 13.7. Price level and temporary military spending, 1705–1918; shaded areas are periods of suspension

period of suspension in Eq. (13.11).[14] In fact, fluctuations in military spending explain virtually none of the variations in inflation over the gold-standard period. Figure 13.7 shows graphically the relation of $\log(P_t)$ to $\tilde{g}_t$.

For making long-range forecasts of inflation, an important issue is whether the level of prices is stationary—that is, whether there is a systematic tendency for the price level to return to a normal value (see Fig. 13.7). Under the gold standard it is conceivable that the price level would be stationary. However, a regression with $\log(P_t)$ as the dependent variable does not reject at the 5% level the hypothesis that the coefficient of $\log(P_{t-1})$ is unity.[15] This finding applies to the gold-stan-

14. A likelihood-ratio test rejects at less than the 1% level the hypothesis that the same model for the inflation rate applies over both subsamples.

15. For example, over 1705–1796, 1822–1913, the result of the instrumental estimation is

$$\log(P_t) = -0.009 + 0.21\tilde{g}_t + 0.943 \log(P_{t-1}),$$
$$(0.008)\quad (0.15)\quad\quad (0.032)$$
$$\hat{\sigma} = 0.063,\quad \text{D.W.} = 1.9.$$

The test that the coefficient of $\log(P_{t-1})$ is unity uses Fuller's (1976, p. 373) distribution, which was discussed before, and applies to the one-sided alternative that the coefficient is less than one. The same outcome with respect to stationarity obtains if the additional lagged variable, $\log(P_{t-2})$, is added to the regression.

dard sample, 1705–1796, 1822–1913, and also to the suspension sample, 1797–1821, 1914–1918. Of course, even a finding that the price level was stationary under the gold standard would not be so useful if there were a nonzero probability (presumably related to $\bar{g}_t$) of shifting to the suspension regime where the price level was nonstationary.

It would be useful for the previous study of nominal interest rates to use the results from Eqs. (13.11) and (13.12) to calculate long-term expected inflation. One difficulty in this procedure is the measurement of the transition probabilities between the regimes. Although the sample is long, it features only two suspensions (a third if 1931 were added) and one resumption (a second if 1925 were included). Hence the sample is still small in this regard.

Budget Deficits

Military Spending and Budget Deficits

In some previous papers I discussed the tax-smoothing theory of government deficits (Barro 1979, 1986a; see also Pigou 1928, chap. 6; Kydland and Prescott 1980; and Lucas and Stokey 1983). Some of the principal conclusions were as follows. First, temporary government spending, as in wartime, would be financed primarily by budget deficits. Thereby tax rates rise uniformly during and after the war, instead of being unusually high during the war. Second, a permanent increase in the ratio of government spending to GNP leads to a parallel increase in tax rates, with no increase in the budget deficit. Third, the government runs deficits during recessions and surpluses in booms to prevent tax rates from being unusually high or low at these times. Fourth, expected inflation has a one-to-one effect on the growth rate of the nominal debt. Thereby the planned behavior of the real debt is invariant with expected inflation. On the other hand, unexpected inflation does not affect the budget deficit and therefore impacts in the opposite direction on the stock of real debt outstanding.

Empirical results for the United States for the period 1916 to 1983 provided reasonably good estimates for the effects on budget deficits from business fluctuations and expected inflation (see Barro 1986a). However, there was less information about the impact of temporary government spending, which was dominated by the observations for World Wars I and II.

It is clear from the previous discussion that the long-term British data are well suited for studying the relation of budget deficits to temporary military spending. On the other hand, the sample does not permit reliable estimates of cyclical effects, because annual data on GNP are available only since 1830 and because the quality of these data before the middle 1850s is especially uncertain. Further, for reasons mentioned earlier, I have not yet been able to use the data to assess the effects from changes in anticipated inflation. Therefore I focus the present study on the relation between budget deficits and temporary military spending.

I calculate the nominal deficit for each year from the difference between the government's total expenditures (including interest payments) and total revenues.[16] I then compute a time series for the stock of public debt outstanding (at "book value") by adding the cumulative deficit to a benchmark stock of debt from the end of 1700.[17] This procedure is necessary because the reported figures on the stock of public debt treat all numbers as par values even when new debt is issued or retired at a discount from par. This problem is especially serious during the Napoleonic Wars and to some extent during the American Revolution, where large quantities of debt were issued at a discount to yield about 5% but were carried on the books as though issued at par (3%).[18] Hence the change in the public debt as recorded far exceeded the true deficit at these times. Then the error was effectively undone later in the nineteenth century when the old debt was eventually redeemed. Thus, by World War I (and before the 1770s), the series that I calculate turns out to be close to the reported numbers on the stock of public debt outstanding. (However, my series is not a market-value construct, because it does not consider the changes in market value that occurred subsequent to the issue date of a security.)

Figure 13.8 shows the ratio of the real public debt (the nominal amount from the start of the year relative to the wholesale price index for the year) to trend real GNP from 1701 to 1918. The ratio rose from about 25% in 1701 to 70% in 1718 (after the War of the Spanish Succession) and declined in peacetime to less than 50% by the early 1740s.

---

16. The data are from Mitchell and Deane (1962, pp. 386–398). The dating of the fiscal years corresponds to that for military spending, as discussed in footnote 4. Given this correspondence, there is no problem in matching the budget deficits with the expenditure numbers.

17. This figure—£14.2 million—comes from Mitchell and Deane (1962, p. 401).

18. See Fenn (1883, pp. 6–9) for the details.

Figure 13.8. Ratio of real public debt to trend real GNP,
1701–1918

Then the ratio reached 90% after the War of the Austrian Succession
(1750) and 140% after the Seven Years' War (1764). Following a decline
in peacetime to 100% in 1775, the ratio rose to over 130% after the
American Revolution (1785). After another peacetime decline to less
than 90% in 1795, the ratio rose to nearly 160% at the conclusion of the
Napoleonic Wars in 1816, and (with the sharp decline in the price level)
to the all-time peak of 185% in 1822.[19] There followed a long peacetime
decline—with only minor interruptions from some small wars—to a low
point of 30% in 1914. Then with World War I, the ratio reached 110%
in 1918.

Figure 13.9 shows more clearly the dominant influence of temporary
military spending on budget deficits. This figure graphs the ratio of the
nominal deficit to trend GNP (trend real GNP multiplied by the wholesale price index), along with the temporary-spending ratio, $\tilde{g}_t$. The figure shows that the relationship is positive and also accounts for the bulk
of fluctuations in the deficit.

19. The reported figures on the stock of public debt indicate that this peak ratio is 275%
rather than 185%. The difference is the extent to which the debt figures—recorded at
par—overstated the deficit during the wartime years. See the discussion above.

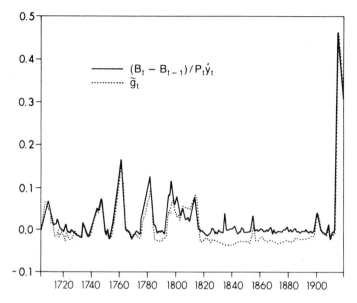

Figure 13.9. Budget deficits and temporary military spending, 1705–1918

The specification of the equation for deficits is

$$\frac{B_t - B_{t-1}}{P_t \hat{y}_t} = b_0 \left(\frac{B_{t-1}}{P_t \hat{y}_t} \right) + b_1 \tilde{g}_t + v_t, \tag{13.13}$$

where B_t is the nominal debt at the end of year t (calculated as above); $B_t - B_{t-1}$ is the budget deficit for year t; P_t is the wholesale price index; $\hat{y}_t$ is trend real GNP; $\tilde{g}_t$ is the temporary-spending ratio as discussed before; and the error term v_t is generated from

$$v_t = \phi v_{t-1} + \eta_t, \tag{13.14}$$

where η_t is white noise and $|\phi| < 1$. Note that the dependent variable in Eq. (13.13) is a deficit–GNP ratio. The coefficient b_0 is the growth rate of the nominal debt that occurs when $\tilde{g}_t$ and v_t equal zero. In a previous analysis (Barro 1979) this rate corresponded to the trend growth rate of real GNP plus the rate of expected inflation. That is, when $\tilde{g}_t = v_t = 0$, the current deficit is set so as to maintain constancy over time for the planned ratio of the debt to GNP. In the present setting I treat the parameter b_0 as a constant. However, nonconstancy of expected inflation is one element that could generate serial correlation of the error term v_t in Eq. (13.13). The omission of cyclical effects, which would themselves be autocorrelated, could also generate this serial correlation. The autogressive form of the error process in Eq. (13.14) is intended to account for these effects.

The estimates of Eqs. (13.13) and (13.14) for 1706–1913 are[20]

$$\frac{(B_t - B_{t-1})}{P_t \hat{y}_t} = \underset{(0.003)}{0.013} \cdot \left[\frac{B_{t-1}}{P_t \hat{y}_t}\right] + \underset{(0.04)}{0.96 \tilde{g}_t}, \tag{13.15}$$

$$\hat{\phi} = \underset{(0.04)}{0.76}, \quad \hat{\sigma} = 0.0087, \quad R^2 = 0.93, \quad \text{D.W.} = 2.0.$$

The first coefficient—0.013, s.e. = 0.003—should equal the trend growth rate of real GNP[21] plus the average rate of expected inflation. In fact, the average growth rate of real GNP from 1701 to 1913 was 1.6% per year, while the average rate of change of the wholesale price index was 0.1% per year. Thus the estimated value of the coefficient on the lagged debt, 0.013, does approximate the trend growth rate of real GNP plus the average rate of inflation.

The estimated coefficient on $\tilde{g}_t$—0.96, s.e. = 0.04—indicates the fraction of temporary government spending (as measured) that is financed by deficits. Note that the estimated coefficient differs significantly from zero but insignificantly from unity. The result indicates that temporary military expenditure was financed by the issue of debt rather than taxes.[22]

20. The value $\hat{\phi}$ is significantly less than one according to Fuller's (1976, p. 373) distribution.

21. I have not allowed for different coefficients in different subperiods, although the average growth rate of real GNP from 1701 to 1770 (0.5% per year) was well below that from 1770 to 1913 (2.1% per year).

22. For much of the sample, the dominant forms of the central government's tax revenues were customs duties and excise taxes—see Mitchell and Deane (1962, pp. 387–388, 392–394) for the data. The tax on land was also significant, amounting to about 20% of total revenue in 1800 but less than 10% by 1840. Income (and property) taxes, begun in 1799, accounted for as much as 15% of overall revenue during the Napoleonic Wars. After lapsing in 1817, income taxes were reintroduced in 1843 at about 10% of total revenue. This percentage reached 15% around 1900 and 30% in 1915. An excess-profits tax for World War I accounted for about 30% of overall receipts. Thus, in order to generate more tax revenues, the government partly raised the rates of existing taxes and partly introduced new types of levies. Also, especially during World War I, there was a tendency for nonmilitary components of governmental outlays to fall during wartime.

The serial correlation coefficient—$\hat{\phi} = 0.76$, s.e. $= 0.04$—presumably picks up factors such as cyclical fluctuations and persisting variations in expected inflation. Thus far, I have no detailed results on these elements.

With World War I included, the results for the period 1706–1918 are

$$\left[\frac{B_t - B_{t-1}}{P_t \hat{y}_t}\right] = \underset{(0.004)}{0.008} \cdot \left[\frac{B_{t-1}}{P_t \hat{y}_t}\right] + \underset{(0.02)}{1.03 \tilde{g}_t}, \tag{13.16}$$

$$\underset{(0.04)}{\hat{\phi} = 0.81}, \quad \hat{\sigma} = 0.0101, \quad R^2 = 0.98, \quad \text{D.W.} = 2.1.$$

These results are similar to those in Eq. (13.15).

As an example of the effect of wartime, from 1757 to 1762 the average value of the temporary-spending ratio $\tilde{g}_t$ was 9.6%. Multiplying by the coefficient 0.96 from Eq. (13.15), the prediction is that the debt–GNP ratio would rise on average by 9.2 percentage points per year during this war. In fact, the ratio rose over the period from 0.74 to 1.39 or by 10.8 percentage points per year.

In peacetime, the variable $\tilde{g}_t$ is negative rather than zero. Hence, instead of predicting a constant ratio of the debt to GNP, Eq. (13.15) says that this ratio will fall in peacetime. This behavior underlies the tendency for the debt–GNP ratio to decline during years that do not involve major wars, as is apparent from Fig. 13.8. For example, from 1822 to 1913, the average value of the variable $\tilde{g}_t$ was -2.1%. Therefore the prediction is that the debt–GNP ratio would fall on average by 2.0 percentage points per year (0.021×0.96). In fact, the ratio fell over this period from 1.85 to 0.30 or by 1.7 percentage points per year.

Budget Deficits versus Government Spending as Determinants of Interest Rates

The present study related interest rates to temporary government purchases, with the method of finance for those expenditures regarded as secondary. However, other theories argue that interest rates respond positively to budget deficits rather than to government spending as such. It would be desirable to use the long-term British data to discriminate between these viewpoints. However, since temporary spending and budget deficits move closely together, as is clear from Fig. 13.9, it is difficult to disentangle the effects of spending from the effects of deficits. Moreover, since the variable $\tilde{g}_t$ is just an estimate of temporary spending, it is even possible that budget deficits are a better measure than $\tilde{g}_t$ of temporary spending. In addition, to the extent that budget deficits represent endogenous responses to recessions or expected inflation, a positive association between deficits and interest rates need not reveal the effect of deficits per se.

Theories that stress the effects of budget deficits on interest rates—such as Blanchard (1985)—also predict an impact from the lagged stock of public debt. This prediction distinguishes the deficit viewpoint from a model that focuses on the effects of current temporary spending. However, as discussed before, the spending theories allow also for effects of lagged expenditures, which would be correlated with past deficits and hence with the accumulated stock of debt. Therefore it remains difficult to discriminate between the two theories.

Over the period from 1730 to 1913 the regression for the long-term interest rate on the deficit–GNP ratio and the lagged debt–GNP ratio is

$$R_t = 3.01 + 5.9 \left(\frac{B_t - B_{t-1}}{P_t \hat{y}_t}\right) + 0.48 \left(\frac{B_{t-1}}{P_t \hat{y}_t}\right), \qquad (13.17)$$
$$(0.27) \quad (1.1) \qquad\qquad\quad (0.22)$$

$$\hat{\lambda} = 0.905, \quad \hat{\sigma} = 0.238, \quad R^2 = 0.90,$$
$$(0.033)$$

$$R^2 \text{ (for } R_t - R_{t-1}) = 0.17, \quad \text{D.W.} = 2.2.$$

Hence, with government-expenditure variables excluded, the current budget deficit and the lagged stock of debt each have significantly positive effects on the interest rate. Also, the fit of Eq. (13.17) is similar to that based on current and lagged temporary purchases in Eq. (13.8).

With the spending variables included the regression becomes

$$R_t = +3.16 + 4.3\tilde{g}_t - 3.9\tilde{g}_{t-1} + 5.4\tilde{g}_{t-2} + 2.2\tilde{g}_{t-3} \qquad (13.18)$$
$$(0.28) \quad (4.0) \quad\quad (3.3) \quad\quad (3.5) \quad\quad (3.4)$$

$$-5.0\tilde{g}_{t-4} + 3.9\tilde{g}_{t-5} + 4.3 \left(\frac{B_t - B_{t-1}}{P_t \hat{y}_t}\right) + 0.34 \left(\frac{B_{t-1}}{P_t \hat{y}_t}\right),$$
$$(2.9) \quad\quad (2.1) \quad\quad (2.2) \qquad\qquad\quad (0.23)$$

$$\hat{\lambda} = 0.906, \quad \hat{\sigma} = 0.232, \quad R^2 = 0.91,$$
$$(0.033)$$

$$R^2 \text{ (for } R_t - R_{t-1}) = 0.24, \quad \text{D.W.} = 2.2.$$

Not surprisingly, the significance attached to each of the spending variables is less than that when the deficit variables are excluded (Eq. 8), and the significance of the deficit variables is less than that when the spending variables are excluded (Eq. 17). For the set of six spending variables, the joint hypothesis that all coefficients are zero leads to the value for $-2 \cdot \log(\text{likelihood ratio})$ of 15.8, which is below the 2% critical value for the χ^2 distribution with six degrees of freedom. For the two deficit variables, the corresponding statistic is 4.5, which is nearly equal to the 10% critical value with two degrees of freedom. In this sense the results indicate some preference for the expenditure variables as influences on interest rates. However, the principal finding is an inability to disentangle the effects of spending from the effects of budget deficits.

Two Episodes of Nonwar Budget Deficits

Because temporary spending and budget deficits move together in wartime, it is natural to search for other experiences that break the collinearity in these variables. In particular, the best experiments would be budget deficits run for no reason—that is, deficits that are not endogenous responses to wartime, recession, expected inflation, and so on. For the present sample, which contains over 200 years of British history, I have been able to isolate two such episodes.

Following the decision in 1833 to free the West Indian slaves, there were large compensatory payments by the British government to slaveowners. The amounts were £16.7 million in 1835 and £4.1 million in 1836.[23] These figures, when divided by the wholesale price index, represented 4.3% and 0.9%, respectively, of trend real GNP. Thus the transfer payments in 1835 were similar in scale to a medium-sized war (see Table 13.1). Because the transfers were temporary, they should be included nearly one-to-one in the concept of the temporary-spending ratio, $\tilde{g}_t$, which so far included only military expenditures. With this adjustment, the measured value of $\tilde{g}_t$ rises in 1835 from -0.033 to 0.010 and in 1836 from -0.035 to -0.026. Using this revision to the $\tilde{g}_t$ variable yields an estimated deficit–GNP ratio from Eq. (13.15) for 1835 of 0.034; the actual value is 0.039. The previous estimate, based on the

23. See Mitchell and Deane (1962, p. 399, note e). Some discussion of the events appeared in Burn (1937, chap. 2) and Fogel and Engerman (1974).

unrevised concept of $\bar{g}_t$, was -0.007. For 1836, the revised estimate for the deficit–GNP ratio is -0.006; the actual value is 0.003.[24] The main point is that the compensatory payments to slaveowners were financed primarily by debt. Thus the budget deficit reacts to temporary peacetime spending in a manner similar to its reaction to temporary wartime spending.

On the other hand, with respect to interest-rate determination, the freeing of the slaves and the payments to slaveowners would be different from temporary military purchases. The freeing of the slaves per se converts some nonhuman assets—that is, ownership rights in slaves— into human capital.[25] With "imperfect" capital markets, this change could raise the desire to save in nonhuman form and thereby reduce market interest rates. However, the financing of the compensation payments by public debt offsets this effect.

The Ricardian view of budget deficits says that the extra public debt is matched by a higher present value of future taxes and thereby has no effect on desired national saving or on interest rates. This view assumes that imperfections in capital markets are unimportant in this context— therefore the view also implies that the freeing of the slaves per se has no appreciable impact on market interest rates. Overall, the Ricardian view predicts no important effect on interest rates from the freeing of the slaves and the associated budget deficit.

The actual path of long-term interest rates was 3.76% in 1831, 3.58% in 1832 (when there was discussion of the pending legislation for freeing the slaves), 3.42% in 1833 (when the emancipation legislation and the compensation package were enacted), 3.32% in 1834, 3.29% in 1835 (when the main compensatory payments were made and the budget deficit was large), 3.35% in 1836, and 3.30% in 1837. Thus, despite the large budget deficit in 1835, there was no apparent impact on long-term interest rates. Short-term interest rates[26]—which are far more volatile from year to year—do show increases after 1833. The path here was

---

24. The previous estimate for 1836, which was 0.022, reflected the large positive residual for 1835—see Eq. (15). If the effect of this residual were eliminated, then the previous estimate would have been -0.016.

25. I am grateful to Levis Kochin for this point.

26. The data are Gurney's rates for first-class three-month bills from Mitchell and Deane (1962, p. 460).

3.69% in 1831, 3.15% in 1832, 2.73% in 1833, 3.38% in 1834, 3.71% in 1835, 4.25% in 1836, and 4.44% in 1837.

The second episode of nonwar budget deficits concerns the debate over income taxes and other levies in 1909 (actually the fiscal year ended March 1910).[27] The dispute over what kinds of taxes to enact and at what levels produced a legislative deadlock during fiscal 1909–1910, which created a one-year lapse in the government's authority to collect certain revenues, especially from the income tax. Therefore, although there was no temporary bulge in expenditures, the sudden drop in receipts, mainly from the income tax, produced a budget deficit of 1.5% of trend GNP in 1909—compare this with an estimated value of -0.4% from Eq. (13.15). This deficit was financed with short-term debt, which was paid off as promised when the uncollected taxes ("arrears") were paid during the following year. The receipt of these backlogged taxes, when added to the regular revenues, generated a budget surplus of 2.0% of trend GNP for 1910 (actually the fiscal year ended March 1911).

The scientific attraction of this episode is that it involves movements in budget deficits that are not confounded by correlated shifts in government expenditures for the military or other purposes. Therefore the behavior of interest rates in 1909–1910 provides information about the effects of a budget deficit per se—although a deficit that was pretty much assured to be temporary and balanced by a surplus the next year. The path of long-term interest rates was 2.90% in 1908, 2.98% in 1909 (when there was a budget deficit), 3.08% in 1910 (when there was a budget surplus), and 3.15% in 1911. These data do not indicate that the budget deficit or surplus had a major effect on long-term rates. For short-term rates,[28] the pattern was 2.29% in 1908, 2.28% in 1909, 3.16% in 1910, and 2.90% in 1911. Hence the short-term interest rate was higher in the year of budget surplus, 1910, than in the year of deficit, 1909.

Overall, one cannot detect a clear relationship between budget deficits and interest rates for these two "natural experiments." In any event, while these episodes are valuable because of the rarity of exogenous deficits, it remains true that the sample of such experiments is small.

27. For a discussion, see Mallett (1913, pp. 298–315).
28. The data are for three-month bank bills from Mitchell and Deane (1962, p. 460).

Observations

The British data from the early 1700s through World War I provide an unmatched opportunity for studying the effects of temporary changes in government purchases. In this chapter I examined the effects of these changes on interest rates, the quantity of money, the price level, and budget deficits. But the data should be useful for many other purposes.

The main findings are as follows. Temporary increases in government purchases—showing up in the sample as increases in military outlays during wartime—had positive effects on long-term interest rates. The effect on the growth rate of money (bank notes) was positive only during the two periods of suspension of the gold standard (1797–1821 and 1914–1918). As long as convertibility of bank notes into specie was maintained, there was no systematic relation of government spending to monetary growth. Similarly, the main interplay between temporary government spending and inflation occurred during the periods of suspension.

Temporary changes in military spending accounted for the bulk of budget deficits from the early 1700s through 1918. This association explains the main increases in the ratio of the public debt to GNP, as well as the decreases that typically occurred during peacetime. Because of the close association between temporary military spending and budget deficits, it is not possible to say with confidence whether interest rates react to temporary spending per se or to the associated deficits.

Over the sample of more than 200 years, I found two examples of major budget deficits that were unrelated to wartime (or the business cycle). One episode featured compensation payments to slaveowners in 1835–1836, and the other involved a political dispute over the income tax in 1909–1910. Because of the "exogeneity" of these deficits, it is interesting that interest rates showed no special movements at these times.

References

Ahmed, S. 1986. "Temporary and Permanent Government Spending in an Open Economy: Some Evidence for the U.K." *Journal of Monetary Economics* 17:197–224.

Barro, R. J. 1979. "On the Determination of the Public Debt." *Journal of Political Economy* 87:940–971.

―――― 1981. "Intertemporal Substitution and the Business Cycle." *Carnegie-Rochester Conference Series on Public Policy* 14:237–268.

―――― 1986a. "U.S. Deficits since World War I." *Scandinavian Journal of Economics* 88:195–222.

―――― 1986b. "The Neoclassical Approach to Fiscal Policy." Forthcoming in *Modern Business Cycle Theory*, ed. R. J. Barro. Cambridge, Mass.: Harvard University Press.

―――― 1987. *Macroeconomics*, 2nd Ed. New York: Wiley.

Barsky, R. B., and L. H. Summers. 1985. "Gibson's Paradox and the Gold Standard." National Bureau of Economic Research Working Paper No. 1680.

Benjamin, D. K., and L. A. Kochin. 1984. "War, Prices, and Interest Rates: A Martial Solution to Gibson's Paradox." In *A Retrospective on the Classical Gold Standard, 1821–1931*, ed. M. D. Bordo and A. J. Schwartz. Chicago: University of Chicago Press, pp. 587–604.

Blanchard, O. J. 1985. "Debt, Deficits, and Finite Horizons." *Journal of Political Economy* 93:223–247.

Burn, W. L. 1937. *Emancipation and Apprenticeship in the British West Indies.* London: Jonathan Cape.

Clapham, J. H. 1945. *The Bank of England*, Vols. 1 and 2. Cambridge: Cambridge University Press.

Deane, P. 1968. "New Estimates of Gross National Product for the United Kingdom, 1830–1914." *Review of Income and Wealth* 14:95–112.

Deane, P., and W. A. Cole. 1967. *British Economic Growth, 1688–1959*, 2nd Ed. Cambridge: Cambridge University Press.

Del Mar, A. 1877. "Standard for Money in the United Kingdom." In *Report and Accompanying Documents of the United States Monetary Commission*. Washington, D.C.: U.S. Government Printing Office.

Evans, P. 1987. "Interest Rates and Expected Future Budget Deficits in the United States." *Journal of Political Economy* 95:34–58.

Feinstein, C. H. 1972. *National Income, Expenditure and Output of the United Kingdom, 1855–1965*. Cambridge: Cambridge University Press.

Fenn, C. 1883. *Compendium of the English and Foreign Funds*, 13th Ed. London.

Fogel, R. W., and S. L. Engerman. 1974. "Philanthropy at Bargain Prices: Notes on the Economics of Gradual Emancipation." *Journal of Legal Studies* 3:377–401.

Fuller, W. A. 1976. *Introduction to Statistical Time Series*. New York: Wiley.

Hall, R. E. 1980. "Labor Supply and Aggregate Fluctuations." *Carnegie-Rochester Conference Series on Public Policy* 12:7–33.

Hansen, L. P., and T. J. Sargent. 1981. "A Note on Wiener-Kolmogorov Prediction Formulas for Rational Expectations Models." *Economics Letters* 8:255–260.

Homer, S. 1977. *A History of Interest Rates,* 2nd Ed. New Brunswick, N.J.: Rutgers University Press.

Judd, K. L. 1985. "Short-Run Analysis of Fiscal Policy in a Simple Perfect Foresight Model." *Journal of Political Economy* 93:298–319.

Kydland, F., and E. C. Prescott. 1980. "A Competitive Theory of Fluctuations and the Feasibility and Desirability of Stabilization Policy." In *Rational Expectations and Economic Policy,* ed. S. Fischer. Chicago: University of Chicago Press, pp. 169–198.

Lucas, R. E., and N. Stokey. 1983. "Optimal Fiscal and Monetary Policy in an Economy without Capital." *Journal of Monetary Economics* 12:55–93.

Mallett, B. 1913. *British Budgets, 1887–88 to 1912–13.* London: Macmillan.

Mitchell, B. R., and P. Deane. 1962. *Abstract of British Historical Statistics.* Cambridge: Cambridge University Press.

Pigou, A. C. 1928. *A Study in Public Finance.* London: Macmillan.

Plosser, C. I. 1982. "Government Financing Decisions and Asset Returns." *Journal of Monetary Economics* 9:325–352.

——— 1987. "Fiscal Policy and the Term Structure." *Journal of Monetary Economics* 20:343–367.

Pollard, S. 1969. *The Development of the British Economy,* 2nd Ed. New York: St. Martin's Press.

Sayers, R. S. 1976. *The Bank of England, 1891–1944,* Vol. 1. Cambridge: Cambridge University Press.

Index

373